MAGI ASTROLOGY:™

The Key to Success in Love and Money

By The Magi Society®

ASTROLOGY REALLY WORKS!

THE MAGI SOCIETY EPHEMERIS

ॐ ॐ ॐ

Other Hay House Titles of Related Interest

ADVENTURES OF A PSYCHIC: The Fascinating and Inspiring
True-Life Story of One of America's Most Successful Clairvoyants,
by Sylvia Browne

BENEATH A VEDIC SKY: A Beginner's Guide to the Astrology of
Ancient India, by William R. Levacy

BORN TO BE TOGETHER: Love Relationships, Astrology, and the Soul,
by Terry Lamb

COLORS & NUMBERS: Your Personal Guide to Positive Vibrations in
Daily Life, by Louise L. Hay

DEVELOPING YOUR INTUITION WITH MAGIC MIRRORS
(book and card pack), by Uma Reed

THE STARS IN YOUR FAMILY: How Astrology Affects Relationships
Between Parents and Children, by Sylvia Friedman

ॐ ॐ ॐ

(All of the above are available through your local bookstore, or may be
ordered by calling Hay House at 800-654-5126.)

Please visit the Hay House Website at: **www.hayhouse.com**

MAGI ASTROLOGY:

The Key to Success in Love and Money

MAGI SOCIETY®

A Division of
Hay House, Inc.
Carlsbad, CA

Published and distributed in the United States by:
Hay House, Inc., P.O. Box 5100, Carlsbad, CA 92018-5100
(800) 654-5126 • (800) 650-5115 (fax)

Editorial: Jill Kramer • *Design*: Jenny Richards

Library of Congress Cataloging-in-Publication Data

Magi astrology : the key to success in love and money / the Magi Society.
       p.   cm.
    ISBN 1-56170-128-9 (trade paper)
     1. Astrology and marriage. 2. Astrology and sex. 3. Astrology and personal finance. I. Magi Society.
BF1729.L6M34   1999
133.5—dc21   98-46503
                                 CIP

ISBN 1-56170-128-9

02 01 00 99   5 4 3 2
First Printing, March 1999
2nd Printing, August 1999

Printed in the United States of America

*The Magi Society dedicates this book to all who
have dreams born out of selfless love.*

*This book is written to help all of us fulfill our dreams,
and to find that special someone with whom
we will happily share and live out such dreams
for the remainder of our lives.*

CONTENTS

Editor's Note: Throughout this book, when dates are written in month/day/year format—e.g., 7/1/67—it should be understood that the dates refer to the 20th century unless otherwise designated—e.g., 10/29/1897.

CHAPTER ONE

☞

Magi Astrology Helps You
Answer the Pertinent Questions in Your Life

What Is Magi Astrology?

The legend of Magi Astrology began at dawn during the spring equinox of 1625. It was then that a small group of Shao Lin monks gathered at a monastery-fort on top of a mountain near the southern coast of China to form a secret society of astrologers, which has the Western name of the Magi Society. Since that time, most of the legendary astrologers of China have been Magi Astrologers. They have been best known for their remarkable ability to predict matters related to marriage, the birth of children, war, and peace. Through hundreds of years, the Magi Society remained a secret society for the very few who were the most gifted astrologers of China. Membership in the society was very limited, and each member passed on their secrets to new members.

Anticipating that the communists would take over China, all of the members of the Magi Society left their homeland between 1945 and 1948. Most settled in Hong Kong and carried on the society's long-standing traditions of advancing astrological knowledge. The society now has a worldwide network of members. A chapter of the society was officially founded in America in 1995. During the last 20 years, through extensive research and the use of high-speed personal computers, the Magi Society has made monumental discoveries in astrology. This has allowed the Society to incorporate immensely powerful and completely new techniques into Magi Astrology. In so doing, Magi Astrology has leaped light years in capabilities.

This is the third book by the Magi Society. It is the first one written to

1

teach the basics of Magi Astrology to the world.

Get ready to enter the magical world of Magi Astrology! It will help you see the universe with an understanding, clarity, and set of perspectives that will truly improve your life. Magi Astrology is a life-altering and life-enriching experience. With it, you'll finally have the astrological tools you need to most prudently deal with all matters pertaining to love and money.

Magi Astrology is easy to understand and master. It contains the new astrological knowledge that will help you finally answer questions such as:

- Is this my soulmate—or just another temporary playmate?
- Will I marry *this* person, and if so, will the marriage be happy and lifelong?
- Is this person the faithful type, or the runaround kind?
- Why do some of us fall in love with the wrong person?
- What is the essence of this individual's personality and character? And how compatible are we together?
- Do the two of us have a mutual destiny together? If so, what is the nature of that destiny? Is it marriage? Just being lovers? Or only friendship?
- Will this extraordinarily sexual relationship end in just another one of those burn-outs and leave a bitter pile of emotional ashes in its wake?
- Will this charmer be there for you through the inevitable bad times, or will you be deserted in your hour of greatest need?
- Will you triumph over your rival for the undying love of the person you want to be with?

The answers to such questions have always been in the stars! And the astounding new knowledge that is a part of Magi Astrology uncovers these answers, finally providing the astrological capabilities needed to understand:

- what it is that makes a prince fall in love with a commoner. And why does a glamorous Hollywood superstar marry a seemingly ordinary person?
- why King Edward VIII gave up the throne of England for Mrs. Wallis Simpson. And why did Elvis Presley, at the peak of his fame, fall in love with 14-year-old Priscilla, and marry *only her*?

- why Prince Charles first married Diana, but then chose Camilla over the princess.

- what made Evita irresistible to Juan Peron.

- why Bill Clinton keeps getting into trouble with women.

The stars' secrets are now finally revealed through the use of Magi Astrology, and by learning it, you can accurately answer all of the above types of questions as they apply in your own life. Magi Astrology can even help you gain the deep insight you need to handle dilemmas such as these:

- Will this relationship improve or worsen? Should you simply break it off right now and end it all together? Or does it deserve another chance?

- When the ecstasy of the physical attraction that you now have with this person wanes, how do you keep the relationship from becoming another one of those fade-aways? How can you replace the sex with the undying selfless love you yearn for and need?

- How can the two of you live together most harmoniously and cooperatively? Is this person capable of a give-and-take relationship, or only a take-and-take disaster?

Good and viable solutions to such problems will actually become clear to you through Magi Astrology's revolutionary new methods of analyzing relationships. Better still, Magi Astrology gives you the ability to *harness the power of the planets* and make them work to your benefit! You can do so by selecting the most favorable times to do something consequential. There is a good time and a bad time to do everything. By learning Magi Astrology, you will know when is the best time to:

- meet your prospective in-laws for the first time.

- get married or engaged.

- initiate a love relationship with someone you might want to marry.

- go on a blind date.

- meet someone new who could be *the one.*

- plan to have a memorable night or a seduction.

Magi Astrology provides you with the ability to use the stars to take command of your life and maximize your chances of fulfilling your dreams. *By absorbing the contents of this book, you will be able to make use of the power of the planets and benefit from them.*

Magi Astrology Solves the Mysteries of Magical Sex

In addition, and especially apropos these day with so many sexually transmitted diseases, Magi Astrology provides you with another significant advantage. You can apply it to help you accurately predict if you are sexually incompatible with someone without having to become intimate. Sex isn't everything. But unless you are a priest or minister, you will probably go through (or have already been through) a stage in your life when sex will be *more* than everything. Fortunately, Magi Astrology has very accurate astrological tools for predicting sexual compatibility. In this book, you will learn that sexual compatibility and attraction are very much astrologically driven and completely predictable. Magi Astrology has such a high level of accuracy in the area of sex that once you master it, you will know:

- if this is someone with whom you can have magical sex.
- when the best time for a seduction is.
- which particular nights or days you should choose in order to have the most memorable lovemaking sessions.
- how you can tell if someone is sexual, supersexual—or not so sexual.
- how you can tell what type of lover someone will be. Will this person be gentle and considerate? Dominant and aggressive? Lethargic or highly energetic? Slow paced and long-lasting? Sensitive or just plain quick and selfish? Awkward or fluid? All of the above? Some of the above?
- when your lover will be most amorous and romantic.

The Magi Society wrote this book to teach you the astrology of emotional and sexual relationships. After you master the material contained in this book, you will understand the *real* astrological reasons for attraction, mind-altering sex, love, and why two persons get married. And you will be able to make use of these new insights to help enrich your life, maximize your chances of having truly fulfilling relationships; and help you find, identify, and marry your soulmate.

Magi Astrology Helps in Matters of Money

Magi Astrology has the tools to help you be as prosperous and financially secure as possible. It can assist you in crucial questions of career and finances such as:

- What profession are you most suited for? When should you make a career or job change? When is the best time to push for a promotion or raise?

- Is your employer the best one for you? Do you have good long-term prospects with this particular company? Or are you better off with another company? If so, which one?

- Is this the right time to start a new business? In what type of business will you be most successful?

- Can you work well with a particular person and become a successful business team, or will you tear each other apart?

- How might you make better investments and improve financially? When is the best time to buy a house? A car? A business?

Magi Astrology versus Traditional Astrology

Most of you reading this book probably have an intuition that astrology really works, but in the past, you may have been at least a little disappointed in the limited capabilities of traditional astrology. This is where Magi Astrology comes in. It has powerful new knowledge that will serve to renew your faith in astrology.

In 1995, the Magi Society's first book, *Astrology Really Works!*, provided proof that *everyone has not just one, but **two** distinct astrological charts*. This fact is now being accepted by most top professional astrologers worldwide. You can just imagine how significant this revelation is. You literally double your knowledge by including your second chart. Have you ever had your second birth chart analyzed? In this book, we will teach you how to analyze *both* of your birth charts, and make use of them to take command of your life in matters of love and money.

This is just one of the many valuable precepts of Magi Astrology. Another powerful tool of Magi Astrology is the use of CHIRON, which was only discovered in 1977. (Note: Whenever we first introduce an astrological term, we will print it in UPPER-CASE LETTERS. It is our way of telling you that the term is defined in the Glossary at the end of this book.) Chiron orbits around the Sun between Saturn and Uranus. It has some of the properties of planets, but also has some characteristics of comets. Chiron has an astrological influence much more powerful than has ever been credited by traditional astrology. You will learn in this book that the position of Chiron in one birth chart and how this position relates to the planets in another person's birth chart is the decisive astrological influence in creating long-term emotional ties between any two persons. In other words: *Chiron is the arrow that points to your soulmate.*

In fact, the Magi Society has just recently discovered that each and every one of us is most likely to fall in love and marry someone who was born with Chiron located in certain positions in the sky. *Chiron is the astrological key to love and marriage.* In this book, we will teach you exactly how to analyze and accurately assess all of this information so that you will know if anyone could, or could not, be your soulmate.

The proper use of Chiron and your second birth chart comprise just two of the new tools of Magi Astrology that this book will teach you. Along with other unique methodologies, Magi Astrology will give you the solutions to problems you always hoped that astrology would provide.

There Is Much More to Astrology Than Sun-Sign Astrology

During the last three decades, the most popular branch of astrology has been SUN-SIGN ASTROLOGY. This is the astrology that focuses on what your Sun Sign is; it is the astrology most popularly used in the astrology columns of magazines and newspapers. Most people believe that Sun-Sign Astrology is all there is to astrology, but it is actually only one small part of traditional astrology. The entirety of astrology is vast in scope and broad in approaches and techniques. Magi Astrology employs the best of these methodologies and adds its own unique precepts. The result is an astrology that goes far beyond normal expectations.

For example, one great advantage of Magi Astrology is that it solves the riddle of Sun-Sign characteristics. Most people are aware of traditional astrology's inclination to assign characteristics and personality traits to various Sun Signs. Although there is a great deal of merit to this approach, the problem has been that some of the attributable traits of a particular sign are inconsistent. For example, a Virgo can be analytical, neat, and meticulous; or a Virgo can be overly critical and picayune. How can you tell which traits a particular Virgo will have? Traditional astrology has left this problem unsolved. But Magi Astrology will show you how to determine if a person will most likely possess the positive traits of a person's Sun Sign as opposed to the negative characteristics of the Sun Sign, and how to use this knowledge to help you in all matters of love and money.

Unless you have read the Magi Society's other books, you will find the techniques of Magi Astrology to be new to you—because they are new—and unique. But they are also simple, reliable, time-tested, powerful, and scientific. And they are easy to understand; you will readily master them once you study the numerous examples in this book.

***By the end of this book, you will find that your ability
to understand and cope with love and money issues
will have dramatically improved.***

Through this book, you can enter the wondrous world of Magi Astrology and learn how to harness the power of the stars and use them to maximize your chances of fulfilling your dreams. The New Age is being born, and all of us at the Magi Society believe that Magi Astrology is an important catalyst to its birth.

CHAPTER TWO

☜

Planetary Geometry Is the Key to Accurate Astrology

One of the secret techniques of Magi Astrology involves PLANETARY GEOMETRY. In spite of this imposing name, it is much simpler than anything you have ever tried to learn about astrology. Here is what it is all about.

Planetary Geometry

Have you ever looked up at the nighttime sky and tried to find any of the planets? Have you ever in your mind drawn connecting lines between the positions of the planets and wondered if the lines and geometric figures thus created have any special meanings? Did you ever wonder if the various angles that the planets make to each other have any influence on life on Earth?

If you have ever done any of those things, then you have already had an intuitive brush with Magi Astrology's principle of Planetary Geometry. It is based on the lines, angles, shapes, and figures that are created when we draw connecting lines between the positions of the planets at the time someone is born. Because the planets are always moving, everybody is born with a unique Planetary Geometry, which is called the NATAL Planetary Geometry, and this has been the secret tool that has given the best Chinese astrologers their legendary capabilities. (Please note that when we refer to a person's natal Planetary Geometry, we will sometimes not include the word *natal* when the meaning is obvious.)

The Magi Society has just recently completed the most extensive and thorough research project into the astrology of personal relationships. As a

9

result, we discovered that a person's Planetary Geometry is the single most powerful astrological influence on the outcome of his or her personal relationships of all kinds. In addition, it is natal Planetary Geometry that is the most accurate indication of the individuality of a person's essence, as well as the likely boundaries of that person's destiny.

Exactly What Is Planetary Geometry?

Planetary Geometry refers to the shapes and patterns that are created when you draw lines connecting the positions of the planets in the sky. If you connect any two planets, you will get a single line; if you connect any three planets, the outline will be a triangle. And if you connect any four planets, the outline will be a quadrangle, and so on. All of these shapes are types of Planetary Geometry. Below you can see some examples.

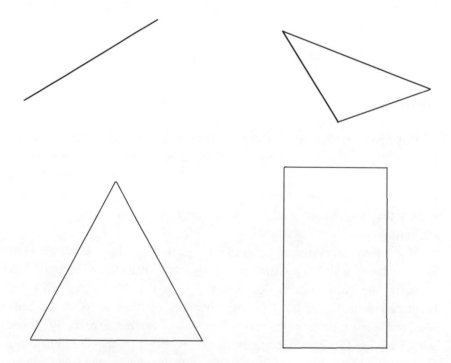

Figure 2A: Four examples of Planetary Geometry

The use of Planetary Geometry has been one of the secrets of the Magi Society. The Planetary Geometry of a particular day provides us with the most important astrological clues as to the significance and meaning of that day. It is also the most accurate clue to the character and abilities of anyone born on that day. The Planetary Geometry of a day is even the best guide for determining whom a person will marry, and all the individuals with whom the person will have an important relationship.

After centuries of devoted research, the Magi Society discovered that each distinctly different type of shape in Planetary Geometry has a special meaning. Magi Astrology uses the various shapes of Planetary Geometry that exist on any day to interpret the most likely meaning of the day. In addition to the actual shape, Magi Astrology also takes into account which specific planets form the shape (we will fully explain this later).

The rules of interpreting Planetary Geometry are simple to understand. For example, from time to time, a group of planets are aligned in such a way that when you connect lines between their positions, they produce outlines that create a symmetrical pattern. Such symmetrical alignments of planets are the most interesting and the most powerful. The following figures illustrate why a pattern is or is not symmetrical.

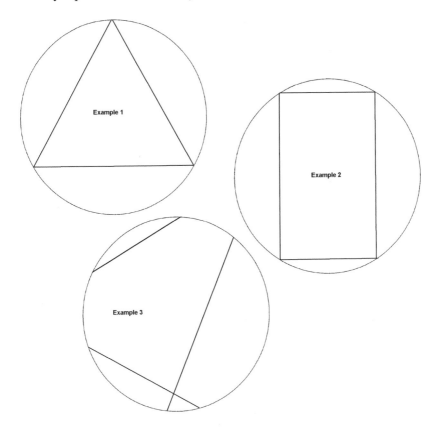

Figure 2B: Three examples of Planetary Geometry

Astrologers learned long ago that a day when a group of planets are positioned in the sky such that they create either the first or second shape is more important than a day when they create the third shape. This is because the first two shapes are symmetrical. Many of you may have intuitively sensed this difference and, therefore, already know this most basic principle of Planetary Geometry and Magi Astrology: *Symmetrical patterns are more significant than those that are not symmetrical.*

See how simple and logical Magi Astrology is? Fortunately, you do not have to know anything about geometry to understand our theories relating to Planetary Geometry. All you need is common sense and you can truly master Magi Astrology. In fact, it is easier to understand and learn than traditional astrology.

Magi Astrology and its unique system of using Planetary Geometry are based on common-sense principles that are logically formulated and scientifically tested. As incredible as it may seem, Magi Astrology can help you learn from the past, understand the present, and provide you with some amazingly accurate predictions about your future—as well as other people's futures. Magi Astrology's system of analyzing Planetary Geometry accurately predicts who you will marry and also gives you the ability to make your marriage and relationships as fulfilling and happy as possible. Most important, Magi Astrology gives you the knowledge needed to harness the power of the planets in order to help you fulfill your dreams! And Magi Astrology does it all without any connection to the occult. In fact, Magi Astrology is completely compatible with Judeo-Christian traditions and beliefs.

This book teaches you Magi Astrology and how to read the language of the stars, but before we get into the particulars, it is helpful if we first learn the most basic principles of astrology in general.

We will start you at the very beginning, and all you need is common sense and a desire to learn. If you can find your way around a city by using a map, you can learn Magi Astrology. We promise that after reading the next two chapters, you will learn so much about astrology that you will be able to teach it to your friends. And you will have fun doing it.

CHAPTER THREE

❦

Learning the Basics of Astrology—the Birth Chart

The most fundamental tool in astrology is what is known as a BIRTH CHART, which is also called an ASTROLOGICAL CHART. This is the chart with a circle and the 12 zodiac signs drawn around the circle; it also includes the positions of the planets. A sample birth chart used in traditional astrology can be found at the end of this chapter on page 35. It is what all astrologers use. We will begin by teaching you what a birth chart is and how to construct it. Then we will teach you how to interpret and evaluate it, and how to use it to better your life.

To some people, the birth chart looks complicated. It is not. In fact, it becomes very simple once you know the history of its origins. The Babylonian astrologers of over 4,000 years ago invented the first birth charts. In this chapter, we will explain how and *why* these Babylonian astrologers designed the birth chart as they did.

The Early Hebrews Were Great Astrologers

About 4,000 years ago, Babylonian astrologers formulated the fundamentals of astrology from which modern traditional astrology is derived.

We should clarify right away that whenever we speak about the "Babylonian astrologers" and use that term, the people we are referring to include the Hebrews from their very beginnings until about the birth of Christ. Babylonia as a land was really ancient Mesopotamia, which was literally "the land between two rivers." These two rivers were the Tigris and the Euphrates. And it was there in "Babylonia" that Abraham, the patriarch of the Hebrews, was born and raised. In Babylonia during Abraham's time, every single person learned astrology. As a result, there are literally dozens of references to the Hebrews' use and respect for astrology in the Old

Testament. For these reasons and many others, the Magi Society is convinced that all the Hebrew prophets of the ancient era were astrologers. If you are skeptical about this, we suggest you study the Kabbala, which is unequivocally Hebrew and highly astrological, with some numerology and mysticism thrown in.

Our main point is that the ancient Hebrews were great astrologers, and contributed greatly to the development of Babylonian astrology, which is the forerunner of modern astrology.

The Origin of Astrology

The Babylonians' interest in astrology originated from their desire to be able to predict the future for their monarchs and themselves. At first they were mainly looking for ways to tell if a day was good for planting a crop, or harvesting one. Along the way, for obvious reasons, the Babylonians quickly became just as interested in trying to predict matters of war and peace, and also natural catastrophes. Was a day good for peace? Was there danger because a war could break out? Or would a day be one that might bring about a major tragedy, such as an earthquake, flood, or assassination? The Babylonians were also very interested in the destiny of all newborn babies and believed that astrology could foretell their future based on the day the infant was born. The Babylonians studied astrology because they wanted to be able to predict whether a baby would be a king, a great warrior—or maybe a very talented musician, poet, or astrologer.

Babylonian Astrologers Looked for Celestial Signs

Have you ever wondered where the word *significant* came from? The first four letters will give you a clue. *Significant* came from the word *sign.* And the actual word *significant* means "something important enough to be worthy of a sign."

What kind of sign? A sign in the sky made by planets or the stars that we can actually see.

The Babylonian astrologers believed that any event really important and historic would be worthy of having its own celestial sign in the sky! This is an interesting belief of the ancients. So pervasive was this belief that the Old Testament of the Bible even talks about and supports this viewpoint. For example, in Genesis 1:14, it says: "And God said, Let there be lights [meaning planets and stars] in the firmament of the heaven to divide the day from the night; *and let them be for **signs*** [authors' emphasis] and for seasons, and for days and years."

Nowadays, most scientists pooh-pooh this belief about "heavenly signs" as nonsense. *But most scientists have never actually investigated the idea.* This book will show you that there is an enormous amount of truth to the belief in celestial signs. It was true then when Genesis was written thousands of years ago, and as you will learn in this book, it is equally valid and true now. Maybe even more so.

The Babylonians believed that MEGA-EVENTS were *always* foretold by celestial signs in the sky. For this reason, the Babylonian astrologers fanatically studied the sky with the goal of being able to recognize such signs when they actually occurred, and predict the precise meaning of the signs. Thus, the Babylonian astrologers began a journey and quest for astrological knowledge that lasted for thousands of years. Along the way, they had to find the answers to many mysteries of the stars. The first such mystery that the Babylonians had to answer was: What *was* a sign, and what was *not* a sign?

The Babylonians decided very early in their work that a celestial sign occurred when something was different and out of the ordinary in the sky. In order to detect when there was a difference that was a sign, the Babylonians realized that they needed to draw and keep maps of the sky on a daily basis, and compare the maps from day to day to look for changes.

They quickly found that the stars themselves do not move perceptibly. So to speak, the stars are "fixed" (called *fixed stars*), and essentially stationary. That did not mean they did not move across the sky. As the Earth rotates, every star moved across the sky. But all of the stars move together; and all the stars' positions remained the same relative to each other. The North Star was always in the same place relative to the other stars. So the positions of all the stars essentially did not change. If there are no changes, there can be no celestial signs because a sign could occur only if something in the sky was noticeably different.

But the PLANETS did move; and the positions of the planets usually moved from one day to the next. By "positions," we are talking about the locations in the sky relative to the fixed stars. When you look up in the night sky and look for a planet, in order to find any particular planet, you have to take into account the fact that each planet has a different position each day. These changes in the positions of the planets were the logical "signs" that the Babylonians were looking for. Therefore, when the Babylonians were looking for changes in the sky that would constitute celestial "signs" that might allow them to predict that a mega-event was coming, they focused their attention on the movement of the planets. (In astrology, the Sun and Moon are referred to as planets. We will continue this tradition for ease of writing.)

The Babylonian Astrologers Invent the Circle . . .

Because the changes in the positions of the planets were possible celestial signs and therefore very important to the Babylonians, they needed a way to keep track of the planets' movements. This was not as easy to do as you might think. Many civilizations tried to devise a reliable way of keeping track of the movements of the planets but did not succeed in doing so. The Babylonian astrologers were the first to accomplish this. To do it, they invented the *circle*.

Have you ever wondered why a circle has 360 degrees instead of 50 degrees or 100 degrees? A circle has 360 degrees because the circle was designed by Babylonian astrologers to be a map of the sky. And there are 360 degrees in a circle because the Sun moves almost exactly one degree a day. The Sun actually moves about 0.9856 degrees per day, but one degree a day was close enough for the Babylonians 4,000 years ago.

Figure 3B at the end of this chapter is an example of how the Babylonians used the circle as a map to help them both record and illustrate the positions of the planets in the sky. The way they did this was both simple and ingenious. Since the planets moved around and around in the sky, they placed the Earth at the center of the circle and drew the positions of the planets on the circumference of the circle. They began to do this more than 4,000 years ago.

The Babylonian astrologers invented and used their circle with its 360 degrees to help them record and illustrate the positions of the Sun, Moon, and the planets every single night for thousands of years as they looked for celestial signs in the sky of impending mega-events.

For thousands of years!

The Stars Were Grouped into Constellations . . .

Sometime early on during those thousands of years, the Babylonians figured out that they needed reference points so that they could easily locate the planets in the nighttime sky. After all, it could be very difficult to find a planet other than the Sun and Moon. For this reason, the Babylonians divided the sky into *constellations*. This way, they had clear guideposts for the positions of the planets. For example, if you wanted to find Jupiter, they might say, "Tonight Jupiter is just a little east of the brightest star in the Taurus constellation."

Originally, the Babylonians believed that they needed reference points over the entire visible sky in order to track the movements of the seven visible planets. So they grouped the visible stars into about 48 different constellations. Then after several hundreds of years of observation, they began to realize that the planets' movements were always limited to a narrow circular band of the sky that was only about 50 degrees wide. The planets did not ever go above or below this 50-degree-wide band. The planets didn't do it then, and they still don't do it now. This 50-degree-wide band in the sky that delineates the boundaries of the movement of the planets is now called the ECLIPTIC. The ecliptic is sort of like the equator, but it is wider, and is in the sky rather than around the Earth. It is most easily defined as the path of the Sun across the sky measured against the stars that are fixed. (Please see Figure 3C at the end of this chapter.) All the planets travel across the sky in such a way that they are normally positioned within this approximately 50-degree-band in the sky.

In these modern times, we know that there are nine planets plus the Sun and Moon. But the Babylonians could only see five of the planets plus the Sun and Moon. These five planets were Mercury, Venus, Mars, Jupiter, and Saturn. Together with the Sun and Moon, we refer to them as the SEVEN VISIBLE PLANETS. Because the seven visible planets rarely moved above or below the ecliptic, the most important constellations became the ones that were within the boundaries of the ecliptic. The ecliptic also became known commonly as the *zodiac*, and the constellations that were within the zodiac became known as the *zodiac constellations*. The Babylonians had 12 of them. They were the ones that covered the path of travel of the planets. Naturally, since the Babylonians were looking for celestial signs, somewhere along the way, these 12 zodiac constellations were also called the 12 *zodiac signs*.

The 12 zodiac constellations were named Aries, Taurus, Gemini, Cancer, Leo, Virgo, Libra, Scorpio, Sagittarius, Capricorn, Aquarius, and Pisces. Legends grew up about them and their origins—legends that became a part of what we now call mythology.

The most important thing to bear in mind about the constellations is that they were initially devised by the Babylonians as guideposts to help them find the planets. Therefore, the Babylonians needed to include the zodiac constellations in their circular maps of the sky. In order to facilitate the drawing of their circles as maps of the sky, the Babylonians assigned a unique symbol to represent each zodiac constellation; in this way, they could just put the symbol of the zodiac sign on the circle rather than drawing a whole lot of stars. Many of you are probably familiar with the symbols for the 12 zodiac constellations. For example, here are the symbols for the Taurus and Gemini constellations:

(The symbols for each planet and sign are shown on page 35.)

Using such symbols worked so well that the Babylonians also assigned a symbol to each planet. When creating maps of the sky, the Babylonians drew the symbols of each zodiac constellation around the outside of the circle and put the symbols for each planet on the perimeter of the circle to show where the positions of the planets were. Figure 3D on page 37 is an example of how the Babylonians used the circle to draw a map of the sky around the time they first did so, over 4,000 years ago.

The illustration represents maps of the sky with the Earth at the center of the circle, the planets at the perimeter of the circle, and the 12 zodiac signs on the outside of the circle, which were used originally as guideposts. The 12 constellation (signs) are each 30 degrees. The degrees for the planets are always numbered from 0 through 29 and never higher than 30, because once a planet moves beyond the 30th degree of any zodiac constellation, it is within the borders of a new zodiac constellation. Such illustrations were meant to be maps of the sky, and they were the first astrology charts that resembled modern-day birth charts.

The Babylonians learned very early that the alignment of the planets on the day a person is born is very important. These circular charts were really the first BIRTH CHARTS, or NATAL CHARTS. The term *natal* means "birth" and is derived from the same Latin word as that which gave rise to another word about birth, *nativity*. The term NATAL PLANETS refers to the positions of the planets that someone was born with.

Why the Circle in Birth Charts Is Divided into 12 Equal Parts

The Babylonians used circles to represent maps of the sky and the positions of each planet. With such maps, we can easily see the constellation (or zodiac sign) that each planet is in. But we can also see from these circle/maps the ALIGNMENTS of the planets to each other. For this reason, we will refer to such charts in the future as BABYLONIAN ALIGNMENT CHARTS, because one purpose was to show the positions of the planets, and their alignments relative to each other and to the zodiac constellations.

This is important because the alignments of the planets to each other are a part of the Planetary Geometry of the charts.

One riddle that has dogged astrologers is the question of how and why the Babylonian astrologers chose to have 12 zodiac constellations, and why each of them were the same size of 30 degrees.

They had a very good reason for doing so. Somewhere along the line, the Babylonian astrologers had made an interesting discovery. They were very interested in the Moon, and they learned that the position of a Full Moon in the sky moved 30 degrees (30 days of the Sun's movement) from one Full Moon to the next. So by having 12 zodiac constellations, each of which was 30 degrees, when the last Full Moon occurred in the 15th degree of one zodiac constellation, then the next Full Moon will occur in the 15th degree of the next one—or at least very close to the 15th degree of the next zodiac constellation.

Each Full Moon actually moves a little less than 30 degrees during each lunar cycle, but 4,000 years ago, 30 degrees was a good enough approximation. In those days, when looking at the Moon, who could tell the difference between 30 degrees and 29.8 degrees? Or 29.1 degrees for that matter.

In other words, as the Moon traveled in the sky relative to the background of stars that were fixed, the Moon became a Full Moon about every 30 degrees that it traveled. In between those 30 degrees of travel, the Full Moon became a three-quarter Moon, a half Moon, a quarter Moon, and a New Moon. And then the Moon became a quarter Moon again and a half Moon again and a three-quarter Moon once again before becoming another Full Moon. And it did all of this in about 30 degrees of movement across the sky, which was the arc of each of the 12 zodiac constellations.

What this all meant was that each LUNAR CYCLE was 30 degrees. This discovery was one of the most important ones in all of astrology. This gave the Babylonians a reason to view the angle of 30 degrees and any multiple of it as having some kind of mystical power. Since there were 12 lunar cycles each year and each lunar cycle was 30 degrees, the Babylonians decided to divide the circle into 12 constellations instead of 10 or 5 or any other number. And this was also the reason that the Babylonians made each zodiac constellation the same size, 30 degrees. This way, with each lunar cycle, the Moon traveled from a particular degree in one zodiac constellation to the same degree in the next zodiac constellation.

The number 12, which was the number of zodiac constellations, became a somewhat mystical number to the Babylonians. In fact, the mysticism of this number was so pervasive that it even extended to surrounding cultures. For example, Christ had 12 disciples, and there were the 12 tribes of Israel. A group of 12 of anything was described as a dozen.

The Babylonians Make Monumental Discoveries

We mentioned earlier that the Babylonians were not the very first astrologers. There were others before them. Well, the Babylonians were also not the only astrologers of their time—almost every ancient civilization had them. Most other astrologers thought that all celestial signs were either visible eclipses, comets, or NEW STARS, such as a nova. For example, it is now known that around the time that Jesus of Nazareth was born, there was a nova, but such celestial events were very rare and unusual. After the nova that heralded the birth of Christ, there was not another one for over 1,000 years. Even comets and visible eclipses were so rare that to limit the definition of celestial signs to only such occurrences rendered astrology virtually useless as a predictive methodology. This was because by using *only* such criteria, celestial signs occurred far less often than the actual mega-events they were meant to predict.

Fortunately for astrology, though, the Babylonian astrologers were much better at research than their counterparts in other cultures. During the time that the Babylonians were improving and developing the way that they drew maps of the sky, they were already drawing and *storing* these daily maps. In addition, they were recording the important events that occurred during each day. Most important, the Babylonian astrologers were also comparing each day's significant events to the changing positions of the planets. For thousands of years, they kept analyzing the positions of the planets on the days when the most historic events happened. The type of events they were interested in included incidents of war breaking out; a peace treaty being signed or broken; a flood, famine, plague, or an earthquake; the birth of someone noteworthy such as a king or great soldier; or the death of such a person. For every day that such a mega-event occurred, the Babylonians studied their circular maps of the planets to detect celestial signs made by the planets. The Babylonians did this for centuries and centuries—and millennia.

To the Babylonians, the whole purpose of all of this work was to see if they could recognize celestial signs in the heavens and predict when something very important was going to happen. Lo and behold, after thousands of years of analyzing and comparing such data, the Babylonians were able to make a series of monumental discoveries that laid the foundation for modern astrology as we know it.

Babylonians Discover the Power of Conjunctions

About 4,000 years ago, the Babylonian astrologers began to make their monumental discoveries. Their first such discovery was that a CONJUNC-

TION of two planets was a celestial sign. On rare occasions, as the planets move around and around in the sky, two planets can come very close together in the sky such that the two planets appear to be right on top of each other. Such an alignment of two planets was given the name CONJUNCTION, and the Babylonians discovered that a conjunction of two important planets was often a celestial sign that a mega-event was going to happen. Figure 3E is an example of what a conjunction looks like in a Babylonian Alignment Chart. It shows that both Venus and Mars are at 15 degrees of Taurus; this means that the two planets form a conjunction, and are CONJUNCT to each other. When this happened, the Babylonians believed that it was probably a celestial sign that something out of the ordinary was about to occur.

The Babylonians' idea that a conjunction was a celestial sign was derived from their long-held belief that an eclipse was a very significant heavenly sign, and from their discovery that a solar eclipse was really a conjunction of the Sun and the Moon. After hundreds of years of investigating eclipses by using their circles, the Babylonians were the first to discover that a solar eclipse was always a conjunction of the Sun and the Moon. When there is a solar eclipse, the Moon is "in front of the Sun" or on top of the Sun—blocking it, and thus eclipsing it. (When there is a lunar eclipse, the Earth is "in front of the Moon" or on top of the Moon—blocking sunlight to the Moon, thereby eclipsing it.)

After this discovery, the Babylonians took the logical next step, which was to apply the concept of a conjunction to the other planets. In so doing, the Babylonians surmised that a conjunction of two planets was a heavenly sign that something important was going to happen or that someone consequential was going to be born. After hundreds of years of fanatically keeping records, the Babylonians found that a conjunction of two planets *did* often signal an important event. It was sometimes a mega-event, but usually it was a MINI-EVENT—something eventful, nonetheless. The special event could be an actual historic event or the birth of a noteworthy person.

Interestingly enough, as we will see later in this book, the Babylonians were essentially correct: A conjunction of two important planets really was, and still is, a celestial sign of something uncommon and out of the ordinary.

Babylonians Discover the Power of Symmetrical Planetary Geometry

As the centuries passed, the Babylonians made another very important discovery. They learned that as the planets move around and around in the Earth sky, an important heavenly sign can come from the *shape* of the figure that was created by connecting lines between the positions of some of the planets. (This forms the Planetary Geometry of the day.) They learned that whenever three or more planets formed a *symmetrical pattern* in the sky, the chances of a mega-event occurring were high. From this they deduced that when planets formed a symmetrical pattern, it was a celestial sign that some significant event was about to take place. Examples of the types of symmetrical patterns the Babylonians considered to be celestial signs are shown below.

Figure 3F: Eight examples of symmetrical planetary geometry

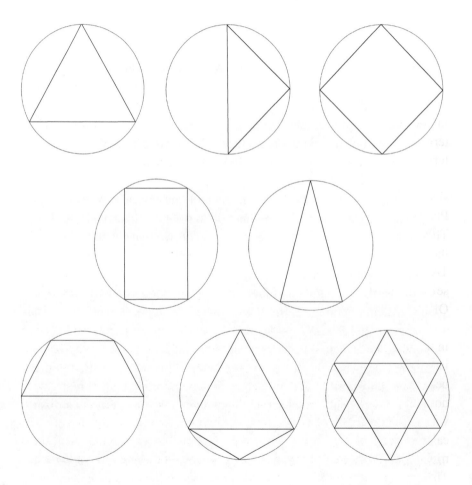

After a thousand of years of fanatical record keeping, the ancient Babylonian astrologers discovered that when the Planetary Geometry of a day included SYMMETRICAL PATTERNS like the ones on the last page, then an extraordinary event was almost sure to happen. The event could be a very *positive* historic event or a very *negative* one. But whatever the event, it would be consequential and have significant impact.

It is helpful to understand exactly how the planets can form such symmetrical patterns. Take, for example, the first symmetrical figure. It is a triangle. But it is not just an ordinary triangle; it is an EQUILATERAL TRIANGLE because each side is exactly the same length. This makes the triangle perfectly symmetrical. The way three planets form such a triangle is when they are each spaced apart by an angle of 120 degrees, which is one-third of the 360 degrees of a circle. In other words, if you look at the sky and see that Jupiter is in one position, and if you turn your head 120 degrees in either direction and find another planet, each of which is ⅓ of the sky away from Jupiter, then the three planets form this special triangle. (Of course, this would assume that you can see through the Earth with some kind of x-ray vision.) In order to easily see if there was a symmetrical pattern, the Babylonians drew lines connecting the planets' positions. All patterns made in this way are examples of Planetary Geometry.

All of the eight figures on the previous page are symmetrical geometric shapes that are examples of what the Magi Society calls SYMMETRICAL Planetary Geometry. Astrologers have given each of them a special name. The first one is called a GRAND TRINE; the second one is a T-SQUARE; the third is called a GRAND CROSS; the fourth is the GOLDEN RECTANGLE, the fifth is a YOD, and the sixth is a GRAND SEXTILE. The seventh is the KITE, and the last is the famous pattern known as the STAR OF DAVID.

There is interesting confirmation that the ancients of Babylonia believed in the power of symmetrical patterns in the sky. We are all somewhat familiar with the Hebrew culture because of the Old Testament of the Bible and because Jesus of Nazareth was born of that culture. But what most of us do not know is that the Hebrew symbol commonly known as the Star of David was actually astrologically derived. The Star of David is really an astrological pattern! It is two perfectly symmetrical triangles, meaning two grand trines. However, one of the grand trines is turned 60 degrees from the other. The entire pattern can be formed when any six of the planets are aligned in the sky such that each planet is spaced 60 degrees apart from the next planet. According to the ancient Babylonians, the Star of David was the most powerful symmetrical pattern of the planets. These astrologers believed that anyone born on a day when the planets formed the Star of David was extraordinarily lucky and would be remarkably powerful.

The Magi Society believes that Samuel, the Hebrew prophet who chose and anointed David as king of Israel, was an astrologer—probably the best one of his time. Even though David was the son of a shepherd, Samuel chose him to be king of Israel because David was born on a day when six planets formed the pattern that is now known as the Star of David. Samuel knew that anyone born on such a day had a great chance of becoming the most powerful person alive, and the most fortunate. Does this mean David really did kill Goliath with a stone? We think so. How lucky and powerful can you get? David was king of Israel and Judah for 33 years, and Israel grew under his reign. Samuel's astrological prediction for David was correct.

The Hebrew prophets were the best astrologers of their times.

An Example of the Power of Symmetrical Planetary Geometry

Unfortunately, no one knows King David's actual birth date, so we cannot really use his birth chart as an example of the power of symmetrical Planetary Geometry. But it is not necessary to use King David's chart as an example. There is no shortage of great examples, because the symmetrical patterns of astrology really work. We will provide you with some to help you understand this very important concept of astrology.

Napoleon Bonaparte was certainly a historic personage. His birth chart is Figure 3G on page 38 at the end of this chapter. (Please note that all birth charts referred to in a chapter can be found at the end of that chapter.) Obviously, someone like Napoleon would fit the criteria of the birth of a very historic person. He impacted the history of Europe for decades. On the day that he was born, there was a symmetrical pattern, a Grand Trine, formed by three of the planets: Mars, Uranus, and Pluto. This pattern is very rare and is an example of the type of symmetrical pattern that the Babylonians believed was a celestial sign that something significant was going to happen. In this case, it was the sign of the birth of the most important man in Europe in the early 19th century. Virtually everyone in Europe during the early 1800s felt the impact of Napoleon's actions.

What this means is that by using and analyzing Planetary Geometry, we would have predicted that Napoleon could have been a very historic personage. Not bad for using a rule of astrology that was formulated more than 4,000 years ago.

The Concept of the Orb, and More Examples of Planetary Geometry

Some of you may have noticed that in Napoleon's birth chart, the Grand Trine, was not exactly perfect. In order to form a perfect Grand Trine, each of the three planets that form a Grand Trine has to be exactly 120 degrees from the other. Such an event almost never happens. The Babylonian astrologers discovered that the planets do not have to form a precisely symmetrical pattern in order to still have a very powerful influence. But the more exact the formation, the more powerful the effect.

The number of degrees that two planets can be short of exactness but will still have a powerful influence, is called the ORB. The orb that the Magi Society prefers most is about three degrees. For example, in the case of Napoleon's chart, Mars and Pluto were 1.5 degrees away from being 120 degrees apart. But Mars and Pluto were within the allowable orb of three degrees to be considered effective in forming one side of the Grand Trine. It turns out that the planets that form each side of Napoleon's Grand Trine were within the three-degree allowable orb. So together, the three planets still form a Grand Trine.

But in fact, there are almost two grand trines in Napoleon's birth chart. There is nearly a conjunction of Neptune to Mars. And Neptune, Pluto and Uranus are very close to the three-degree orb of forming a second Grand Trine. When so many planets are involved in one shape, we call the result COMPLEX PLANETARY GEOMETRY. And we give more leeway in the orb for such figures. In Napoleon's case, we regard him as having two Grand Trines. The power of Napoleon's natal Planetary Geometry explains why Napoleon was able to have so much impact on all of Europe. He was born with two Grand Trines.

The formation of a Grand Trine in the sky also signaled the beginning of World War II. Adolf Hitler sent his Nazi German army to war on September 1, 1939, by invading Poland (Figure 3H). On that day, Mars, Neptune, and Uranus formed a grand trine in the sky and is another example of the power of symmetrical alignments and how Planetary Geometry accurately foretold of a true mega-event. How much more of a mega-event can you get than the start of a world war?

Symmetrical Patterns Are Examples of the Most Powerful Form of Planetary Geometry

The Babylonian style of alignment charts for the day Napoleon was born and the day that Hitler invaded Poland are good examples of how useful Planetary Geometry really is to astrology. All alignments of planets in the sky are forms of Planetary Geometry, and Grand Trines are among the most consequential and powerful. When a Grand Trine is formed, it almost always has a noticeable impact.

As other examples of what we mean by consequential Planetary Geometry, on page 39 at the end of this chapter (Figures 3I and 3J), we have provided the Babylonian style of alignment charts for the two most devastating earthquakes ever to hit the United States. They were both in San Francisco. Notice that on both dates, three planets formed one of the symmetrical patterns that we showed you on page 22. On the days of both San Francisco earthquakes, three planets formed the exact same symmetrical shape, a pattern called the T-square. The only difference is that one T-square is the mirror image of the other and is therefore rotated 180 degrees. But they are both the same shape of symmetrical pattern.

"Coincidences" such as these encouraged the Babylonians to believe in the power of symmetrical patterns and to continue to search for astrologically based celestial signs as a way of predicting the days when significant events would occur.

How Planets Can Form an Important Geometric Pattern

We understand that some of you are completely new to astrology and may not fully understand how any geometric pattern is actually formed by the positions of the planets. For the sake of those of you who still do not fully understand how these geometric figures are formed, we hope the following explanation will help:

For the Babylonian Alignment Chart of the 1906 San Francisco earthquake, note that Neptune and Uranus are on opposite sides of the circle, about 180 degrees apart, and Mercury is in between the two planets, about 90 degrees from each. In terms of the actual positions of the planets in the sky on that fateful day, this chart tells us that Uranus and Neptune were on opposite sides of the Earth, and were therefore about 180 degrees apart. At the same time, Mercury was located in the sky at about the halfway point between Uranus and Neptune. If you draw a line in the sky connecting Uranus and Neptune, Mercury is in the middle of that line.

Babylonian Astrology Was Missing Key Planets

Some of you might be thinking that these examples are not truly representative, and are chosen only because they work. But we assure you that

Planetary Geometry and astrology do work. We prove it at the end of the book by using Planetary Geometry as well as some new concepts that are unique and powerful tools of Magi Astrology.

However, we understand why some of you might have doubts at his time. After all, you might be thinking, *If the astrology of the Babylonians was always as accurate as the few examples given so far, then why isn't astrology recognized and respected as a science?* How come there is no college or university giving out degrees in astrology?

There is an answer to all such questions, and it is a very simple and understandable one. The main reason is that the Babylonian astrologers had one very major shortcoming: They did not know about three very important planets. Pluto was not discovered until 1930. Neptune was discovered in 1846, and Uranus in 1781. These three planets are sometimes referred to collectively as the NEW PLANETS. Not knowing about these three very important new planets was a crippling handicap for the Babylonian astrologers.

Take, for example, the day that started World War II, September 1, 1939. On that day, there was a Grand Trine of Mars, Neptune, and Uranus. We have already explained that a Grand Trine was one of the Babylonians' sure-fire celestial signs of an impending significant event.

But if you did not know about Neptune and Uranus, there would be no grand trine, and the Babylonians did not know about Neptune and Uranus. Therefore, on that most historic of days, even though symmetrical patterns would have worked perfectly, the Babylonians would not have known that there was a symmetrical pattern in the sky—not without Neptune and Uranus. They would not have seen the sign in the sky that would predict that momentous day!

The Babylonian astrologers were right about the importance of symmetrical patterns made by the planets, but they did not know about enough of the planets to hold on to this belief. Even worse, they would think they were wrong. Trying to do astrology without all of the planets is like trying to write a doctoral thesis with a three-year-old's vocabulary, or like trying to spell words without half the alphabet. You are very limited in what you can do. But the rules are valid, nonetheless.

Because of this insurmountable disadvantage, the Babylonians, and virtually all other astrologers since them, have groped for other ways to use the planets as a predictive methodology. They devised many other tools for astrology, most of which were useless, or even worse, just plain wrong. And in so doing, astrologers took some very wrong turns and did something that resulted in another of the main reasons why astrology is not studied in the universities: *Most astrologers set aside the Babylonian Alignment Charts in favor of the HOROSCOPE CHART.*

There Are Disadvantages in Using Only Horoscope Charts

A horoscope chart is the type of astrological chart that is used today in virtually all astrology magazines and books. It still has the Babylonian circle with its 12 parts. But the 12 parts represent HOUSES and are *usually not equally divided into 30-degree segments.* The major problem with such charts is that you cannot look at them and easily pick out a symmetrical pattern of planets. You cannot easily visualize the important alignments and Planetary Geometry made by the planets, the way you can with a Babylonian Alignment Chart.

It was the Babylonians themselves who also designed the original horoscope charts. They were meant to be used in addition to the alignment style of charts, but they are not as useful as the original alignment charts.

To master the contents of this book, it is not necessary to understand what horoscope charts are. For those of you who want an example of one, please look at Figure 3K on page 40. We have provided you with a horoscope chart of the invasion of Poland by Hitler's armies on September 1, 1939. Please compare the horoscope style of birth chart to the Babylonian Alignment Chart for the same date. Notice that in the horoscope chart, you cannot easily see that there was a grand trine on that date. In fact, it is even difficult to determine where the positions of the planets are in horoscope charts because each of the 12 houses is represented as being the same size, even though each house has a different number of degrees. This means that the relative proportional distances between the planets is not easily discernible. In a horoscope chart, the planets are not placed in the positions that they actually were in the sky, but are placed according to their house positions. Nonetheless, astrology magazines use horoscope charts all the time.

We think there is a use for horoscope charts, but only when they are displayed *side by side* with a chart similar to the Babylonian Alignment Charts. By itself, a horoscope chart makes it easy to miss the crucial Planetary Geometry. Besides, certain popular styles of horoscope charts give some people headaches because they actually reverse the numbers that indicate the degrees of the planets. That's right—in some such charts, the astrologers actually reverse the numbers that indicate the degrees of the planets because the numbers are written along the radii of the circle. Confused? So are most people. But don't worry, we don't use them in our books, and you do not need to understand them to master Magi Astrology.

The Babylonian Alignment Charts were designed so that you cannot help but notice the most important Planetary Geometry of the planets. But unfortunately for astrology and the world, these charts have not been used by the majority of astrologers for a very, very long time. The Magi Society regards their disuse as a major setback for astrology and one of the main reasons astrology is not more widely accepted than it is. If astrologers had kept the faith and continued the prevalent use of Babylonian-style alignment charts, then certainly when the new planets were discovered, the whole world would understand the importance of Planetary Geometry, and know that astrology really works.

Astrology Has No Uniform Definition for Time of Birth

You cannot have a horoscope chart without the time of birth. This is because it is the time of birth that determines the ascendant and midheaven, and none of the 12 houses are able to be calculated without the ascendant. The houses are the key to horoscope charts. However, there is a very real problem that the astrological community has not yet come to grips with. Astrology has not defined time of birth.

There cannot be horoscope charts without a time of birth, and yet astrology does not have a uniform definition of what time of birth is. Is it the time that the umbilical cord is cut? The time any part of the baby first leaves the womb? The time the baby first gasps for air and cries? Is the time of birth when the baby first opens its eyes and is aware of the world? Or is it when the soul incarnates into the body? And when is that? Or, is it another parameter—perhaps one that we have never thought of? Astrology is not sure.

Not only do astrologers not have a uniform definition of the time of birth, but the nurses and doctors who fill out birth certificates do not share the same standards for determining time of birth. To make matters even more confusing, most birth times are written as an afterthought, from memory, once the delivery team is certain the baby is healthy. How accurate is the memory when there is so much vital work to be done during the delivery process?

Magi Astrology Is Very Accurate Even Without a Time of Birth

For every 12 minutes of time, the ascendant and all the houses are shifted about three degrees. Three degrees is the orb that we use. This means that if a birth time is inaccurate by 12 or more minutes, the horoscope chart can be misleading or entirely invalid. For this reason, the Magi Society decided long ago that it was necessary to develop and perfect a form of astrology that can be highly accurate and helpful when only a *date* of birth is available, without requiring a *time* of birth. We believe that we have achieved this through Magi Astrology. We have done so by concentrating on the Planetary Geometry of a birth chart, and greatly advancing the techniques used to evaluate Planetary Geometry.

By focusing our research on Planetary Geometry, the Magi Society made one of the most exciting discoveries in the astrology of love and all relationships. We learned that the pieces of Planetary Geometry created by the planets when we were born are very much like pieces of a jigsaw puzzle; everyone was born with such jigsaw pieces. Another person's Planetary Geometry will either fit our pieces, or not, and it is this fit (or nonfit) that ultimately determines the outcome of all of our relationships. We all fall in love with those who were born with Planetary Geometry that fits ours. We also learned that the planets actually point to our soulmate and the person we will marry. The astrological planet that tells us all this is Chiron.

Chiron Is the Planet That Points to Your Soulmate!

Chiron is so new that it was discovered only in 1977, eight years *after* man first landed on the Moon. But just as the Babylonians were greatly handicapped because they were not aware of Uranus, Neptune, and Pluto, traditional astrology has been equally lost without using Chiron. Astrologers have given the following symbol to represent Chiron:

By combining the use of Chiron with Planetary Geometry, we finally have the astrological answers to the mystery of why we love those we do, and whom we will marry. To give you a glimpse of how we can do this, let us look at the birth charts of Figures 3L and 3M. These charts are similar to those we have already seen, but in each of them, there are two symbols (representing planets) inside of a square. The squares are our way of saying that the planets belong to someone else's birth chart. In Figure 3L, the chart is that of Clark Gable with two of Carol Lombard's natal planets drawn in (Lombard's Sun and Chiron). Lombard's actual birth chart is Figure 6C on page 150. In Figure 3M, the chart is that of Humphrey Bogart, with two of Lauren Bacall's natal planets drawn in (Bacall's Chiron and Neptune). As you can see, by drawing connecting line between some of the planets of both of these superfamous married couples, we get Grand Trines, which are signs of a match made in the heavens. The key component of these two Grand Trines was Chiron, *and Chiron is the key piece of the jigsaw puzzle of marriage. Chiron is the arrow that points to your soulmate,* and we will devote almost a hundred pages to this subject so that you will know how to determine whom Chiron points to in your chart.

Now that you have had a preview of one of the principles of Planetary Geometry as it relates to relationships, let us return to providing you with step-by-step detail.

Combined Planetary Geometry Is the Astrological Key to Love

When each person is born, the planets create a unique natal Planetary Geometry. If there are certain types of symmetrical patterns in this geometry, the person has a greater-than-normal chance of becoming historically significant. In this regard, a person's Planetary Geometry gives us a sign of the likely boundaries of that person's destiny from the historical perspective.

In addition, every person's Planetary Geometry also has an overriding influence on that person's relationships of all kinds. This is because we are all most attracted to, and most compatible with, persons whose natal Planetary Geometry fits together in certain ways with our own Planetary Geometry, like a jigsaw puzzle. Let us explain this in detail.

If you take one person's Babylonian-style alignment chart and *overlay* it and *superimpose* it on top of another person's Babylonian-style alignment chart, you create what the Magi Society calls a COMBINED ALIGNMENT CHART (CAC). With a CAC, you can see the positions of both persons' natal planets because both are drawn on a single combined chart. In this way, you can visually determine if the overlay of the two charts creates symmetrical figures like the ones we showed you earlier on page 22. If they do, then the two persons whose planets combine to form such symmetrical patterns have a good chance of being lifelong lovers, the type that Hollywood used to make movies about. In other words, there is a good chance that the two people will both feel like they are soulmates, will fall in love, and will eventually marry. Examples of all this are Carole Lombard and Clark Gable, and also Lauren Bacall and Humphrey Bogart.

The combining of the natal planets of Clark Gable and Carole Lombard formed a Grand Trine. So did the natal planets of Humphrey Bogart and Lauren Bacall. Both of these symmetrical patterns are celestial signs of a lifelong and historic romance. That is why we still hear about Gable and Lombard, and about Bogie and Bacall.

Just as a symmetrical pattern formed during a day usually creates a very powerful influence for that day, a symmetrical pattern that is formed by combining the natal planets of two persons creates a very powerful and special relationship— one that is likely to be life-altering for both persons.

In this book, for emphasis and simplicity, a CAC will contain all the natal planets of one person, and only the most important planets from the other person. When two individuals' charts are combined to form a CAC, the patterns and shapes formed by their combined planets is called COMBINED PLANETARY GEOMETRY. The Grand Trine is an example of the type of Combined Planetary Geometry that exists in the CAC of most lifelong married couples. This means that we can analyze a CAC to help us identify the person we will marry. The Magi Society has found that the shape of the patterns formed when you combine two persons' natal planets is a very accurate indication of the type of relationship that the two persons are most likely to have.

Gable and Lombard formed a Grand Trine, an indication of compatibility and harmony. But a T-square is not good; a couple that forms one is likely to have a tumultuous relationship. The T-square shape is the one that we saw in the charts of the two earthquakes of San Francisco.

This means that you can predict the probable outcome of a relationship between two people by analyzing their Combined Planetary Geometry. In this book, we will learn all about the different kinds of Combined Planetary Geometry and what they each mean.

But using combined alignment charts to successfully analyze relationships requires another very key component. The key component is CHIRON, a new astrological planet.

Chiron Has a Special Impact on Personal Relationships

Just as the Babylonians were at a severe disadvantage in their study and practice of astrology without the three new planets, modern astrologers have been at a disadvantage in trying to analyze relationships without using and understanding Chiron. Chiron is an astrological body just like the Sun, Moon, and the planets. But *Chiron is by far the most important planet when it comes to relationships.*

> ***Chiron is the arrow that points to your soulmate!***
> ***The position of Chiron in a birth chart is the best clue to***
> ***marriages, spouses, children, and all family ties.***

In 1977, astronomers discovered Chiron. Originally, astronomers thought that Chiron was a planet. Some astronomers and skeptics of astrology said that the discovery of Chiron would put an end to astrology. They were very wrong. Instead, we will see in this book why Chiron will give birth to a resurgence of astrology unseen since the days of Johannes Kepler, when astrologers were respected and influential advisors to European and Asian monarchs.

Chiron is not a planet in the astronomic sense. But just as the Sun and Moon are not true planets and yet have profound astrological influences, so does Chiron. And just as Uranus, Neptune, and Pluto were all very important "new" pieces of the secret of the stars, so is Chiron. Whenever astrology discovers and makes use of a new piece of the astrological puzzle, some old mysteries become easily understood.

For example, Figure 3N is the Babylonian Alignment Chart for December 7, 1941, the day Japan attacked Pearl Harbor. This chart includes Chiron, and from now on, all of our charts will include Chiron.

Note that when Chiron is included, the chart for the Pearl Harbor attack clearly has a Grand Trine formed by Chiron, Mars, and Sun! So the ancient Babylonian laws of astrology were right again. On both of the most important days that started World War II, there was a Grand Trine in the sky. A Grand Trine is one of the most powerful symmetrical forms of Planetary Geometry, so this is another indication that symmetrical Planetary Geometry is a celestial sign that a mega-event could occur. (The shape of the Planetary Geometry by itself does not tell us if the event is good or bad, but you will learn later on how to use other tools of astrology to foretell or explain the actual nature of the mega-event.)

In this book, you will also see again and again that the recent discovery of Chiron and its incorporation into astrology will explain what astrologers could not explain before its discovery. By including Chiron, astrologers can do more than ever before.

Although Chiron is *always* important, Chiron is most important when it comes to matters involving relationships between two people. In any *relationship,* be it one relating to love, sex, friendship, or business, Chiron is the most important planet. It is so crucial, that in about 80 percent of all married couples, the positions of Chiron in the birth charts were the most reliable signs of whether the couple would or would not marry each other. We will explain all of this later on in the book.

Planetary Geometry Provides a Broad Range of Information

You now know how the Babylonians constructed a birth chart, and you also can see why they formulated their charts in the way they did. The next step is to understand how to analyze and *interpret* the birth chart.

Knowledge of how to *interpret* birth charts is remarkably helpful in improving all of our relationships. The key to accurate interpretations is Planetary Geometry. By learning how to assess the Planetary Geometry of a day, we can determine if it is a good time to get engaged or married; or if it is a propitious day to *look* for a job or *start* a new job or business. We can even determine if it is a good day to seduce a particular person, or meet or make love to someone for the first time.

That's right—there are good and bad days to do every type of activity or endeavor—and we know which is which through an analysis of the Planetary Geometry of the planets on any day.

In addition, by evaluating the Planetary Geometry of any day, we can determine the inner tendencies of anyone born on that day. Is the person likely to be reliable, honest, and faithful? Or is the person an incurable runaround and a heartbreaker? Is he or she cerebral and practical, or instinctual and emotional? Stable or unpredictable? Sexual or intellectual? All of the above, at different times—or too much of one and not enough of the other?

The answers are in the stars, and it's all in the alignment of the planets and the Planetary Geometry that the planets create. In the next chapter, we will begin to show you how to interpret birth charts by using Planetary Geometry.

ॐ ॐ ॐ

Symbols for the 12 signs and the planets

♈	ARIES	♎	LIBRA	☉	SUN	♄	SATURN
♉	TAURUS	♏	SCORPIO	☿	MERCURY	♅	URANUS
♊	GEMINI	♐	SAGITTARIUS	♀	VENUS	♆	NEPTUNE
♋	CANCER	♑	CAPRICORN	♂	MARS	♇	PLUTO
♌	LEO	♒	AQUARIUS	♃	JUPITER		
♍	VIRGO	♓	PISCES				

Figure 3A: Sample chart of USSR founded 12/30/1922

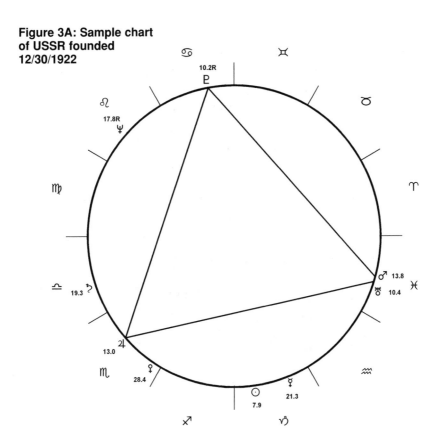

Figure 3B: Circle was invented by Babylonians to map the sky

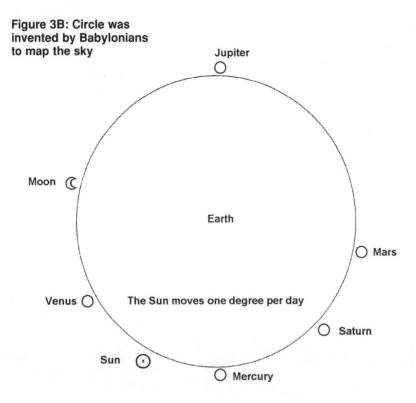

Figure 3C: The positions of the planets in the sky are limited to a band of about 50 degrees. Only the Moon, Venus, Mercury, and Mars can go outside this band, and then only by a few degrees.

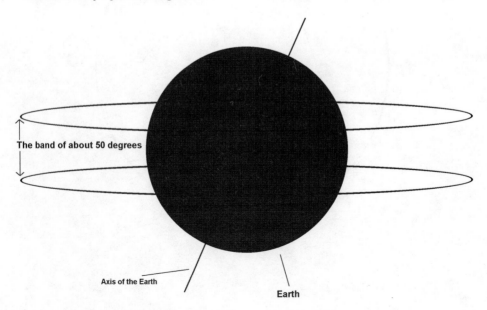

**Figure 3D:
Babylonians divide
to circle into 12
constellations of 30
degrees each.**

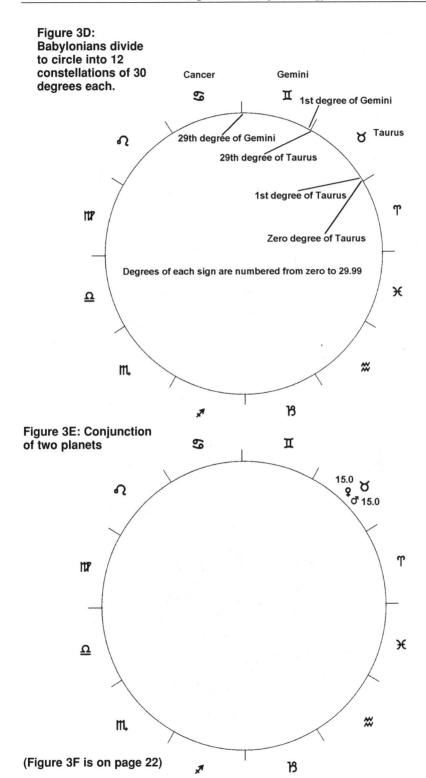

Cancer

Gemini

1st degree of Gemini

29th degree of Gemini

Taurus

29th degree of Taurus

1st degree of Taurus

Zero degree of Taurus

Degrees of each sign are numbered from zero to 29.99

**Figure 3E: Conjunction
of two planets**

15.0 ♀ ♉
♂ 15.0

(Figure 3F is on page 22)

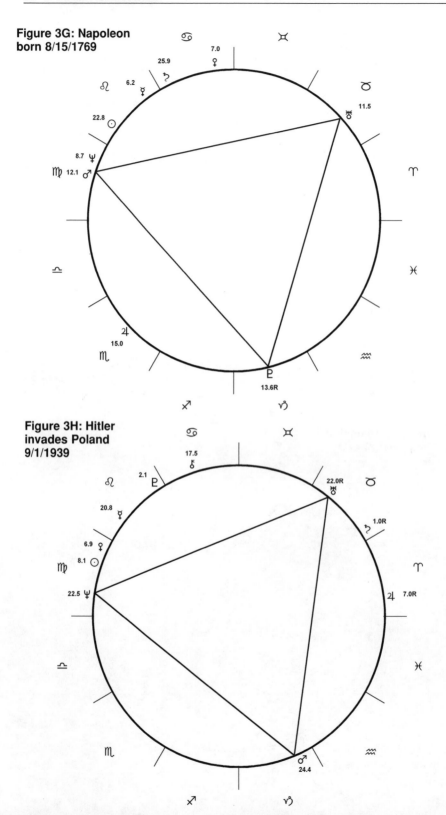

Figure 3G: Napoleon born 8/15/1769

Figure 3H: Hitler invades Poland 9/1/1939

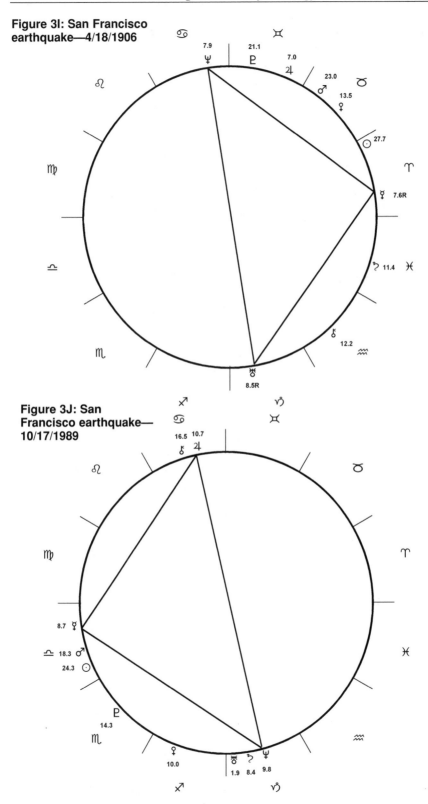

Figure 3I: San Francisco earthquake—4/18/1906

Figure 3J: San Francisco earthquake—10/17/1989

Figure 3K: Horoscope chart for time Hitler invaded Poland, 4:45 A.M., 9/1/1939

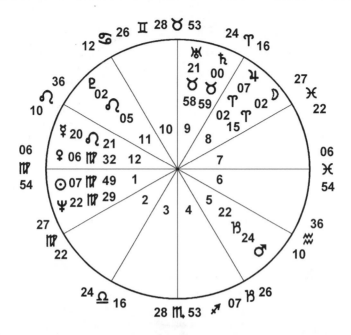

Figure 3L: Gable and Lombard Combined Chart

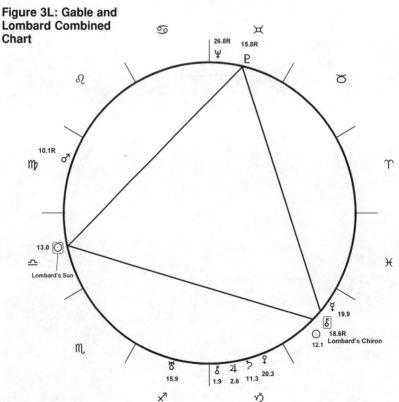

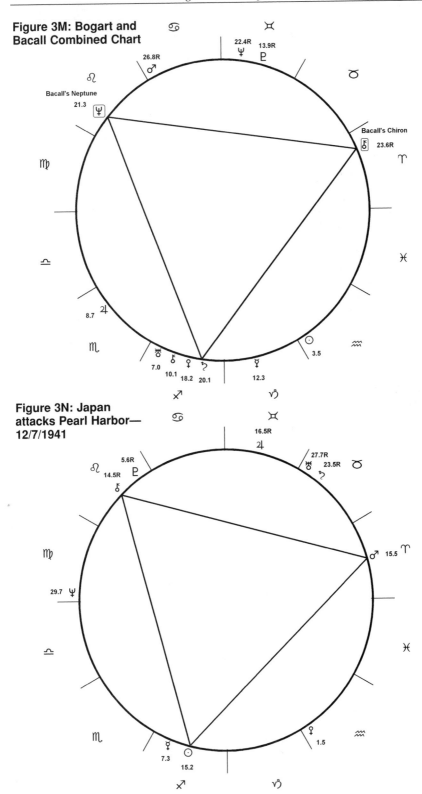

Figure 3M: Bogart and Bacall Combined Chart

Figure 3N: Japan attacks Pearl Harbor— 12/7/1941

CHAPTER FOUR

༄

How to Interpret a Birth Chart

For decades now, many millions of people have been fascinated with SUN-SIGN ASTROLOGY. Sun-Sign Astrology is that portion of traditional astrology that primarily uses SUN SIGNS as a predictive tool. Those of you who have applied it to the problems in your daily lives already know that Sun-Sign Astrology is very limited in its ability to help you. But Magi Astrology answers some questions that Sun-Sign Astrology cannot, such as:

- Why do some people have the best character traits of their Sun Signs, and others have the worst?

- Why do you get along with some Leos but not others? And some Scorpios but not others?

- Why are some Taurians stubborn and obstinate beyond all reason, while others are not stubborn; but instead, are reliable, steadfast, and tenacious in their endeavors? How come some Cancerians are so sensitive that they cannot take a joke, while others are sensitive in a sensual way and are darn right irresistible?

During the 1970s, Sun-Sign Astrology became very popular even though it left all such questions completely unanswered. Together with Horoscope Astrology, Sun-Sign Astrology comprises the basic tools of traditional astrology. But even the entirety of traditional astrology lacks the ability to adequately help us in matters of love and money. In this book, we will teach the parts of Magi Astrology that help you accurately answer many important questions about the people in your life—for example:

- Why are some people so intelligent, and others almost illogical?

- Why are some people so hyper-emotional that you don't feel safe being around them, while others are so stable you would almost consider them boring?

- What is it that makes one person simply exude sexuality—so much so you are excited by their mere presence—while others leave you so cold you would rather just go to bed. Alone.

- Why are some individuals so much fun to be with, while others are just wet blankets?

- What makes someone extraordinarily artistic or talented, while others are not the slightest bit artistically oriented?

You will be able to answer all of the above questions and more by learning how to evaluate Planetary Geometry. But first, we want to give you a mini-lesson on Sun-Sign Astrology and its shortcomings.

Sun-Sign Astrology Has Limited Capabilities

Many of you are probably aware of the general public's love affair with Sun Signs. Here are the 12 commonly known signs and some identifying characteristics of persons born under the signs:

- **Aries**: Adventuresome, impulsive, fearless, impatient, abrupt, zealous; has strong initiative and is a person of action.

- **Taurus**: Persistent, strong-willed, loyal, immovable, unchanging, trustworthy, reliable.

- **Gemini**: Punctual, gregarious, sociable, nervous, changeable, provocative, spontaneous.

- **Cancer**: Cautious, protective, sensitive, moody, emotional, home-loving, maternal or paternal.

- **Leo**: Forgiving, dramatic, snobbish, a conspicuous spender, has excessive self-esteem, generous.

- **Virgo**: Meticulous and organized, fussy and hypercritical, honest, conscientious, trusting.

- **Libra**: Gracious, harmonious, peace-loving, indecisive, unreliable, judgmental, loves luxury.

- **Scorpio**: Determined, intense, jealous, suspicious, secretive, passionate.

- **Sagittarius**: Fun-loving, optimistic, adaptable, manipulative, greedy.

- **Capricorn**: Ambitious, prudent, a good planner, frugal, not usually fun to be with, good provider, self-reliant.

- **Aquarius**: Idealistic, kind, free-spirited, needs regular change and independence. The least predictable sign.

- **Pisces**: Compassionate, understanding, agreeable, careless, weak-willed, dependent on others.

During the last three decades, literally thousands of astrology books and hundreds of magazines have pushed the importance of Sun Signs to the very limit by applying it to compatibility—that is, trying to tell us which other Sun Signs we are, or are not, compatible with. Astrology owes a debt of gratitude to these magazines and books for helping to keep astrology in the minds of the public and expanding the borders of its popularity.

For most of us, our only real glimpse of astrology is Sun-Sign Astrology. But there is a drawback to this type of astrology. Many individuals who have tried to apply it to questions of compatibility know firsthand that Sun-Sign Astrology falls far short of being able to offer solutions to the ever-pressing problems related to love and human relationships. The magazines that publish astrology columns have wisely realized and accepted this short-coming. That is why such columns are written more for entertainment purposes and for fun, as opposed to pretending to provide serious advice. Sun-Sign Astrology is just too general and too limited. For example, are you compatible with every Leo and incompatible with every Scorpio? Of course not. The fact is, you are compatible with some Leos and not other Leos; and we are all compatible with some people of every sign, and totally incompatible with some other people of every sign. So, obviously, Sun-Sign Astrology has severe limitations.

If astrology is to be truly useful and fulfill at least some of our needs, it has to be able to tell us whether or not we are compatible with *this particular Leo, or that particular Scorpio,* and so on, which is precisely why this book was written. The knowledge we provide will help you answer such questions accurately, helpfully, and with clarity.

In the past, in an attempt to answer specific questions, astrology books have expanded compatibility analysis to include not just the Sun Sign, but also the rising sign (or ASCENDENT), the Moon Sign, the Venus Sign, and the Mars Sign, and so on. For instance, are you compatible with someone whose Sun and ascendent are in Leo, and whose Moon is in Taurus and has Venus in Virgo? Although at first, one might think that this approach would be helpful, it is actually so confusing that rather than answering questions, this methodology creates all kinds of unanswered questions without ever helping you get closer to the answers of your original questions. If you've tried it, you already know its shortcomings. There are just too many conflicting interpretations to such an approach.

For example, the other person's Moon in Taurus is very compatible to your Sun, and is about average in compatibility to your Moon, but it is not good for your Mars or Venus. The other person's Venus in Leo is very compatible to your Venus and Moon, but not for your Mars or Sun. And your ascendants are only so-so in compatibility. So what does this all mean?

Confusion is what it means.

Besides these problems with Sun-Sign Astrology, there is that universally unresolved question: Why do people fall in love with someone who is not their "type"? We all have friends who have cut out magazine pictures of their supposed type for years, and dreamed about meeting him or her. Then they fall in love with someone who bears no resemblance to that fantasy.

Why?

To answer this question, and to find the astrological reasons to compatibility, emotional relationships, love, and marriage, the Magi Society recently concluded a three-year study of personal relationships. This study analyzed the birth charts of about 25,000 couples, of which over 17,000 had lifelong marriages lasting at least 20 years; and about 2,500 were engaged or living together for at least one year but never got married. There were almost 1,000 couples who broke up but later eventually married. We also researched about 5,000 couples who were married but later divorced. Whenever possible, we included in our research the birth charts of all of the subsequent spouses of divorced individuals. The study ultimately analyzed the birth charts of a little more than 55,000 persons. The results of this study were earthshaking.

We found out conclusively that it is not our Sun Signs, but our Planetary Geometry that determines who we are most harmonious with and who we will marry. By comparing the Planetary Geometry of the birth charts of any two individuals, we can accurately evaluate the nature and destiny of the relationship that two individuals are most likely to have. Planetary Geometry was also found to be the crucial astrological influence to emotional, sexual, spiritual, communicative, and intellectual compatibility issues.

For thousands of years, astrologers have been seeking to unlock the secret celestial signs of love and marriage. It is Planetary Geometry that

gives us such signs, but in order to master it, it's necessary to first understand Planetary Geometry's most important components, which are called
PLANETARY ASPECTS.

Planetary Aspects

As we discussed earlier, the Babylonians began studying astrology primarily to help them accurately predict which days were going to be historic or
significant. But after they began to study astrology, the Babylonians became
much more ambitious. They wanted to be able to predict not just *whether* certain days were going to be historic, but also precisely and exactly *why* the day
would be. For example, would a particular day be a day of peace or of war?
And what would be the destiny of a person born on that day?

The Babylonians studied astrology for thousands of years to try to discern the answers to such questions, but they never did fully achieve their
goal. As we mentioned, it was impossible for them to do so because they
did not know about Uranus, Neptune, and Pluto—and they did not know
about Chiron. You simply cannot accurately predict what will happen without knowing about these planets. But while the Babylonian astrologers were
trying to achieve their goal, they did succeed in discovering PLANETARY
ASPECTS. A planetary aspect is a *meaningful* alignment of just two planets. Let us explain the details of how they are formed.

We all know that the planets are constantly moving around and around
in the Earth sky. After thousands of years of observation and looking for
celestial signs, the Babylonians discovered that whenever any two planets
were aligned in the sky in such a way that the angle between them was any
one of seven specific angles, then the chances of an uncommon event
occurring was very high. The Babylonians called the alignments of two
such planets a *planetary aspect*. Modern astrologers simplify the term, and
we often just call them ASPECTS. An aspect occurs whenever any two
planets are aligned in the Earth sky at any of the following seven angles:

0 degrees	called a ***conjunction***
30 degrees	called a ***semi-sextile***
60 degrees	called a ***sextile***
90 degrees	called a ***square***
120 degrees	called a ***trine***
150 degrees	called a ***quincunx***
180 degrees	called an ***opposition***

Figure 4A at the end of this chapter is intended to help you understand how aspects are formed. Please look at this figure and note that the circle is marked off at each of the above seven different angles, from 0 degrees to 180 degrees. As the planets move around in the sky, if any two planets are positioned so that the angle of their alignment is any of these seven angles, then the two planets form what astrologers call a *planetary aspect.* The angle is measured by drawing a line from the Earth to each of the planets, then measuring the angle of these two lines. When measuring the angle between two planets in a circle, there are always two possible angles; the sum of both of these angles always equals 360 degrees. When measuring the angle of an aspect, astrologers always use the smaller angle. Therefore, there is never an aspect greater than 180 degrees because astrologers always use the smaller angle.

The seven angles that can create aspects were very special to the Babylonians, and they are called ASPECT-ANGLES. Since every one of them is divisible by the number 30, we sometimes refer to them collectively as 30-DEGREE-TYPE ANGLES. To the Babylonian astrologers, whenever two planets were aligned at any of the above seven aspect-angles, a planetary aspect was formed, and that was a celestial sign that an uncommon event would occur.

Planetary aspects are so important that we want to make certain you understand them, so we will explain them again. Bear in mind that the planets are constantly moving around and around in the sky. As they move, the angle of alignment between any two planets will change. A planetary aspect occurs whenever any two planets are aligned in the sky such that they are both in the same degree of the same zodiac constellation (sign), or the two planets are in the same degree of any two different zodiac constellations. When two planets are aligned in this manner, they MATCH DEGREES, meaning that the two planets are in the same degree of the constellations (or signs), and form a planetary aspect.

Planetary aspects are the simplest type of Planetary Geometry. Intricate Planetary Geometry is comprised of several individual aspects. The Planetary Geometry created by a single aspect is just a line connecting the two planets. To get this line, we simply draw a line between the two planets that form an aspect, just as we drew lines in the charts with Grand Trines or T-squares in the last chapter. For example, every line in Figure 4B represents a planetary aspect and connects the planets that form the aspect.

The Babylonians discovered that whenever two planets matched degrees (formed an aspect), it was consequential, and an uncommon event would probably occur. The uncommon event would not be as important as when several planets formed a symmetrical pattern, such as a Grand Trine. Therefore, when planets matched degrees, it was viewed as a sort of MINI-SIGN as opposed to a celestial sign. The Babylonians chose to call these mini-signs by the term *planetary aspect*. The discovery of planetary aspects was monumental because it led the Babylonians to another discovery. They found out that when there was a planetary aspect formed in the sky, they could sometimes predict what would happen depending on which two planets formed the aspect. They found out that different types of things happened during planetary aspects, and the type of thing that happened was dependent on which two planets formed the aspect. This led to their next discovery, called PLANETARY SYMBOLISMS.

Planetary Symbolisms

The subject of planetary symbolisms is covered in most astrology books and is even touched on in the horoscope columns of many magazines. For this reason, anyone who is at least a little familiar with traditional astrology will know the basics of planetary symbolisms. However, we have written this book so it will be understood by someone who knows absolutely nothing about astrology. For this reason, we will begin our explanation of planetary symbolisms at the beginning, about 4,000 years ago.

As we've said, the Babylonians had been fanatically watching the skies for thousands of years. Somewhere along the way, they came upon an incorrect, but understandable notion. Since the planets moved, but the stars did not, they thought that each planet was so different from the stars that every planet must have been ruled by one of the many gods of their several religions. Since Mars was the only planet that was red, and blood is red, they believed that Mars was connected to war and warriors, since both cause the shedding of blood. Venus, the morning star, is so exquisitely radiant that the Babylonians believed Venus was their god of beauty and love. Mercury was the fastest-moving planet, so the Babylonians made Mercury their god of speed and messengers. Jupiter is the brightest planet; this gave the Babylonians the idea that Jupiter was associated with their religion's most powerful god. Saturn was the only planet that had a slightly oval shape. It looked like a shield, and the Babylonians thought Saturn had something to do with shields and was ruled by the god in their religion that was responsible for armor.

Because of these associations of the planets to the gods of their religions, the Babylonians began to ascribe certain powers to each planet, and they called such "powers" RULERSHIPS and SYMBOLISMS. For example, Venus had rulership over matters of love and beauty, and Mars had rulership over war and the soldier. It was then that the Babylonians conceived of the idea that when any two planets formed a planetary aspect by matching degrees, the gods of those two planets were getting ready to do something that would have an impact on life on Earth. In other words, the Babylonians thought that when two planets formed a planetary aspect, the gods of those two planets were giving us a celestial sign that they were about to act and that something uncommon was about to happen.

All of this led to the idea that it was possible to predict the future by looking for planetary aspects and taking into consideration which planets, or gods, were forming the planetary aspect. For example, when Venus and Mars formed a planetary aspect, it meant that the god of love and beauty and the god of war and warriors were going to do something that would impact this world. To the Babylonians, one possibility was that a beautiful (Venus) warrior (Mars) would be born. Another possibility was the birth of someone who loved (Venus) war (Mars). Basically, the Babylonians devised a rule of interpreting aspects: *Combine and integrate the symbolisms of the planets.* This rule is called the *Rule of Combining Symbolisms.* By employing this rule, in addition to the two possibilities above, a Venus-Mars aspect could also mean that it was a time when people on Earth would love (Venus) war (Mars) and therefore act with unusual belligerency, causing a war to break out. Or, it could be a time when people would love (Venus) soldiers (Mars).

That is how the Babylonians made their predictions using astrology. Since they thought that the planets had divine connections, the term *divination* was used to refer to this method of attempting to predict the future.

That was 4,000 years ago. Humankind has now known for a long time that the planets have no connection whatsoever to any gods, and the planets have no special powers of any kind. But the most fascinating and amazing feature of astrology is that this method of prediction actually worked more often than not. In this age of modern science, it is unfathomable that the Rule of Combining Symbolisms could possibly be fruitful, but this method of prediction had enough accuracy to withstand the test of time—about 4,000 years' worth of time. Is it all just coincidence and superstition? How did astrology survive all these years if it was all based on a superstitious belief that the planets were associated with gods?

Why Has Astrology Survived Over 4,000 Years?

The Babylonians' theory of why planetary aspects worked was all just superstition because they incorrectly thought that the planets were gods. But the Rule of Combining Symbolisms is quite useful. We did not know the reasons why this rule worked 4,000 years ago; and we still do not know why. But the rule works, which is why astrology has survived for so long.

The ancient Babylonians were unaware of Magi Astrology, Uranus, Neptune, Pluto, and Chiron; and they were wrong about the planets being gods. Yet their astrology has survived the Mongols, the Crusades, the Dark Ages, the Middle Ages, the Renaissance, the Industrial Revolution, and the age of science. Babylonian astrology has survived persecution by the Jesuits and the Roman Catholic Church, the ban by communism, and the ridicule of modern science. It has even survived the attack by the intellectuals and the established educational institutions.

The astrology of the Babylonians survived because it works. This does not mean that all of Babylonian astrology works. They had many erroneous ideas that we won't discuss in this book. But the Babylonian Rule of Combining Symbolisms to interpret planetary aspects was, on the whole, quite valid—and some of the symbolisms or rulerships that they ascribed to the planets are still useful tools even now. The main reason is that the Babylonians were actually the first to devise and implement *empirical methodology*, which is the basis of modern science.

The Babylonians Derived Symbolisms Empirically

As astounding as it may seem, when two planets form an aspect, astrologers can actually often predict the impact and effect of the aspect's influences. Astrologers can do this because the probable range of the results of any planetary aspect is dependent on which two planets form the aspect, and because *different planets have different influences.* We have already explained that the original reason the Babylonians thought each planet had different influences is because they thought the planets were associated with the gods of their religion, and each god had a different set of powers or rulerships. This *theory* was obviously wrong. But even though the gods of the Babylonian religions never existed, some of the *symbolisms* and rulerships of the planets still worked.

The reason these symbolisms are still useful is that the Babylonians derived them as a result of thousands of years of observation and experience. This method is actually the same as the *empirical methodology* of modern science. The word *empirical* means "observed." The simplest and most basic step of scientific methodology is to observe what occurs, design some method of quantifying the observations, and devise a formula to fit the observations and predict future results. In a very real sense, the Babylonian astrologers obtained their symbolisms in this very way. For example, we learned in the last chapter that Pearl Harbor was bombed when the Sun and Mars made a planetary aspect of 120 degrees called the trine. The Babylonians had figured out that the Sun represents the day, and Mars represents war. Thus, when the Sun and Mars form an aspect, to the Babylonians it means a day (Sun) of war (Mars). There were lots and lots of days of war in the era of the Babylonians, so they had an enormous amount of data about the planetary aspects that existed on days of war. Many of them had aspects formed by Mars and Sun, and it is that fact that gave the Babylonians the idea that Mars rules war.

The Babylonians used their mammoth amounts of records to help them derive their rulerships and symbolisms for the planets.

How to Predict the Meaning of Each Planetary Aspect

The idea that different planets have different influences should be at least a little familiar to most of you who have read some astrology columns in magazines or newspapers. For example, you are probably familiar with astrology's concept that Venus rules attraction, romance, and desire; whereas Mars rules sex, war, and aggression. These differences between the planets' powers are called their symbolisms, or sometimes they are called rulerships. Each planet has its own unique set of symbolisms and rulerships. Astrologers use a planet's particular symbolisms to interpret the results and effects of a planetary aspect that is formed by any two planets. When two planets form an aspect by matching degrees, we can usually accurately predict the meaning of an aspect simply by *combining and integrating the symbolisms* of the two planets that make up the planetary aspect.

For example, when Venus and Mars create a planetary aspect (by being in the same degree of the constellations, thus matching degrees), then astrologers interpret the meaning of the Venus-Mars aspect by combining and integrating the symbolisms of Mars to the symbolisms of Venus. Venus symbolizes desire, and Mars is symbolic of war. By combining these two symbolisms, we get an interpretation of "desire and war." The next step is to integrate these symbolisms; when we do that, we get "desire for war" or "desire of war." But what is most important is that we can use any of the valid symbolisms of a planet in our interpretation; this means that each aspect has a range of interpretations. Another possible interpretation of an aspect formed by Venus and Mars is "attracted to aggression." This is because Venus rules attraction as well as desire, and Mars is ruler of aggression as well as war. Also, a more palatable interpretation of the Venus-Mars aspect is "desire for sex," since Mars rules sex, and Venus symbolizes desire.

So we can combine any of these symbolisms to interpret the influence of a Venus-Mars aspect. In this way, each planetary aspect has a RANGE OF VALID INTERPRETATIONS, and the variation is dependent on the range of the symbolisms of the planets that form the aspect. We will discuss this in more detail later in this book.

To many of you, all of this may be new and not fully understandable yet, but we will give many more examples as we continue. So please don't get stuck on the issue of how to interpret aspects. Just read on.

Enhancement Aspects Are the Most Powerful

Although there are seven possible angles that form planetary aspects, some angles are more important than others. The Babylonians knew right away that the conjunction and the trine were special. The trine and the conjunction are planetary aspects because they are formed when two planets are 0 or 120 degrees apart, respectively. But these two aspects were not like any of the other aspects.

The Babylonians realized that the conjunction was the most powerful aspect. This made sense because even before the Babylonians discovered the other six angles of aspects, they regarded a conjunction by itself to be a celestial sign due to the fact that the conjunction is what occurs between the Sun and Moon during a solar eclipse.

They also viewed the trine as exceptional. A Grand Trine consists of three trines and is the most powerful celestial sign that can be formed by three planets. This must have been the reason that the Babylonians correctly surmised that a single trine by itself was also at least a little special, although it was not quite as special as the conjunction.

The Magi Society has confirmed that of the seven different angles of planetary aspects, the trine and the conjunction create the strongest and most beneficial influences. For this reason, Magi Astrology has given them a special name. Both the trine and the conjunction are a special type of aspect called an ENHANCEMENT ASPECT, and we call the actual angles of these aspects ENHANCEMENT ANGLES. Both the 120-degree angle and the 0-degree angle are enhancement angles.

Enhancement aspects are the most powerful aspects and also the most beneficial. You will see in chapter 7 when we teach you about your second birth chart that there are other ways to form enhancement aspects. But until then, an enhancement aspect is formed when two planets are aligned in a trine or conjunction. They deserve a special name because they are the most important and most powerful planetary aspects.

ॐ ॐ ॐ

We are beginning to accumulate a lot of terms that may be unfamiliar to you. Please remember that there is a complete glossary at the back of this book. Every astrological term used in this book is defined and listed there in alphabetical order.

ॐ ॐ ॐ

Planetary Aspects Influence Sun-Sign Characteristics

Earlier in this chapter, we discussed some of the shortcomings of Sun-Sign Astrology. But as amazing as this type of astrology can be, it is severely restricted in capabilities and is often confusing. Remember the first two questions of this chapter? They were:

- Why do some people have the best character traits of their Sun Signs, and others have the worst?

- Why do you get along with some Leos but not others? And some Scorpios but not others?

Well, the answers are always in the stars, and since you've now learned about planetary aspects, you are finally ready to *understand* some of the answers. Now that you're familiar with enhancement angles, we can explain that each Sun Sign has good characteristics, and each has tendencies that are not as desirable, *but a person is most likely to have the Sun Sign's better attributes when the person's Sun makes an enhancement angle with any other planet.*

For example, if someone is born a Virgo, and the person was also born with the Sun in conjunction or trine to any planet, then that person will most likely manifest the better facets of Virgos. This means that the person will be most likely to be orderly and meticulous, neat and discriminating, punctual and responsible, and loyal and stable. When someone has an enhancement aspect of any planet to the Sun, that person is said to have an *enhanced sun.*

But the most important astrological indications of anyone's personality and character are the actual planetary aspects that a person is born with. Planetary Aspects are indications of the uncommon characteristics of that individual's personality. At one time, this belief was so universally accepted that it worked itself into the English language! That is why we talk about the "aspects of a person's character."

Natal Aspects Give Us Insights into a Person's Character

The ability to interpret an aspect is an amazingly useful part of astrology. One of the reasons is that we can use this knowledge to predict some of the probable characteristics of any person based on the person's natal aspects (see glossary). People tend to resemble at least one of the valid interpretations and characteristics of the aspects that they are born with. For example, Adolf Hitler was born with a Venus-Mars aspect. Remember that an aspect always foretells something out of the ordinary and not something that is average in nature. So in the case of the Venus-Mars aspect, someone who is born on a day that has this aspect can manifest an *abnormal* desire for war and aggression. Adolf Hitler is a perfect example. He was born with a very exact conjunction of Mars and Venus (see Figure 4C).

We can also use planetary aspects to predict or explain the historical significance of a day. Once again, Adolf Hitler is a very good example. Hitler became chancellor of Germany on January 30, 1933, when Mars was nearly exactly 120 degrees from Venus, and formed a trine (Figure 4D). On both days—Hitler's birth and his first day as chancellor—there was the same planetary aspect, with a nearly exact planetary aspect formed by Mars and Venus! On both of these days, Venus and Mars were in the same degree of the Zodiac constellations, which meets the criteria for creating a planetary aspect. We now have two of the key astrological reasons for World War II.

The odds against two birth charts having such exact planetary aspects of Mars and Venus is greater than 10,000 to one. If you were a good astrologer at that time, and you used Magi Astrology in your work, you would have known that Hitler's rise to power in Germany was very likely to lead to war!

Different Planets Have Different Symbolisms

The Babylonians discovered that different planets have different symbolisms, and they also found out what some of the most important symbolisms were by analyzing the effect of planetary aspects. It is easy to duplicate the type of data that led the Babylonians to such remarkable discoveries.

For example, please look at the Babylonian Alignment Charts for the day that Hitler invaded Poland, the day Hitler became chancellor of Germany, the day Napoleon Bonaparte was born, and the day that Japan attacked Pearl Harbor. We can easily discern that there was at least one Grand Trine on all four of those very historic days.

But what is even more important is the fact that the planet Mars was a component of each of the Grand Trines. There were also two conjunctions (the most important aspect) in the four charts, and Mars was a component of both of them. There was a conjunction of Mars in the chart of the birth date of Napoleon, and for the day Hitler became Germany's chancellor. Mars is a component of more planetary aspects in these four charts of war than any other planet, and only Mars is the common denominator of each symmetrical pattern (the Grand Trines) in all four charts of these superhistoric days.

Common sense would tell us that Mars probably has something to do with war. Let us go further.

At the end of this chapter, we have also provided you with the Babylonian Alignment Chart for another important date that led to World War II. It is the chart for September 27, 1940 (Figure 4E). It is not very well known, but that was the date that Adolf Hitler as Germany's chancellor, Benito Mussolini as leader of fascist Italy, and Emperor Hirohito of Japan signed a treaty—a very, very unusual treaty.

Guess what the treaty was.

It was a war pact between Germany, Japan, and Italy to conquer and divide the world between them. Japan would be given greater Asia, and the rest of the world would belong to Germany and Italy. However, each nation had to go and conquer those areas through wars, and each of the three nations' leaders pledged to not interfere in each other's wars. In essence, these three obnoxiously power-hungry despots agreed to help each other in a worldwide war of conquest. The treaty has been called the Axis Pact because the three countries were referred to as the Axis nations, as opposed to the U.S., Great Britain, France, and so on, who comprised the Allies.

As was the case with the planetary aspects of the other four days of war that we already looked at, the planetary aspects of the day of the Axis Pact also revolved around Mars. It was a pact to wage a worldwide war, and there were two planetary aspects made by Mars on that day. Mars was conjunct to Neptune, and Mars was trine to Uranus.

Most of us would think that this type of data would lead one to surmise that Mars had something to do with war. That is also the way the Babylonians viewed it.

The charts mentioned above are examples of the type of data that led the Babylonians to discover that Mars probably had an influence over matters of war. Now we're only showing you five charts, which is not enough to allow anyone to be sure whether Mars symbolizes war. This is because we only have room in this book for a few interesting examples. But the Babylonians had well over 1,000 years of charts, data, and experience when they came to their conclusion that Mars ruled war.

It was from similar examples and data that the Babylonians discovered some of the other key symbolisms of the planets.

By the way, the Planetary Geometry of the Axis Pact deserves special mention. On that day, Mars was conjunct to Neptune, and both planets were trine to Uranus. This is an example of what Magi Astrology calls a CON-JUNCTED TRINE. This is a special shape of Planetary Geometry, and each special shape has a different level of power. In the hierarchy of the power of the different shapes of Planetary Geometry, the Conjuncted Trine ranks just below the Grand Trine in power. So this is a very powerful pattern. In fact, we will see that this is a key pattern in the astrology of love relationships.

Dynamic Symmetrical Patterns

On page 72, we illustrated two types of symmetrical patterns that the planets can form. The difference between the type A patterns in Figure 4F and the type B patterns of Figure 4G is that the type A patterns are such that each side of each pattern is a planetary aspect, but not every side of the patterns of type B are aspects. Both types of patterns are symmetrical, but common sense would tell us that the type A patterns are much more powerful than the type B kind. This is exactly the case, and that is why we call them DYNAMIC. In this book, each of the symmetrical patterns that we have seen in the charts of our examples have been dynamic symmetrical patterns, and therefore extraordinarily powerful.

The Babylonians Discover Some Crucial Symbolisms

Although using historic dates in astrological research in the way we did is very enlightening, it also has its limitations. You cannot obtain the full scope of a planet's symbolisms by using the birth charts of only mega-events of history. You also need to include the birth charts of special people and ordinary people. For at least a thousand years before the Babylonians made the discoveries of the key symbolisms of the planets, it was decreed by many Babylonian monarchs that the birth dates of every newborn child should be recorded, and it was these records that allowed them to effectively determine a wide range of the symbolisms of the planets.

The Babylonian astrologers were meticulous in their record keeping and took great pains to detail what happened to each child. Did a female child become beautiful and have a happy marriage? Did a male child become a good farmer or soldier? Or perhaps a musician or poet? Did a child have a long and successful life? Or did the person die young in battle or for another tragic reason, such as a disease?

From all of these records, the Babylonians were able to determine some of the most important symbolisms of the planets that we are aware of, and a majority of these symbolisms were so well derived that they still work today.

For example, it was the Babylonians who discovered that Venus had an effect on attraction, desire, beauty, and partnerships; and that one of Jupiter's symbolisms was that it bestowed good luck and the horn of plenty, which are pretty important symbolisms to know.

An Important Symbolism Is Validated

We have been talking about war a lot, but let us now look at peace. In recent times, the Magi Society's research has confirmed some of the useful symbolisms for Jupiter. We learned that peace was most likely to occur when the Sun and Jupiter made enhancement aspects. An enhancement aspect, remember, makes up two of the seven angles of planetary aspects. In *Astrology Really Works!*, our first book, the Magi Society confirmed the Babylonians' discovery that on days when the Sun and Jupiter formed a conjunction or a trine, peace was much more likely to exist than on other days. As it turns out, the most significant days of peace usually occur on days when Jupiter and the Sun form an enhancement aspect. Perhaps even more important is the fact that prominent persons of peace are usually born on days when Jupiter and the Sun form an enhancement aspect.

Here are some examples. The three most important days for peace in this century were the two days that ended the two world wars in Europe, and the day that marked the end of the Cold War. In *Astrology Really Works!*, we provided our readers with the birth charts of these three momentous days, showing that there was a trine of Jupiter and the Sun on each of those days. We will not duplicate those charts in this book, but we will give you the dates. World War I ended November 11, 1918; World War II ended in Europe on May 7, 1945; and the Cold War ended on November 4, 1989.

Since the publication of our first book, the most important day for peace in Europe has been December 14, 1995, the day of the Dayton Peace Accord, the peace treaty that ended the war in Bosnia. The treaty was signed in Dayton, Ohio, because President Clinton was in Dayton, and all the other signatories met there for that reason. That day had a Sun-Jupiter enhancement. Here, again, a very important day for peace came about when there was an enhancement aspect of Jupiter and the Sun.

The Valid Range of Interpretations

The reason Magi Astrology regards a Sun-Jupiter enhancement as signifying a day of peace is because we interpret enhancement aspects by *combining and integrating* the symbolisms of the two planets that form the aspect. One of the symbolisms of the Sun is "the day," and one of the symbolisms of Jupiter is "peace." Therefore a Sun-Jupiter enhancement is a sign of a day (Sun) of peace (Jupiter). We want to use this example to illustrate a concept of Magi Astrology that we call the VALID RANGE OF INTERPRETATION. There are always at least several interpretations for any planetary aspect. An interpretation is valid so long as we use the validated symbolisms of the planets. Therefore, a day when there is a Sun-Jupiter enhancement cannot validly be interpreted as a day of war because war is not a symbolism of Jupiter; it is a symbolism of Mars. But if a day had a Sun-Mars enhancement, then it could be a day of war. For example, the day that Japan attacked Pearl Harbor had a Sun-Mars enhancement.

All planets have a number of symbolisms. The Sun symbolizes the day, but one of its other symbolisms is that of a "person." Jupiter symbolizes peace, and also forgiveness and good fortune, among other things. This variation of symbolisms for a planet is essential to astrology because each planetary aspect can be interpreted according to the various symbolisms of the planet. It is these symbolisms that determine the valid range of the interpretations of any aspect.

For example, a Jupiter-Sun enhancement can mean a day of peace or a person of peace because the Sun symbolizes both the day and the person. Let us give you some examples of persons of peace with Jupiter-Sun enhancements. In our opinion, three important men of peace in this century are Mikhail Gorbachev, Oral Roberts, and Billy Graham. Each of them was born on a day with Jupiter trine the Sun. Rev. Graham was born on November 7, 1918; and Rev. Roberts was born on January 24, 1918.

Most historians agree that Mr. Gorbachev was the driving force in ending the Cold War. Under every other Soviet leader who preceded Gorbachev, an end to the Cold War would have not only been impossible, it would have been unthinkable. Mr. Gorbachev was born on March 2, 1931, and there was a very exact trine of Sun and Jupiter on that day.

And in our opinion, as America's two leading evangelists, Oral Roberts and Billy Graham are important men of peace. These examples help us realize that *a natal aspect is often a sign of the character of the person.*

This does not mean that everyone born on a day with a Sun-Jupiter enhancement is a person of peace. We all have free will, and we can interact with every planetary aspect that we are born with in whatever way we chose, except that we almost always stay within the range of valid interpretations.

Magi Astrology Is Consistent with Free Will

One of the biggest questions astrologers have had to face concerns how much power, if any, a planetary aspect has over the NATIVE. (The term *native* in astrology refers to the person born with the natal aspect.) In other words, was Hitler destined to live a life of aggression and war because he was born with a nearly exact Venus-Mars conjunction?

The answer is no. We all have free will to lead our life morally and ethically. We explained earlier that each planet has quite a few different symbolisms, and that there is a valid range of interpretations for any planetary aspect. This means that each planetary aspect can result in quite a few different interpretations, with some being more palatable than others. We believe strongly that each of us has the free will to choose how each of our natal aspects is manifested, within the valid range of interpretations. The following examples will help you understand what we mean.

Every planet has a large number of symbolisms and a broad range of them. Venus has other symbolisms besides desire and love. Astrologers have known for a very long time that Venus also symbolizes money, beauty, seduction, grace, and harmony. Mars also has other symbolisms besides the two we have already discussed. Along with war and aggression, it rules muscles, energy, the body and bodily motion, dance, physical labor, athletics, and professional sports. Any of these symbolisms can be used to interpret a planetary aspect, and anyone born with any aspect can choose whatever interpretation he or she prefers to be manifested, as there are always many choices of manifestations of any aspect. As an example, the Venus-Mars aspect can mean:

- money (Venus) from professional sports (Mars);
- a beautiful (Venus) body (Mars);
- love (Venus) of muscles (Mars);
- love (Venus) of sex (Mars);
- love (Venus) of sports (Mars);
- beautiful (Venus) muscles (Mars);
- graceful (Venus) bodily movements (Mars);
- harmony (Venus) of muscles (Mars), which means coordination;
- energetic (Mars) desires (Venus);
- energy (Mars) for love (Venus);
- energy (Mars) for seduction (Venus); and
- any combination of the other symbolisms of Venus and Mars. You'll see shortly that both planets have quite a few other important symbolisms.

So which interpretation is the "correct" one for a particular person with the Venus-Mars enhancement aspect? The answer is that any person with any natal aspect has the free will to choose which possible interpretation will be manifested. The person can also choose to have multiple manifestations, meaning that more than one interpretation is valid at the same time.

Every Natal Aspect Is a Sign of a Gift or a Special Talent

After an enormous amount of research, the Magi Society discovered that without exception, every aspect can provide the native with unusual talents and skills (if the native works hard to improve himself or herself). The Magi Society believes that all of us can use each and every natal planetary aspect to help us obtain a special talent or skill, or we can be *influenced by* the presence of the planetary aspect in our birth chart. The choice is ours. Hitler was weak-willed in this regard, and he let his Venus-Mars aspect get the better of him. He could have harnessed the power of the aspect to provide him with a special talent, such as graceful bodily movements, money from sports, a beautiful body, and so on. But instead, he took the most undisciplined and immoral route and ended up with a love of war. This was *his* choice, not the stars'.

The Symbolisms of Each Planet Must Be Consistent

Each planet has a range of symbolisms. In order for astrology to be valid, each and every symbolism of a planet must be consistent. The consistency of all the symbolisms of each planet is one of the most important rules of Magi Astrology. Let us explain what we mean.

The astrological concept of symbolisms is very similar to the idea that each of the 12 zodiac signs has a different impact and effect on our personalities. These different influences of the 12 signs are very much like the different symbolisms of the planets. However, whereas the influences of each sign concentrate on personalities, the symbolisms of all of the planets cover the whole of life and every possible aspect of life. This includes tangibles as well as intangibles.

In astrology, there is a planet that is symbolic of each type of idea, special talent, skill, ability, feeling, mood, science, study, language; and each type of knowledge, profession, career, and status (such as being married or divorced). There is also a planet that symbolizes each part of the body; each element, mineral, living organism, plant, drug; and each type of thing that human beings build or make, such as airplanes, nuclear weapons, telephones, computers, rubber tires, clothes, and automobiles. Everything is a symbolism of one of the planets—absolutely everything.

The symbolisms of the planets are the heart and soul of astrology. The planets are like words, and their symbolisms are the definitions of the language of the planets and stars. Just as each word in a language has a set of definitions, each planet has a set of symbolisms, or definitions. In astrology, everything conceivable is covered and included among the symbolisms of the planets. Since there are only 11 planets, in order for astrology to cover all facets of life, each planet must have quite a few symbolisms. *However, every symbolism of any one planet must always be consistent with all of that planet's other symbolisms. This last rule is vital for the integrity of astrology, and also its accuracy.*

Take, for example, the symbolisms of Jupiter. We pointed out earlier that both Billy Graham and Oral Roberts were born with a Sun-Jupiter aspect, and we used them as examples of men of peace, which is an interpretation of the Sun-Jupiter aspect. Although Billy Graham and Oral Roberts are not renowned worldwide as men of peace per se, they are known to be men of Christianity, and Christianity has a message of peace. For example, Christianity teaches us: If someone strikes you, turn the other cheek. If everyone followed such teachings, there would be peace on Earth, and good will toward all men. Therefore, it is *consistent* for Jupiter to symbolize both peace and Christianity. Jupiter also symbolizes forgiveness, which is necessary for peace, and is also a centerpiece of Christian teachings.

Such examples should help you understand what we mean when we say that the various symbolisms of a planet have to all be consistent. You might ask: What would be inconsistent? If, for example, Mars symbolized war *and* gentleness, that would be inconsistent. If Jupiter symbolized Christianity *and* revenge, that would be inconsistent. If Jupiter symbolized good fortune *and* losses, that would be inconsistent. As it turns out, Jupiter is symbolic of forgiveness, and Saturn symbolizes revenge and losses.

The symbolisms of Magi Astrology are completely consistent. This allows a range of interpretations that are consistent with each other. This is a very important concept to understand because every planetary aspect can be interpreted using any symbolism of the planet. This also means that the influence of a planetary aspect varies, and the range of variation is determined by the range of valid and consistent symbolisms of the planets.

Symbolisms for the Planets

It is very helpful for you to have at least a general idea about the most important symbolisms of all the planets so that you can learn how to use them to help you deal with matters of love and money. Symbolisms are so important that we will devote more time to them later on in this book. For now, please just *get an idea of the range of the symbolisms of the planets, and glance* through the following symbolisms of the planets so that you will have a general idea what each planet is all about. These are Magi Astrology's symbolisms and rulerships for the planets. If you have studied astrology's symbolisms, you may notice that there are some differences between these symbolisms and the ones in other astrology books. We are only *listing* symbolisms in this chapter, but in later chapters, we will also explain why we believe the planets have some of the symbolisms that they do.

- **Venus** symbolizes attraction of all kinds, infatuation, desire, attachment, and emotional needs. Venus has dominion over intimacy and sexual energy and desire in the woman; it also signifies sex appeal, beauty, grace, fashion and being fashionable, socializing and sociability, and partnerships and the act of unification (such as a wedding), but not the marriage itself. Venus has dominion over *combining* and coordinating different things, including parts of the body, countries, companies, ideas, and any two things whatsoever. Venus rules the companion and companionship, friendship and friends, being together, joining, cooperating, and merging; also possessions, money, social standing, jewels and adornment, and luxury. This is very interesting: Venus rules seduction, the act of making love, female sexuality and sexual energy in the woman; and it is representative of charm, harmony, and a sense of humor. Venus is a BENEFIC, and therefore symbolizes good luck and elevated levels. A benefic is a term of ancient astrology referring to a planet that is highly beneficial and one that brings good luck or high levels of something beneficial and helpful, as well as victory and championships.

- **Mars** represents the body and muscles, motion, bodily movements and activity, energy, initiative, the sex drive (especially in men), war, weapons of war, aggression, anger, violence, temper, belligerency, the soldier, the warrior, violence, accidents, sudden disruptions (including accidents), competitiveness, athletic competition, and the athlete. Since Mars rules the body, it has dominion over what we do with the body, such as athletic endeavors, dance and ballet, and also pure physical labor. Mars is associated with pure *physical* attraction of the body, as distinguished from emotional and even sexual attraction. Venus rules female sexuality, but Mars is the ruler of male sexuality. Mars governs initiative and being a person of action, as opposed to indecision and excessive contemplation. It also rules the dancer and farmer, laborer and carpenter, and any profession that has a primary requirement of using the body. Mars signifies crudeness, vulgarity, macho attitudes, and the he-man.

- **Pluto** is the ruler of sexuality, lust, obsessive desires, and the sex organs. (This overlaps in some ways with Mars, which symbolizes pure physical attraction, but there is a difference.) Pluto is also representative of power; the establishment; and things that enhance or preserve power, such as atomic energy and weapons, politics, great success, big business, corporations, and advertising. Pluto signifies dictatorships and oppression, as well as the state of being oppressive; this leads to Pluto signifying the super ego and undeserved self-esteem. Pluto represents the ingredients of great wealth, such as investments, the banking industry, the loaning of money, the issuance of debt, and the ability to pay it back; as well as most financial instruments, such as bonds and mortgages. It also represents gambling and betting, the trading of financial instruments of all types and profits therefrom. It provides the ability to take advantage of and capitalize on something in order to make a profit. Pluto has dominion over drastic changes that are true upheavals, and in this regard, it represents beginnings and endings. Pluto rules obsessions of all kinds, including emotional and sexual ones. Also, Pluto is ruler of the actual sex act, as opposed to lovemaking and seduction, which are ruled by Venus. Venus seduces you; Pluto simply throws you on the bed and says, "Take off your clothes." Pluto is, therefore, symbolic of sexism and male chauvinism.

- **Neptune** rules longevity and anything that has to do with the long term, including true love and long-term relationships (but not marriage, because Chiron rules marriage). It is Neptune that imparts sensuality to women. Neptune also represents creativity, inspirations, and whatever inspires. Neptune has dominion over morals, ethics, and ethical behavior and standards; it signifies sensitivity and gentleness. Neptune rules electricity and electrical devices, and whatever involves the sea and water, such as shipping. More important, Neptune governs health, medicines, and anything that increases life expectancy or improved health; as well as regeneration, healing, and anything that increases longevity. This leads to Neptune's rulership of serenity, tranquility, and safe passage, as well as stability and peacefulness at home. Neptune is the planet of youthfulness and being young at heart, spirit, and body. It is Neptune that rules the act of procreation and reproduction; as opposed to Venus, which rules the act of making love and seduction. Neptune is also different from Pluto, which rules the sex act itself. Neptune signifies all long-term assets, such as inheritances, copyrights and patents; and whatever comes from the ground, such as minerals, oil, plants, and food. It is Neptune that rules long-term financial security. Neptune also symbolizes doctors, nurses, pharmacists, and all artistic and creative professions.

- **Jupiter** is symbolic of fulfillment, good fortune, success, enrichment, prayers answered and dreams coming true, peace and forgiveness, wisdom and good judgment, reliability and being honorable, promises kept, the law, the principle of order, morality, generosity, fairness, gratitude, faithfulness, selfless-ness, compassion, optimism, and hope. Jupiter is symbolic of Judeo-Christian religions, Providence, grace, power benevo-lently used, self-sacrifice, selflessness, as well as protection and the protector. Jupiter is also representative of truth and true genius, the leader, royalty, expansion of what is good or help-ful, and contraction of what is bad and harmful. Jupiter is the most powerful benefic (Venus is second), and it improves and helps every planet it makes an aspect with.

- The **Moon** has rulership of emotions, fluctuating moods, the psyche, the subconscious, greed, fear, capriciousness, and uncontrollable urges. Because of all of these rulerships, it fol-lows that the Moon is representative of fanaticism and illogical beliefs and actions.

- **Mercury** governs communication and writing, the mind, intel-ligence, design, logic, expression, poetry, singing, and music. Mercury also rules teaching; and the conveying of ideas, mes-sages, announcements, and conferences. Because Mercury was the Roman god of speed and messengers, Mercury rules speed and swiftness, travel, transportation, and all vehicles of trans-portation (including airplanes, cars, and railroads). Since Mercury rules traveling, it also represents exploring and explo-ration—including the exploration of the mind and space; and exploring for minerals, oil, and gas. Mercury has dominion over very important parts of the body, including the brain, ears, eyes, respiratory system, nervous system, and the reflexes. Mercury signifies the teacher, writer, singer, architect, and any profession that has a primary requirement of use of the mind or that requires the act of communicating. Mercury's rulership of the mind extends to anything that mimics the mind, such as cal-culators, computers, and computer software.

- **Uranus** is symbolic of freedom and independence and the urge for both; and is representative of excitement and thrill seeking. Uranus also signifies change and what is new, including the news. Also, it represents astrology, because it is the study of changes in planets' positions, which creates new things. Since change can be revolutionary, Uranus is representative of everything that is new or innovative, including discoveries. Along these lines, Uranus symbolizes what has changed the world, such as inventions and technology, flying, space travel, and aeronautics. But the most important rulerships of Uranus are that of fame, the public, and whatever has to do with the public—such as the mass media, broadcasting, and the entertainment business. Uranus is representative of what is worldwide, pervasive, and universal in nature or status, and publicity and publicizing. It is Uranus that signifies the globalization of anything, and it is also symbolic of being massive in general size or amounts. In our bodies, Uranus is ruler of what our body does to adjust to changes; this means Uranus rules balance, eye-hand coordination, and depth perception; but it overlaps with Mercury in these areas.

- **Saturn** is symbolic of too much or too little of something, and never just the right amount. It is also the planet of control and dominance, and the desire for control and dominance over others. Saturn represents restrictions and constriction—contraction of what is helpful, and expansion of what is harmful. It governs scientific thinking and whatever is contrary to Judeo-Christian traditions. It is symbolic of obstruction, limitations, shortages, destruction, losses, mistakes, hindrances, disruptions, bad luck, dissolutions, and breaking apart. It is also representative of revenge, selfishness, and narrow-mindedness. Saturn is the planet of deception; and signifies temptation, deceit, deceitfulness, the occult and attraction to the occult, and also confusion. Saturn also governs frustration, disappointment, being unhappy, as well as hatred and repulsion. What's interesting to note is that Saturn signifies temptations of all kinds and being *unable* to resist them. Saturn is also a sign of being below average, in a weakened status, in ill health, and in a state of diminished vitality and/or capacity. There are problems in this world, so there has to be a planet that signifies them—and Saturn is the one that does.

- **Chiron** is the planet that has rulership over emotional ties, marriages, weddings, the family, spouses, and children. It represents the target of a person's *romantic and marital interest.* Chiron also has rulership over promises and commitments of love, including engagements and marriage vows. It governs fertility and pregnancies, and the act of giving birth to *children in marriage.* Chiron rules the marital and romantic instinct and desire of romance, as well as romance itself. It also signifies karmic bonds and intuitive trust. Chiron has dominion over charisma and a person's public image; and being noteworthy, esteemed, distinctive, and distinguished in appearance. Chiron is ruler of your career and how you choose to make a living, as well as where you could be most successful. It also signifies your earning power, the economy, and economics. Chiron imparts extraordinary qualities. It also represents life, death, and reincarnation, and it is symbolic of the future. *To say that Chiron is a very important planet is an understatement!*

- **The Sun** symbolizes the actual person, day, or entity of the astrological chart. In this regard, the Sun can also represent a relationship, a marriage, a corporation or partnership, a contract, a time period, and anything else that is able to be represented. If you do not understand this, you will after all the examples that are provided later in this book. The Sun also has rulership over crucial parts of the body, such as the heart and circulation system, as well as vitality and the essence of the person.

You can see that some of the symbolisms of the planets can combine to form some very interesting interpretations for the aspects. Knowing these symbolisms and how to interpret aspects will be crucial to our ability to deal with all matters of love, money, relationships, and careers.

☙ ☙ ☙

Figure 4A: There are 7 angles that create (planetary) aspects

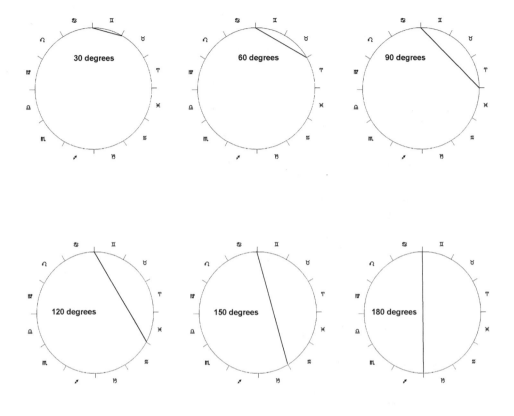

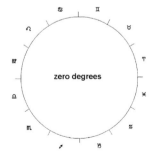

When two planets are aligned in the sky such that they form any of these seven aspect angles, lines like these are drawn connecting these two planets to emphasize that an aspect exists.

Figure 4B: How a Grand Trine is formed

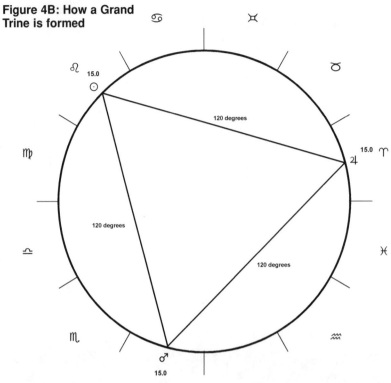

Figure 4C: Adolf Hitler born 4/20/1889

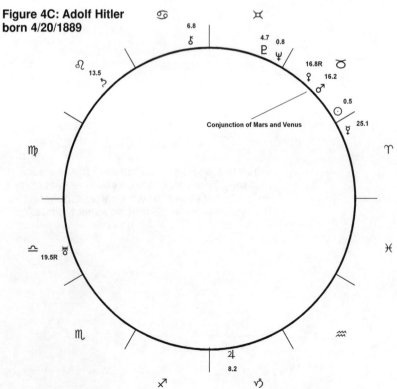

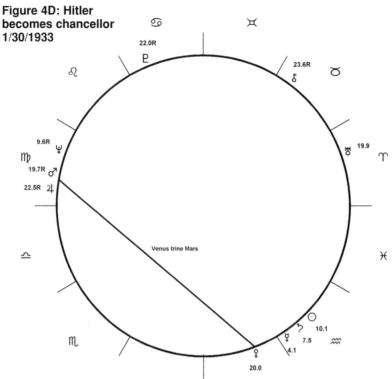

Figure 4D: Hitler becomes chancellor 1/30/1933

Venus trine Mars

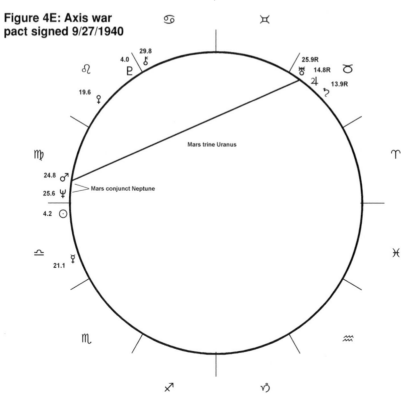

Figure 4E: Axis war pact signed 9/27/1940

Mars trine Uranus

Mars conjunct Neptune

Figures 4F and 4G: Two types of symmetrical Planetary Geometry

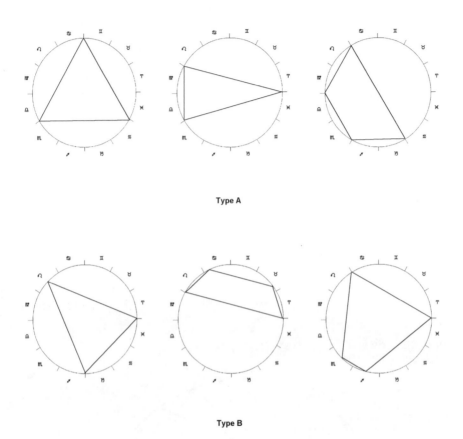

Type A

Type B

In the above figures, each straight line (aspect line) inside the circles represents an aspect. Each circle has 12 signs, and the dividing point of each sign is marked with a short hash line; there are 12 such lines, and each one is 30 degrees apart from the next one.

All of the aspect lines of the type A figures are 30-degree-type angles (0, 30, 60, 90, 120, 150, or 180). Therefore, the type A figures are dynamic and very powerful. Each of the type B figures has at least one line that is not a 30-degree-type angle. Such figures are not dynamic, and are less powerful than dynamic ones.

CHAPTER FIVE

❦

How Planetary Geometry Affects
Love and Money Issues

Every planetary aspect that someone is born with is a reflection of the character of the person. The great advantage of knowing about planetary aspects and symbolisms is that we can now answer questions such as these:

- Is this person the runaround kind or the marrying kind?

- What makes this person tick? And what is this person's true nature?

- Are we sexually compatible? Also, for how long?

- Who can I have a fling with so that there will be no entanglements or repercussions?

- In what career or business can I be most successful?

- What are my very special talents, and how can I best apply them?

In this chapter, we begin to learn how to use aspects (which is the simplest form of Planetary Geometry) and the symbolisms of the planets to help us answer questions such as the ones above.

We begin with a discussion of how to understand the overriding traits of a person's personality by analyzing the planetary aspects of the day the person was born.

Sexual Planets and Sexual Aspects

It is a simple fact: some people are just more sexually oriented than others. There are those who can live without any sex for a long time; and there are those who cannot stand to go without sex for just a few days. This can cause unbreachable incompatibility.

Magi Astrology's rules of interpreting planetary aspects can forewarn us about such a problem. Quite often, in a love relationship, one person wants and needs much more sex than the other, and this difference in sexual needs and desires can destroy an otherwise good relationship. This is certainly not the only form of sexual incompatibility, but this type of sexual incompatibility is the easiest thing to determine when you know Magi Astrology. That is because the sexual needs and capacities of a person are readily predictable by analyzing a person's planetary aspects, especially the ones that include a SEXUAL PLANET.

There are three sexual planets, meaning that there are three planets whose influences cover areas of sex. They are Venus, Mars, and Pluto. If a person was born with an aspect formed by any two of these planets, then that person has a SEXUAL ASPECT and is highly sexual, meaning that the person both needs, and is capable of, a high degree of sexual activity in a relationship. To many such persons, quantity is quality, and if they have a partner who cannot supply the quantity, they too often go and find someone who can supply it. Love and emotional attachment is usually a secondary issue to such people.

To be more specific, any aspect formed by any of the following three pairs of planets creates a Sexual Aspect, and a person who was born with any such aspect is usually a very sexual person, meaning that the person needs and can provide more sex than most, in terms of quantity:

- Venus and Pluto can mean desire (Venus) for the sex act (Pluto);

- Mars and Pluto can mean energy (Mars) to do the sex act (Pluto); and

- Venus and Mars can mean desire (Venus) and sexual energy (Mars).

From the symbolisms of astrology, it is easy to see why these three *pairings* of planets create Sexual Aspects. As usual, the enhancement aspects are the most powerful in this regard. If someone was born with any of these aspects, especially if they are enhancement aspects, then they have Sexual Aspects and are usually highly sexual persons.

Who is an example of a person born with a Sexual Aspect?

- Madonna! (no surprise).

- Prince Charles (surprised?).

- Also Prince Charles's mistress, Camilla Parker-Bowles.
  She has all three of the Sexual Aspects. This explains a few
  things, don't you think? Especially when you take into
  account that Princess Diana had *no* Sexual Aspects.

We will talk at greater length about these people later in this book. The important lesson now is that if someone was born with a Sexual Aspect, they are highly sexed, meaning they are capable of and demand more sex. If you are looking for great amounts of sex, they can provide it. The downside is that people with Sexual Aspects are less likely to remain faithful than those who do not have them—much less likely!

A Sexual Aspect makes the person less able to resist sexual temptations. Even worse, a Sexual Aspect makes the person search for and seek out new sexual conquests and experiences—or just a new sex partner. Sexually Aspected persons (those born with Sexual Aspects) are proud of their sexuality and sexual prowess and tend to look forward to showing off their capabilities to someone new.

There are, of course, other forms of sexual compatibility and incompatibility besides the type we have just discussed, and some of them are more important than this type. Later in this book, we will explain how to accurately assess whether two persons are sexually compatible in other ways.

An Astrological Reason Why Men and Women Differ about Sex

In general, the average man is more sexually oriented than the average woman. There is an astrological reason for this. There are some aspects that affect men in a different way from women. Specifically, the Mars-Neptune, Mars-Uranus, and Mar-Chiron aspects are *male sexual aspects,* but they are not sexual aspects for women. In other words, we interpret these three aspects differently for men than women when it comes to predicting sexuality. For women, the Mars-Neptune and Mars-Chiron aspects increase the female urge for a family and to want to become pregnant, but they do not increase the desire for sex, nor do they enhance sexual capacity. Women with these two aspects focus on bearing children and not on the sex act. The Mar-Uranus aspect in women provides more energy, but this energy is not specifically sexual in nature.

On the other hand, of the three Sexual Aspects we previously listed, the Venus-Pluto aspect has a stronger sexual influence on the woman than the man. In fact, the Venus-Pluto aspect is a FEMALE SUPER SEXUAL ASPECT along with Venus-Mars; whereas the MALE SUPER SEXUAL ASPECTS are Mars-Pluto, Mars-Neptune, and again, Venus-Mars. These findings of ours are consistent with the fact that the male sexual planet is Mars, and the female sexual planet is Venus. Venus-Mars is a Super Sexual Aspect for both men and women.

Incidentally, Madonna was born with a Female Super Sexual Aspect. Most women who are born with one will not marry a man who does not have a Sexual Aspect, because men who don't simply cannot keep up with women who do. We will see later on in this book that Madonna's men have Male Super Sexual Aspects. And so does Bill Clinton.

The Romance Planets and Romance Aspects

There are also planets that help give birth to, fortify, and strengthen love and harmony between two persons. There are three such planets, and we call them ROMANCE PLANETS. Like the Sexual Planets, the Romance Planets are the ones you would expect from their symbolisms. Chiron, Venus, and Neptune are all Romance Planets. Chiron is the most important and most powerful, but the other two are not far behind—and all three play a crucial role in all emotional relationships. Like the Sexual Planets, the Romance Planets combine to make a special type of aspect. Whenever any two of them create an aspect, they create what we call ROMANCE ASPECTS. Any aspect that is created by any pairing of Chiron, Venus, or Neptune is a Romance Aspect, and people who are born with such aspects have a very strong desire and need for love and relationships; they do not want to be alone, and most *cannot* be alone. Such persons almost always want to be married and have a family, or at least be in love. For these reasons, they fall in love the fastest. Obviously, confirmed bachelors do not have Romance Aspects in their birth charts. Just so there is no confusion, here is a listing of the Romance Aspects:

- Chiron and Venus can mean desire (Venus) for marriage (Chiron) and children (Chiron);
- Venus and Neptune can mean desire (Venus) for long-term relationships (Neptune); and

- Chiron and Neptune can mean long-term (Neptune) marriage (Chiron) or romance (Chiron).

Here, again, there is a difference between how women and men react to aspects. There are four other pairings of planets that create Romance Aspects, but they apply only to women. Sun-Venus, Venus-Moon, Sun-Chiron, and Moon-Chiron are all FEMALE ROMANCE ASPECTS but do not influence the man in the same way. These four aspects induce women to be more romantic and more desirous of meaningful relationships, marriage, children, and a family. Men are oblivious to such influences from these particular aspects.

In a man, the Sun-Venus aspect is a sign of beauty without the special overtones of romanticism that their female counterparts have. The Sun-Chiron and Moon-Chiron aspects are signs of men who would be good fathers, but again, these characteristics are not attached to romanticism. It is just the way most men are.

Such facts help us understand the gap between the way women and men view heterosexual relationships. Men are more sexual in part because there are more Sexual Aspects that work on men; and women are more romantic and are in greater need of meaningful relationships because there are more Romance Aspects that affect them. However, women are also more romantic because men are men and women are women. This mystery makes life more intriguing.

Are You Planning a Seduction? Take Advantage of Seduction Aspects!

Are you planning a seduction? Well, we have *great* news. Your chances of exhilarating success will be greatly increased when you entice and tempt someone at a time when the planets form SEDUCTION ASPECTS. This is because the planetary aspects that exist at any time in the sky influence how we all feel.

Different aspects in the sky have different influences on all of us. If you think back, you will no doubt recall times when it seemed as if the whole world was on a nastiness binge; everyone was in a bad mood. And, there were other times when it seemed that the whole world was in a helpful and cooperative kick; everyone was in a good mood. Such times are predictable by analyzing the planetary aspects of the day. For whatever reason, planetary aspects are signs of the general mood of everyone around us. Of course we all put our own spin to this, so some of us are not as affected as others, but we are all influenced at least a little by the planetary aspects of a day. That is the cause of those times when almost everyone seems either happy or sullen.

For example, when Japan attacked Pearl Harbor, there were two aspects that spelled *war*. Mars and Sun formed a trine, and Chiron and Mars were in trine. Not only were these signs that there could be war, but they were also indications that the level of belligerency worldwide would be well above normal. The U.S. declared war on Japan. Germany and Italy declared war on the U.S., who then declared war on them. See what we mean? The Sun-Mars trine and Mars-Chiron trine lasted through all these declarations of war.

But fortunately, there are also days when the world generally feels romantic and more loving. Such days are good times to seduce someone or to make love. We all feel more romantic when a Seduction Aspect is in the air. In other words, when a Seduction Aspect is formed by the planets in the sky, everyone will feel more inclined to *fall* in love and feel more inclined to *make* love, including the person who is the target of your seduction. On a day when a Sexual Aspect is in the sky, everyone has more sexual energy. Try it—it works! When we make love during a Seduction Aspect, our lovemaking is more fluid, more exhilarating, and more satisfying. We also want more romance and sex. The Magi Society has been doing this for hundreds of years. Why do you think there are so many Chinese?!

Seriously, here are the five Seduction Aspects:

1. Sun enhanced by Venus, a time (Sun) for seduction (Venus);

2. Moon enhanced by Venus, a mood (Moon) for seduction (Venus);

3. Venus enhanced by Neptune, a time for sensual (Neptune) desires (Venus);

4. Venus enhanced by Mars, a desire (Venus) for sex (Mars) and sexual (Mars) seduction (Venus); the joining (Venus) of bodies (Mars); and

5. Mars enhanced by Pluto, energy (Mars) for the sex organs (Pluto).

Bear in mind that it is Venus that is the ruler of seduction. Each of these Venus aspects elevates our romantic desires and increases our need to be with someone. The Mars-Pluto aspect is sort of like a dose of Viagra, but it also works on women. We all have more sexual energy and are all more susceptible to being seduced under the influence of any of these five aspects.

You may have noticed that two of these aspects are also Sexual Aspects; this means that days when such aspects exist are definitely times you want to mark your calendar in red—for romance and passion!

The period of time when an aspect is formed and within orb is called the ASPECT'S TIME, or just ASPECT TIME. The aspect time of Seduction Aspects are the best times to seduce anyone.

To help you make use of this information, we have provided a LOVE CALENDAR at the back of this book. It contains the best days for love and seduction for five years. Try it out; we think you will love these days. The Love Calendar also warns you of days when love relationships could be tumultuous. The best way to handle such days is to be understanding and not do anything drastic; just let the days pass by, and don't make waves.

When referring to the best times to do things, there is a branch of astrology that specifically deals with choosing the most favorable times to engage in specific types of activities. It is called ELECTIONAL ASTROLOGY. Let us focus on this subject next.

Electional Astrology

Electional Astrology is the branch of astrology that deals with the selection of specific days to engage in any particular type of activity. Astrologers believe that there are good days and bad days to do anything. This belief is based on an idea that originated from the ancient Hebrew prophets. They believed that when a man and woman were married using a specific set of rituals, then the couple was reborn together in a new form, and the astrological chart of the wedding date becomes the chart of the marriage (called the MARRIAGE CHART or WEDDING CHART). Their lives were then as dependent on the Marriage Chart as their own birth charts. This idea was conceived as early as 4,000 years ago, but became most important when the Hebrews began to anoint kings (since the same theory applied to this act).

From the days of Abraham until about the birth of David, the Hebrews did not have kings. Instead, they were led by men of high moral stature, those whom the Hebrews believed had direct access to their Lord. Moses, Joshua, and other early famous leaders of the Israelites were never kings. The last group of such leaders of the Hebrews are referred to as the judges, all of whom were regarded as prophets. Samuel was the last of the judges, and it was he who anointed Saul as the first king of Israel, and also David as Saul's successor.

We already explained that we are certain that Samuel was a great astrologer. Samuel believed in the importance of choosing the most favorable days for weddings such that the newlyweds would be *reborn* with the most favorable astrological charts. So when he had to crown the first king of Israel, it was natural that Samuel did it on a very favorable day, and also did it in a way so that the king would be reborn with a new astrological chart—and one that was a great one.

This idea of rebirth and new charts defies logic, but it works when it is done right. To the Hebrews, the key to the rebirth process of the coronation is the invocation of God and the anointing of the head with holy oil. This tradition was regarded as so sacred that every single monarch of England has been crowned in this way. Modern historians agree that such a coronation ritual is meant to represent that the individual symbolically dies to be reborn again in a new form. What the historians do not usually realize is that this all originated from astrological beliefs held by ancient Hebrew prophets.

The criteria used by the Hebrew prophets to evaluate if a day was good or bad had to do with the planetary aspects of the day. They were correct about this. By analyzing the planetary aspects of a day, you can tell if a day is a good one to get married or be coronated. But the usefulness of Electional Astrology has grown far beyond such limited types of events. Nowadays, astrologers correctly believe that the theories of Electional Astrology can be applied to *any* activity. There are good days and bad days to do absolutely anything and everything, and it all depends on the Planetary Geometry of the day. There are good and bad days to look for a job, start a new job, make love, negotiate a contract, open a bank account, make a speech, have a medical procedure performed, begin a medication, buy a house, pay off a loan, go on a blind date, start a romance, take a trip, and so on.

We just explained that when there are Seduction Aspects or Sexual Aspects, it is a good time to make love. We are not saying that you should not make love unless such aspects exist. However, if your love sessions have been normally good, then if you do make love during any of those types of aspects, the results will be fabulous.

All of this is important, but where knowledge of Electional Astrology becomes most crucial is when we engage in any activity for the *first time*. At that time, the Planetary Geometry that exists when we first do something becomes the birth chart of that type of activity for the rest of our lives. Such is the case with the coronation of a monarch. Also, when we get married, the planetary aspects and geometry of the day we are wed becomes the astrological chart of our marriage, and therefore becomes the Marriage Chart.

What is the rationale behind the idea of a Marriage Chart? We have all felt days when there is a smooth and vibrant energy in the air and everything goes right. Astrologers believe that such days are good days to begin things because by commencing something new on such a day, you capture and *preserve* whatever energy the day has that makes it so wonderful. This energy that a day has is dependent upon the alignment of the planets and the Planetary Geometry of that day.

Have you ever wished you could preserve a feeling or moment? You can. In this book, you will learn how to select and preserve the energy of such days. In so doing, you can actually harness the powers of the planets and use them to your advantage. This is one of the keys to success in love and money.

Electional Astrology teaches us that there are some days that are good to do certain things, and there are days that are not good to engage in a certain type of activity. The Old Testament even talks about this: "To every thing there is a season, and a time to every purpose under the heaven . . . A time to love, and a time to hate; a time of war, and a time of peace" (Ecclesiastes 3,1 and 3,8).

And the stars will give us signs to tell us when the best time is to do anything.

Theory of Natalization

Astrologers have never given a name to their theory that when a person engages in a distinct type of activity for the *first time,* the birth chart of that time becomes the birth chart for that person's actions for that type of activity. It is useful for astrology to have a name for this theory. We will call it NATALIZATION, because the action taken has a birth, and therefore is born, or NATALIZED. Both words are new to the English language, but they are necessary for the growth and understanding of astrology and its theories. Since scientists ascribe a name and term to all of their concepts, it's only fitting that astrologers do the same.

Natalization occurs whenever anyone engages in any type of activity for the very first time. For example, when Michael Jordan first touched a basketball, that moment in time became the birth chart of Michael Jordan as a basketball player—for his entire life. Similarly, when two people make love for the first time, the birth chart of that time is the birth chart of their love-making relationship.

Electional Astrology Explains a Baffling Mystery

By employing the theory of natalization, a good astrologer can explain how Hitler somehow was able to lead his whole country into a lunatic war. This is because the chart of the day Hitler became Germany's chancellor was extraordinarily powerful and was preserved through natalization. Hitler's own chart was not powerful, but the chart of the day he became chancellor was powerful enough to be able to lead a whole nation almost unquestioningly into a devastating war. That chart had two symmetrical patterns—it had two grand trines! There were two very significant celestial signs in the sky, which was just like Napoleon's birth chart. Napoleon was also able to lead his nation in a lunatic war. In both cases, there were celestial signs in the sky that warned us of this possibility. Also, in both cases, there were two Grand Trines in the sky with Mars as the key planet. The odds against this being a coincidence are well over ten million to one.

You Can Harness the Power of the Planets!

Magi Astrology's greatest value is that it helps us harness the power of the planets and use them to maximize our chances of fulfilling our dreams.

We can make use of the Theory of Natalization to utilize the power of the stars to our advantage in both affairs of love and money. For example, we can choose an especially favorable astrological day to get married or start a job or business. By doing so, we preserve and retain the power of the favorable Planetary Geometry in our marriage, job, or business.

There is a twist to this that is important to understand. Sometimes, one very important action that is natalized overrules another less important action that was natalized.

For example, if two persons make love before getting married, the birth chart of the wedding overrules the earlier chart of the first time they made love. The chart of the first time two persons make love is referred to as their LOVEMAKING CHART, or LOVE CHART. The Love Chart will rule their relationship until this chart is overridden by a Wedding Chart, and then the wedding chart takes precedence. If the two persons never get married, but they've made love, then their Love Chart is the primary chart that rules their relationship.

If two people never make love, the chart of their relationship is based on the moment they first see each other. This is the COMPANIONSHIP CHART. If two people have never met, then the chart of their relationship would be that of the first time they spoke on the phone or corresponded, even by mail or e-mail. We call this the Distant Relationship Chart. However, once they meet, the Distant Relationship Chart is superseded by the chart of their first meeting, which then becomes their Companionship Chart.

Nothing supersedes the Marriage Chart unless there is a divorce; then the Love Chart is back in force, and the chart of the wedding is dissolved. Once a marriage is dissolved through a divorce, the Marriage Chart can never be revived. If the same two persons get married again, they have a new Marriage Chart, which has the Planetary Geometry of the day of their second wedding.

The most useful part of all of astrology is to be able to harness the power of the planets and improve our chances of fulfilling our dreams by choosing the best times to natalize a crucial activity. Very often, the success of an individual is the result of the power of that person's Marriage Chart, or the chart of the day the person began a job or business. Later in this book, you will learn how to maximize your chances of happiness and success by choosing the best times to natalize something very important.

Our Planetary Aspects Are Signs of Our Essence

Our NATAL ASPECTS are the planetary aspects that existed at the time we were born, and our Natal Planetary Geometry is that which existed at the time of our birth. (But for simplicity in writing, we will omit the word *natal* when it is obvious what we mean.) For a very long time, astrologers have known that our aspects reflect our character; as we mentioned previously, this is one reason why people still talk about "an *aspect* of that person's character."

We've explained that we can accurately determine the range of influence of any aspect by combining the various symbolisms of the planets that create an aspect. For example, if Venus and Uranus form an aspect, then the aspect can mean:

- money (Venus) from the entertainment business (Uranus);
- famous (Uranus) good looks (Venus);
- desire (Venus) for independence (Uranus); or
- changes (Uranus) of love relationships (Venus).

It can also mean any other combination of the symbolisms of Venus and Uranus. It is even possible for someone with the Venus-Uranus aspect to reflect all of the above. Interestingly enough, the two persons who most perfectly fit all of the above interpretations are Elizabeth Taylor and Warren Beatty. Both of them were born with the Venus-Uranus conjunction, which is a sign of someone who prefers to change lovers and not be with any individual for an extended period of time. The term *extended period of time* also has a much shorter duration in the minds of natives of Venus-Uranus aspects. (A native is the person born with the aspect.)

Taylor and Beatty handled their Venus-Uranus conjunctions a little differently. This is because men and women react somewhat differently to the influences of the aspects. Because Taylor is a woman, she has the greater need to be married; women have the biological clock ticking and the instinctual desire for children. So, Taylor got married and divorced eight times. That is a lot of "I do's" and a lot of "I no longer do's." It takes something uncommon in a person to be able to go through all of these marriages without going bonkers. It is the Venus-Uranus conjunction Taylor was born with that not only helped her through all those marriages and divorces, but also spurred her on to keep getting married. Most of us go through heartaches when we break up with anyone we have loved. However, the Venus-Uranus person usually breathes a sigh of relief and relishes the thought of their next love partner.

So far, Warren Beatty hasn't said "I do" more than once. But he did say "I won't" a whole lot of times—a lot more than eight times. And most of these times, his "I won'ts" were probably Shermanesque, meaning they were unequivocal. (General Sherman, you might recall, did not want to be president of this country, but others wanted to draft him for the nomination. He stopped that movement when he made his now famous statement: "If nominated I will not run. If elected, I will not serve.")

What this tells us is that your chances of marrying someone are dramatically decreased if that person has the Venus-Uranus natal aspect. It also means that if you do marry such a person, the person could get the seven-year itch in seven months.

We believe that none of the above is the actual result of an influence by the Venus-Uranus conjunction, but rather this conjunction is a sign of the soul and what the person is really like. We also want to repeat that astrology is not an exact science and everyone has free will. The wind may blow one way, but a person can decide to walk against the wind. Similarly, a person can go against the normal attributes of a natal aspect. It would be best for a person to learn to be a reflection of the best interpretation of their natal aspects. For example, Venus-Uranus could be "love (Venus) for the world (Uranus)."

In addition, when analyzing natal aspects, it is imperative to take into account all of the natal aspects that a person was born with. Some aspects cancel each other out or are overpowered by another one or more aspects.

What is an aspect of fidelity and steadiness in love relationships? The aspect that is the most reliable indication of loyalty and faithfulness is the Venus-Jupiter enhancement. This aspect's many interpretations include that of loyalty (Jupiter) and fidelity (Jupiter) in unions (Venus). Our research shows that persons born with the Venus-Jupiter enhancements are involved in fewer divorces than any other aspect. Also, weddings that take place with this aspect are the least likely to end up in divorce; this is due to natalization of that aspect and preserving the energy of the aspect.

A person's natal planetary aspects are such useful indications of the person's character and essence that we devote a whole chapter of this book to interpreting each and every aspect.

It is now time to discuss the "why" and "how" of planetary aspects. How can they possibly work, and why do they exist? Do they have real power, or are they just a sign of something out of the ordinary? Ever since their discovery 4,000 years ago, they have been a mystery, and they remain mysterious, untouched by any conceivable scientific explanation. It is this inconceivability that makes scientists so skeptical about them. But we have proven that they work in the last chapter of this book. So what can we give you as an explanation for why they work?

Our Theory about Planetary Aspects

Why do aspects work? Why are they accurate indications of the character of the native (the person born with the aspect)?

The Magi Society theory in this regard is probably the most controversial of all. We believe that the world is designed by a God that is a Benevolent Providence, and we believe that astrology is one of God's Benevolent Designs. We believe in the God of Judeo-Christian tradition and that such organized religions have been a mainstay in helping the world to understand the value of moral teachings. Modern civilization owes its laws, social order, prosperity, and its very existence in large part to the sacrifices of ancient Jews and Christians. They were the ones who led the way toward the abolition of the actual sacrificing of humans to pagan gods. They also led the way to giving women an equal status with men (although we still have further to go in this regard). It is the Jews who brought into this world the belief that one man should have one wife, and that there is one God. There really is something very special about these ancient Jews, and Christ was born as one of them. It is Christ who was the first to teach us that God loves us. Millions of Jews and Christians literally gave their lives to stand up for these beliefs. Considering their sacrifices, the debt that we owe them is unmeasurable.

It has been almost 2,000 years since Christ was born unto us. Since then, his message has been distorted. Isn't everything after so long a period of time? We have one very big problem with a particular doctrine of some organized Christian religions. We do not accept or believe in the concept of hell and damnation. It is time we did away with this. Almost all parents love their children so much that they would forgive them for anything. Could God and Christ be any less forgiving and understanding than most parents? We are sure that God and Christ are more forgiving and understanding than any of us can ever be, or even conceive to be. Is it consistent with the love and forgiveness that Christ taught us that we would be punished forever for failing in our lives here on Earth? We think not.

So then the question is, what happens when we die?

We believe that our souls survive death and that we come back to learn what we did not learn the previous time. We either come back here or go to another world God designed for us. This means we believe in reincarnation. The reason that this is a subject of an astrology book is that we believe that astrology has a lot to do with the day we come back to this world. *We can only come back on a day that has the planetary aspects that match our souls!* In other words, if we were warlike, we can only come when there is an aspect that reflects the warlike nature. If we are peaceful, we can come back when there is an aspect that reflects this peace within our souls.

What this all means is that our Planetary Geometry really comprises celestial signs of what we are really like. Our Planetary Geometry, including all of our planetary aspects, is an indication of what our souls have been in our last life. But we all have a chance, in every life and at any time, to improve what we are. The easiest step in that improvement is to upgrade to a better interpretation of our aspects. This is why we took such pains to detail what we mean by the *valid range of interpretations* for any aspect. Every aspect has some good interpretations, and some not as good. But we all have the free will to choose to be the best interpretation of each of our aspects.

In this book, we occasionally write about how aspects have powers and influences, but we never really mean or believe that they actually do have powers in and of themselves. We always mean that they are signs. We think a Benevolent Providence designed these signs to guide us. And He also went one step further. God made use of planetary aspects and designed it so that every planetary aspect is also a gift from Him of a special talent and skill.

Planetary Aspects Are Indications of Special Talents

One of the most exciting and helpful benefits of mastering Planetary Geometry and the symbolisms of the planets is that not only are they invaluable in matters of love, they also help us in all matters of money. Also, these tools of Magi Astrology can solve one of the biggest questions in all of our lives:

- What career should I pursue? How can I obtain the most personal satisfaction and make the most money?

In the past, some individuals have relied on aptitude tests and career counselors. Others were pushed in a particular direction by parents or circumstances. It is a real shame that so many of us do not ever discover what we are best at—or only find out after decades of trial and error. But there is a much better way. God designed astrology to give each of us great talents—every single one of us! And the stars give us signs showing what these talents are. We just have to learn how to read them.

Too often, we toil and struggle at a dead-end job that we neither enjoy nor are suited for. But by the grace of God, we are all born with special abilities, and we are all born with whatever we need to be very successful in *something*. However, we must find out what that *something* is, work very hard at it, and never give up. Our Planetary Geometry and the symbolisms of Magi Astrology are very accurate tools that will give us the best clues to what and how we can achieve the greatest success. We can analyze our Planetary Geometry to help us determine the career where we can each achieve the greatest amount of success, as well as gain the fullest sense of enjoyment and satisfaction.

Some examples will help you readily understand exactly what we're talking about. The Babylonian Alignment Charts of these examples are at the end of this chapter. We start with Mikhail Baryshnikov and Ted Turner, both of whom have achieved super success in a particular field of endeavor, and their Planetary Geometry explains exactly why they were able to do so.

Mikhail Baryshnikov

Mikhail Baryshnikov is widely regarded as the greatest classical ballet dancer of recent times—and his Planetary Geometry predicted it! Baryshnikov was born with a Sun-Mars quincunx (Figure 5A). Any aspect of Sun and Mars is an indication of an unusual ability in careers ruled by Mars; one such career is dancing. The reason Mars rules dance is that it rules the muscles and the body, and dance requires both. Mars also rules bodily movements, which is what dance is.

But you might correctly be thinking that Mars also rules war, the soldier, athletics and the athlete, and other things. Therefore, you might ask, what makes Baryshnikov a dancer instead of a soldier or athlete?

The answer is: It's because of the rest of his Planetary Geometry. Baryshnikov was born with a truly extraordinary DYNAMIC SYMMETRICAL PATTERN. We explained earlier that a symmetrical pattern is dynamic if all of the planets of the pattern match degrees. Please look at Baryshnikov's birth chart on page 114 and note that Venus, Neptune, and Pluto form a symmetrical pattern; and each planet matches degrees, thus making aspects to each other. This particular pattern is called a YOD. Only Magi Astrology has formulated a set of simple rules to guide us in interpreting geometric patterns. The special talents imparted by any Yod can be understood by combining and integrating the symbolisms of the three planets that create the Yod. Venus is symbolic of grace and beauty; Neptune rules artistry and creative skills; and Pluto rules sexuality and the ability to capitalize on and make money from a talent. Together with the Sun-Mars aspect, the three planets in symmetrical pattern create a dancer who can dance in a way that has grace (Venus) and beauty (Venus), is artistic (Neptune) and creative (Neptune), is sexy (Pluto), and can make money (Pluto) doing it. The Venus-Neptune-Pluto alignment imparts grace and beauty that is simultaneously creative, talented, and sexy. Baryshnikov's abilities in this regard are truly extraordinary because a Dynamic Symmetrical Pattern provides the greatest talents and skills.

But there is even more. Baryshnikov has another Dynamic Symmetrical Pattern. It is a Golden Rectangle formed by Jupiter, Saturn, Uranus, and Mercury, and this also greatly enhanced his ability to be the world's premier ballet performer. Uranus rules coordination and balance; and Mercury rules reflexes, the eyes, and respiration. Jupiter improves whatever it is in aspect with; and when Jupiter and Saturn are activated and on the same wavelength in any dynamic pattern, the two planets create the symbolism of "unlimited" (which is something we explained in the *Magi Society*

Ephemeris). All together then, these four planets endowed Baryshnikov with unlimited abilities in matters requiring coordination and balance, and reflexes and eye-body skills. Hence, Baryshnikov's Natal Planetary Geometry was uniquely suited to help him become the best classical dancer of recent times.

Ted Turner

Ted Turner's Planetary Geometry also precisely defined his area of greatest ability (Figure 5B). Turner is the man responsible for bringing us CNN (the Cable News Network) and TBS (the Turner Broadcasting System). He revolutionized news broadcasting with CNN and its round-the-clock news programming, which is now seen worldwide, even in China and Russia. CNN is the most widely broadcast television channel in the world. In addition, Turner brought the baseball games of the Atlanta Braves to all of America and made the Braves the most watched baseball team ever. He recently sold his interests in TBS and CNN to Time Warner and became wealthy enough to make the biggest donation in history—about a billion dollars—to the United Nations. All of this fits perfectly with his Planetary Geometry.

Like Baryshnikov, Turner was born with a Yod; Turner's Yod is comprised of Uranus, Mercury, and Mars. Can you believe it? This Yod is symbolic of broadcasting (Uranus)—both news (Mercury) and sports (Mars)—and means that Turner was best suited for that business.

Turner also has a conjunction of Venus and Sun; quite often, this aspect makes the person very attractive because Venus rules beauty. By most standards, Turner fits that manifestation of the Sun-Venus aspect.

Also, Turner's Sun is squared by Jupiter. Jupiter rules generosity, so this aspect can help us figure out why Turner made the biggest charitable contribution in history.

Ralph Nader

In our first book, *Astrology Really Works!,* we went into great detail about how to interpret natal aspects. While doing research for that book, we carefully analyzed the Planetary Geometry of every person who had a truly extraordinary talent or ability. We found that these people always had Planetary Geometry that defined their unique capabilities. We discovered that every highly talented artist was born with the Planetary Geometry that symbolizes the specific talent the artist possesses; every great athlete has the Planetary Geometry that is necessary to become a great athlete in their particular sport; every great businessman has the Planetary Geometry to excel in the particular business in which the person achieved the greatest success. Planetary Geometry even works on careers you would never dream could be predictable through astrology.

For example, Ralph Nader has been the foremost consumer advocate in America (born 2/27/34; chart not shown). He is not a businessman or politician or entertainer or athlete. He is a consumer advocate. What could the Planetary Geometry of a consumer advocate possibly be? A Saturn-Pluto aspect! Nader was born with a natal aspect of Saturn quincunx Pluto. This is the aspect that means limitation (Saturn) of big business (Pluto) and power (Pluto). So Nader is successful as a consumer advocate because he has a special ability to limit big business, and counter big business's accumulation of power. Nader also has Jupiter quincunx to Mercury, which endows him with the ability to communicate (Mercury) very well (Jupiter) and to be able to give very noble (Jupiter) speeches (Mercury) about fairness (Jupiter) and integrity (Jupiter).

See how amazing natal aspects and Planetary Geometry are? They are *SIGNS* and clues as to how we can achieve the maximum success. So if you are wondering what career path to take, look at your stars, meaning look at your Planetary Geometry. But don't worry if you're not sure how to interpret it. We still have a lot to teach you about how to do that.

Businesses Also Have Birth Charts

Electional Astrology and knowledge of Planetary Geometry can also help you maximize your chances of success if you are planning to start a business.

Corporations also have birth charts. Through the process of natalization, when a company is first created, the astrological chart of that time of creation (date of incorporation) becomes the chart of the corporation, and the Planetary Geometry of the chart determines the ability of the company to make money.

Have you ever wondered why AT&T failed in the computer business? And why IBM failed in the copying machine business? Are you surprised that Dell Computer and Compaq each sell more personal computers than IBM? And why is it that some companies can grow by making massive acquisitions, while others cannot?

By now you know that the answers are in the stars. But do you know why? If you're thinking that it's because of aspects, you are correct.

A company must be *incorporated* on a day that has the necessary planetary aspects that enable it to be especially prosperous in a particular business or activity, or else it will not be able to compete in that business. Like a person, a company can only succeed at what the aspects allow. There can be a number of different areas in which one can achieve success, but companies—and all of us—are able to achieve the most success in an area in which our strongest planetary aspects endow us with the specific abilities we need. As always, let us give you some examples in order to clarify what we're saying.

General Electric and Exxon

General Electric and Exxon are two of the most profitable corporations in the world. Exxon is the world's largest oil company, and in terms of the value of its stock, General Electric is the world's most valuable corporation. Both companies were founded about a hundred years ago, when Neptune and Pluto made a conjunction (Figures 5C and 5D). This conjunction is a very rare event; the next Neptune-Pluto conjunction will not occur until the 24th century. There is a general rule in astrology: The rarer the alignment of the planets, the more meaningful and more powerful the alignment is. The Neptune-Pluto conjunction is very meaningful and very powerful, and gave rise to the birth of two of the most powerful and preeminent companies in the world. It is their Neptune-Pluto conjunctions that enabled GE and Exxon to be supersuccessful in the businesses that they dominate. Both companies make their money in the exact way that the Neptune-Pluto conjunction would predict.

The Neptune-Pluto conjunction signifies the ability to capitalize (Pluto) and make profits (Pluto) from Neptune-related areas. Neptune rules oil, and Exxon is synonymous with oil and is known worldwide as the largest oil company. Neptune also rules electricity, and General Electric (GE) is the number-one company in the world in electrical equipment, such as power plants and light bulbs. Neptune also rules medical equipment, and GE invented and is the sole manufacturer of MRI equipment, electrical devices that are used to diagnose diseases. This equipment has revolutionized medicine in the 1990s.

Another symbolism of Neptune is that of financial security, so the Neptune-Pluto conjunction means financial security (Neptune) from big business (Pluto) and the ability to compete (Pluto). Exxon and GE are two of a handful of companies with AAA credit ratings. Obviously, as predicted from their Neptune-Pluto conjunction, Exxon and GE are extraordinarily secure financially.

The important lesson to learn is that the Planetary Geometry of the birth chart of a corporation will foretell that company's distinctive abilities, just like a person's Planetary Geometry.

Exxon and GE were both incorporated on a day that had a Yod, which is the same Dynamic Symmetrical Pattern that exists in the birth charts of Baryshnikov and Turner. GE's Yod is the most powerful because there is a conjunction of Neptune and Pluto at one corner of the Yod; in effect, GE has two Yods, or a DOUBLE YOD. In Magi Astrology, we have a special way of interpreting a Double Yod. Essentially, we simply combine and integrate the symbolisms of all four planets, just the way we have already learned to do, but we place special emphasis on the conjunction. GE's Double Yod provides it with the unique ability to attain worldwide (Uranus) success (Jupiter) through big business (Pluto) in Neptunian areas, such as electricity and electrical appliances, and medical equipment that is electrical in nature, and especially through inventions (Uranus).

GE also has a Mercury-Uranus aspect that empowers it with the resources and expertise to prosper in broadcasting (Uranus) and news dissemination (Mercury). This is one reason why GE's purchase of NBC has been so astoundingly profitable and rewarding.

In the case of Exxon, its Yod is a part of a larger pattern of Planetary Geometry. On the day Exxon was founded, there were five planets that matched degrees. Besides Mars, Venus, and Mercury, which form the Yod, both Neptune and Pluto also matched degrees. These five planets are all in aspect to each other, meaning that each of these five planets made an aspect to each of the other four planets. Such an alignment of five planets is remarkably unusual and powerful. Astrologers had never focused on this sort of alignment before, so it was up to the Magi Society to give a name to such alignments.

In *Astrology Really Works!,* we named such alignments PLANETARY SYNCHRONIZATION. A planetary aspect occurs whenever any two planets match degrees. Planetary Synchronization occurs whenever three or more planets match degrees. Common sense tells us that the more planets there are in a synchronization, the more powerful it is. Exxon's five-planet synchronization has awesome power. That is the main reason why Exxon is the largest and most profitable oil company in the world.

Amazingly, Exxon's synchronization of five planets specifically enabled the company to be the world leader in oil exploration and marketing. Synchronizations are interpreted in the same way a Yod is: We simply combine and integrate the symbolisms of the planets that comprise the synchronization. The five planets that are in synch on Exxon's birth date are Neptune, Pluto, Venus, Mercury, and Mars. Of these five planets, three are directly related to oil. Neptune rules oil, Mercury rules exploration, and Mars is the ruler of drilling. You might wonder why Mercury signifies exploration. It does so because Mercury was the Roman god of traveling, and traveling is a requirement of land exploration. No other planet's symbolisms come even close to exploration. As for Mars being the ruler of drilling, this follows logically from Mars' rulerships of body movements and labor-intensive activities. Also, drilling for oil is attacking the ground; this is very much a part of the symbolisms of Mars.

Together, these five planets IN SYNCH mean money (Venus) from the big business (Pluto) of oil (Neptune) exploration (Mercury) and drilling (Mars). Exxon also has the remarkably powerful aspect of Jupiter trine Chiron, representing a successful (Jupiter) career (Chiron).

We refer to the chart of a corporation as a *business chart*. The birth charts of the founding of a partnership or the signing of a business agreement are also considered business charts.

Why Russia Is Having So Much Economic Trouble

The world will be a much safer place when the Russians have a true free market system and an economy that is stable. This may take a while longer than most think, but we hope that the Russians don't give up trying. Perhaps what we say will be encouraging.

America is now the premier economic power in the world, and its most powerful corporations are known worldwide. The whole world knows about Coca-Cola, GE, Boeing, Microsoft, Merck, 3M, Procter and Gamble, Exxon, IBM, and others. Can you name a Russian company? Almost none of us can. But except for Microsoft, all of the above superpowers of the U.S. economy were founded at least 50 years ago. You have just learned that the Neptune-Pluto conjunction is one of the reasons for the unmatched success of GE and Exxon in their respective businesses. The competitiveness and super success of these companies were achieved in large measure because of their awesome Planetary Geometry. It took two centuries for America to build its economy and competitiveness based on corporations that were founded on the most favorable Planetary

Geometry. Unfortunately, since Russian companies have only been formed for less than a decade, they do not yet have enough companies with strong astrological charts to be able to have a strong free market economy. Over time, Russia will. In fact, during the first decade of the 21st century, there are superb aspects that will allow Russia to form companies that should rival any in the world, if Russia retains free enterprise.

The Planets Can Be Feminine, Masculine, or Neutral

Astrologers have long believed that each of the 12 zodiac signs is either feminine or masculine. In much the same way, Magi Astrology believes that each planet is masculine or feminine, except that some can be neutral. This has a bearing when interpreting characteristics and personality, because when the Sun matches degrees with a planet, the masculine or feminine nature of the matched planet will influence the character of the person. Mars and Pluto are the most masculine planets, and Neptune and Venus are the most feminine planets. This means that people who are born with an aspect of the Sun and Mars, or Sun and Pluto are the most masculine people in the zodiac. Those born with an aspect of the Sun and Neptune, or the Sun and Venus are the most feminine people in the zodiac.

But this is only one astrological factor, and it is important that we not give it too much emphasis when rendering an interpretation. Each planetary aspect and other astrological factors must be taken into consideration— even the sex of the person. After all, the male and female hormones still work according to the sex of the individual.

Here are all the planets listed by masculine or feminine tendencies:

- Mercury: masculine
- Venus: very feminine
- Moon: feminine
- Mars: very masculine; the most masculine planet
- Jupiter: neutral
- Saturn: masculine
- Chiron: neutral
- Uranus: feminine
- Neptune: very feminine; the most feminine planet
- Pluto: very masculine

The Sun is neutral.

From time to time, we will apply this knowledge of the masculine and feminine influences of the planets to help us understand how to most completely and accurately comprehend the meaning of planetary aspects.

It can be very useful information, because men and women love in different ways. The love of a woman is more idealistic, lasts longer, is more giving, less sexual, and more family oriented than the love of a man. But like everything else that has to do with humankind, these are only generalities. There are men who have the capability to love in the same way that women usually do. We can tell if a particular man is such a person by the aspects he was born with. For example, the Venus-Neptune aspect is such an indication. Both planets are feminine; they mean long-term (Neptune) and feminine (Neptune) love (Venus).

Planetary Synchronization Is the FOCUS of Every Chart

In any powerful chart, there are usually several important aspects, and it is sometimes difficult to determine what the FOCUS of the chart is. The focus of a chart is the most crucial Planetary Geometry of the chart, the one that is most defining, and the one that the other alignments are subordinate to. There is a very good general rule of Magi Astrology that will help us determine the focus of a chart:

> *Whenever there is a planetary synchronization,*
> *it is usually the focus of a chart.*
> *If there is more than one synchronization,*
> *then the one that is most exact is the focus.*
> *If there is no synchronization,*
> *then the aspects are the focus of the chart.*
> *The more exact the aspect, the more important the aspect.*

We should point out that all dynamic symmetrical patterns are also planetary synchronizations, because all the planets match degrees and are therefore in synch to each other. Bearing this is mind, if you look back at every chart in this book, you will see that the focus of every chart is a synchronization. That is how important synchronizations are. Each synchronization can be interpreted by combining and integrating the symbolisms of each of the synchronized planets.

Planetary Geometry Is the Astrological Key to a Successful Marriage

Marriages have birth charts, also. The birth chart of a marriage is that of the time the wedding occurred. Like everything else that has a birth chart, the likely attributes and characteristics of the marriage will be indicated by the Planetary Geometry of the Wedding Chart. And this is the key: *A marriage cannot be happy or lasting without the Planetary Geometry that will enable it to be so.*

The Planetary Geometry of a Wedding chart will determine if the couple will want to stay married or get divorced. It will define the boundaries of the type of marriage that the couple will have, as well as the strengths and failings of the marriage. Believe it or not, the Planetary Geometry of the Wedding Chart will even influence the success or failure of the careers of both persons and will have an effect on the type of professions that either of the two spouses will be able to engage in prosperously. For these reasons, it is crucial that we choose the day we get married and make certain that it has the Planetary Geometry needed to help us to fulfill our dreams for the marriage, and for our lives.

What Planetary Geometry should one try to include when choosing a wedding date? We devoted a chapter to this very question in *Astrology Really Works!* Later in this book, we will again go into considerable detail on how to select the best possible wedding date. One of the criteria that is most helpful when making such a choice is SUPER ASPECTS, which is our next subject.

Super Aspects

Planetary aspects are the building blocks of complex Planetary Geometry. Every aspect is important, but some are more important than others. There are quite a few possible pairings of planets that can make aspects. The most powerful ones are SUPER ASPECTS. The term *SUPER ASPECT* was introduced in *Astrology Really Works!,* which identified 12 aspects that were generally the most useful and helpful for anyone or anything to have, including weddings. These 12 aspects were collectively referred to as Super Aspects, and gave everyone who was born with one of them a jump-start on achieving the maximum success. Here are the 12 Super Aspects:

1. Jupiter enhancement of Pluto
2. Venus enhancement of Pluto

3. Pluto enhancement of the Sun
4. Uranus enhancement of Pluto
5. Jupiter enhancement of the Sun
6. Jupiter enhancement of Venus
7. Jupiter enhancement of Uranus
8. Jupiter enhancement of Neptune
9. Uranus enhancement of Venus
10. Neptune enhancement of Venus
11. Uranus enhancement of the Sun
12. Neptune enhancement of the Sun

After monumental research, the Magi Society discovered that each and every one of these 12 Super Aspects is a significant help to anyone blessed enough to be born with one. But the key is that they are equally helpful for businesses and marriages (with two exceptions to be discussed).

Of these 12 Super Aspects, the Jupiter-Pluto enhancement and the Jupiter-Uranus enhancement were given special names because they were the most special. The Jupiter-Pluto enhancement was named the SUPER SUCCESS ASPECT because it was measurably more powerful than any other aspect in helping the native achieve super success. Seven out of eight of America's richest men (as determined by *Forbes* magazine in 1995) were born with that aspect. This makes sense from the symbolisms of Jupiter and Pluto, since Pluto rules power, big business, and profits from business and competition; and Jupiter rules enrichment, success, and good fortune. All of the eight billionaires listed in *Forbes* as the richest individuals in America made their fortunes in big business, the way their Jupiter-Pluto aspects would predict.

We gave the name SUPER FAME ASPECT to the Jupiter-Uranus enhancement because almost half of the preeminent actors in Hollywood have been born with that aspect. Uranus rules fame and the entertainment business, so once again, the symbolisms of the planets accurately predict the gifts and talents that this aspect signifies. Since another symbolism of Uranus is politics, this aspect also bestows great political skills. For example, Bill Clinton and Newt Gingrich were born with this aspect.

When we wrote *Astrology Really Works!*, we decided not to include Chiron because the book was already breaking so much new ground that its addition would have been an information overload. Now that we have introduced you to the power and the true symbolisms of Chiron, we need to add three more aspects to the list of Super Aspects. They are all CHIRON ASPECTS, meaning they are aspects where Chiron is one of two planets that form the aspect. The three additional Super Aspects are the Jupiter-Chiron and Venus-Chiron enhancements—and also the very rare Chiron-Pluto enhancement.

Jupiter-Chiron is just as powerful as Jupiter-Pluto in certain ways. In any business that deals with the general public, this is the best aspect to pick when choosing a day for starting the business because the aspect bestows a fabulous public image (ruled by Chiron).

The Venus-Chiron enhancement is also one of the most powerful of all aspects for a Business Chart. The most logical interpretation is that of a career (Chiron) involved in making money (Venus). It can also lead to powerful charisma (Chiron). What may be the most important characteristic of this aspect is that Chiron works extraordinarily well with Venus because of the harmony of some of their rulerships. Chiron rules free enterprise and earning power, and Venus rules money. The combination of these two planets leads to a Super Aspect for business. For example, both Intel and Compaq have the Venus-Chiron enhancement aspect.

Chiron-Pluto signifies a career (Chiron) that is profitable (Pluto) and powerful (Pluto), as well as being charismatic (Chiron). Obviously a Super Aspect.

Choosing the Best Planetary Geometry for Matters of Love and Money

We have already explained that every marriage and business has a birth chart and that the destinies of both are very much dependent on the strengths or weaknesses of their Planetary Geometry. For this reason, it is of utmost importance that we understand the merits and benefits of each type of Planetary Geometry, as well as the problems associated with each.

The simplest form of Planetary Geometry has to do with planetary aspects. No matter how complex the Planetary Geometry, it is always simply comprised of individual planetary aspects, and we can understand the likely effect of any Planetary Geometry by analyzing each planetary aspect separately. Since planetary aspects are the building blocks of all the more interesting and most powerful symmetrical patterns and complex Planetary Geometry, it is helpful to understand the implications and powers of each such aspect. For this reason, toward the end of this book, we provide you with the most appropriate principal interpretations of every aspect as they relate to matters of love and money.

The general rule is that the 15 Super Aspects are each very helpful to have in any chart, but there are exceptions when it comes to relationship charts. The Uranus aspects are the exceptions. It is not good to have a Sun-

Uranus or Venus-Uranus aspect in a Wedding Chart because Uranus imparts a desire for independence and change, which is detrimental to the longevity and stability of a marriage. On the other hand, the Venus-Neptune and Jupiter-Chiron Super Aspects are particularly good for Wedding Charts. Venus-Neptune helps engender and sustain long-term (Neptune) romance (Venus) and attraction (Venus); Jupiter-Chiron increases the chance of a successful (Jupiter) marriage (Chiron) and peaceful (Jupiter) family (Chiron). We will detail all of this in chapter 15 so that you will be proficient in knowing how to choose the planetary aspects that you desire for a relationship or business chart.

Using Magi Astrology to Help You Marry the Person of Your Dreams

Believe it or not, you can actually use Magi Astrology to help you harness the power of the stars in order to improve your chances of marrying the right person. One way to do this is to select a perfect day to meet *the one* or to make love for first time. You have learned from our Theory of Natalization that each of these acts creates a birth chart. If one of these birth charts has very powerful Planetary Geometry, a marriage is likely to occur.

When two persons begin a relationship, they only have one astrological chart that rules their relationship: the COMPANIONSHIP CHART. It is the chart of the time when the two persons' eyes first meet. The Planetary Geometry of that instant of time is the most influential astrological force on the outcome of the relationship that ensues, until the two persons make love for the first time. Then *that* time becomes the astrological chart of their love relationship, and this chart CO-EXISTS with the Companionship Chart. We will refer to this second chart as the LOVE CHART. The Love Chart, the Companionship Chart, and the Wedding Chart are all examples of RELA-TIONSHIP CHARTS. (Sometimes we will refer to the Wedding Chart as the Marriage Chart.)

If a Companionship Chart and/or the Love Chart have very powerful Planetary Geometry, then the chances of marriage are greatly increased. The reverse is also true. Let's take a look at the Companionship Chart of three really well-known couples who have had superfamous marriages: John F. Kennedy (JFK) and Jacqueline Bouvier; Evita and Juan Peron; and Bianca and Mick Jagger. Their Companionship Charts and Love Charts are good examples of how superpowerful Planetary Geometry can propel two people toward getting married. This information may help *you* marry the person of your dreams.

Evita and Juan Peron

Andrew Lloyd Webber's very entertaining movie *Evita* informed us that Evita met Juan Peron on the evening of January 22, 1944 (Figure 5E). During the few years prior to this meeting, Evita had slept her way up the social and political ladder. Peron also maneuvered his way right up near the top of that ladder. When Evita and Peron met, he still had a live-in lover, but Evita succeeded in making such an impression on him that he ousted this woman that very evening, quite literally kicking the poor soul out in the middle of the night. Evita spent that very night at Peron's home.

Was Evita so irresistible that any man would do what Peron did?

We don't think so. Evita was attractive, but she was no Helen of Troy. Astrologically speaking, Evita and Peron were very attracted to each other. In the next chapter, we will begin to explain the astrology of attraction and learn why two persons are irresistibly drawn to each other. However, we think that the main reason Evita was able to oust her rival (the woman living with Peron) in such a cavalier fashion was that the Planetary Geometry of the time she met Peron was overwhelmingly powerful. There was a Double Grand Trine!

It is amazing how powerful a Double Grand Trine is.

On that night when Evita first met Juan Peron, the Sun, Neptune, and Uranus formed one Grand Trine; and a second Grand Trine was formed by Mars, the Sun, and Neptune. The first Grand Trine foretold of a relationship (Sun) that would be enduring (Neptune) and could create changes (Uranus), and that would be well known (Uranus) and political (Uranus). When a relationship is long term in nature and can create change, it means that it is a relationship of significant consequences. How prophetic!

The second Grand Trine adds to the power of the relationship. The presence of Mars in this other Grand Trine makes the chart aggressive and bristling with energy—never at a loss for initiative. With Evita and Peron, there was no room for hesitation or excessive deliberation. You can just imagine Evita saying, "Juan . . . be a good man and kick the other woman out for me—tonight!"

We can bet that Evita and Juan made love that first evening. Why else do you kick someone out in the middle of the night? This means that the time of their Love Chart is only about six hours later than that of their Companionship Chart. In the six or so hours from the time they met until the time they first made love, the planets that create the two Grand Trines essentially did not move, except for the Sun. The Sun moves about ¼ of a degree in six hours. Mars moved much less, and Uranus and Neptune moved much, much less. This means that the very powerful Planetary Geometry of their Companionship Chart also existed in their Love Chart. The movement of the Sun actually made the Grand Trines more exact and, therefore, more powerful. The Grand Trines were strong enough that Evita and Juan got married and became Argentina's most famous couple.

By the way, on that night, there was also a Seduction Aspect, but it was in the second chart. Remember, we explained in chapter 1 that there is always a second birth chart. We explain what such charts are in chapter 7, where you will see why the night the Perons met was a fabulous one to make love, and why there was extraordinary sexual energy in the air. You see, there are times to make love, and there are times to read a good book or watch a good movie—alone.

Bianca and Mick Jagger

Another couple who probably made love on the night they met are Mick and Bianca Jagger. We do not know this for a fact, but we cannot imagine Mick pussyfooting around, can you? Especially when he was only 27 years old, single, and at the peak of his game. Mick met Bianca on September 22, 1970, in Paris (Figure 5F). He may or may not have been with long-standing paramour Marianne Faithful at the time. But that would not have stopped Mick from consummating a relationship.

Mick was the quintessential bachelor. So what kind of Planetary Geometry was in their Companionship and Love Charts so that Mick Jagger was moved enough to marry Bianca? It must have been enormously powerful—and it was. Pluto was in conjunction to the Sun with Neptune sextile to both. This alignment meant that there was a Planetary Synchronization of the Sun, Neptune, and Pluto. We have explained that Planetary Synchronizations are interpreted by combining and integrating the symbolisms of the planets that make up the synchronization; if there are conjunctions, we emphasize them. This particular synch meant a powerful (Pluto) and obsessive (Pluto) relationship (Sun) that would be long-lasting (Neptune).

There was also a Synchronization of Jupiter, Chiron, and Uranus, meaning the relationship would move toward a successful (Jupiter) and famous (Uranus) marriage (Chiron). That's for sure. They got married less than eight months later. Five months after that, and only eleven months after they first met, Bianca gave birth to their daughter, Jade. We told you Mick doesn't pussyfoot around. (Aspect lines connecting Jupiter, Chiron, and Uranus are not drawn. Sometimes we will not highlight the less important aspects.

JFK and Jacqueline

Our next example is that of JFK and Jacqueline, who met on May 8, 1951. The chart of that date is Figure 5G. If you look at the chart at the end of this chapter, and if you have not read *Astrology Really Works!*, you might be surprised by the fact that there is a whole second set of planets drawn in the middle of the circle. Remember when we said that everyone and every thing has a second birth chart? The planets inside the circle represent the second birth chart for the day JFK met Jacqueline. In chapter 7, we will fully explain what such second birth charts are all about and teach exactly how to analyze and interpret them. But we wanted to include this second chart to remind our readers that there is always a second chart, and we will refer back to this particular second chart later.

Let us get back to the normal chart with just the circle. Like the Mick and Bianca Jagger Love Chart, there was a synchronization of the Sun, Neptune, and Pluto. Obviously, the same interpretation is also valid here. There was also a Synchronization of Saturn, Venus, and Mercury. This is not a good set of planets to have in synch. It can lead to limited (Saturn) love (Venus) and communication (Mercury). From what we have learned about Camelot and their relationship, this synch accurately foretold of a lonely relationship, one that lacked depth of love and ease of discourse. But we also know now that neither JFK nor Jacqueline were looking for a very close emotional relationship in marriage. JFK wanted his many affairs with a variety of women, and a wife who was capable of furthering his political ambitions; and Jacqueline was mesmerized with power and wealth. So the match was good enough, and the synch of the Sun, Neptune, and Pluto was powerful enough for them to exchange vows—with at least one set of fingers crossed.

By the way, the Companionship Chart and Love Chart co-exist with the Marriage Chart, meaning that the three charts all have an influence on the marriage. But the Marriage Chart is the most consequential.

Important Days Have Celestial Signs

The Engagement Chart is the chart of the day that an engagement is publicly proclaimed, or when the announcements are sent out. This is an important day, and the Planetary Geometry of this day often gives us signs as to whether the couple will actually get married. If they are engaged but not meant to be married, there will usually be a detectable celestial sign to that effect on the announcement date.

We can use Jacqueline Bouvier as an illustration of what we mean. Very few people know this, but she was once engaged to a gentleman named John Husted, Jr. The engagement was made public on January 21, 1952 (Figure 5H), and was broken off three months later. As you can see from the chart of this announcement, there was a Planetary Synchronization of Mercury, Jupiter, and Uranus. Note that the shape of the Planetary Geometry formed by these three planets is the same as the ones that existed during the two San Francisco earthquakes, whose charts are Figures 3I and 3J. This shape is called a T-square, and it is powerful, but it has negative consequences, just like the two earthquakes. Also, it is a sign of an unblessed time.

So far, in all of our examples of interpreting Planetary Geometry, we've derived the interpretations by combining and integrating the symbolisms of the planets that form the geometry. But none of the examples of how we interpret Planetary Geometry had this T-square shape before. We looked at T-squares in the two charts of the earthquakes, but we did not actually interpret them. It is time to do that because T-squares need to be interpreted quite differently. This is because T-squares are one of the few shapes of Planetary Geometry that are TURBULENT.

Turbulent Planetary Geometry

If all Planetary Geometry were helpful, then the world would not have earthquakes. However, we all should have suspected from the charts of the two San Francisco earthquakes that the T-square is not a beneficial form of Planetary Geometry—and it is not. In fact, whenever any three planets form a T-square, and whenever any four planets form a Grand Cross, the planets are in an alignment that creates problems, and they do not act harmoniously or cooperatively together. For this reason, such geometry needs to be interpreted differently from the other shapes.

This is very consistent with the ancient rules of Babylonian astrology. Thousands of years ago, the Babylonian astrologers believed that some of the seven angles that form aspects were bad, and some were good. They had made the decision that the aspects made by the angles of the conjunction and trine were the most helpful and favorable aspects; and they judged the aspects made by squares and oppositions to be unfavorable aspects. They also were wary of the quincunx or semi-sextile. But they thought the sextile was the equivalent of a weak trine—favorable, but not as strong.

Although the system that the Babylonians used, which divided aspects into good or bad aspects, has some value, it was never able to be developed into a working interpretive tool. Magi Astrology has developed a much more sophisticated system, and we believe we have a more valid system of interpreting different angles of aspects. We will explain the details of our system later in this book. But for now, we wish to explain how to understand the impact of the T-square and Grand Cross (a Grand Cross is really two T-squares). We want to be able to refer to these two shapes collectively, so we have given them the names of TURBULENT GEOMETRY, TURBULENT SHAPES, or TURBULENT PATTERNS.

For thousands of years, astrologers, to their credit, have correctly emphasized that these two shapes in the sky are important celestial signs of danger and/or problems. The Magi Society has formulated a method of accurately predicting the influence of Turbulent Geometry. We use a concept we call *negatization*. Let us illustrate what we mean by negatization, with a few examples.

A Turbulent Shape existed on both days of the San Francisco earthquakes; the same shape was also present on the day that the engagement of Jacqueline Bouvier to John Husted, Jr. was announced. The shape was a T-square, and the one that existed on the announcement date was formed by an opposition of Mercury to Uranus with Jupiter in square to both Mercury and Uranus. Our normal system of prediction would be to combine the symbolisms of these three planets and come up with an interpretation something like a successful (Jupiter) public (Uranus) announcement (Mercury). But because the shape formed by these three planets is a T-square, we *negatize* the symbolisms of Jupiter. The result is an interpretation of an unsuccessful (the negatization of the normal symbolisms of Jupiter) public (Uranus) announcement (Mercury). Or. it could mean an unfortunate public announcement or an ill-fated public announcement. Obviously, since the engagement was definitively broken off in just a few months, the sign that the stars gave was correct when interpreted in this way, with the negatization.

Turbulent Patterns During an Eclipse

As another example of how we judge the meaning of a turbulent pattern, please take a look at the chart of the lunar eclipse of August 6, 1990 (Figure 5I), which is at the end of this chapter. It should be obvious that there was a Grand Cross at that time, and it was comprised of the Sun, Pluto, Mars, and Moon. This was the eclipse that warned astrologers about Iraq's invasion of Kuwait and the financial turmoil that immediately followed. You probably recall that oil prices went through the roof, and stock prices fell to the basement. It was an unbelievably accurate sign, and some astrologers did predict the meaning.

Many astrologers believe that the alignment of the planets (especially eclipses) directly impacts our lives. But the Magi Society firmly believes that astrological alignments are celestial signs to guide us as to what is likely to unfold. This makes more sense, because the eclipse occurred a few days *after* Iraq invaded Kuwait on August 2. If the eclipse was the cause, the eclipse would more logically occur before or during the attack. In any case, the sign that the eclipse gave us was remarkably precise. Using the rules of Magi Astrology, the Grand Cross meant that this was a period of time (Sun) of fanatical (Moon) war (Mars) to attain power (Pluto). The fact that the shape was a Turbulent Shape means we add the negatization. So we add the word *unsuccessful* or *unfortunate* or *ill-fated*, and so on.

When we look back at the Grand Trine of the day of the Japanese attack on Pearl Harbor, we realize why the attack was so successful. It was a Grand Trine, and not a turbulent geometric shape. The same is true of the Nazi invasion of Poland. Grand Trines tend to be a sign of successful and powerful undertakings, even if it is war. Grand Crosses and T-squares tend to be a sign of problems that may result from a tragedy or a war, or unsuccessful attempts at waging war.

Squares and Oppositions Are Turbulent Aspects

There are only a few Turbulent Shapes. We already know about the T-square and the Grand Cross. Every Turbulent Shape is comprised of only aspects that are squares and oppositions. This should tell us something about squares and oppositions. Since the very early stages of the development of Babylonian astrology, astrologers have always divided the seven angles that form aspects into good or bad angles. Since that time, almost all astrologers have interpreted all squares and oppositions by using negatization. So we will sometimes refer to the square and opposition as Turbulent Aspects.

For example, the Jupiter-Chiron square in the chart of the announcement of the Jacqueline Bouvier/John Husted engagement meant an unsuccessful (Jupiter when negatized) engagement (Chiron). The Sun-Mars square told us there was no energy (Mars when negatized) to the plan (Sun) or announcement (Sun) itself.

(You may have noticed that when we negatize a symbolism, we essentially OFFSET the symbolism, so sometimes we will just call a negatized symbolism an "offset.")

Similarly, when we look at the eclipse of August 6, 1990, we can use the oppositions of Venus-Saturn and Saturn-Chiron to help us predict that there would be loss of life (Chiron) and loss of money (Venus). Since Saturn is the only planet with symbolisms that are normally negative, when dealing with any Turbulent Aspect that is formed by Saturn, the negative attributes of Saturn are *emphasized* in any negatization, rather than offset. For Saturn-Chiron, this method results in interpretations of *very tragic* loss of life, as opposed to just tragic loss of life. For Saturn-Venus, we get a prediction of very *large* losses of money.

Another example of how we interpret Turbulent Aspects is that of the solar eclipse of August 22, 1998 (Figure 5J). The Planetary Geometry of this eclipse was a clear celestial sign of impending worldwide financial turmoil. On August 17, 1998, Boris Yeltsin's administration decided to let Russia's currency (the ruble) be devalued. This was a catalyst for a run on Russian banks, because everyone went to their banks to withdraw their money and exchange their rubles for dollars. The result was a near collapse of the Russian banking system, with most banks actually closing their doors on August 27 and 28. The financial crisis in Russia led to fears of a return to communism and a worldwide collapse of stock prices. Our stock market had its biggest one-day drop in the Dow Jones Industrial Average on August 31, 1998. However, our financial markets held up well compared to problems in the rest of the world. The Brazilian stock market was cut in half while the Japanese market hit a 15-year low.

The solar eclipse that was a sign of all these crises had a Venus-Uranus opposition, signifying worldwide (Uranus) loss (negatization) of money (Venus). There was also a Saturn-Pluto quincunx. (The quincunx is a Turbulent Aspect when Saturn is a component.) The result of this aspect is shrinkage (Saturn) of big business (Pluto) and profits (Pluto).

Hundreds of millions of people lost trillions of dollars during just a few weeks after the eclipse. But if you knew Magi Astrology, you could have predicted what would happen, and you could have taken appropriate measures.

Avoid Turbulent Aspects

One of the best ways to apply our knowledge of Turbulent Aspects is to help us achieve the best marriage we are capable of. From the astrological point of view, the most powerful influence on marriage is the Planetary Geometry of the wedding date, and one thing we do not want in a Marriage Chart is a bunch of Turbulent Aspects. At the end of this chapter, we gave you the wedding charts for Clark Gable and Carole Lombard, and John Lennon and Yoko Ono. As you probably know, Lennon died after being shot, and Lombard died in a plane crash. Both deaths occurred while the two individuals were married.

The Gable/Lombard Marriage Chart has two very exact oppositions. One was formed by Jupiter and Neptune, translating to a lack of (Jupiter with negatization) longevity (Neptune). The other opposition was Mars-Chiron, warning of an accident (Mars) that leads to loss of life (Chiron rules life, but there is negatization so we use the term *loss of life*). Trines and conjunctions are good aspects, but there was not a single trine or conjunction in the Gable-Lombard Marriage Chart.

There were two conjunctions in the Lennon/Ono Marriage Chart, but the two conjunctions were in opposition to each other, creating four oppositions. The results of these four oppositions were as follows:

1. Jupiter opposed to Sun=unfortunate wedding
2. Jupiter opposed to Chiron=ill-fated marriage
3. Uranus opposed to Chiron=turbulent relationship
4. Uranus opposed to Sun=a wedding noteworthy for the wrong reasons

Besides these Turbulent Aspects, each of these two famous weddings took place when there was a strong quincunx formed by Saturn. Now remember that Saturn is the one planet that is a sign of pain and problems. Gable married Lombard when Saturn was quincunx to Neptune, indicating that there would be a limitation (Saturn) on longevity (Neptune). The marriage did not make it to its third anniversary. The Saturn quincunx aspect in the Lennon wedding chart was Saturn-Pluto, which was indicative of a tragic (Saturn) end (Pluto) to the marriage. *When a quincunx is a Saturn aspect, it is a Turbulent Aspect!*

Marriage Charts are so important that we will come back to them later on in this book. In the meantime, if you have just checked the Planetary Geometry of your relationship charts, such as a Wedding or Love Chart, and have found Turbulent Aspects in them, please do not jump to any conclusions yet. Enhancement aspects in a chart can overpower Turbulent Aspects if there are enough of them. In addition, remember when we explained that we all have a *second* birth chart? A marriage also has a second chart that co-exists with the Babylonian-style-alignment chart and could be much more favorable. We will begin to discuss this second chart in chapter 7, so please do not get depressed if your existing Relationship Chart is not the best. You only need one of the two charts to be very favorable.

Besides the various Relationship Charts, there are other very powerful influences related to whether or not two persons will have a blessed relationship. They are called LINKAGES, which we will discuss in the next chapter. But first, we want to give you some good news about all the planetary aspects that you were born with.

Personal Versus Historic Aspects

While you were reading the last few sections about the problems inherent in Turbulent Aspects, you might have been worried about having them in your own birth chart. But we have great news for you in that regard. No planetary aspect is bad when it is in the chart of a living being.

The Magi Society has a theory about planetary aspects that is derived from a great deal of research. The database we use for our research is enormous. In fact, outside of government institutions, the Magi Society has the largest database of birth dates of talented people that we are aware of. It is so large that it includes the birth dates of almost every extraordinarily talented person in every artistic and professional field. More specifically, our database is comprised of every professional athlete who has ever played football, baseball, basketball, and hockey in the U.S.—and almost every great dancer, musician, singer, actor, poet, writer, politician, inventor, and scientist, as well as most supersuccessful entrepreneurs. We even have the birth dates of almost every racehorse that has competed in the U.S. as a thoroughbred in the last two decades (the birth dates of horses are called *foaling dates*).

From this enormous database of birth dates of exceptional individuals, we have uncovered the following facts:

- The more talented the person, the more planetary aspects the person has.

- The more talented the person, the more exact the planetary aspects are.

- The angle of the planetary aspect is not important; squares and oppositions can be just as helpful as trines and conjunctions.

Our research shows that there are virtually no highly talented individuals who do not have very exact planetary aspects. What is most interesting is that a high percentage of very talented successful people have not only Turbulent Aspects, they even have Turbulent Planetary Geometry. This does not mean that astrology is inconsistent in that Turbulent Aspects are good for us to be born with, but are nonetheless signs of upcoming problems. Instead, what this means is that Planetary Geometry has a different effect on women and men than on historical events. In other words, Turbulent Aspects are signs of turbulence from the historical and current events perspective, but people who are born on those days are not negatively affected by the Turbulent Aspects. Instead, all aspects, even Turbulent Aspects, are signs of uncommon abilities and skills. This is an idea that is new to astrology, but it is the only explanation that fits the facts.

The facts are that almost every supertalented individual was born with at least one nearly exact planetary aspect, usually several. The angle of the aspects are not important. The angle can be enhancement or turbulent, or any other 30-degree-type angle. The more aspects a person has, the more talented the person is. The more complex the Planetary Geometry, the more talented the person. Even Saturn aspects are indications of inherent special abilities.

Because of all of this, it is necessary to distinguish between an aspect that someone is born with, as opposed to an aspect that exists on a day when events occur. That is why we have developed the terms PERSONAL ASPECT and HISTORIC ASPECT. A Personal Aspect is one that a living thing is born with, and a Historic Aspect is one that exists when something happens. All Personal Aspects are interpreted in the same way no matter what the angle of the aspect. We simply combine and integrate the symbolisms of the planets that comprise the aspect. There is never any negatization or offset, and when we are dealing with Personal Aspects that are formed by Saturn, we use the better symbolisms of Saturn.

However, Turbulent Aspects that are Historic Aspects are interpreted with the negatization, or offset, and *a Saturn aspect that is a quincunx is a Turbulent Aspect when it is a Historic Aspect.*

Every Personal Aspect Can Endow Us with a Special Talent

The net result is that there are no negative Personal Aspects. To help illustrate how we interpret Personal Aspects that are Turbulent Aspects or

Saturn Aspects, at the end of this chapter (Figures 5M through 5Q), we have given you the Babylonian style-of-alignment charts for five of the best athletes who ever played their particular sport. They are:

- Michael Jordan—basketball's all-time best player

- Wayne Gretzky—hockey's all time-best player

- Rod Laver—the number-one male tennis player in history and the only person to ever win two Grand Slams (which means that he won all four major events in one calendar year—twice)

- We also give you the charts of both Steffi Graf and Martina Navratilova, because opinion is divided as to which of these two women is the best female tennis player in history.

Each of these five all-time greats has very powerful Planetary Geometry comprised of very exact aspects. We will use an analysis of Michael Jordan's Planetary Geometry as a guide for the others:

— Jordan has Synchronized Planetary Geometry of Chiron, Mars, and Pluto. This provides him with the ability to have a career (Chiron) in competitive (Pluto) athletics, and also extraordinary energy (Mars), because the synchronization of Mars enhances Mars enormously. The Mars-Chiron aspect endowed Jordan with noteworthy (Chiron) energy (Mars) such that he can have a successful career (Chiron) in sports (Mars). Jordan thrives on competition and pressure, and he is at his best when the game is on the line. This is predictable from his Venus-Pluto trine, which is love (Venus) of competition (Pluto). Also, the Venus-Pluto aspect helps him to be a champion because it signifies victory (Venus) in competition (Pluto).

Most of us fold under extreme competition; Jordan does not, and Magi Astrology gives us another reason why. His Saturn is square to Neptune, which means that he will not give an inch. The reason that this aspect is interpreted in this way is that Neptune is symbolic of being gentle and impressionable. Saturn's square to that reduces such characteristics (Saturn rules reduction), thereby making the person hard-nosed and immovable. We had explained much earlier that we all have the free will to use our Personal Aspects the way we choose, within the valid range of interpretations. This was Jordan's choice. More power to him.

Jordan also has Uranus quincunx Mercury, which is the aspect that most specifically helps him to be a great basketball player. Mercury rules the nervous system, eyes, and ears; this leads to Mercury also being ruler of reflexes, and the sense of balance. Uranus rules change as well as our ability to make changes and adjustments to our body when we are in movement; thus, Uranus rules coordination and the ability to judge distance and spatial relations. When Mercury and Uranus cooperate by being in aspect, it endows the native with the ability to direct the body to make the changes needed to score the winning basket.

One of the few persons with more championship rings than Jordan is Bill Russell; he also has an enhancement of Uranus and Mercury, along with more planetary aspects than almost anyone else.

— Graf, Gretzky, and Navratilova all have very similar Planetary Geometry to Jordan's, which is why they are all so well suited for sports. Laver's Planetary Geometry is somewhat different. He derived his championship abilities from the two Dynamic Symmetrical Patterns. The Sun, Neptune, Uranus, and Saturn form one; and Jupiter, Pluto, and Venus create the other. All five of these great athletes have Turbulent Aspects and Saturn Aspects, and all five were helped by them.

Every Personal Aspect Includes a Gift from God

As we mentioned in *Astrology Really Works!*, the Magi Society believes that every Personal Aspect is a gift from a Benevolent Providence, endowing a special talent to the native. When we came into this world, God gave each of us *gifts* of special talents. Our Planetary Geometry is a celestial sign to tell us the nature of the special talents that we are blessed with. The last chapter of this book provides irrefutable proof of the validity and power of planetary aspects and other forms of Planetary Geometry, and shows that they are signs of great abilities. We provide proof in both a scientific way and in a way that the average person can understand.

In the next chapter, we will begin our exploration of the astrology of love and attraction, and what the signs are that tell us if two people will or will not get married. But before we move forward to that subject, we would like to ask you to ponder a few thoughts.

Astrology is a system of celestial signs, but why are there such signs? We believe the reason is that astrology was designed by a Benevolent Providence. If this is the case, there should be other evidence of Benevolent Designs of a Benevolent Providence—and there is plenty of that. You just have to notice the *signs of such designs*. Here is one that you really cannot get too far away from.

Water, Water Everywhere . . .

Scientists have been regularly announcing supposed startling discoveries. They think that they've found traces of water on other planets and some of their moons as well. To such scientists, the implication is always that there is a chance that life existed in these places, and therefore, we on Earth are not so unusual and certainly not unique.

The Magi Society is always amazed by the brilliance of scientists in some areas, and even more amazed at the lack of brilliance among these same scientists in other areas. Since when is a trace of water a sign that we are not unique? The requirement for intelligent life to exist is not *traces* of water—but water, water everywhere—huge amounts of *drinkable* water.

The only way to get drinkable water is the way we get it on Earth— through the cycle of evaporation and rain. It so happens that the amount of water on Earth is enormous enough, and the temperature and atmospheric pressure of Earth is favorable enough, so that contaminated water is constantly being purified through the process of evaporation, condensation into clouds, and then the return to Earth as pure and drinkable rain. We call this the RAIN CYCLE. Without this cycle, even the most primitive and basic life forms could not have possibly developed. We believe that this Rain Cycle is so unique to Earth and so efficient at providing us with life-sustaining drinkable water that it is also some kind of celestial sign. It is a sign of God's presence, and of his love and Benevolent Design.

So the next time you read or hear that scientists have found traces of water someplace not on Earth, and they think there is life because of this, call and ask them how much water is needed to have enough for a Rain Cycle. There is a need for water, water everywhere, or there is no chance for life like ours. If the Earth were flat, the water on this world would cover the entire surface of Earth and would be about a mile high. That is how much water is needed for real life. Earth is truly unique. That is because Earth was uniquely designed by Providence—and so is astrology. So if you look at your astrological chart and think you have been short-changed, it is not the case. Everyone has been given gifts, and all of our aspects are gifts. We just need to work hard to harness them.

Incidentally, one day, probably not too long from now, some scientists will be sure to claim that they have "created" life forms with some gases, other chemicals, maybe some electrical charges, and certainly with a little water. But would that make Earth less unique? We don't think so. Especially when you take into consideration other conditions, such as the fact there is just enough salt in the oceans to prevent bacteria from infesting them, but not too much salt to prevent fish from flourishing. Also, the oxygen content of the air on Earth is just enough so that humankind could make use of fire, but there is not too much oxygen that fire would be uncontrollable. Everything on Earth seems to have been designed with a perfect balance that favors life—everything—from the trees that bear fruit, to the minerals and the supply of oil, to the vast oceans filled with seafood and the lands filled with animals that humankind has made use of.

Lately, even in the scientific community there has been much talk about how perfectly balanced the entire universe is, and that this must all mean that there is a Designer. So much so that *Newsweek* devoted a cover article to this subject (July 20, 1998). "Physicists have stumbled on signs that the cosmos is custom-made for life and consciousness. It turns out that if the constants of nature—unchanging numbers like the strength of gravity, the charge of an electron and the mass of a proton—were the tiniest bit different, then atoms would not hold together, stars would not burn and life would never had made an appearance." To say nothing about the Rain Cycle, et cetera.

❦   ❦   ❦

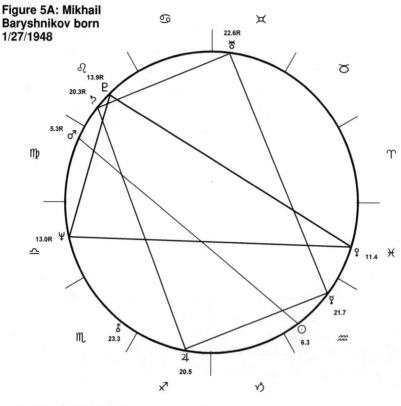

Figure 5A: Mikhail Baryshnikov born 1/27/1948

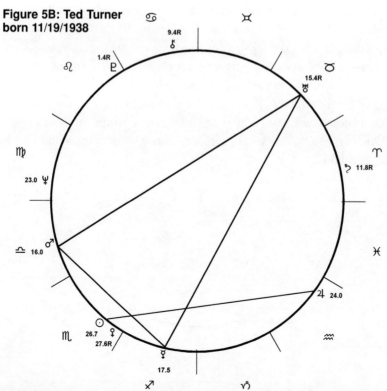

Figure 5B: Ted Turner born 11/19/1938

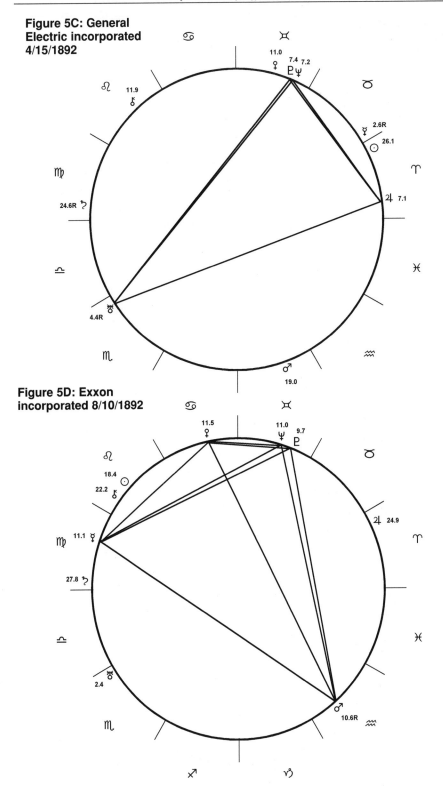

Figure 5C: General Electric incorporated 4/15/1892

Figure 5D: Exxon incorporated 8/10/1892

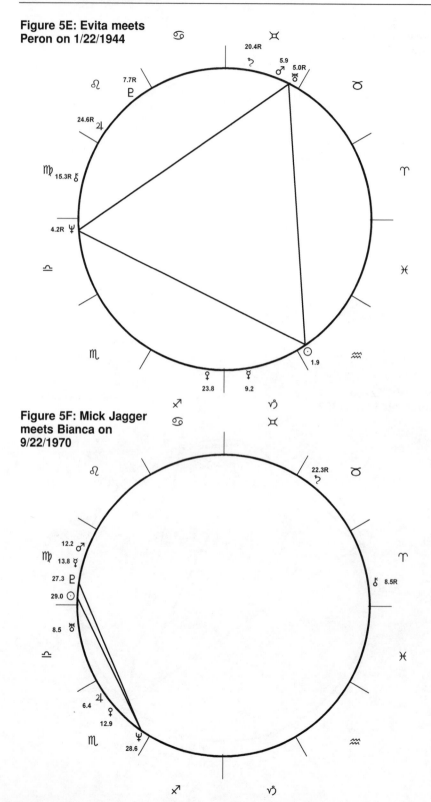

Figure 5E: Evita meets Peron on 1/22/1944

Figure 5F: Mick Jagger meets Bianca on 9/22/1970

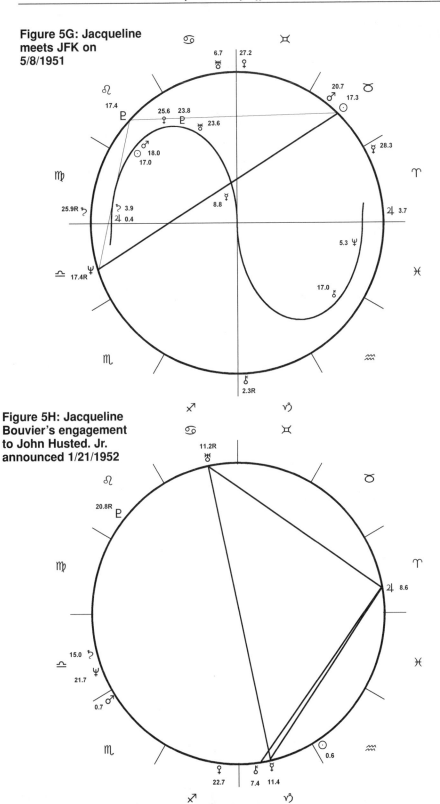

Figure 5G: Jacqueline meets JFK on 5/8/1951

Figure 5H: Jacqueline Bouvier's engagement to John Husted. Jr. announced 1/21/1952

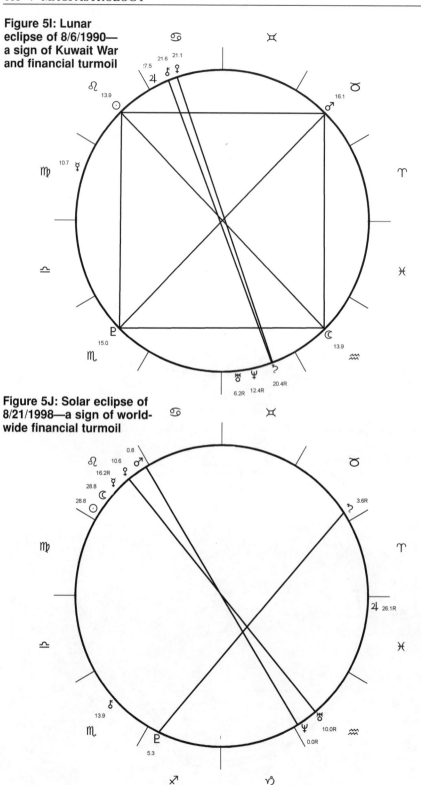

Figure 5I: Lunar eclipse of 8/6/1990—a sign of Kuwait War and financial turmoil

Figure 5J: Solar eclipse of 8/21/1998—a sign of world-wide financial turmoil

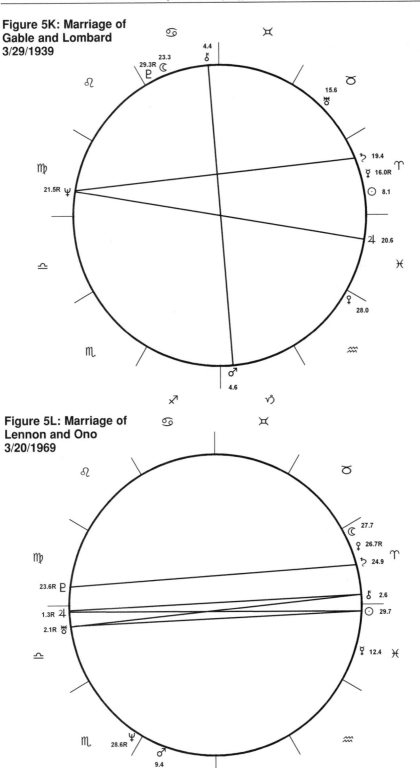

Figure 5K: Marriage of Gable and Lombard 3/29/1939

Figure 5L: Marriage of Lennon and Ono 3/20/1969

**Figure 5M: Michael
Jordan born 2/17/1963**

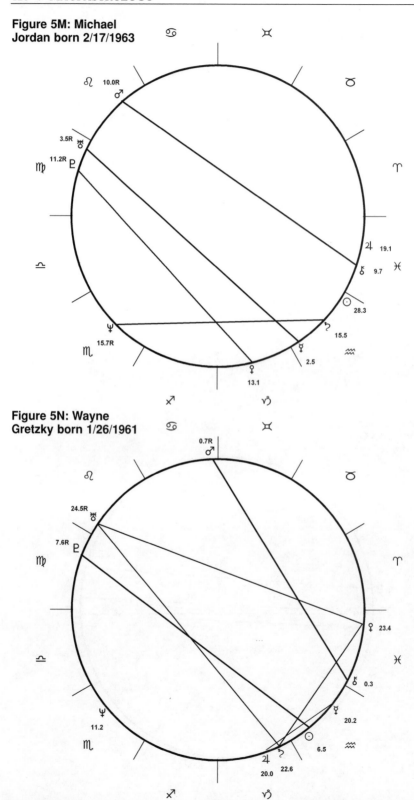

**Figure 5N: Wayne
Gretzky born 1/26/1961**

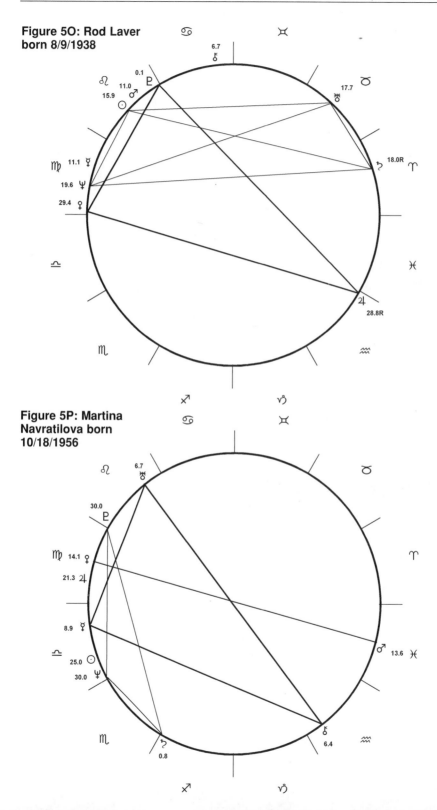

Figure 5O: Rod Laver born 8/9/1938

Figure 5P: Martina Navratilova born 10/18/1956

**Figure 5Q: Steffi Graf
born 6/14/1969**

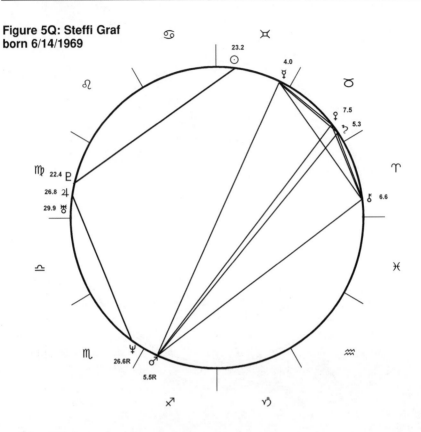

CHAPTER SIX

❧

Chiron Is the Arrow that Points to Your Soulmate!

A re you undecided about a relationship? Or at least a little confused? Magi Astrology can help! Are you wondering if the person you think you love is the one you should marry? Do you wonder if there is someone else out there who could be better for you and be your real soulmate? We will show you how to resolve those dilemmas in this chapter.

Every day, millions of individuals are asking questions such as these:

- Should I break off this relationship now, or give it another chance?

- Why did I fall in love with someone who is not my type?

- What is it that creates that unique vibrant attraction between two people that everyone refers to as "chemistry"?

- Even more important, what is it that creates that magical bond and love between two people such that they marry and become partners for life?

- What is the destiny of our relationship? Are we soulmates, great lovers, just playmates, or friends?

- How is it that a pauper will marry a billionaire, and a commoner will marry royalty?

- How do ultra-glamorous superstars of Hollywood choose their spouses?

- Why is it that sometimes when I look at someone, I think, *That is a gorgeous person, but he/she does nothing for me?*

- *Will I marry this person . . . or will it be someone else?*

These are the most important questions in a love relationship. From the very beginnings of the history of courtship and marriage, humankind has tried to find a way to accurately answer these questions. Our ancestors have used oracles, tea leaves, incantations, turtle shells, burnt ashes, and everything you can think of to try to answer such questions—but to no avail. Through the centuries, literally millions upon millions of women and men have truly spent the very best years of their lives in relationships that never resulted in marriage and family. Or even worse, they spent years in failed marriages and broken families. Most of these people wish that they had those years back and that they could undo their mistakes.

The problems have gotten much worse in recent times. The divorce rate has risen to around 50 percent. Now, more than ever before, there is a greater chance that we will devote ourselves to a significant other who ends up with someone else. It seems very unfair. The emotional pain can be unbearable, and the years wasted are irreplaceable, especially for women who want a family. When a dream is shattered and cannot be put back together, it immobilizes us, affects us negatively in every segment of our lives, and can leave wounds or scars that never fully heal.

Is there a way to avoid this pain?

We cannot *guarantee* that if you use Magi Astrology you will not ever go through a nearly paralyzing heartbreak. But we really believe we can help you *significantly* reduce the chances of going through such emotional torture. We are also confident that we can greatly improve your chances of attaining your dreams. You deserve it; we all do.

There are two areas in which we can be of the greatest help to anyone looking for happiness in love. The first step is to be realistic about a relationship. If we are not deluded by others and do not mislead ourselves, then we will not be as disappointed if a relationship unravels. This is because we will not have invested too much of our soul into a doomed relationship. In order to do so, we need to understand who we are with, know what we want out of a relationship, accurately assess what is possible with the relationship, and not be deceived by anyone, including ourselves. We can take a great step toward achieving all of this by mastering the Magi Astrology taught in this book.

The second step to achieving happiness in love is more exciting and proactive. It involves learning Electional Astrology the Magi way so that we can harness the power of the stars and use it to plan our lives and become more successful in our relationships than we would be had we not done so. For example, we can choose an extraordinarily favorable day to get married that could truly change and benefit our lives.

We've already started teaching you the basics of Electional Astrology, and we will bring you more information later on. In this chapter, we will focus on learning the Magi Astrology techniques that will help you be realistic about a relationship. You will learn to identify which of your relationships have the potential for marriage, and which do not. You will also learn about a key astrological factor that makes relationships long-lasting. Through the newest techniques of Magi Astrology, you finally have an objective way to answer the question: *Will I marry this person . . . or someone else?*

The Magi Society Has Done Massive Research

We explained earlier that as research for this book, the Magi Society recently concluded a study of the astrology for all types of relationships, especially those involving love, sex, and marriage. As far as such research projects go, it was both the most extensive project that we know of, and also the most successful. It was made possible only because of the Magi Society's worldwide network of members, who are linked together through the Internet, and because of the recent availability of massive databases of relevant information.

The research project was given the name "Magi Astrology Compatibility Study," or MACS. The most important discovery to come out of MACS is that the position of Chiron in your birth chart is the single most important astrological influence on long-term relationships of all kinds, including those involving love and marriage.

If you are not familiar with Chiron, it is probably because most people were born before it was discovered in 1977. Chiron is like a planet even though it is not; Chiron is sort of a comet that has some of the features of a planet. What is crucial is that the Magi Society's research project discovered that Chiron has a very powerful astrological impact, and it is the position of Chiron when you were born that is the key to whom you will marry, and who will marry you.

Chiron is the arrow that points to your soulmate!

Chiron is the celestial sign of your soulmate. By the end of this book, you should be able to accurately evaluate which person in your life Chiron is pointing to.

EDITOR'S NOTE

The position of Chiron in your birth date is so important and so hard to obtain that we have included 16 pages of data in this book so that you will be able to find the position of Chiron on any date from 1920 to 2015. A set of data or book that contains astrological positions is called an EPHEMERIS. At the end of this book, we provide a complete ephemeris for Chiron.

You may also want to know the positions of all the other planets on certain days, such as on your birth date and the birth dates of people you know. The publishers of this book, Hay House, Inc., also publish the *Magi Society Ephemeris.* That book will give you the positions of all the other planets for the 50 years ending in 1999. Once you buy the *Magi Society Ephemeris,* you can use a coupon in that book to also obtain the additional data for the positions of the planets for the years 1901 to 2009.

Hail, Chiron—The Long-Awaited Astrological Key to Love and Marriage

Chiron has astrological influences even though it is not a planet. That is neither new or unusual; the Moon and the Sun are not planets either, and they have very powerful astrological influences. What is new and exciting about Chiron is that it has the most important influence on long-term relationships and on marriage. Chiron is also the ruler of spouses and children.

If you have been disappointed in traditional astrology in the past because it has been unable to help you resolve questions about your relationships, you will just love learning about Chiron. Chiron is the long-awaited missing link to the astrology of relationships of all kinds!

We shall see throughout the rest of this book that the position of Chiron in your birth chart will determine who you will or will not marry, and who you can and cannot be successful business partners with. Just think how valuable such information is!

Ever since the first breath of astrology over 10,000 years ago, astrologers have been looking for the astrological secrets behind romance, love, and marriage. But they never found it—until now.

In the last few chapters, we learned the basics of astrology. You now know how to construct a Babylonian Alignment Chart, and you can see how useful it is for predicting the significance of any day. You also learned how to pick out the planetary aspects of a day, and how important they are in birth charts, Wedding Charts, and Electional Astrology. You are now ready to learn the special techniques of Magi Astrology that will help you find answers and solutions to your queries and problems in the most crucial matters of love and money. We will first deal with the issues concerning love, and we will begin with the mystery of attraction. Let's see why we're intoxicatingly attracted to one person—but not to another.

Planetary Geometry Is the Mainspring of Attraction

Even if two people look almost the same and act almost the same, you will always be more attracted to one of them than the other. There is something intangible yet very real that defines the essence of a person, and it is not the way the person looks or acts.

When you are attracted to a person, it is the person's "energy" and essence that you are drawn to. But what is it that defines the essence and "energy" of an individual? This is an astrology book, so we believe that the essence of a person is defined by the positions of the planets at the moment of that person's birth.

Everyone's natal Planetary Geometry is different, and no one can truly imitate anyone else. Take Elvis Presley, for example. Elvis is the most imitated person of this century. His appeal is so great that literally dozens of men have made a living from imitating him. However, no one has ever fooled the audience, and no one ever will because it is impossible to successfully pretend you are someone else. Every person is unique and defined by their astrological chart. It was Elvis's unique Planetary Geometry that allowed *him* to sing about "a hunka hunka burning love" without being laughed off the stage. Instead, women screamed and fainted with burning love for him.

So when we are attracted to someone, it is the person's unique Planetary Geometry that somehow creates that magnetic attraction that we feel for him or her. Most of us refer to this attraction as "chemistry," but it is really PERSONAL ENERGY.

What is personal energy? It is one of the many things that scientists have not been able to detect, but which is just as real as what they *can* detect with their instruments. The Magi Society cannot detect it either. It may be that no one will ever invent, develop, and build an instrument that will be able to detect personal energy, but that doesn't matter because we will always be able to "read and see" our personal energy since it is reflected by our natal Planetary Geometry. It is not unusual for science to be unable to detect something powerful and significant. There are many examples of science being unable to detect what we know must exist. As an example, we refer to birds and the "energy" that they use to navigate in flight. Although this is an astrology book, we think it will be very helpful if we relate a true story about flying birds to explain what we mean.

The Wonder of How Birds Navigate in Flight

A member of our Society had a bird that he kept in a cage in a very large room. He would always keep the cage door open, and the bird would regularly spend time at a window that was at the opposite end of the room where the cage was located. Every day, for a couple of years, the bird continually flew from the cage to the window and back. One day, while the bird was at the window, the cage was moved two feet closer to one wall. In the normal course of the bird's routines, it flew from the window to where the cage normally was. Amazingly, it did not notice that the cage was not there. Instead, it flew unsuspectingly right onto the spot where the perch of the cage usually was, and actually stretched its feet out to the nonexistent perch, stopped flying, and tried to land and retract its wings. When the bird started to fall, it squawked loudly, opened its wings, and flew back to the window. However, it did so by first taking the same route as if it were leaving the door of the cage. After being at the window for a short while, it once again attempted to land on the perch that was no longer there.

The bird went through an exact repeat of what had already transpired earlier. It still did not know that the cage had been moved. After spending a little more time at the window, the bird again flew back to the area that was normally occupied by the cage, but this time it took a slower and more deliberate approach. It circled the area previously occupied by the cage and squawked loudly again before returning directly to the window. The bird finally used its eyes and could see the cage was no longer in its usual place, but it did not give any indication that it was aware that the cage was just two feet away.

What this tells us is that birds do not navigate by sight. Instead, they have some unknown sense that science has no knowledge of. When you think about it, this must be the case, because when a bird is in a forest, it could not possibly navigate by sight alone. How do they find their nests? They do not do it the way we would. They don't think, *My nest is on the fourth branch of the oak tree that is the eighth tree just east of that very tall redwood.* In real life, a bird can be chased by a hawk, and it can scavenge for food far from home, yet it very easily finds its way back to its little nest, hidden on some *indistinguishable* tree, unerringly. How?

Birds probably have some unknown sense that allows them to hone in on a kind of "energy marker," and they can find these markers from thousands of miles away. That's why the swallows continually come back to Capistrano—and they've been doing it for thousands of years.

Birds are by no means the only animals who can navigate using an unknown system. Whales, penguins, seals, and many species of fish also do it. This is even more unfathomable because navigating the oceans is much more difficult than by air or land. You cannot possibly *see* where you're going. Yet whales have been known to migrate almost 10,000 miles—flawlessly.

There are many such wonders that science has no clue about—and personal energy and astrology *are* examples of such wonders. We may not have instruments that detect them, but so what? We also cannot detect whatever the birds use to navigate. So if a skeptic of astrology asks you how astrology could possibly work, just smile and retort, "Don't the swallows always return to Capistrano?!"

Personal Energy Is Another Wondrous Mystery

Just as swallows navigate through some unknown wondrous system, astrology works in some unknown and wondrous way. Each of us has a unique personal energy that is directly related to the particulars of our souls. We have learned that certain events can only occur at certain times, and the sign of those times is the Planetary Geometry of the planets in the sky. In a similar way, each of us can only be born at a time when the Planetary Geometry is in line with our personal energy. This would mean that the positions of the planets when we were born are reflections of our souls. If we are peaceful in nature, we are born under planetary aspects that reflect our inner peace; if we are aggressive in nature, we are born under aspects that signify aggressiveness. Each planet represents its own unique symbolisms that are translated into some form of energy, which varies depending on the planet's position relative to Earth. The positions of the planets at the moment we were born are referred to as our NATAL PLANETS, and these positions are the ones that are in our astrology charts. Every person has a set of natal planets that are a sign of their personal energy. It is this personal energy that creates the attraction that makes two persons fall in love. *This means that each natal planet is an arrow that points to who we are most attracted to.* The mechanisms of these arrows are called INTERASPECTS.

Interaspects

Interaspects are astrological signs of attraction or friction between two people. Here is what they are all about.

We have discussed the fact that when two planets in the sky are aligned at any of the seven different aspect-angles, the two planets form an aspect. In the same way, whenever one person's natal planet is aligned at an aspect-angle to another person's natal planet, the two natal planets form an interaspect. An interaspect is a meaningful alignment of two planets, one from one birth chart, and the other from another person's birth chart.

A simple illustration will help you fully understand this concept. John Kennedy, Jr.'s chart is Figure 6A on page 149. His natal Mars is at 18.5 degrees of Cancer. Figure 6B is Carolyn Bessette-Kennedy's birth chart, with John's natal Mars added inside the small square. This is an example of a CAC. John's Mars forms a Grand Trine with Carolyn's Chiron and Neptune. John's Mars also forms interaspects with her Sun, Pluto, and Uranus.

Interaspects act just like aspects. The two natal planets forming the interaspect become interactive and create a noticeable influence that the two persons feel when they are in close proximity to each other. This results in what most of us refer to as *chemistry*. Depending on the angle and the natal planets that form the interaspect, the feeling that the interaspect creates can be anywhere from magically exhilarating to darn right revolting.

We can accurately interpret the probable result of the interaspect by using the same type of rules that we use to interpret planetary aspects. To get the actual probable meaning, we combine and integrate the symbolisms of the planets that create the interaspect.

Since there are 11 natal planets and 7 different aspect-angles, there are a lot of chances for two persons to create interaspects. There are usually at least a half dozen interaspects between any two persons. When we are referring to the two persons who form interaspects, we call them CONNECTED PERSONS. Every interaspect has an influence on how the two connected persons feel and react to each other. Interaspects are the key to compatibility as well as attraction.

The concept of interaspects is not new and has been used by astrologers for a long time. Those of you who have studied the astrology of relationships already know what an interaspect is. But since we want our book to be understood by readers who know little or nothing about astrology, we are going to delve into a little more detail about interaspects in order to make sure all of you understand them.

How Interaspects Are Formed and Interpreted

At the end of this chapter, we have provided you with the Babylonian-style birth charts for Clark Gable and Carole Lombard (Figures 6C and 6D). Their combined chart is Figure 3L on page 60. Note that Gable's natal Pluto is at 15.8 degrees of Gemini, and Lombard's Sun is at 13.0 degrees of Libra. These two planets in the two different charts are within 3 degrees of being exactly 120 degrees apart. Just as a planetary aspect has an orb, so does an interaspect. The Magi Society uses an orb of three degrees for interaspects. This approximate 120-degree alignment between these two natal planets is within orb of being one of the seven aspect-angles that create aspects. Since every angle that creates aspects also creates interaspects, Gable's Pluto and Lombard's Sun form an interaspect, and is called a Sun-Pluto trine (the same terminology as for regular aspects themselves).

Gable's natal Pluto is also trine to Lombard's natal Chiron, which is located at 18.6 degrees of Aquarius. This is a second interaspect between these two superfamous lovers. They also have a third interaspect that is a trine. Gable's Sun is trine to Lombard's Sun, creating a Sun-Sun trine.

Every interaspect has an effect on the two people who create the interaspect (connected persons). We can accurately predict the results of interaspects by using the same rules of interpretation that we use for planetary aspects. Again, this is because interaspects work in ways that are very similar to aspects. Each interaspect creates a different range of influences, and the range of valid interpretations depends on the range of symbolisms of the planets that form the interaspect. You can foretell what area of a relationship any interaspect will most likely impact simply by knowing which planets create the interaspect and the symbolisms of the planets.

For example, since Mars and Venus are two of the Sexual Planets, any interaspects created by them will very likely influence sexual attraction between the connected persons. Traditionally, astrologers have taught that when one person's Mars is conjunct or trine to another person's Venus, the two persons can have magical sex together. The astrologers are right.

But just like a planetary aspect, an interaspect has a range of valid interpretations and can have a multiplicity of manifestations. This means that the Mars-Venus interaspect also can signify that the two persons can be great dance partners because they can have combined grace of motion. We understand this when we recall that Venus rules grace and Mars rules dance and bodily movements. Another reason that this interaspect creates good dance partners is that the interaspect creates unified (Venus) body movements (Mars). That's also why the interaspect is good for sex.

As another example, the Venus-Pluto interaspect can result in desire (Venus) for the sex act (Pluto), desire for power (Pluto), love (Venus) of earning power (Pluto), obsessive (Pluto) desires (Venus), and any other interpretations that fit within the range of the symbolisms of Venus and Pluto.

Planetary Linkages Are the Most Beneficial Interaspects

We explained in the last chapter that in Magi Astrology there are seven angles that can form a planetary aspect, and that all aspects that people are born with can be helpful in providing a special talent. But this is not the case with the seven angles of interaspects. When it comes to interaspects, some angles are good and some are not so good. The two enhancement angles (conjunction and trine) form the most harmonious and beneficial influences. *So does the quincunx.* An interaspect that is a trine, conjunction, or quincunx is very helpful in improving compatibility and increasing harmony between the two people whose natal planets form such an interaspect. Such interaspects create a strong LINK between the two individuals. For this reason, in Magi Astrology, we call such interaspects by a special name: PLANETARY LINKAGES. A planetary linkage is a type of interaspect, and it is formed when the angle between two different persons' natal planets are 0, 120, or 150 degrees. An orb of 3 degrees is allowed. When we are referring to the angles, the angles of 0, 120, and 150 degrees are collectively referred to as LINKAGE ANGLES. Such angles will quite literally link one person to another in a harmonious way and create long-term attraction and compatibility.

Planetary Activations Can Be Problematic Interaspects

Interaspects that are formed by the angles of 90 and 180 degrees create a very different result from the linkage angles. The Magi Society calls the 90- and 180-degree angles ACTIVATION ANGLES, and we call the interaspects formed at those two angles PLANETARY ACTIVATIONS. We call them activations because the two planets activate each other, but in a different way than if the angle was a linkage angle. A planetary activation creates attraction between two people, but the attraction is fickle and usually burns out somewhat quickly, maybe even by the next morning. That's right—it can be that short-lived. This may help to explain a lot of experiences in some people's lives.

An example may help you understand this concept. Traditional astrology's favorite interaspect is Venus and Mars. In our research, the Magi Society found a marked difference between a Venus-Mars linkage and a Venus-Mars activation. Between a woman and a man, both interaspects can result in a level of sexual attraction that is impossible to ignore. However, if the interaspect is at an activation angle, the sexual attraction deteriorates quickly, often with unpleasant consequences. Instead of love (Venus) of sex (Mars), an activation can erode to belligerent (Mars) desires (Venus). The outcome is still within the valid range of interpretations of the interaspect, but is obviously not desirable.

It is important to make a distinction between Planetary Linkages and Activations. Planetary Linkages between any two natal planets will create *long-term* harmony and attraction. Planetary Activations will create *short-term* attraction, and what initially appears to be harmony, but the apparent harmony often degenerates into conflicts of interest and incompatibility. Obviously, it is much better for two people to have linkages than activations.

Just as planetary aspects that are 30 and 60 degrees are not that important, we do not consider interaspects created by the 30- and 60-degree angles to be important.

Interaspects have been used by astrologers for quite a while, and traditional astrology has been very correct in stressing the importance of interaspects when evaluating a relationship between any two connected persons.

Romance Linkages: The Key to Long-Term Attraction and Marriage

Any two planets can form a planetary linkage or activation. Linkages are more favorable than activations. The significance of a linkage depends on which planets create the linkage, although every linkage between two persons increases compatibility and enhances emotional ties between the connected persons. However, in all matters of love and marriage, the most helpful linkages that two persons can have are ROMANCE LINKAGES. There are four Romance Linkages, and they are:

1. Venus links Chiron, meaning uniting (Venus) into a family (Chiron) or combined (Venus) destinies (Chiron).

2. Venus links Neptune, meaning long-term (Neptune) attraction (Venus) and attachment (Venus).

3. Chiron links Neptune, meaning long-term (Neptune) marriage (Chiron).

4. Jupiter links Chiron, meaning successful (Jupiter) marriage (Chiron).

When a woman and man form two Romance Linkages, there is the likelihood of a significant romance between the two persons. Note that Chiron is a part of three of these linkages and is the most important Romance Planet.

Super Linkages

A linkage is formed between two persons whenever one person's natal planet is aligned at a linking angle to any natal planet of the other person. Linkages are important, but a SUPER LINKAGE is much more powerful and is a concept unique to Magi Astrology.

Two people form a Super Linkage whenever one person has a planetary aspect, and the other person has a natal planet that forms a linkage angle to any of the two planets of the aspect.

In essence, a Super Linkage occurs when one person's natal planet links with another person's natal *aspect*. There are always three planets involved in a Super Linkage. An example of this is the Super Linkage between Clark Gable and Carole Lombard. On page 31, we first explained what a Combined Alignment Chart is. The Gable-Lombard Combined Alignment Chart is on page 40, and their individual charts are Figures 6C and 6D at the end of this chapter. As the charts illustrate, Gable was born with an aspect of Sun trine Pluto, and Lombard's Sun forms a linkage with Gable's

Sun-Pluto trine by being at a linkage angle (120 degrees) to Gable's Pluto. This creates a Super Linkage. Lombard's Sun also forms a linkage angle to Gable's Sun, thus forming a second linkage. To form a Super Linkage, it is necessary to have three planets and only one linkage. We also allow a slightly wider orb (up to 4 degrees).

A Super Linkage always has three planets and two interaspects, and at least one of them has to be a linkage (120, 150, or 0 degrees). The other interaspect can be any other angle, even an activation angle.

Whenever the natal planets of any two persons form a Super Linkage, it is the astrological focus of the relationship between the two connected persons. Once you learn how to analyze Super Linkages, you can finally answer the question: *Will you marry this person?*

This is because if a Super Linkage includes a Chiron Linkage, then the chance of a marriage between the linked persons is uncommonly high. A Chiron Linkage is one formed between Chiron and another planet. Chiron is the magical ingredient that results in marriages. In our research, we discovered that most married couples form a Super Linkage that has a Chiron Linkage. We call such a Super Linkage a ROMANTIC SUPER LINKAGE. It is by far the most powerful and reliable astrological indication of whether two persons will get married. We also discovered that couples who break up without getting married usually do not have Romantic Super Linkages. This is so important that it bears repeating:

Couples who form Romantic Super Linkages are likely to get married!

Once you learn how to analyze Romantic Super Linkages, you will know the likelihood of whether two persons will get married. How awesome is that? To help you understand exactly what we mean by all this, we will use ten examples of very famous couples and detail how to detect and interpret the Romantic Super Linkages that they have.

John F. Kennedy, Jr., and Carolyn Bessette Kennedy

As the only son of JFK, John, Jr. had been America's most eligible bachelor. He did not get married until he was 36 years old, leaving a trail of broken hearts and tabloid speculations. When he finally did marry, it did not surprise anyone in the Magi Society, as he had been dating Carolyn Bessette for some time. There were rumors that they had split up, but the two of them have TWO Romantic Super Linkages. Breaking up is hard to do when two people have Romantic Super Linkages. When such persons are apart, each one feels lonely and unfulfilled, and they cannot stop thinking about each other. That's why such persons usually end up walking down the aisle to exchange wedding vows.

Let's see step by step how to detect Romantic Super Linkages. As always, all of the charts we refer to are at the end of that chapter. Please look at the birth chart of Carolyn Bessette Kennedy (Figure 6B). You cannot have Super Linkages without aspects, so we begin by looking for her aspects. She has Pluto and Chiron forming an aspect because the two planets are 180 degrees apart. They are both in the 18th degree. Carolyn also has a second very powerful aspect because her Sun and Pluto are trine to each other.

Carolyn actually has more powerful aspects than just those two. She has a conjunction of Mars and Venus, and she also has Chiron trine Neptune. And finally, her Jupiter is quincunx to her Neptune. Carolyn has a lot of very powerful planetary aspects, which we would expect since she is a very gifted woman, and each planetary aspect is a gift from God.

So far, we have noted that Carolyn has five powerful planetary aspects. *The aspect that is usually the most important in a relationship is the one that is formed by Chiron.* Such aspects are called CHIRON ASPECTS.

Carolyn has two Chiron aspects, and one of them is her Chiron-Pluto opposition. Note that John's Mars makes a trine to the Chiron of Carolyn's Chiron-Pluto opposition. In other words, if we overlay his chart on top of hers, John's Mars is nearly exactly trine to her Chiron. His Mars is 120 degrees from Carolyn's Chiron. To help you see this linkage, we have drawn John's Mars inside of Carolyn's chart; his Mars has a rectangle around it and is 120 degrees from Carolyn's Chiron. This is a linkage angle and forms a CHIRON LINKAGE between John's Mars and Carolyn's Chiron. In describing the way these planets align with each other, we say that John's Mars links to Carolyn's Chiron-Pluto aspect. This alignment of their natal planets form a Romantic Super Linkage and is the most reliable astrological sign that two persons could marry. A Romantic Super Linkage can be formed in one of the following two ways:

1. One person has a Chiron-aspect, and the other person has a planet that links to Chiron.

2. One person has an aspect, and the other person's Chiron links
    to one of the planets that forms the aspect.

In both cases, there is a Chiron Linkage.

A Romantic Super Linkage always includes a Chiron linkage. It is the presence of the Chiron linkage that creates the maximum attraction and mutual romantic interest.

However, the result of Romantic Super Linkages is not just attraction. It also promotes harmony, being in tune with each other, trusting each other; and feeling empty, lonely, and lost without each other. It creates the compatibility and dynamics for lasting love to develop between the two persons. Most of all, it creates the need for each other, and only each other, such that the relationship advances to marriage.

Guess what? There is another Romantic Super Linkage between John and Carolyn. John's Mars also forms another Romantic Super Linkage with Carolyn's other Chiron aspect, her Chiron-Neptune trine. In this case, Mars is trine to both her Neptune and her Chiron, and links with both planets. This particular interalignment forms a Grand Trine, which is the most powerful Combined Planetary Geometry. In fact, if you look back to the Combined Alignment Chart of Gable and Lombard, there was a Romantic Super Linkage there, and it also formed a Grand Trine. The existence of a Romantic Super Linkage that forms a Grand Trine makes the marriage destined—almost like it was written as a sign in the heavens.

John's Mars is actually 3.1 degrees away from a trine to Carolyn's Neptune, which means that it is 0.1 degrees out of orb when using our 3.0-degree orb. But when there is special Planetary Geometry like a Grand trine, we give the orb of one (but only one) alignment a little leeway (and only a little).

As we mentioned earlier, for more than a dozen years, John reigned supreme as America's most eligible bachelor, and one year, *People* magazine even rated him as the sexiest man alive. When he finally got married, he wed a woman with whom he created two Romantic Super Linkages and a Grand Trine. This is an example of the power of such linkages and Planetary Geometry.

What we find highly encouraging is that every single person, without exception, has someone with whom the planets form irresistible Romantic Super Linkages. One day (or enchanted evening), everyone will meet someone whose natal planets will form a Romantic Super Linkage. Then—magic! At that time, the couple will forget all the hurt they may have already experienced. They just have to be patient, have faith, and wait for the right person—and not get too depressed, anxious, or make any disastrous mistakes while they're waiting.

A Romantic Super Linkage is the stars' clue to whom we will marry. Romantic Super Linkages create both attraction, harmony, and that aching, irrepressible desire to be with that person when he or she is not there. A Romantic Super Linkage between two people is what creates the rapturously enthralling and vibrant feeling that some refer to as "chemistry" or "attraction" or even "love." People tend to get married when they feel that way.

Carolyn and John Kennedy, Jr. have two Romantic Super Linkages. We think that is a key factor in why they fell in love deeply enough to get married. In fact, a Romantic Super Linkages is so powerful that it can even make a king abdicate his throne in order to marry someone.

The Duke and Duchess of Windsor

To many people, the most celebrated romance in the history of the 20th century is that of King Edward VIII and Mrs. Wallis Simpson. This king abdicated his throne, and he did it in order to marry Mrs. Wallis Simpson. She was a very intelligent, charming, and attractive American who would have made a very suitable wife for almost any man—except for the fact that she'd been married—twice.

This made her unsuitable in her time—especially for the King of England. Nowadays, it might seem commonplace, but their romance began not very long after the Victorian era, when it was unseemly for the King of England to even be *seen* with a divorcée. But it was worse than that. She wasn't just a divorcée—she was a remarried divorcée who was still in her second marriage—not to mention a "commoner."

The couple met before Edward became king. She, as Mrs. Wallis Simpson, was at his side when he became king at his coronation in January of 1936. Edward was told by cabinet ministers that the British public would not tolerate their king having a mistress, let alone one who was married. At the time, a marriage to Simpson was generally considered to be beneath the dignity of the crown of England. Defiantly, the couple went on a cruise together in August of 1936. However, there were powers in England's politics who viewed this open affair as intolerable, and used it as a means of forcing an abdication. The "powers that were" succeeded. So, Edward abdicated his throne, accepted exile terms, and married Wallis in France on June 3, 1937. The couple became known as the Duke and Duchess of Windsor.

What is it that made Wallis Simpson so irresistible to King Edward, so different from any other that a king of England gave up his throne and agreed to being exiled? The answer, of course, is always in the stars, and the stars' answer is Romantic Super Linkages.

You cannot have a Romantic Super Linkage without Chiron, so the first step in looking for Romantic Super Linkages is to look for Chiron and Chiron aspects. Wallis Simpson had a Chiron-Neptune trine and a Venus-Chiron trine. Lo and behold, King Edward's Jupiter linked twice with her Chiron-Neptune aspect by being trine to Chiron and conjunct to her Neptune. (We have added King Edward's Jupiter to Simpson's chart, and it has a rectangle around it. Please see Figure 6F.)

Once again, a superfamous married couple has a Romantic Super Linkage; it was this astrological factor that created the magical attraction and trust necessary for this well-known marriage. It also created that longing to be with one person and only that person. Nobody is immune from that feeling—not even kings. Royals need love just as much as the rest of us.

At this point, or perhaps even earlier in the book, some of you may have wondered why we choose superfamous couples and superhistoric dates as our examples. As you must know by now, the Magi Society is certain that astrology really works. If this is the case, the principles of astrology should be verifiable in virtually all of the most extreme cases. The more extreme an example, the more obvious it should be that astrology works. Therefore, the extreme cases will be the best examples to use as teaching tools. Besides, is anyone really interested in the Super Linkages formed by Harriet and Paul Nobody? To be honest, nobody is interested in the Nobodies.

So here is another extremely famous example who had a Romantic Super Linkage.

Grace Kelly, Prince Rainier III of Monaco, and Oleg Cassini

As our next example, we will discuss a love triangle that was formed by Grace Kelly, Prince Rainier III, and Oleg Cassini. As almost all of you probably know, the famous actress Grace Kelly married Prince Rainier III to become Princess of Monaco. But before the marriage, and actually just before she met the prince, she had been dating fashion designer Oleg Cassini. According to most accounts of Princess Grace's life, she had been dating Cassini for some time and was seen with him all over France before meeting Prince Rainier III. Even though she was apparently serious about Cassini, once she met Prince Rainier, it did not take long for Grace and the prince to fall in love and decide to marry.

What a triangle: Grace Kelly, the irresistibly beautiful Queen of

Hollywood; Oleg Cassini, the very dashing and supersuccessful fashion mogul of world renown; and Prince Rainier III, a real live prince who owned the most glamorous casino in the world. Even though it was a triangle for only a very brief time, what a story it would have made for today's tabloids. If Chiron had been discovered before then, and if you knew Magi Astrology, you could have written for such tabloids because you could have explained why Grace Kelly was so very attracted to *both* men. More important, you could have accurately predicted that she would choose the prince. You would have known all this because all of the answers were always in the stars—and the stars' answers were readable through Magi Astrology and the Super Linkages of the three people involved in the triangle.

So let's look at the stars, by which we mean their birth charts. The first chart we should look at is that of Grace Kelly, since hers is the pivotal chart. It is her chart that must have linked with both men. Her Chiron is in 11.6 degrees of Taurus, and it is opposed to Mercury. She does not have any other Chiron-aspect (Figures 6G–6I).

If we are to overlay Oleg Cassini's chart on top of Grace Kelly's chart, and do the same with Prince Rainier III's chart, we would see that both men were born with their natal Venus conjunct to Grace's Chiron—both men. This is not a coincidence. The position of both men's Venus create Romantic Super Linkages because each man's Venus was conjunct to the Chiron of Grace's Chiron-Mercury opposition.

So why did she chose one man over the other?

Was it because one was a prince? We do not think so. Grace Kelly was already essentially the undisputed Queen of Hollywood, and most people considered Hollywood a better place to be than the tiny principality of Monaco. In order to marry the prince, Grace had to give up her life in Hollywood because she had to take on the duties of being a princess—and you could not be a princess and a movie star at the same time. This means that like Edward VIII, Grace Kelly abdicated a throne of sorts, as well as her career, to marry the one she loved.

But why?

Magi Astrology gives us the astrological reason Grace was willing to make great sacrifices to marry Rainier. It was because she actually had two Romantic Super Linkages with the prince.

As we all know, there are many levels of intensity for attraction. There is attraction, and then there is that magical, mystical irresistible *ATTRACTION*. One Romantic Super Linkage is enough to create attraction of the irresistible kind. But two of them—wow! (Just like John Kennedy, Jr. and Carolyn.)

Grace Kelly and Prince Rainier III formed two Romantic Super

Linkages. We have already explained how the first one was formed. The second one was created in the following manner. Grace had a natal aspect formed by her trine of Pluto and Sun, and Prince Rainier III's natal Chiron formed a linking angle (quincunx) to her Sun, which is part of her Sun-Pluto aspect. This formed the second Romantic Super Linkage.

Only Chiron can create Romantic Super Linkages. Without Chiron involved in a Super Linkage, the attraction is still very strong, but it is Chiron's influence in the linkages that creates the magical bonds of love and harmony that results in marriages. And, it is Chiron that mystically creates the circumstances that push such couples toward marriage. If Chiron is not involved, the result is just Super Linkages—nothing to sneeze at, but it does not have the same intensity and magical qualities that Chiron adds.

Together, Grace Kelly and Prince Rainier III had two Romantic Super Linkages. No wonder they got married. Oleg didn't have a chance once Grace met the prince. Grace Kelly had one Romantic Super Linkage with Oleg; this was a sign of the extreme attraction that they had. They dated seriously and talked about getting married, and they may very well have been married if Grace had not met someone with whom she had two Romantic Super Linkages.

In Grace Kelly's natal chart, we added the prince's Venus and Chiron, and put rectangles around them. You can see how perfectly these two planets fit into Grace's chart—almost like a piece of a jigsaw puzzle, and in many ways, that is how to view each natal planet. Incidentally, you might have noticed that Oleg Cassini's Sun is almost exactly in the same position as Prince Rainier III's Chiron. This created a Super Linkage with Grace Kelly, but it was not a Romantic Super Linkage, because only Chiron can do that. When there is a Romantic Super Linkage, the earth shakes and mountains are moved—and lasting, binding love emerges.

Other Superfamous Examples

We cannot run out of examples of Romantic Super Linkages, because most married couples have them. But for this book, we chose the following additional examples because they are instructive and of special interest:

- Elvis and Priscilla Presley
- Kim Basinger and Alec Baldwin
- Richard Gere and Cindy Crawford
- Paul Newman and Joanne Woodward

- Clark Gable and Carole Lombard
- Humphrey Bogart and Lauren Bacall
- Evita and Juan Peron

The charts of all these couples are at the end of this chapter. We have simply provided the Combined Alignment Chart for each couple. Such charts can look overcrowded if all of both persons' natal planets are included; for this reason, we drew in only the linking planets for one person, and the complete set of planets for the other person.

All of the couples above have at least one Romantic Super Linkage. We will explain how each of the couples form Romantic Super Linkages so that you can check to see if *you* have such interalignments to someone in your own life.

৺ ৺ ৺

- Elvis and Priscilla Presley had a Romantic Super Linkage because Priscilla has a Sun-Neptune trine, and Elvis's Chiron was conjunct her Sun and trine her Neptune.

Some of you might be wondering why Elvis Presley and Priscilla got divorced if they were so well matched. There are two astrologically based reasons.

First of all, besides Romantic Super Linkages, there are other very important astrological influences on love, harmony, and compatibility. We have not yet explained all of them, but they all need to be taken into consideration when making an important decision on matters of love. So please bear with us while we take a little time and explain each of the most important astrological factors one by one. By the end of this book, you will understand these other important astrological criteria—and you will learn how to use them all together in order to help you in your daily lives, especially in matters of love and money.

The second reason the marriage of the Presleys failed is that they didn't get married on a favorable astrological day. We already learned how important Marriage Charts are. The Planetary Geometry of the Marriage Chart has a profound influence on the ultimate success, nature, and character of the marriage. We will see later in this book that the Marriage Chart of the Presleys was a very weak one. Romantic Super Linkages will tell us if two persons will fall in love and get married, *but a marriage is unlikely to be successful unless the wedding takes place on a very favorable astrological day.*

"Astrologically favorable" means a day with Planetary Geometry that enhances and maximizes the chances of a successful marriage. However, we should point out that even a great Marriage Chart does not guarantee a happy and lifelong marriage, or even a long-term marriage. What we have found is that getting married on a perfect day minimizes the chance of *outside* influences destroying a marriage. The right wedding date helps bring about financial security and successful, happy children to the marriage.

But every marriage also needs to be nurtured from within. This requires that both spouses forgive and understand each other and work hard at sustaining the marriage. No relationship works without forgiveness and understanding. That is, and always has been, the most important key to success and happiness in love.

However, there are enormous advantages to knowing about Romantic Super Linkages. Such knowledge can save us heartache and pain. We all have friends who wish they did not let a relationship drag on for as long as it did before they broke up. If you do not have Romantic Super Linkages with someone and you're having problems with the relationship, you should seriously reevaluate the relationship based on your acquired knowledge of Magi Astrology *after you finish this entire book and master its contents.* Please do not give up on a relationship or do anything drastic until you've read the rest of this book. Like relationships themselves, the astrology of relationships has several dimensions. So far, we have only touched on two of these, Super Linkages and Planetary Geometry. We will learn about the additional parts of the puzzle later on. As with anything else in life, we need to analyze the entire picture before coming to any conclusions.

౪ ౪ ౪

Getting back to examples of Romantic Super Linkages:

- Joanne Woodward has a Chiron aspect formed by her Saturn and Chiron. They form a trine and are only 0.8 degrees apart. Paul Newman's Jupiter is at 9 degrees Capricorn, trine to her Chiron and conjunct to her Saturn, forming a Romantic Super Linkage.

- Clark Gable was born with an almost exact opposition of Pluto and Uranus. This aspect created his most powerful aspect, and Carole Lombard's Chiron was trine to Gable's Pluto, within the three-degree allowable orb. This created a Romantic Super Linkage, forming the necessary chemistry between them such that the king of Hollywood would marry the blonde actress.

- Bogie and Bacall also had a Romantic Super Linkage. Bogie's Saturn was trine Bacall's Neptune and Chiron.

- As for Kim Basinger and Alec Baldwin, they form a Romantic Super Linkage because Alec's Chiron is trine to Kim's Mars and Jupiter. Kim's Mars and Jupiter form a planetary aspect that is a trine, and it is only one degree apart.

- Juan Peron formed a Romantic Super Linkage with Evita. His Jupiter was conjunct to her Neptune, which was trine to her Chiron. We need to simplify the language in describing these linkages. In the future, we might simply say that Peron's Jupiter links to Evita's Chiron-Neptune aspect.

- Cindy Crawford is a very beautiful and successful woman. *Forbes* magazine tells us that at one point she was the highest-paid model in the world, but women do not envy her for that. What women do envy is that she was lucky enough to have been married to Richard Gere. He and Cindy Crawford are so personable, gorgeous, and successful that both of them could have married almost anyone they wanted. Why did they choose each other? Of course the reason they got married was in the stars. Cindy's Chiron is trine to Richard Gere's Venus and Chiron, and Richard's Venus and Chiron form a trine. All together, this creates two Romantic Super Linkages.

As you can see, each of these superfamous couples has a Romantic Super Linkage. Hopefully, from these examples, you have learned enough to know whether you make such linkages with someone. Then you will also know whom you will probably marry. But please also always bear in mind that the birth chart of the marriage is what determines a successful marriage. That is the reason why two of the couples we've talked about (Richard and Cindy, and Elvis and Priscilla) got divorced.

A few pages ago, we explained that in addition to Romantic Super Linkages, there are other equally powerful astrological influences on attraction, love, and compatibility. In the next few pages, we will explain one of them.

Combined Planetary Geometry

An interaspect is an elementary form of Planetary Geometry. Super Linkages are a much more powerful and advanced form of Planetary Geometry than interaspects. In the next few pages, you are about to see an even more powerful and advanced type of Planetary Geometry.

Super Linkages are all part of what we call COMBINED Planetary Geometry, or just Combined Geometry. This is because Super Linkages can only be formed if we *combine* the geometry of the charts of two people. Although Romantic Super Linkages are the most common and pivotal astrological influences that promote marriages, there are other astrological factors that do so. One of these other factors is SYMMETRICAL COMBINED GEOMETRY, which is formed whenever the planets of two individuals' charts combine to form a symmetrical pattern. Symmetrical Combined Geometry is the most powerful of all the astrological influences on love and compatibility.

In fact, all of the couples we have discussed in this chapter have Symmetrical Combined Geometry. If you look at the actual combined alignment chart of John, Jr. and Carolyn Bessette on page 150, you will easily see that by combining their planets, there is Symmetrical Combined Geometry because there is a Grand Trine formed by combining their planets.

John and Carolyn's two birth charts actually combine to form several amazing symmetrical patterns; we do not show it, but there is a Golden Rectangle. In fact, there are two Grand Trines. In the last chapter, we learned about the enormous power of synchronized symmetrical geometry formed by the planets on a given day. It can create historic consequences and foretells extraordinary possibilities for a day. Just as a Grand Trine, or any symmetrical pattern, is very powerful in the chart of any particular day, there is also enormous power when a symmetrical pattern is formed by combining the planets of two birth charts.

When Symmetrical Combined Geometry occurs in a combined chart, the power of the symmetry creates exceptional compatibility and harmony between the two persons who form such geometry. It engenders and promotes truly remarkable ease in the relationship of the two people. If the geometry is CHIRON BASED, meaning if Chiron is a component planet of the symmetrical patterns, then the symmetrical alignment of the combined geometry magnifies any desire to make a commitment that would make the relationship permanent. In other words, the presence of Chiron in the Combined Geometry creates a desire in the two people to link together permanently and get married. All three of the Symmetrical Combined Geometry made by John and Carolyn are Chiron based!

ॐ   ॐ   ॐ

We have already accumulated a lot of new terms and concepts, and it would be difficult for anyone to grasp them all immediately. Please don't let this discourage you. *Do not hesitate to use the glossary at the back of this book.* Magi Astrology is really very simple, and we promise you that you will understand it all as you read on and see the examples we provide. The rewards of this knowledge are enormous and can help you immeasurably. Also, you may want to discuss the material in this book with friends and co-workers and see how well it works in their lives and on their relationships. By analyzing their relationships, you will gain a greater understanding of the material in this book.

Examples of Symmetrical Combined Planetary Geometry

In each of the examples of the ten couples we discussed in this chapter, by combining the charts of both partners, Symmetrical Combined Geometry is formed. In seven of the couples, the Combined Geometry includes a Grand Trine, which is the most powerful shape of Symmetrical Combined Geometry. (We have shown you only the Grand Trines.)

We should point out that the shape of the combined Planetary Geometry does not have to be a Grand Trine to be effective; a combined Grand Trine is probably the most helpful and most powerful. But any symmetrical pattern that is formed by the overlay of two charts creates what we call COMBINED SYMMETRY. There is Combined Symmetry when a symmetrical pattern exists in a combined chart, so long as at least one planet is contributed by each person's chart. If the Combined Symmetry is Chiron based, this promotes a special ease and harmony in the relationship whereby the two people are more likely to both want a lifelong relationship.

The Most Important Planets in Combined Geometry

When you're analyzing a Combined Alignment Chart and looking for clues as to the exact nature of the stars' influence on a relationship, it can sometimes become confusing because it is hard to tell which Combined

Geometry is the most important to a relationship. To help us sort all this out, we need to bear in mind that both the power and precise nature of all Combined Geometry is dependent on which planets make up the geometry (referred to as the Planetary Composition).

As we stressed earlier, Chiron is the most important planet in creating long-term relationships. The impact of the planets is listed below in their order of importance to a relationship:

1.	Chiron	7.	Saturn
2.	Venus	8.	Mars
3.	Neptune	9.	Mercury
4.	Sun	10.	Pluto
5.	Jupiter	11.	Uranus
6.	Moon		

What the order of this listing tells us is that a Combined Geometry that includes Chiron is always more important than one that does not have Chiron. The second most significant Combined Geometry that any couple can have is one that includes Venus, and the next after that is one that includes Neptune. And so on.

A Grand Trine in the sky does not tell us if the day is good or bad; it is only a sign that the day is too important to be ignored. However, Grand Trines in Combined Geometry are not only important, but also very helpful. The Grand Trine is the most harmonious symmetrical pattern. Sometimes, a couple will have a conjunction at a corner of the grand trine. This makes it much more powerful and creates a Double Grand Trine. The more planets that form a symmetrical pattern, the more helpful the pattern.

There is a symmetrical pattern that is powerful but actually is not helpful. It is the T-square. When two persons form a T-square, it is a sign of attraction and disharmony. The T-square is the only combined symmetrical pattern that we have found to not be helpful to a long-term relationship. We call it TURBULENT COMBINED GEOMETRY. It creates a great deal of attraction, so we have to be careful about it since we are all very attracted to someone with whom we form it. The T-square creates a roller-coaster relationship and flip-flops back and forth between extreme attraction and extreme antagonism. Unless you want to have an up-and-down relationship, you should get off, or better still, not get on at all. We will see an example of this later when we discuss Marilyn Monroe and Arthur Miller.

A Message of Hope for All Who Are Still Seeking their Soulmates

Romantic Super Linkages and Combined Symmetry are both part of the broad concept of Combined Planetary Geometry. They are tools of Magi Astrology that obviously work very well. However, we are not trying to prove they work. There is no way for us to prove anything that involves your own emotions and feelings, but you can prove it to yourself by checking on the Combined Planetary Geometry that you make with the people in your life. If you do so and apply the techniques you have already learned, you will understand things about your past and present relationships you did not previously comprehend.

The key to compatibility is in the Combined Planetary Geometry that two persons form. Like pieces of a jigsaw puzzle, one person's planets must fit with those of another. And if they do . . . then MAGIC. This is how a prince falls in love with a pauper, and why many of us fall in love with someone who is not our type. The fact is that we are all most attracted to and most compatible with those with whom we form Romantic Super Linkages and Symmetrical Combined Geometry—and these are both original precepts of Magi Astrology.

We regard all of this as great news, because it means that there really are soulmates—and we do not have to be beautiful or rich for someone to be attracted to us and love us in the way we want and need. We just have to find that person with whom we have the right Combined Planetary Geometry!

So far, we have dealt with only Babylonian Alignment Charts. But we mentioned in chapter 1 that we all have two birth charts. What a wonderful thought! It means that you have another chance to have great planetary aspects and form great Romantic Super Linkages with someone you love. You'll begin to learn about your second birth chart in the next chapter.

Magi Society Computer Software

The Magi Society has computer software that will greatly help you analyze the Combined Planetary Geometry and all the interaspects between you and another person. It is called *MagiSoft,* and it will accurately display and print all interaspects and Combined Planetary Geometry. It can be difficult for most of us to do this type of analysis by hand without computers. We want to make it easy for you to check on the interaspects that you make with anyone else. For this reason, we are making our computer software available to those who have bought *this* book, and/or our other books published by Hay House, Inc. A special coupon is at the back of this book on page 435 so that you may obtain this Magi Society computer software.

☙ ☙ ☙

Figure 6A:
John Kennedy, Jr.
born 11/25/1960

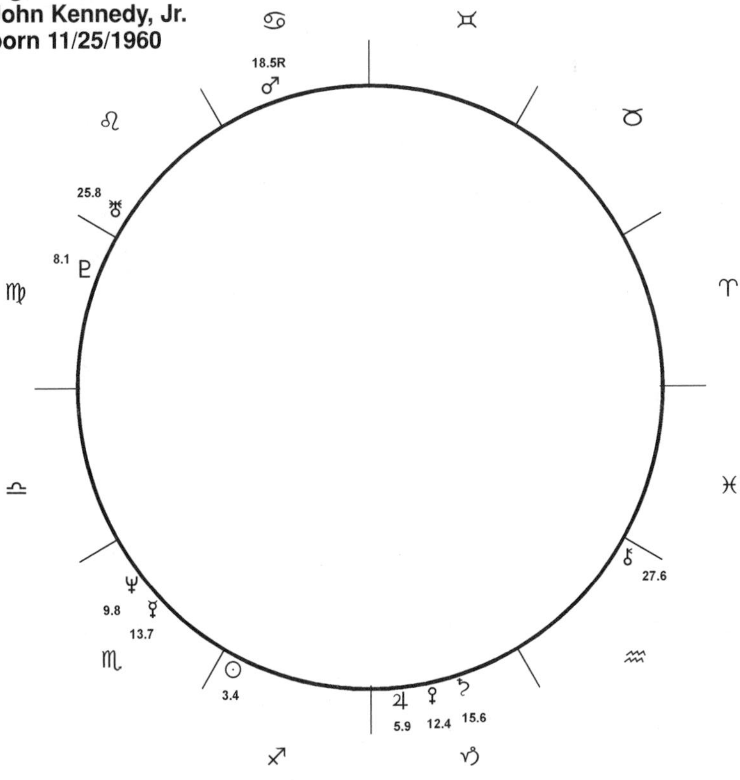

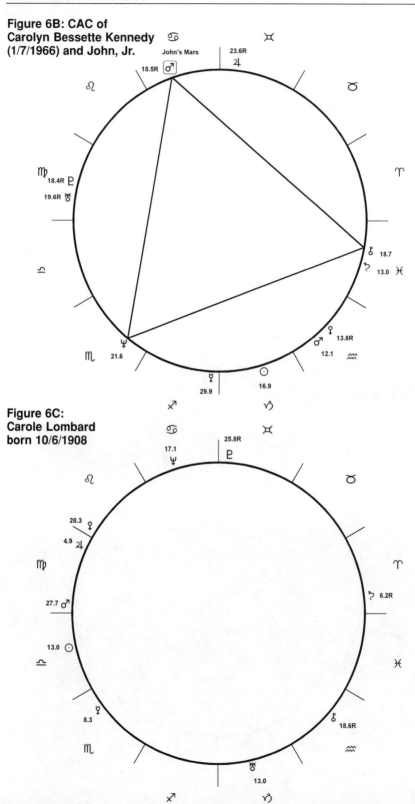

Figure 6B: CAC of Carolyn Bessette Kennedy (1/7/1966) and John, Jr.

Figure 6C: Carole Lombard born 10/6/1908

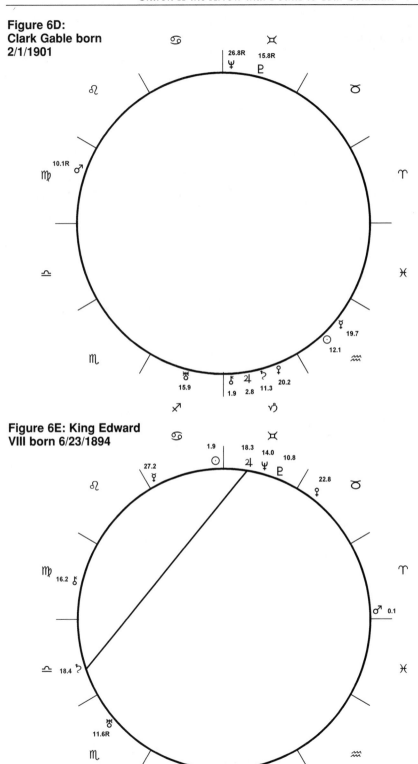

Figure 6D:
Clark Gable born
2/1/1901

Figure 6E: King Edward
VIII born 6/23/1894

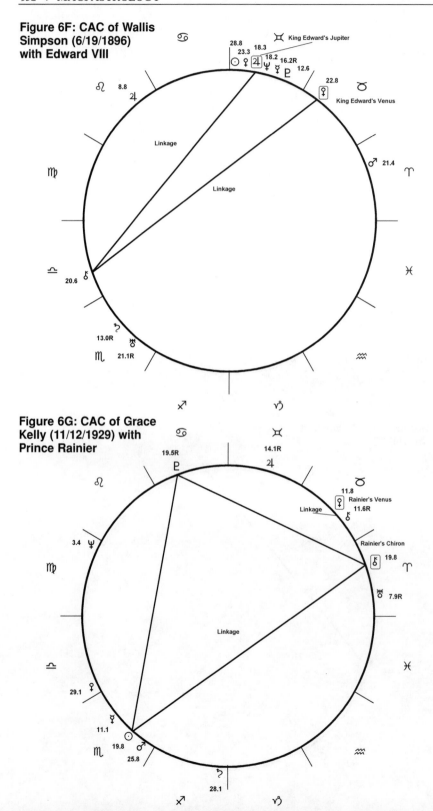

Figure 6F: CAC of Wallis Simpson (6/19/1896) with Edward VIII

Figure 6G: CAC of Grace Kelly (11/12/1929) with Prince Rainier

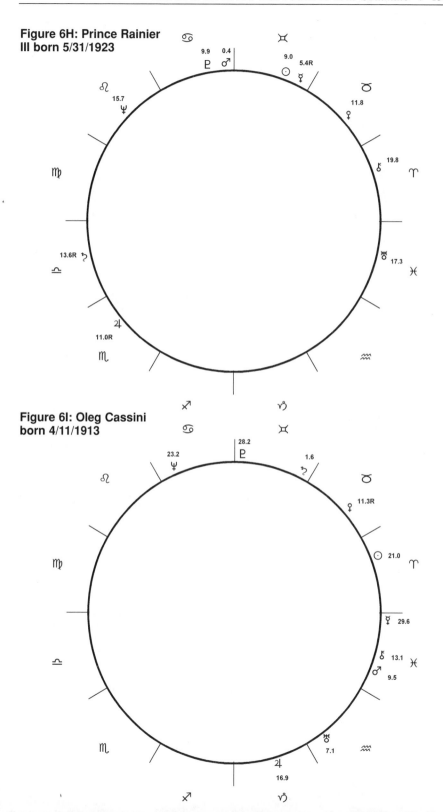

Figure 6H: Prince Rainier III born 5/31/1923

Figure 6I: Oleg Cassini born 4/11/1913

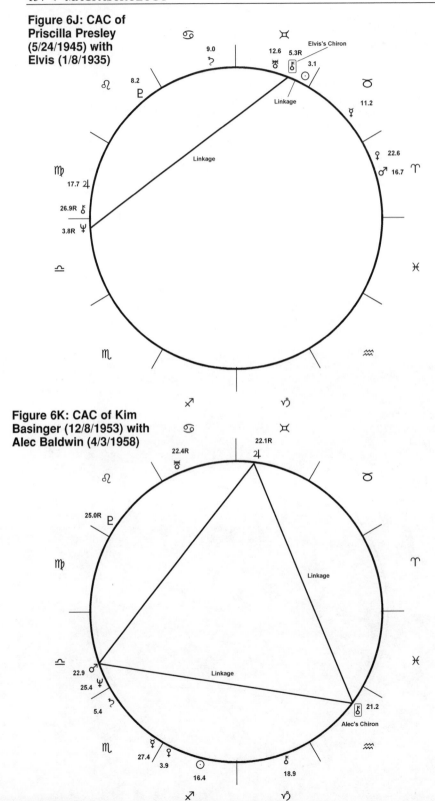

Figure 6J: CAC of Priscilla Presley (5/24/1945) with Elvis (1/8/1935)

Figure 6K: CAC of Kim Basinger (12/8/1953) with Alec Baldwin (4/3/1958)

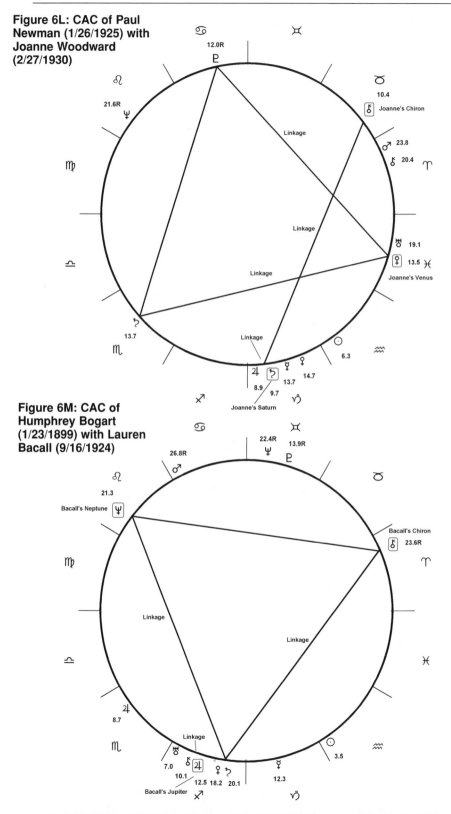

Figure 6L: CAC of Paul Newman (1/26/1925) with Joanne Woodward (2/27/1930)

Figure 6M: CAC of Humphrey Bogart (1/23/1899) with Lauren Bacall (9/16/1924)

**Figure 6N: CAC
of Richard Gere
(8/31/1948) with Cindy
Crawford (2/20/1966)**

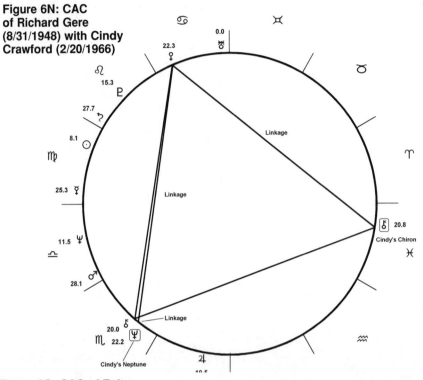

**Figure 6O: CAC of Evita
(5/7/1919) and Juan Peron
(10/8/1895)**

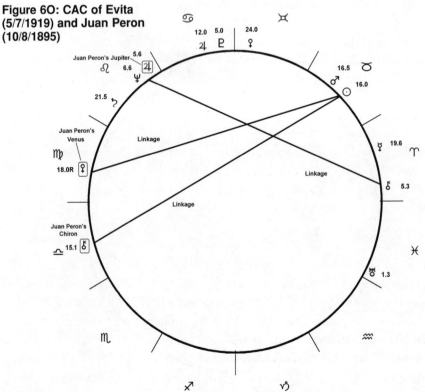

CHAPTER SEVEN

ॐ

We All Have a Second Birth Chart

We know that all of the planets, including Earth, revolve around the Sun, and the Moon revolves around the Earth. These movements of the astrological bodies cause the alignment and locations of the planets in the sky to change moment by moment, hour by hour, day by day, and so on. In other words, the apparent (or visible) positions of the planets in the sky are always changing.

The most fundamental premise of astrology is that the movement and the positions of the planets in the sky have a strong impact on what happens on Earth. For this reason, it is imperative to know the positions of the planets at any given time. All astrological charts that utilize the circle, including the Babylonian Alignment Charts, are designed to give you the positions of the planets. But what very few people know is that such charts only give you half of the positions; the other half is completely missing, even though it is just as important. Let us explain what we mean.

The planets each move both horizontally and vertically in the sky, but astrologers have been taking into account only the horizontal movement of the planets and have ignored the vertical movement. When astrologers talk about what sign the Sun is in, they are talking about only the HORIZON-TAL POSITION of the Sun. Astrologers have always believed that the horizontal positions and movement of the planets have an influence on life on Earth. They are correct on this point. But the VERTICAL movement and positions of the planets must also have an influence and should also be taken into consideration in any astrological analysis.

A map always has two coordinates, the horizontal and the vertical. An astrological chart is also a map—a map of the sky. Each planet moves a little bit horizontally, and at the same time it also move a little bit vertically. Therefore, all astrological charts should provide both the horizontal and vertical positions of the planets. However, the astrological charts used by the Babylonians and by traditional astrology all use only the horizontal coordinates of the planets. These charts are missing the vertical positions, and it is these positions that create your second birth chart. Just as a person will not get where he or she wants to go by using only the horizontal coordinates of a map, an astrologer will also get lost if he or she only uses the horizontal coordinates of a planet.

When astrologers say that they are a Leo or a Scorpio, what they really mean is that the horizontal coordinate of their Sun was in Leo or in Scorpio on the day they were born. When astrologers say that their Mars is in Gemini and their Moon in Virgo, they are really referring only to the horizontal coordinate of these planets. It is these horizontal coordinates in the sky that all astrologers since the Babylonians have marked down in the circle of an astrological chart, but the vertical coordinates are equally important.

Let us give you an example of the effect of the vertical position and movement of the planets. It is the vertical position of the Sun that creates the variance in the length of the day and the length of the night as we go from one season to the next. During the course of a year, the Sun's vertical position moves and varies by slightly under 47 degrees. When the Sun is at its highest position, the day is the longest and we begin the summer. When the Sun is at its lowest position, winter begins and the day is shortest.

What Creates Our Second Birth Chart

Astronomers refer to the horizontal locations of the planets as the LONGITUDES, and the vertical positions of the planets as the DECLINATIONS. Astrology has adapted the same terminology. In traditional astrology, the longitudes are used to create the charts that have the circle. These charts include all horoscope charts and Babylonian-style alignment charts. It is the horizontal positions of the planets (the longitudes) that are drawn around the circumference of the circle. In Magi Astrology, we use the declinations to create our second birth chart. To distinguish between the two different types of birth charts, all horizontal-position birth charts are referred to as ZODIAC SIGN CHARTS; the vertical-position chart is called the DECLINATIONS CHART.

We all have two astrological charts. This is good news for all of us because we all have a chance for more planetary aspects and more special abilities. It also gives us a whole new chance to form Romantic Super Linkages with someone. This is one reason why you should finish this book before making any drastic decisions about your relationships.

In our first book, the Magi Society unequivocally proved that astrology *does* really work, and we were able to do so only because we used both the vertical *and* the horizontal positions of the planets. Our book proved that the vertical positions of the planets are just as important as the horizontal ones when it comes to astrological influences. Therefore, we all have two birth charts.

Until we published *Astrology Really Works!*, most astrologers did not include an analysis of the Declinations Chart when making astrological interpretations. But since the publication of that book, many astrological organizations and magazines are now recommending the use of declinational interpretations to their members and readers.

So, we all have an entire second astrological chart. It is the Declinations Chart, and it has most of the facets of the Zodiac Sign Chart. In other words, the Declinations Charts have planetary aspects, Planetary Geometry, planetary synchronizations, linkages, Super Linkages, and Romantic Super Linkages. Interestingly enough, it is the Declinations Chart that is more likely to tell us about the sexual nature of any relationship we have. That's why we haven't yet talked much about sex, sexual attraction, and compatibility. We needed this extra tool to understand these issues.

A Sample of a Declinations Chart

Let's see what a Declinations Chart looks like. There is a sample of one on page 164 (Figure 7A). As you can see, there is a complete set of planets on the chart, and each planet has a number next to it that designates the actual declination, in degrees, of the planet (the vertical coordinates). Here's how we determine the positions of the planets for the Declinations Chart:

We just explained that the declination of the Sun is what determines how long there is daylight each day. The variance in the declination of the Sun from the longest day to the shortest day is about 47 degrees. The declination of the Sun is highest on the first day of summer and lowest on the first day of winter. The declination of the Sun is in the middle of these two points at the first day of spring and also at the first day of the fall season. This middle point is called the EQUINOX PLANE and is used as the zero point when measuring declinations. That is why we have the terms *spring equinox* and *fall equinox*. The declination of the Sun is measured using units of degrees north or south of this equinox plane (essentially the CELESTIAL EQUATOR). The position of the Sun rises from this zero point to about 23.5 degrees above it when going from the first day of spring to the first day of summer. During this time, the declination of the Sun is rising from zero to 23.5 degrees NORTH DECLINATIONS. After the first day of summer, the declination of the Sun decreases as the vertical movement of the Sun brings it back down to the equinox plane on the first day of autumn, and the declination of the Sun is again zero. After that day, the Sun's vertical motion brings the Sun lower and lower in declination until it reaches about 23.5 degrees SOUTH DECLINATIONS on the first day of winter. Afterwards, the Sun's declinations goes back to zero, and it repeats the entire cycle. The most important feature of the Sun's movement is that it moves up and down. The declinations of all the planets also move up and down.

The Magi Society designed a Declinations Chart to mimic the up-and-down motion of the planets in the sky. To map and illustrate such movements and positions, the Magi Society decided to use a sine curve because this type of curve moves up and down (please refer to Figure 7A). Like the Zodiac Sign Chart, planetary symbols are used to illustrate the position of each planet.

In a Declinations Chart, the actual degrees of north or south declination for each planet are noted alongside the symbols of the planets. More than 99 percent of the time, the planets are within about 25 degrees either north or south declination.

There you have it—your second astrological chart (Figure 7A). We call it your DECLINATIONS CHART to distinguish it from your Zodiac Sign Chart.

If you do not understand this concept, don't worry. Few astrologers really understand how the declination of a planet is calculated. That is because they do not have to calculate these positions. They simply use an ephemeris, which lists the declinations of all the planets on a periodic basis. All you really need to do is understand that there is a second set of planetary locations that forms a second birth chart, and know how to read a Declinations Chart so that you can overlay one on top of the other to look for aspects, Planetary Linkages, and Super Linkages in the declinations—which is quite simple. *Declinations Charts are easier to use than Zodiac Sign Charts—much easier!*

Basically, you don't need to know the "why" of the second birth chart. You only need to know what the second birth charts look like and how to use them in matters of love and money. As we go on, we will give you so many examples that you will surely understand how to use everyone's second birth charts by the end of this book.

The Magi AstroChart

The Zodiac Sign Chart represents one coordinate of the position of the planets, and the Declinations Chart represents the other coordinate of the planets. In order to advance astrology to two dimensions as simply as possible, the Magi Society has developed a special way of drawing birth charts so that a single drawing has both the Declinations Chart as well as the Zodiac Sign Chart. Such a chart is called a MAGI ASTROCHART, and all the birth charts in this book from this point on are examples of them. Please examine Figures 7B and 7C at the end of this chapter. They are the Magi AstroCharts of both President Bill Clinton and Bill Gates (the world's richest man). Clinton and Gates are obviously two of America's most powerful men, and we chose them to illustrate a point about the importance of the Declinations Chart.

The greatest advantage of a Magi AstroChart is that it combines your Declinations Chart with your Zodiac Sign Chart (Babylonian Alignment Chart) into a single integrated and easily viewable chart. This is accomplished by placing a person's Declinations Chart inside the circle of the Babylonian Alignment Chart. Both the Babylonian Alignment Chart portion and the Declinations Chart portion have a full set of planets, one set representing the horizontal position (longitudes) of the planets and the other set representing the vertical position (declinations). For this reason, in a Magi AstroChart, there are *two* full sets of planets.

There is a horizontal line running across that cuts the circle in exactly half. This line represents zero degrees of declination, which is the declinational position of the Sun at the spring equinox, as well as at the fall equinox. The zero-degree line is the EQUINOX LINE. The declinations are measured either north or south of the Equinox Line. This means that there are two possible positions of each numeric degree; there is a ten-degree north and a ten-degree south declination.

There Are Planetary Aspects in the Declinations Chart

We explained in chapter 4 that a planetary aspect is a meaningful alignment of planets. A meaningful alignment of planets can occur in the declinations as well as the circle (longitudes). Planetary aspects occur in the declinations whenever two planets are both in the same degree and also on the same side of the Equinox Line, such as Bill Clinton's Jupiter and Chiron. Astrologers call such a planetary aspect a PARALLEL. The two planets are referred to as being parallel to each other. When two planets are in the same degree but on opposite sides of the Equinox Line, like Bill Gates's Jupiter and Chiron, we say that the two planets are CONTRA-PARALLEL to each other. This alignment also creates a planetary aspect in the declinations, and the aspect is called a contra-parallel.

Both the parallel and the contra-parallel are the equivalent of the conjunction in the Babylonian Alignment Chart (although the contra-parallel is not as strong as the parallel). This means that the parallel and contra-parallel are not only planetary aspects, but they are also enhancement aspects. Since astrology is consistent, this also means that such declinational planetary aspects are interpreted the same way as the enhancements are in the Babylonian Alignment Charts; you simply combine and integrate the symbolisms of the planets that comprise the aspect.

Let us use an example to help illustrate what we just said. In Figure 5G of chapter 5, we provided the declinations for the day that JFK and Jacqueline Bouvier first met. If you look back to that chart, you will notice that the Sun was in 17.0 degrees north declinations and Chiron was in 17 degrees south declinations. This means that these two planets formed an aspect and there was an exact contra-parallel of the Sun and Chiron because these two planets were in the same degree and matched degrees. This aspect can be interpreted as signifying that it was a day (Sun) of marriage (Chiron) and spouses (Chiron) and children (Chiron). There is no question that it was such a day because they got married, became each other's spouse, and the marriage produced children. See how important the declinations can be?

Planetary linkages and interaspects are also created and interpreted in a similar manner. The north and south side of the declinations can be viewed as being similar to a sign of the zodiac, but there are only two "signs" in the declinations, as opposed to 12 of them in the longitudes. Interaspects between two persons exist wherever the declination of one person's natal planet is parallel or contra-parallel to the declination of any of the other person's natal planets. An ORB always applies in astrology. The orb that the Magi Society prefers to use for the declinations is 1.2 degrees. Those of you who have read our book *Astrology Really Works!* will probably notice that the 1.2-degree orb is less than the orb we recommended in that book. At the end of chapter 12, we explain why we chose to use and introduce declinations with the wider orb in our first book, and also why we have now decreased its size.

In chapter 4, we discussed the fact that an enhancement aspect was formed whenever two planets are in trine or in conjunction, but we also said at the time that there were other ways to have an enhancement aspect. We now know that there are also enhancement aspects formed in the declinations. The term *enhancement aspect* was introduced in *Astrology Really Works!* and is defined as an aspect that is created by any two planets that are aligned in one of the following four angles:

1. Trine
2. Conjunction
3. Parallel
4. Contra-parallel

Enhancement aspects are the most powerful and beneficial aspects, and we interpret them by simply combining and integrating the symbolisms of the planets that create the aspect. The term *enhancement aspect* is now gaining popularity among the world's leading astrologers.

There Are Also Planetary Linkages and Synchronizations in the Declinations Chart

In essentially all ways, the declinations work just like the longitudes. In other words, the rules and laws of astrology that work in the Babylonian Alignment Charts also work in the Declinations Charts.

Just as there are Planetary Linkages formed by our natal planets in the longitudes (Babylonian Alignment Charts), our natal planets in the declinations also form Planetary Linkages. And, just as there are Super Linkages in the Babylonian Alignment Charts, these linkages are also in the Declinations Charts. Both Planetary Linkages and Super Linkages are just as strong in the declinations as in the longitudes—sometimes even stronger. Also, just as the presence of Chiron makes Romantic Super Linkages in the longitudes, Chiron has the same effect in the declinations. More specifically, Planetary Linkages and Super Linkages occur in the declinations in the following manner:

We explained in chapter 6 that whenever you overlay two individuals' birth charts on top of the other, and a planet in one person's chart is aligned at a linkage angle (at a 0-, 120-, or 150-degree angle) with any of the other person's planets, you create a Planetary Linkage in the Babylonian Alignment Charts. With the Declinations Charts, there is a Planetary Linkage whenever a pair of natal planets from two different charts are parallel or contra-parallel to each other. Both forms of Planetary Linkage promote attraction, harmony, and compatibility between two persons. In the declinations, a Super Linkage is formed whenever there is a Planetary Linkage between two persons, and one of them has another planet that is parallel or contra-parallel to the two linked planets. If any of the three planets is Chiron, there is a Romantic Super Linkage.

The one difference between the Zodiac Sign Chart and the Declinations Chart is that there are no activations in the Declinations Charts.

Declinations Charts are just as important as Babylonian Alignment Charts. With them, we literally double our knowledge of astrology, and we can explain what seemed inexplicable before. With such charts, we can finally explain why Prince Charles divorced Princess Diana to be with Camilla Parker-Bowles, and why Madonna married Sean Penn and had an affair with Dennis Rodman. Their Magi AstroCharts are at the end of the next chapter, which deals with the astrology of sexual attraction and mind-altering sex.

♋ ♋ ♋

Figure 7A: Declinations Chart of Bill Gates born 10/28/1955

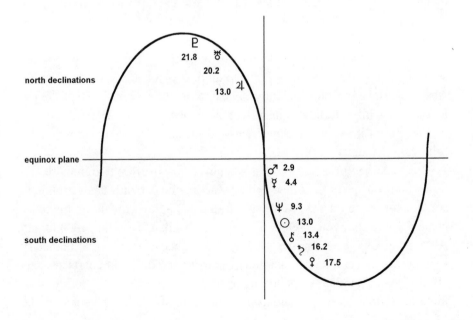

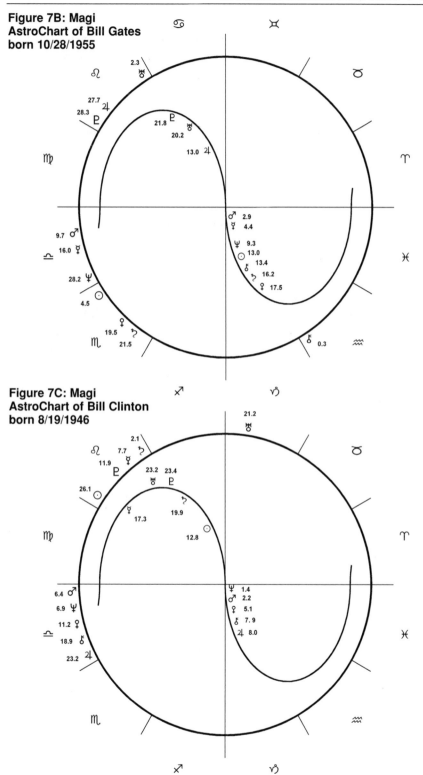

Figure 7B: Magi AstroChart of Bill Gates born 10/28/1955

Figure 7C: Magi AstroChart of Bill Clinton born 8/19/1946

CHAPTER EIGHT

☙

The Astrological Secrets of Magical Sex

We have all wondered: *What is it that really creates that mind-altering sexual ecstasy that is so hard to find?* We are also intrigued by the following questions:

- When is the best time to seduce someone?

- When is the best time to plan on having a memorable night of love and boost a relationship?

- What is it that makes someone truly sexually compatible with me, and be in tune to my needs, emotionally and physically?

- For women, more often than not, timing can be every thing when it comes to making love. So, how can I, as a woman, find a man who has that perfect timing and sensitivity?

- What makes two bodies work as one during lovemaking, where each knows the other's urgent and intense desires and fulfills each other spontaneously and instinctively—every step of the way?

- As a man, what gives me the extra energy to allow me to give a woman a whole night and morning of love that she will forever look back upon with fond remembrance?

- What makes one person much more sensual or sexual than another—or much more mechanical and awkward than another? What makes one person either much more understanding and caring than another—or much more selfish than another?

- What makes a man supervirile? What causes a woman to be
  sexually insatiable?

The answers are always in the stars, so read on. . . .

Sexual Linkages

In chapter 6, we discussed the power of Planetary Linkages and Super
Linkages, and the fact that Chiron creates the longest-lasting unions. This
is due to the symbolisms of Chiron, which rule marriage, spouses, the family, and long-term relationships.

However, Chiron does not have sexual overtones. In fact, a very hand-
some man and a beautiful woman can have very strong Romantic Super
Linkages, yet still have limited sexual attraction to each other, resulting in
a nearly platonic relationship after the usual short spurt of initial sexual
activity.

The Magi Society's research helped us unlock the secret of rapturous
sex, as well as enduring sexual attraction and lasting, high-quality lovemaking. The key is SEXUAL LINKAGES. As a result of the our research
into relationships, we have discovered that Sexual Linkages create the
greatest sexual attraction and are responsible for the most satisfying sexual
exhilaration—so much so that some people mistake all of this for love. A
Sexual Linkage is one that is between any two of the three Sexual Planets.
We explained that of the 11 planets, 3 of them have significant sexual symbolisms and are Sexual Planets. They are Venus, Mars, and Pluto. The three
SEXUAL LINKAGES are created whenever the following pairs of planets
form a Planetary Linkage:

1. Venus and Pluto—obsession is the key to this linkage. This
    is the strongest of all of the connections in creating obsessive
    and *undying* sexual attraction, and is the longest-lasting,
    most obsessive Sexual Linkage, because of the symbolisms
    of Pluto.

2. Mars and Pluto—this linkage is marked by intensity, peak
    sexual satisfaction, and the greatest sexual energy, resulting in
    daily sessions of multiple acts of sex. This linkage creates the
    highest level of rapturous sex—the intensity reached during
    climaxes is so high you will never forget it. However, this
    linkage does not create attraction because it does not have

Venus involved; it is Venus that rules attraction. As a result, the sex eventually burns out with this linkage.

3. Venus and Mars—traditional astrology regards this as the best linkage for sex, but those who have experienced all three linkages tell us that the other two are better by both quality and quantity by a slim but noticeable margin. Yet the Venus-Mars linkage can come close to the obsessive qualities of Venus-Pluto linkages, and in addition, can bring a couple close to the dizzying sexual heights of the Mars-Pluto linkage. The other two are stronger in each of their own ways, but this Venus-Mars linkage combines the features of both, although at a noticeably lower level of intensity.

These three Sexual Linkages create sexual attraction and chemistry, and these three are responsible for magical, ecstatic sex—the kind that makes some women even faint. When you meet someone who is sexually irresistible and find the sex to be euphoric, then it is almost always because the two of you have one or more of these three Sexual Linkages.

If you have ever felt awkward when making love to someone, chances are that the two of you did not have any of these three linkages. For whatever reasons, when you have any of these Sexual Linkages with a lover, the lovemaking is more spontaneous and fluid; the two of you are in synch every step of the way, and you are aware of each other's urgent needs and know just how to fulfill them. The result is magical sex.

That is one reason why Sexual Linkages are important.

Depending on the character and priorities of the persons involved, sometimes Sexual Linkages are a more potent cause of marriage than Romantic Super Linkages. It all depends on how important sex is to the persons involved. That depends in large measure on whether they have any Sexual Aspects (please see page 74 to refresh your memory about them).

Examples of Famous Couples with Sexual Linkages

We already learned that Madonna was born with the Female Super Sexual Aspect, so sex is very important to her. It doesn't mean that she has no other requirements; she is too intelligent to have only one yardstick. However, the material girl is a very sexual woman, and many of us envy her.

Madonna exudes sexuality. She does so in public—for example, when she appears bare-breasted at a fashion show. She exhibits her sexuality on stage and in her videos by performing with more sexual overtones than any other female superstar. Is it all just an act and a publicity gimmick? No. We are certain that Madonna's public persona is due to her true inner personality—and we know this from her Magi AstroChart

Madonna's very high level of sexuality is the result of her declinational aspect of Venus parallel to Pluto, which means desire (Venus) for sex (Pluto). It also means obsessive (Pluto) desires (Venus), powerful (Pluto) seductive abilities (Venus), and powerful female sexuality (Venus). As we explained in chapter 5, a Sexual Aspect gives the native both the desire and capability for extraordinary amounts of the highest-quality sex. In fact, the Venus-Pluto enhancement is a Female Super Sexual Aspect. Lucky Madonna—and her men as well! Now, even more people will envy her.

Madonna and Her Men

By knowing that Madonna has a female Super Sexual Aspect, we would expect that she would choose her men for sexual reasons—at least much more so than the average woman would. This would mean that she must have Sexual Linkages with Sean Penn, the only man she has married, and Sean Penn must also have a Sexual Aspect or else he could not have met Madonna's requirements. The material girl needs a lot of high-quality sex.

Guess what? Madonna has all three Sexual Linkages with Sean Penn— and all three are in their Declinations Charts. Sean Penn has a Male Super Sexual Aspect—also in the Declinations Chart. Lucky him, too!

As we explained in the last chapter, the parallel and the contra-parallel are the equivalent of the conjunction and the trine. This holds true in all facets of astrology, including Planetary Linkages and aspects.

Madonna has all three of the Sexual Linkages to Sean Penn. Please look at Madonna's Magi AstroChart at the end of this chapter (Figure 8A); you should focus on her declinations and notice that Madonna was born with both her Venus and Pluto close together at around 20 and 21 degrees of north declinations. Sean Penn has his Mars and Pluto at around 20 and 21 degrees of north declinations. We gave you Penn's birth chart (Figure 8B) and noted that his Mars and Pluto made three sexual linkages with Madonna. An orb of 1.2 degrees is allowable in both aspects and linkages in the declinations. Here are the Sexual Linkages that Madonna has with Sean Penn:

• Madonna's Venus is parallel to Sean's Pluto.

- Madonna's Pluto is parallel to Sean's Mars.
- Madonna's Venus is parallel to Sean's Mars.

Sean Penn was born with a Male Super Sexual Aspect; he was born with Pluto parallel to Mars. So now we know that Madonna and Sean must have had fabulous nights together—and days, too. However, as we mentioned, the material girl seeks out men she is sexually drawn to. That was also the case with basketball star Dennis Rodman.

The Magi AstroChart of Dennis Rodman is on page 179, Figure 8C. The thing to notice is the placement of his Mars and Pluto in the declinations. Dennis Rodman's Mars and Pluto are in degrees 20 and 21 of north declinations. If this sounds familiar to you, it's because both planets are in the same positions as the Mars and Pluto of Sean Penn. Hence, Madonna had the same three Sexual Linkages with Dennis Rodman that she had with Sean Penn, more or less. There are always differences between the Planetary Linkages made with two different charts, but in these two cases, the Sexual Linkages are about as similar as they can be. Also, Dennis Rodman has the same Male Super Sexual Aspect that Sean Penn has, so he could also meet Madonna's requirements in that regard.

So Madonna and Sean Penn had all three Sexual Linkages. Was that the reason they got married? We don't think so. Sex is sex, and sexual energy and attraction are based on the Sexual Planets, but love and marriage are based on Chiron. Chiron Linkages are key to the feelings of love and trust that are needed for two individuals to get married. This leads us to a special type of Chiron Linkage that we call a Magical Linkage. Madonna has such a linkage with Sean, but that will be a subject of our next chapter. This one is devoted to Sexual Linkages.

Princess Diana and Prince Charles—a Mismatch in Sexuality

We stated in the first chapter that Magi Astrology explains why Prince Charles is so bonded to Camilla Parker-Bowles—and the reasons would amaze a lot of us. What we are about to say will probably also surprise Charles's mother, the Queen of England.

Prince Charles was born heir to the British throne. As far as thrones go, the crown of England is the most coveted one of our time. Because Charles was born with the expectation of becoming king, he was skillfully trained to play the role of the crown prince. This meant that he was trained in the art of projecting the public image of a caring intellectual. He was taught well, and he learned well.

However, underneath the public image, the real Prince Charles is revealed by Magi Astrology, which shows that the prince was born with— oh my God—*two* Sexual Aspects. Or does he have *three* of them?

Clearly, Prince Charles was born with at least one Male Super Sexual Aspect (Figure 8D). He has Mars contra-parallel Pluto, but he also has a trine of Mars and Pluto, with an orb of about four degrees. In Magi Astrology, this is too wide an orb to be considered effective enough to rate as an aspect, unless the native (the person with the aspect) has another enhancement aspect that is comprised of the exact same two planets. That is the case with Prince Charles. Under such circumstances, there is a CUMULATIVE EFFECT. By itself, the Mars trine Pluto is too far apart and off by too many degrees to have the power to be considered a planetary aspect, but the alignment does have power, and it increases the power of the Male Super Sexual Aspect that he does have in the declinations, making that aspect almost a Super Super Sexual Aspect. In addition, he has Uranus contra-parallel Mars, which is a male Sexual Aspect, so sex is very important to Prince Charles— and this is precisely the reason why he divorced Diana.

Please look at the Magi AstroCharts of these two royals at the end of this chapter. Of special importance is the fact that Diana was not born with any Sexual Aspect. Also, note that when you overlay their two charts, the combined chart does not have any Sexual Linkages—not even one.

Uh-oh . . could it be that the princess turned out to be too demure for Charles's liking? And could it be that sex is number one on Charles's priority list?

Now take a look at the Magi AstroChart of Prince Charles's lifelong mistress, Camilla Parker-Bowles (Figure 8F). Camilla was born with two Sexual Aspects—and she nearly has a third! She clearly has Pluto parallel Venus, as well as Venus parallel Mars. In addition, her Mars is pretty close to being parallel to her Pluto. And, of course, you will recall that the Venus-Pluto enhancement is the Female Super Sexual Aspect and is the one that Madonna has.

So Camilla is more to Prince Charles's liking in the sexual area. They are both *highly* sexual persons, and Diana was not. However, what really created the apparently all-consuming sexual obsession that Charles has had for Camilla is that the two of them have Sexual Linkages—all three of them. Whoops! On closer examination, they have four of them—and maybe there are even more because of a cumulative effect.

Camilla and Prince Charles have the following Sexual Linkages (Charles's Mars and Pluto are added to Camilla's chart to help you see these):

- They have an exact Pluto-Venus Sexual Linkage, since Prince Charles has his Pluto at 23.1 degrees, and Camilla's Venus is also at 23.1 degrees. This is essentially an exact linkage, and is the most powerful of the Sexual Linkages. The closer to being exact that this or any other Planetary Linkage is, the stronger the power of the linkage. With the prince and Camilla, it is about as close as you can get. This is also the Sexual Linkage of obsessions, which explains the intense nature of their relationship.

- Camilla and the prince also have the Mars-Venus Sexual Linkage because Camilla's Venus at 23.1 degrees is linked to Prince Charles's Mars at 24.0 degrees. The two planets are on the opposite sides of the declinations, but this forms a linkage because they match degrees.

- They also have the Mars-Pluto Sexual Linkage. Camilla's Mars at 22.0 links with Prince Charles's Pluto at 23.1 degrees. As if this linkage was not powerful enough, the two of them have another one. Camilla's Pluto at 23.6 links to Charles's Mars at 24.0. Such double linkages have awesome added power. In fact, they are so rare but so powerful that we need to give them a special name: DOUBLE LINKAGES. So, Prince Charles and Camilla have a Double Linkage of the Mars-Pluto Sexual Linkage.

As if all of the above was not enough, Camilla's Mars is about 4.5 degrees away from making a trine to Prince Charles's Venus, providing a cumulative effect to the Mars-Venus Sexual Linkage that they already have.

Poor Di. She didn't have a chance!

So, finally, through the tools of Magi Astrology, we now know the real reasons for Camilla and Charles's obsessive union and why the relationship revolves around sex, just as England's tabloids have said.

Once again, the answer was in the stars. You just have to know how to read them. These examples also demonstrate to us the enormous influence of Sexual Aspects and Sexual Linkages.

England Has a Very Sexual Royal Family

In England, the fact that Prince Charles has the Male Super Sexual Aspect may come as a surprise to some, but anyone who reads the British tabloids would not be at all surprised to learn that Prince Charles's younger brother, Prince Andrew, rivals Camilla in the number of Sexual Aspects each was born with. Prince Andrew has been long regarded as the playboy of Britain's royal family, so much so that few in England were surprised when the young prince squired one steamy woman after another in his pre-marriage days. At one time, Prince Andrew even had a very public affair with a soft-porn star. This prompted the tabloids to remark that as far as Prince Andrew was concerned, sex wasn't the most important part of a relationship; it was the *only* part of a relationship. Let's see what our new knowledge of astrology can reveal about Prince Andrew. (He was born on 12/19/60; chart not shown.)

Wow—Prince Andrew was born with four Sexual Aspects, including a Male Super Sexual Aspect. No wonder sex has been so important to him. He has Mars contra-parallel Pluto, Venus contra-parallel Pluto, Mars parallel Venus, and Mars conjunction Venus. When someone like Prince Andrew has so many Sexual Aspects, he will rarely marry anyone who does not match him in sexuality.

As you can see, Sarah Furguson (born 10/15/59, chart not shown) was not a match for Prince Andrew in this area, as far as natal aspects are concerned, because she only has one Sexual Aspect. However, a woman is often able to keep up with a man who is more sexual than she is, although the reverse is not usually the case. So, Sarah was able to meet Prince Andrew's requirements because she was sexual *enough*. But Prince Andrew had dated a dizzying number of women. What made him so attracted to Sarah?

Well, they have two Sexual Linkages. Her Pluto is parallel his Venus and also his Mars. In addition, her Venus is almost conjunct his Pluto. It is only a shade farther than the three-degree orb we allow, but since they already have a Venus-Pluto linkage in the declinations, the near conjunction counts as a cumulative aspect and raises the power of the Venus-Pluto linkage to a much higher level. Only about one out of fifty women will have both the Sexual Aspects that Sarah has, as well as the Sexual Linkages that Sarah makes with Prince Andrew. That is quite a few women to have to experiment with before finding an equal—even for Prince Andrew.

Lucky Prince Andrew. He is a prince of England and he has Sexual Aspects. We wonder what Prince Andrew did in a previous life to deserve all this!

Princess Di and Dodi Fayed

Princess Di and Prince Charles were married in 1981, separated in 1993, and they were officially divorced in 1996. As far as most of us know, Princess Di had only one significant relationship after her separation. It was with Dodi Fayed, the man she was killed with in the car crash in 1997. We already explained that Prince Charles and Di were a sexual mismatch. We have assumed that this mismatch was a strong driving force, at least in Prince Charles's desire to get divorced. He obviously wanted to be with Camilla, who is a highly sexual woman making multiple sexual linkages with Charles. Charles and Diana had no sexual linkages, and Diana was more of a lady in the Victorian sense.

But as the old saying goes, a lady in one man's bed may not be a lady in another man's bed. British and American tabloids quoted Di as telling her friends that she just could not get enough of Dodi. Is there truth to this, or did the tabloids' sources exaggerate? We can figure out the answer by look-ing at Dodi and Di's Magi AstroCharts (Dodi's is Figure 8G).

Di and Dodi had a sexual linkage—just one. However, one is enough when you have been in a conventlike set of circumstances as Di had been—that is, with the world watching your every move, sexual or otherwise. Actually, one Sexual Linkage is enough even if you've been around the block a few times. The Sexual Linkage that Di and Dodi had is close to being exact. Di's Pluto was less than one-half degree from Dodi's Mars in the declinations.

Conclusion

Our conclusion is great news for everyone: YOU DO NOT HAVE TO BE GORGEOUS OR SUPER SEXY TO ATTAIN THE HEIGHTS OF MAGICAL SEX. You just have to find a partner with whom you make sex-ual linkages. If you are also both loving and unselfish, the rest will flow naturally.

Now, some more conclusions we derived from our research: We looked at every famous married couple that we had birth dates for, as well as the ones who were in our research project. There were over 25,000 of them in our recent study; plus about another couple of hundred thousand from the Magi Society's data that was accumulated since 1625. It was a mountain of data to analyze. We are very thankful for computers and computer software.

Our data goes back to 1625, and we found a difference in the linkages that prevailed in different time periods. Most significantly, a marked change occurred after the Victorian era. It was after that time that sexuality became more important in the choice of marriage partners. The percentage of married couples who had Sexual Linkages was significantly higher after the Victorian era than before or during it. This makes sense, because before and during the Victorian era, women were not supposed to enjoy sex, and pre-marital sex was abnormal, as opposed to these days, when it is quite commonplace.

The level of married couples with Sexual Linkages was at its highest around 1970, just after the introduction of the birth control pill and during the early years of the sexual revolution. This level tapered off dramatically beginning in the mid-1970s. Our data shows that during the last ten years, the occurrence of Sexual Linkages in married couples has now been holding steady at a level that is *not* significantly higher than what would occur by mere random chance. They occur more often than norm, but not so much more often that they can be considered a factor in the way we now choose our marriage partners. Once again, as was the case for most of the last couple hundred years, Sexual Linkages are becoming less important as a factor in deciding whether two people get married. However, Romantic Super Linkages do occur in the Combined Alignment Charts of married couples significantly more often than by random chance.

A Sexual Linkage is least important in a marriage where both persons are gorgeous. It seems that being superattractive creates enough sexual attraction without Sexual Linkages—but we all suspected that. Also, if a couple has a Romantic Super Linkage, they are likely to get married regardless of whether they have a Sexual Linkage.

If you have a Sexual Linkage with someone, it does not mean that you are more likely to marry the person. It only means that you have a higher-than-normal level of sexual attraction to that person, and that sex with the person is better than with most. However, sex is sex, and sex does not equate to love, nor does it ultimately *become* love. A Romantic Super Linkage is a sign that love could develop. Of course, if you have both with someone, then all the better. Lucky you.

However, if you have only Sexual Linkages and no Romantic Super Linkages, it would be advisable to accept our advice that there is a high probability that the relationship is one-dimensional, and that marriage is unlikely. A long-term relationship is also unlikely. In fact, if there are not any Super Linkages of any kind, a long-term relationship of any kind is probably inadvisable, but we must caution that there are still other significant astrological factors to take into consideration when assessing a relationship, and we will learn about them in the rest of this book.

Our studies provided us with some discoveries, which can be of guidance to you:

Most successfully married couples are comprised of two people who match each other in Sexual Aspects. Usually, either both persons have at least one Sexual Aspect, or neither person has a Sexual Aspect. Otherwise, there is a mismatch in sexuality, and this usually leads to a breakup *before* marriage or a breakup *after* marriage.

The vast majority of long-lasting marriages are between two persons who form either no Sexual Linkage, or just one Sexual Linkage, regardless of other factors. Marriages between couples who have more than one Sexual Linkage end in divorce even more often than the already very high divorce rate. It seems that when two people have more than one Sexual Linkage, the sex becomes too important a part of their relationship. There is not enough room for much else to develop, such as love and understanding. In a sense, this is a shame, but maybe God designed it this way so that we would learn that there really is much more to a relationship than sex.

Marriages between two people who do not have any Sexual Linkage can work out great. Of all the marriages we looked at in recent times, those which have been between two persons who do not have any Sexual Linkages actually have a higher median duration than those with Sexual Linkages. In other words, they usually last longer—about 20 percent longer on average. This is significant. It seems that such couples have focused their relationship on areas other than sex, and the relationship has benefited from the broader focus.

There Are Drawbacks to Sexual Aspects

If you were not born with a Sexual Aspect and you feel sort of left out, please don't feel that way. Here's why.

Most women were not born with Sexual Aspects. Only a little over a third of women are. About two-thirds of men have one because there are more Sexual Aspects that only work on men. It seems that there is a disadvantage being born with a Sexual Aspect because such men and women are more likely to get divorced, and their marriages have a shorter median duration, meaning the marriages last fewer years on average. The same is true with respect to the love relationships of such persons. A person with a Sexual Aspect tends to have relationships that have a lower life expectancy than a person without a Sexual Aspect. As a matter of fact, the more Sexual

Aspects a person has, the shorter the duration of the person's relationships. Perhaps this is due to the fact that having a Sexual Aspect gives a person the urge to seek new sexual partners. Obviously, this urge is not conducive to long-term relationships and commitments of love.

It seems that when someone has more than one Sexual Aspect, the person pursues sexual fulfillment to the detriment of many other areas of life. Such persons need to understand their tendency, and muster the willpower to control it.

Figure 8A: Madonna born 8/16/1958

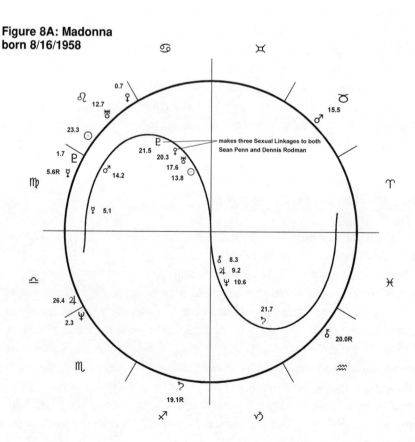

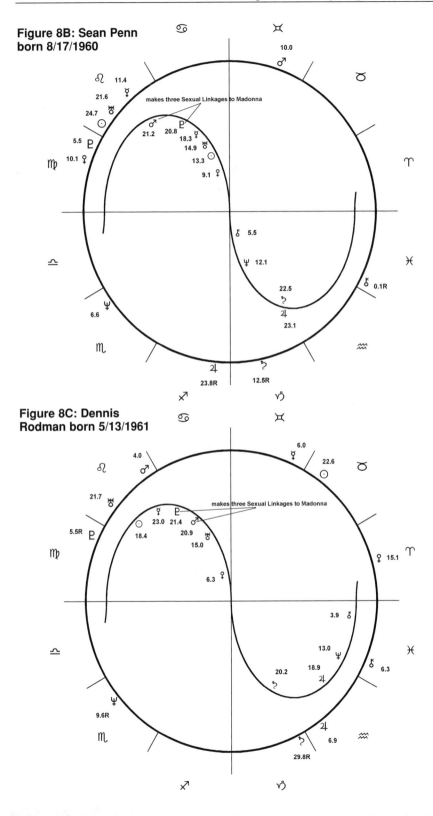

Figure 8B: Sean Penn born 8/17/1960

Figure 8C: Dennis Rodman born 5/13/1961

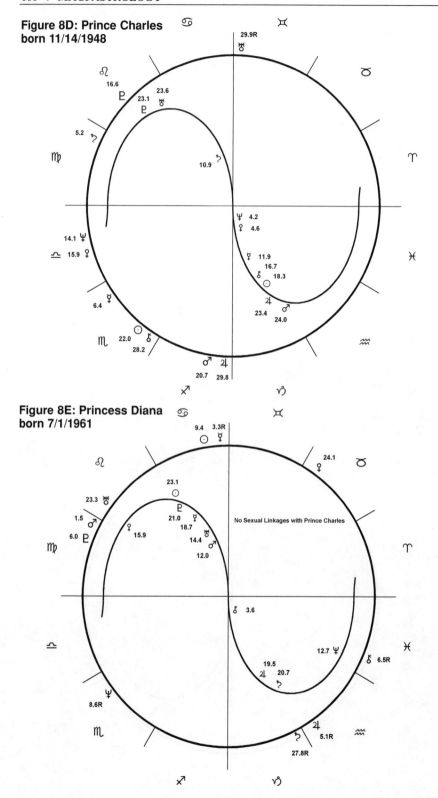

Figure 8D: Prince Charles born 11/14/1948

Figure 8E: Princess Diana born 7/1/1961

No Sexual Linkages with Prince Charles

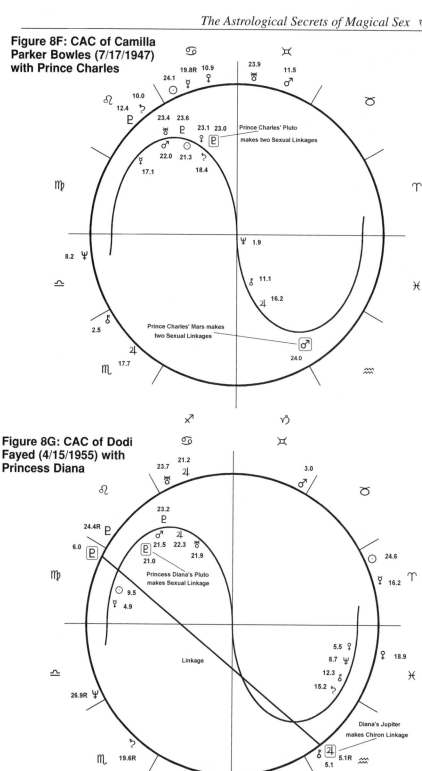

Figure 8F: CAC of Camilla Parker Bowles (7/17/1947) with Prince Charles

Prince Charles' Pluto makes two Sexual Linkages

Prince Charles' Mars makes two Sexual Linkages

Figure 8G: CAC of Dodi Fayed (4/15/1955) with Princess Diana

Princess Diana's Pluto makes Sexual Linkage

Linkage

Diana's Jupiter makes Chiron Linkage

Chapter Nine

⌘

Special Linkages That Are
Signs of Love and Intimacy

We have discussed the fact that a Romantic Super Linkage requires three planets, and they are the most reliable indications of lasting love and probable marriage. But there are some linkages formed by just two planets that are almost as powerful in creating marriages. We are referring to the MAGIcal Linkage, Cinderella Linkages, the Cupid Linkage, Lifetime Linkage, and the Linkage of Trust. Each of these linkages has its own unique spin, and each deserves its own consideration.

The Venus-Chiron Linkage Is Magical

In matters of love, the most important of the linkages are the four Romance Linkages. These four linkages have their own special powers and add a little magic to the relationship of the linked persons. Of these, the Venus-Chiron Linkage is the most powerful and beneficial of all.

The Venus-Chiron Linkage is a Romance Linkage. When it comes to relationships and especially marriages, this linkage is by far the most powerful individual linkage. This linkage creates desire (Venus) for marriage (Chiron) or the union (Venus) of spouses (Chiron). The Venus-Chiron linkage appears more often in married couples than any other linkage, including the three Sexual Linkages. For this reason, it is justifiable to call this linkage a *marital* linkage. However, the Venus-Chiron Linkage is also the most powerful and helpful one that two persons can have when it comes to affairs of money. For these reasons, in Magi Astrology, we refer to the

Venus-Chiron linkage as the MAGICAL LINKAGE because it seems to have something truly magical about it. Two people who have this linkage have a special bond and make great business, as well as marriage, partners.

Examples of the MAGIcal Linkage

Getting back to Madonna, we should emphasize that although she has the Female Super Sexual Aspect, the material girl would not have married anyone she did not love. Madonna was very much in love with Sean Penn. How do we know? Sean Penn and Madonna have the Venus-Chiron MAGIcal Linkage. Of all the individual linkages, Venus-Chiron *is the linkage that is the most reliable sign of marriage.* Sean's Venus is contra-parallel to her Chiron.

The Venus-Chiron MAGIcal Linkage is one of the four Romance Linkages. Madonna and Sean also had another Romance Linkage in that Sean's Chiron is linked to Madonna's Neptune. In fact, they have a Romantic Super Linkage because Sean's Chiron links to Madonna's Venus-Neptune square. Together, these three astrological bonds were strong enough for Madonna, who was the undisputed female icon of the 1980s, to marry Sean.

So Madonna married Sean not just because of the three Sexual Linkages they had. We told you the material girl did not marry just for great sex.

Princess Diana and Prince Charles Had Two MAGIcal Linkages

When we add our knowledge of the Venus-Chiron MAGIcal Linkage to the knowledge we already have, we can understand relationships nobody else has been able to explain, such as why Prince Charles married Diana even though he was so sexually bonded to Camilla Parker-Bowles.

The answer is always understandable when you master Magi Astrology. Charles married Diana because they had the Venus-Chiron MAGIcal Linkage—twice.

His Venus is contra-parallel her Chiron, and his Chiron is contra-parallel her Venus. This means that they had a DOUBLE LINKAGE. As this example illustrates, Double Linkages have extraordinarily special power. The Venus-Chiron linkage is the most powerful Romance Linkage and signifies linked (Venus) destinies (Chiron). Even after they were divorced, nothing could unlink their mutual destinies because of the two sons that their marriage produced.

What the Venus-Chiron Double Linkage tells us is that although there was no lasting sexual attraction between Diana and Charles (they had no Sexual Linkages), they did actually believe they were in love at one time. After all, they were married 12 years before their official separation, and royal watchers say that they did indeed appear to be the quintessential couple. In the beginning, they were not faking their happiness, but when Diana found out about Charles's regular trysts with Camilla and he refused to give them up . . .

Of all the two-planet linkages, the MAGIcal linkage is the most reliable sign that a long-term relationship is likely. Check this out for yourself and see which persons in your life form the MAGIcal linkage with you.

The Venus-Chiron Linkage Is Really Very Magical

Prince Charles and Princess Diana were not alone in being a royal couple with the MAGIcal Linkage of Chiron and Venus. They are not even alone among royal couples in having a Double Linkage of Venus-Chiron. The power of this one single linkage is so awesome that an examination of royal weddings reveals that this linkage existed in *all* of the most important royal weddings in recent times. In fact, a Double Linkage of Chiron and Venus exists between Queen Elizabeth and Prince Philip, and the Venus-Chiron Double Linkage also linked Grace Kelly with Prince Rainier III!

The Combined Alignment Chart of these two other royal couples are at the end of this chapter (Figures 9A and 9B). As you can see, Queen Elizabeth and Prince Philip have a Double Linkage of Chiron and Venus in the declinations. The Queen's Chiron is nearly exactly parallel to her husband's Venus, and her Venus is within orb of making a contra-parallel to her husband's Chiron, thus creating a very rare Double Linkage of Chiron and Venus.

In the case of the Rainiers, Princess Grace's Chiron was close to being exactly parallel to her husband's Venus, while her own Venus was within orb of making a contra-parallel to her husband's Chiron. So all three of the most famous royal couples of the last 50 years had a Double Linkage of Chiron and Venus.

To paraphrase an old saying, you don't have to be a rocket scientist to figure out that the Venus-Chiron MAGIcal Linkage has special meaning. It is so important that we will repeat ourselves and state again that the Venus-Chiron Linkage is the linkage that occurs more often than any other in married couples. The Venus-Chiron MAGIcal Linkage is so powerful that it can overpower what outwardly appears to be a total mismatch. When you meet a husband and wife who are so different you have to keep asking if they're married, chances are that they have the Venus-Chiron MAGIcal Linkage. Below are two of the most famous examples of such marriages in the 20th century.

The Owl and the Pussycat

For the benefit of you readers who are not familiar with the phrase "the owl and the pussycat," it is used to refer to a marriage between two individuals who are such opposites that almost nobody understands why they got married.

In recent times, there have been two couples who have attracted the most attention as far as being in an owl-and-pussycat marriage. One is the marriage of Marilyn Monroe, the sex goddess, to Arthur Miller, the Pulitzer Prize-winning intellectual. More recently, there was the marriage of Christie Brinkley, the uptown girl who was a superstar model, to Billy Joel, the very popular singer who was about a half foot shorter. He was super-successful, but he was not considered to be uptown by many tabloids. Personally, we think Billy Joel *is* very uptown and do not understand why journalists thought the marriage was one of contrasts, except for the height difference. But then again, we looked at the marriage from the viewpoint of Magi Astrology.

In both cases, the two couples formed the MAGIcal Linkage. However, we should not limit our analysis to just that one linkage. At this point, we have discussed most of the major astrological influences that promote love and marriage between two people. We know about Romantic Super Linkages, Symmetrical Combined Geometry, and Sexual and Romance Linkages. Each of these linkages is defined as a form of Planetary Geometry because they all create specific types of shapes and lines in the Combined Alignment Charts. We will call these four astrological influences NUPTIAL Planetary Geometry. We should now be able to use all of them to help us learn how to analyze our own relationships. Let's use the two owl-and-pussycat marriages as examples from which to learn more about using Nuptial Planetary Geometry.

When Opposites Attract

When opposites attract, astrology is always the key to the reasons why such individuals feel enough love and trust to marry each other, especially when they are as superfamous as our case studies. We will discuss three very famous examples.

In the case of Christie Brinkley and Billy Joel, their Combined Alignment Chart has all four forms of Nuptial Planetary Geometry. No wonder the uptown girl and Billy Joel immediately fell in love (Figure 9D)!

Christie Brinkley was born with a conjunction of Venus and Sun. Using our interpretation method of combining the symbolisms of these two planets to interpret what this aspect is a sign of, we get a beautiful (Venus) person (Sun). Nobody would disagree with that! This is one of her most important aspects. Billy Joel's Neptune is trine to this conjunction, thus creating a Super Linkage. It also creates a shape of Planetary Geometry that we call a Conjuncted Trine. We have already noted that this particular type of Planetary Geometry is almost as powerful as the Grand Trine.

Similar to the three royal couples we just discussed, Christie and Billy also have *two* of the Venus-Chiron MAGIcal Linkages. Billy's Venus trines Christie's Chiron. In addition, Billy's Chiron is parallel to Christie's Venus—another example of a Double Linkage of Chiron and Venus!

They did not miss out on the sex, either! Billy's Venus is very close to being in exact contra-parallel to Christie's Mars, thus creating a Sexual Linkage.

On top of all of this, a Double Grand Trine is formed by Brinkley's Sun-Jupiter trine, and by Billy Joel's Neptune being in trine to her Sun-Jupiter trine. This is a Double Grand Trine because Brinkley's Venus conjuncts her Sun. Remember that when we are looking at complex Planetary Geometry, an orb of four degrees becomes acceptable because we are allowed a little leeway on one pairing.

In interviews with Christie and Billy, both of them have always said that from the moment they met, they were in love. Because of Magi Astrology, we now know why.

They had all four types of Nuptial Planetary Geometry needed for sustained attraction, enduring harmony, and understanding, as well as the sexual attraction necessary to add spark to a marriage. And they got married pretty quickly. Unfortunately, they got married on March 23, 1985, and that was not a favorable astrological day. Because astrology really works, they eventually got divorced. We will discuss this Wedding Chart later on.

Marilyn Monroe and Arthur Miller

Marilyn Monroe and Arthur Miller also had all four types of Nuptial Planetary Geometry (Figure 9C).

Arthur Miller was born with the very powerful conjunction of Jupiter and Chiron, which gave him a fabulous (Jupiter) public image (Chiron). Marilyn Monroe's Saturn linked to this conjunction, thus creating a Romantic Super Linkage, which is the number-one indicator of marriage.

They also formed a combined Conjuncted Trine, which is Symmetrical Combined Planetary Geometry even though it is not as obviously symmetrical as a Grand Trine. It is a very narrow equilateral triangle.

The marriage of Monroe and Miller was also foretold by their MAGIcal Linkage; Arthur's Venus was almost exactly contra-parallel to Marilyn's Chiron.

Believe it or not, Marilyn was not born with any Sexual Aspects. Her ability to project sexuality came from her natal aspect of a Venus-Chiron conjunction. This is a Romance Aspect and provided her with charismatic (Chiron) beauty (Venus). Arthur Miller did not have a Sexual Aspect either, but the couple did have a Sexual Linkage. Arthur Miller made a Sexual Linkage with Marilyn Monroe because his Mars was parallel to her Pluto.

Unfortunately, they also formed a T-square in their Combined Geometry. Miller was born with a Venus-Neptune Square, and Monroe's Chiron was opposed to his Venus and square his Neptune. Any T-square is bad, but this was awful because of the Venus-Chiron and Neptune-Chiron activations. In chapter 15, we give you interpretations for all linkages and activations.

The Perfect "10" Marries Her Perfect Match

There is another very famous couple that has been considered unusual. We are referring to Bo Derek, star of the film *10,* and her now late husband John Derek. Monroe and Miller were opposites because of their personas— Miller was the superintellectual, Monroe was viewed by the public as the "dumb blonde." Brinkley and Joel were viewed as opposites by the press as being the uptown girl and not-so-uptown boy. In the case of Bo and John Derek, they were considered opposites because of age.

They met when Bo was very young. She was a perfect "10" and only 16. He was 46. That made him three times as old as she. In an effort to avoid controversy, John spirited her off to France and married her when she turned 18, which meant that he was 48. When he turned 60, she was only 30. John has been referred to as a Svengali ever since Bo married him, but we think that those who referred to him as such were a little jealous. Wouldn't most men be jealous of someone who was married to Bo Derek, Linda Evans, and Ursula Andress as John was?

So, what made an exquisitely beautiful 16-year-old girl who was a perfect 10 fall in love with a 46-year-old man—even if he was also a 10?

If you guessed that the answer is in the stars—you're right! An analysis of Bo and John's Combined Alignment Chart, as with each of the other examples, will help us have more and more confidence in the accuracy and power of Magi Astrology.

The most important astrological basis for this famous couple's attraction and compatibility was Symmetrical Combined Geometry—with eight planets. (Their combined alignment chart is on page 198.) They had four linkages that were trines, and these four trines formed two parallelograms in a symmetrical pattern. Also, note that the overall figure is eight planets, with each person contributing four of them—a near-perfect symmetrical shape of eight planets. As we explained, each of the two-planet linkages helps to create harmony and attraction. With eight of them . . . well, remember that the more planets in linkage, the more the two people are in synch.

The fact that Chiron was one of the planets in this eight-planet symmetrical pattern strengthens the geometry's ability to produce a marriage.

Even though Bo Derek was very convincing when she played the role of a young and very sexually oriented seductress in the film *10*, Bo herself does not have a Sexual Aspect. This makes sense because no 48-year-old man can keep up with an 18-year-old woman who has a Sexual Aspect. John, who died in 1998, was born with the Venus-Pluto Sexual Aspect; this means he had enough sexual energy when he got married at 48 for a normal woman. Bo and John had the Venus-Pluto Sexual Linkage because Bo's Pluto was parallel John's Venus. This all added up to just enough spice for a very young woman who did not regard sex as the centerpiece of a marriage. She looked for love and harmony, and she got it. They did not have the Venus-Chiron Romance Linkage, but their Chiron-based eight-planet symmetrical Combined Planetary Geometry gave them all the harmony and compatibility they needed, by a wide margin. They were married for the entire balance of John's life, which was 24 years.

Of course, another reason Bo and John's marriage lasted as long as it did lies in the strength of the day they got married. This is explained later on in this book in chapter 16.

There are four other particular pairings in linkages that we should know about because they are truly unique. The Lifetime Linkage is one of them.

The Lifetime Linkage

From the symbolisms of Magi Astrology, we would expect that a linkage of Chiron to Neptune would create a very long-term relationship. This is because in Magi Astrology, Neptune is the planet of longevity and anything that is long term. Therefore, the Neptune-Chiron Linkage would mean a long-term (Neptune) partnership (Chiron). This linkage usually bonds the two persons in such a way that they are likely to have a long-term relationship. Even though the relationship is not always lifelong, we call this linkage the LIFETIME LINKAGE.

The Chiron-Neptune linkage is a Romance Linkage but is the least romantic of the Romance Linkages. By itself, this linkage does not guarantee that there will be intimacy between the linked persons. (The Venus-Chiron MAGIcal Linkage almost guarantees intimacy between a man and woman.) But it creates long-term partnerships. It could be in the form of marriage, it could be a business partnership, or it could simply be a long-term friendship. The details of the partnership would depend on the other linkages that two people have. For example, are there Sexual Linkages or other Romance Linkages, or are there linkages good for making money together? (We will deal thoroughly with money-making linkages later.)

We believe that the Neptune-Chiron Linkage is important enough to warrant special attention as well as its own name because it occurs very often in long-term relationships.

Now we come to the Cinderella Linkages. They are very interesting and also somewhat magical.

The Cinderella Linkages

Do you have friends who dream about marrying a millionaire? Tell these friends they can use Magi Astrology to maximize their chances of doing so. This is because they can improve their chances if they find a millionaire with whom they form a Cinderella Linkage. Otherwise, they don't have a chance. Also, tell your friends that they need to be born with the Cinderella Aspect. That is also important.

Have you ever noticed that some women seem to attract all the rich men, and *only* the rich men, while other women seem to date one financial flop after another, and even lend these guys money they never get back?

There is an old saying that goes: *It is just as easy to fall in love with a rich man as a poor man.* Guess what? That is not true. Maybe that's why we don't hear it spoken much anymore.

What we are about to say might be discouraging to some of you who have dreamed about marrying wealth. Our research resulted in the discovery that there are three linkages that are most powerful in creating a Cinderella, so we call them Cinderella Linkages. They are the MAGIcal Linkage, the Jupiter-Chiron linkage, and the Chiron-Neptune linkage. Each of these three linkages greatly increases the chances of a marriage occurring where the marriage would elevate one person to a much higher level of money or social standing.

In addition, there are two CINDERELLA ASPECTS. They are the Chiron-Neptune enhancement and the Venus-Chiron enhancement.

Again, because Magi Astrology really works and because the symbolisms of Magi Astrology are consistent, the Cinderella Linkages and Cinderella Aspects are both the ones we would expect to act in this manner, according to their symbolisms. Here is how we can interpret the three Cinderella Linkages and two Cinderella Aspects:

- The Jupiter-Chiron linkage is a Cinderella Linkage because it means success (Jupiter) and good fortune (Jupiter) from marriage (Chiron) and from a spouse (Chiron).

- The Venus-Chiron MAGIcal Linkage is also a Cinderella Linkage because it means money (Venus) and social standing (Venus) through marriage (Chiron) and because of a spouse (Chiron).

- The Chiron-Neptune linkage is symbolic of security (Neptune) from marriage (Chiron), which usually means a Cinderella has been born through marriage; this is also the Lifetime Linkage.

- The Chiron-Neptune Cinderella Aspect means financial security (Neptune) from marriage (Chiron).

- The Venus-Chiron Cinderella Aspect means money (Venus) and social standing (Venus) from marriage (Chiron).

Some of the most famous examples of Cinderellas in this century are the women we have already discussed in this book. In every single case, these women either have a Cinderella Linkage to the husband that made them each a Cinderella, or she was born with one of the Cinderella Aspects—or both.

- Princess Diana was a real live Cinderella, and she was born with Neptune trine Chiron, a Cinderella Aspect. We already know that she had two Cinderella Linkages to Prince Charles because of the two Venus-Chiron linkages.

- Carolyn Bessette is as much of a Cinderella as anyone who has married royalty, since the Kennedys are essentially America's royal family. Although Carolyn came from a very respectable social background, it was not on a par with the Kennedys. She was born with the Cinderella Aspect of Chiron trine Neptune.

Here is the best one of all:

- Mrs. Wallis Simpson was born with both of the Cinderella Aspects. Her Chiron is trine her Venus, and also trine her Neptune. In addition, she and King Edward VIII formed two Cinderella Linkages! His Jupiter trined her Chiron, and his Venus linked with her Chiron through the quincunx angle. So the woman who became the Duchess of Windsor by marriage was born with both Cinderella aspects, and the man who made her a Duchess linked to her with two Cinderella Linkages. Doesn't astrology amaze you sometimes when you know what to look for?

- Evita Peron was born with only one Cinderella Aspect (Chiron trine Neptune), but one is enough—especially if you find someone to make the Cinderella Linkage with. Her Chiron is trine to Juan Peron's Neptune. She did not marry royalty, but she did marry someone who was a possible choice as president of her country, and he *did* become president. Anyway, his social standing when they got married was so much above hers that you have to judge her to be a Cinderella.

• Priscilla Presley was the daughter of an officer in the U.S. armed forces who was of field rank stature. Obviously, she came from a very respectable family and was comfortable, but Elvis made her one of the most envied women in the world by marrying her. Priscilla entered an entirely different world overnight. Didn't they refer to Elvis as the king? Priscilla is a very capable woman and has been very successful in the management of Elvis's estate, but she can thank her lucky stars for Elvis. And she can thank her Cinderella Linkage and aspect. Elvis's Chiron was trine her Neptune to create the Cinderella Linkage. She was born during a Chiron-Neptune PLANETARY ECLIPSE.

A planetary eclipse is a term we introduced in *Astrology Really Works!* It refers to a condition where one planet appears to eclipse another planet in the sky. It occurs when two planets are close to being in the same degree of the Zodiac Sign Chart and the Declinations Chart at the same time. Obviously, this means that there is a conjunction and a parallel simultaneously. When two planets are close to this type of alignment, it is a celestial mini-sign. Due to the cumulative effect, neither the conjunction nor the parallel has to be within normal orb for the planetary eclipse to be effective. In Priscilla's case, her parallel of Neptune and Chiron is close enough so that it counts as an aspect when we add the near conjunction of Chiron and Neptune.

Cinderella Linkages work for men, also. In fact, Cinderella Linkages usually occur whenever one person is significantly raised (through marriage) to a much higher social or financial standing.

Does this mean that if marrying well is very important to some people, and they do not have the Cinderella Aspect, they should slit their wrists? Of course not. They might find someone who makes the Cinderella Linkage to them, but they should realize that the odds are against them marrying "extraordinarily well." To be forewarned about this is very valuable knowledge. Now, instead of waiting for a better-heeled prospect that will never come, people without Cinderella Aspects can concentrate on the prospects that are already there. Besides, we should all take heart in the fact that money really is *not* everything, and happiness is not based on it. Look at Elvis and Prince Charles. Besides, with Magi Astrology, we think that anyone can pick a good enough wedding date so that they can all build their own nest at least comfortably enough to marry for love and not money. We are not promising millions, but we do think a firm grasp of Magi Astrology can improve everyone's financial well-being. This means that there is no longer a reason to marry for anything other than love. That is great news and will be part of the attributes of the coming New Age.

The Linkage of Trust

Anther special linkage we want to pay special attention to is the Linkage of Trust.

Chiron and Sun create the Linkage of Trust. Again, this is perfectly consistent with the Magi Astrology symbolisms for the planets, since Chiron rules trust. A normal interpretation of this linkage is a trusted (Chiron) person (Sun). Like the Lifetime Linkage, the exact nature of a relationship between the linked persons would depend on the other linkages involved.

The Linkage of Trust is a very good linkage to have with someone so long as the person you have it with is trustworthy. Unfortunately, this is not always the case. When you think that a friend of yours is blind to someone's faults, chances are pretty good that it is because of this linkage. For this reason, if you have such a linkage with someone, you have to be more careful than usual to protect yourself against being blind to the person's shortcomings. So if you have trusted friends who are telling you that you are blind to someone's faults, and you have a Linkage of Trust with that person, you should be very careful to avoid financial dealings with that individual.

The Cupid Linkage

There is another special linkage that is highly romantic but not quite as powerful in the marriage department. It is the Sun-Venus linkage. This linkage is indicative of attraction (Venus) to the person (Sun). Since Venus rules seduction, intimacy, desire, and attraction, this linkage is dynamically powerful in that sexual intimacy between the two connected persons is highly likely. However, because Chiron is not involved in this linkage, neither person is moved to desire marriage. Bill Clinton and Monica Lewinsky have two of these linkages. It deserves a special name—the CUPID LINKAGE—because the arrow of Cupid's bow is symbolic of the pain this linkage often causes. When a man and woman have this linkage but not much more, someone usually gets hurt because neither marriage nor a real relationship is in the stars; Chiron is a spectator. But the Cupid Linkage does create a very high level of romantic interest and instant intimacy. For this reason, we will add this to the list of Romance Linkages.

Summary

We have enough special linkages now that so that it is very useful to provide a summary. Here it is, from the beginning:

Sexual Linkages:
- Venus and Pluto
- Mars and Pluto
- Venus and Mars

Romance Linkages
- Venus and Chiron (MAGIcal Linkage)
- Jupiter and Chiron
- Chiron and Neptune (Lifetime Linkage)
- Venus and Neptune
- Sun and Venus (Cupid Linkage)

Cinderella Linkages:
- Venus and Chiron
- Jupiter and Chiron
- Chiron and Neptune

Linkage of Trust:
- Sun and Chiron

Cupid Linkage:
- Sun and Venus

ॐ ॐ ॐ

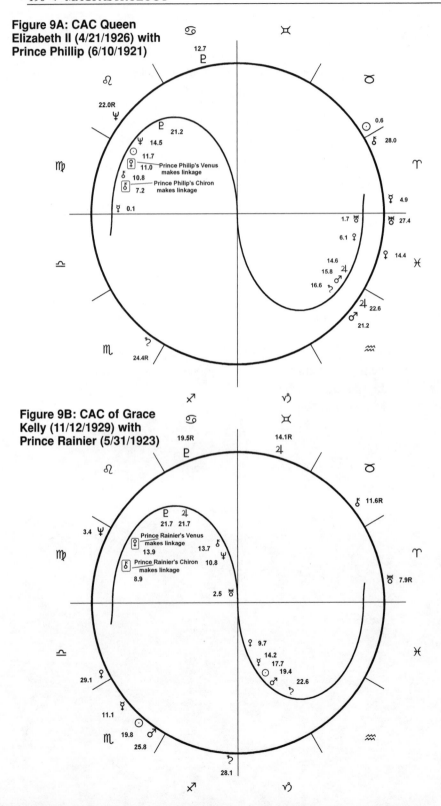

Figure 9A: CAC Queen Elizabeth II (4/21/1926) with Prince Phillip (6/10/1921)

Figure 9B: CAC of Grace Kelly (11/12/1929) with Prince Rainier (5/31/1923)

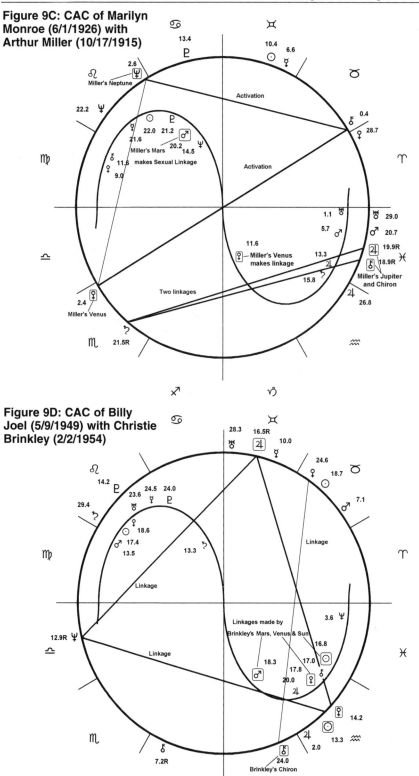

Figure 9C: CAC of Marilyn Monroe (6/1/1926) with Arthur Miller (10/17/1915)

Figure 9D: CAC of Billy Joel (5/9/1949) with Christie Brinkley (2/2/1954)

Figure 9E: CAC of John Derek (8/12/1926) with Bo Derek (11/20/1956)

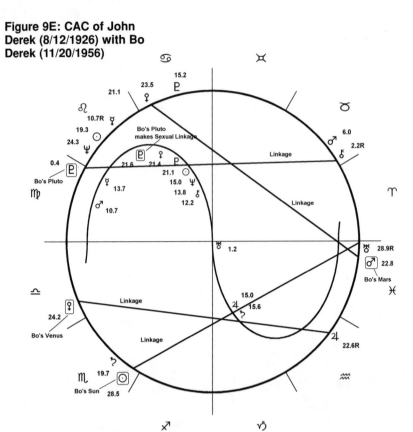

CHAPTER TEN

๛

Maximize Your Success with Golden Linkages

We are now going to apply the principles of Magi Astrology to the attainment of a successful career. This can be done through what we call GOLDEN LINKAGES, which are one of the recent discoveries of the Magi Society's research. They can help you create the most prosperous and rewarding partnerships in any career or profession that you would like. Whether your employer or partner is a corporation or a person, they all have birth charts, and we all make linkages, activations, and other forms of Combined Planetary Geometry with our employer or partner. Just as certain linkages create certain results in a personal relationship, it is also the case that certain linkages create certain predictable results in a business relationship.

Activations are more likely to be harmful than helpful, but all linkages are helpful. There are some types of linkages in a business relationship that are remarkably helpful in making money and attaining recognition and achievement. The linkages that are most helpful in achieving success are called GOLDEN LINKAGES. For example, Bill Gates has Golden Linkages with Microsoft, and Michael Dell has Golden Linkages with Dell Computer.

The exciting part of all this is that it means that you can use Golden Linkages to harness the power of astrology to help you maximize your success. The first step is to go into partnership or work for someone with whom you make Golden Linkages, even if that someone is really a corporation.

Golden Linkages

There are only five Golden Linkages:

1. The Venus-Chiron MAGIcal Linkage
2. The Jupiter-Chiron Cinderella Linkage
3. The Jupiter-Pluto Linkage
4. The Pluto-Chiron Linkage
5. The Venus-Pluto Linkage

If you form any of the above linkages with someone, then you have a Golden Linkage with that person. It means that you can make money with that person, and the person can make money with you and for you. Remember, please, that only five angles of interalignment create linkages; they are the four enhancement angles plus the quincunx. The orb we allow for the declinations is 1.2 degrees, and with the longitudes, the orb is 3 degrees.

Here, again, as always, Magi Astrology is consistent because the linkages that are golden are the ones you would expect to be that way according to the Magi symbolisms of the planets. Here is how each of the Golden Linkages are interpreted:

1. Venus-Chiron means money (Venus) from partnerships (Chiron).
2. Jupiter-Chiron means successful (Jupiter) partnerships.
3. Jupiter-Pluto means being successful (Jupiter) at business (Pluto) together, and making profits (Pluto) together; the reason we say "together" is because of the linkage.
4. Pluto-Chiron means a partnership (Chiron) for profits (Pluto).
5. A Venus-Pluto linkage means money (Venus) from business (Pluto) together.

As we have already explained several times, the valid range of the predictable influences of aspects are determined by the range of the symbolisms of the planets that comprise the aspect. This same rule applies to the valid range of interpretations for linkages, and the symbolisms used are the same for both linkages and aspects. For this reason, all linkages have influences that are similar to that of a natal aspect formed by the same planets, but the influence is on the connected persons as a unit. In other words, a Jupiter-Pluto linkage acts on the connected persons as a unit in a very similar way that a natal enhancement aspect of Jupiter-Pluto acts on the person born with the enhancement (the native). Using the symbolisms of the planets, this would mean that linkages involving two planets, both of which have symbolisms including money, success, and power, should create a linkage that has golden qualities. This happens to be the case. For this reason, the following five linkages also enhance earning potential:

1. A Venus-Neptune Linkage means long-term (Neptune) money.

2. A Venus-Uranus Linkage means money from the public (Uranus).

3. A Venus-Jupiter Linkage means good luck (Jupiter) in matters of money.

4. A Jupiter-Uranus Linkage means a high level (Jupiter) of fame (Uranus). In this world, fame is a child and product of success.

5. A Jupiter-Neptune Linkage means high levels (Jupiter) of long-term financial security (Neptune) and success (Jupiter).

As always, we prefer to be able to refer to a specific group of linkages collectively, so we call these five the SILVER LINKAGES, and we call the Golden and Silver Linkages, collectively, the SUCCESS LINKAGES. One Golden Linkage is about equal in power to two Silver Linkages.

If you have one Golden Linkage with someone, it means you can make money with that person. Obviously, if you have two or more of them with one person, you should encourage the person to become partners with you. From our extensive research, we have found that the most successful partners in the world almost always have two or more Golden Linkages.

But the best news of all is that you can harness the power of Golden Linkages by starting a business chart on a day that makes Golden Linkages with you. It worked for Bill Gates and Michael Dell (of Dell Computer). Together, they are worth more than $55 billion.

Bill Gates and Microsoft Corporation Have Golden Linkages

According to *Forbes* magazine, for several years now, Bill Gates was not only the wealthiest person in the United States, he was also richer than anyone else in the world. Gates is the founder of Microsoft Corporation, which has a stock value second only to General Electric. In other words, the total value of all of the stock of Microsoft Corporation was worth more than any company in the world except for General Electric. This is quite an accomplishment. It is all the more impressive when we take into consideration the fact that Microsoft was only founded in 1981, and other companies such as Exxon, IBM, DuPont, and AT&T have been around for an average of 100 years.

Bill Gates first incorporated Microsoft on June 25, 1981, in Washington State (Figure 10A). In 1986, Microsoft "went public," meaning that the company sold shares of its stock to the public and legally obtained a listing of its shares on a regulated "exchange." Attorneys generally advise entrepreneurs that if they are going to take their company "public," they should change the company's domicile to Delaware where the laws are most favorable for corporations. In other words, they should set up a new company under the laws of Delaware and transfer all the assets of the old company to the new Delaware company. Microsoft did this in 1986. A new Microsoft Corporation was formed on September 19, 1986 (chart not shown), and it acquired all of the assets of the original Microsoft company. The reason we discuss all this is because Bill Gates's Combined Geometry is different with the two different corporations, but he had Golden Linkages with both of them.

With the original Microsoft Corporation, Bill Gates's birth chart created two Golden Linkages. There was the Jupiter-Chiron linkage, and there was also a Venus-Pluto linkage.

The new Microsoft Corporation also forms two Golden Linkages with Bill Gates, but it is much better than just the average two linkages. They have a Double Golden Linkage of that amazing MAGIcal Linkage. Gates's Venus is contra-parallel to the new company's Chiron, and Gates's Venus is also quincunx to the company's Chiron.

Gates did very well with the first Microsoft, but he made more than 99 percent of his net worth through the new Microsoft. That MAGIcal Linkage is indeed very magical.

If you had been able to invest $10,000 in Microsoft stock at the initial public offering price, 11 years later your investment would have been worth over $2.5 million. This is an example of the power of Golden Linkages—and hard work and a lot of good decisions. Golden Linkages help people to make the right decisions—that's how they work. But we should make it clear that there is nothing that replaces hard word and devotion to your career. Diligence, perseverance, integrity, plus the Golden Linkages is the necessary combination for super success.

Michael Dell and Dell Computer Have Golden Linkages

There is actually a company whose stock price has performed even better than that of Microsoft's; it is Dell Computer Company. If you had invested $10,000 in Dell at the public offering price, your stock would have been worth $5 million in less time.

Microsoft's most famous product is the Windows operating system. Almost everyone in the U.S. knows about it. Less than one-tenth of American adults know that Dell Computer is the most successful direct marketing computer seller in the world (although everyone on Wall Street knows this).

Michael Dell is to Dell Computer what Bill Gates is to Microsoft, but even more so. Like Microsoft, Dell Computer was reincorporated when the company went public. And like Bill Gates, there are spectacular Golden Linkages between Michael Dell and both of the Dell Computer Companies. They are even better than the ones that Bill Gates has with Microsoft.

With the original Dell Computer, Michael Dell created two Golden Linkages. They are Jupiter parallel Chiron and Jupiter trine Pluto. With the new Dell Computer Company (Figure 10B), Michael Dell makes these three Golden Linkages:

1. Jupiter parallel Chiron
2. Venus trine Chiron
3. Pluto parallel Chiron

There are also two Silver Linkages.

What we should learn from this is that if you are forming your own company or a partnership, you must choose a date that has a birth chart that will form at least one, and preferably two or more, Golden Linkages to your own birth chart. That is the only way you might achieve success on the level of Bill Gates and Michael Dell.

However, not everyone wants to, or should, form their own company. Most of us work for an employer, but you can make use of the Golden Linkages of Magi Astrology to be as successful as possible as an employee. You can do this by including Golden Linkages in your criteria when choosing a job. Of course the usual other important considerations should not be ignored. Job description, growth opportunity, the financial health of the employer, and salary plus benefits are not to be ignored, but Golden Linkages give you an edge over other employees. You are likely to be better treated and more successful with a company that forms Golden Linkages with you.

Figure 10A: CAC of Original Microsoft Corporation (6/25/1981) with Bill Gates (10/28/1955)

Figure 10B: CAC of Dell Computer Co. (10/22/1987) with Michael Dell (2/23/1965)

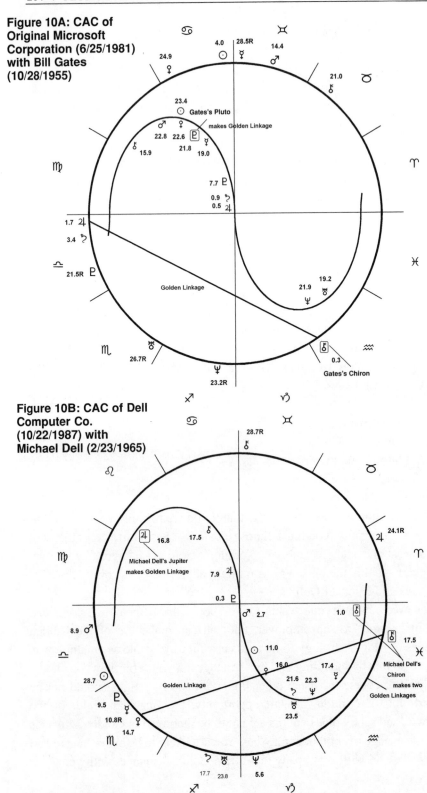

CHAPTER ELEVEN

Fulfill Your Dreams with Help from Magi Astrology

Do you have a dream? Do you fantasize that you are performing in front of a huge audience and everyone is mesmerized by your artistic talents? Do you dream that you can enthrall the public with your singing voice? Your dancing ability? Your acting skills and charisma? All of the above?

Take heart, because Magi Astrology might just be your key to achieving such dreams, and any other ones that you may have.

Have you ever attended a rock concert of a world-class musical group and watched as the singers and musicians enchant and almost hypnotize the audience? Have you ever wondered how these bands do it?

By mastering Magi Astrology, you will know what helps these bands captivate their audiences. You will also learn how to take the first step toward being able to do so yourself. These bands are comprised of members who make Golden Linkages to each other. In fact, all of the most successful bands that have ever been formed are comprised of members who make at least one Golden Linkage to every other member of the band!

Just as Golden Linkages work between employer and employee, they work between people who are business partners. Actually, they work even better.

Golden Linkages and other helpful linkages have been the key to the success of the most popular musical groups in the world. As examples, we have chosen popular music's three most successful bands. They are the Beatles, the Rolling Stones, and Fleetwood Mac. A band is a partnership; each member of the group is a partner of every other member. The membership of the Rolling Stones and the Fleetwood Mac has changed from time to time, but the most successful lineups of these two bands, as well as the Beatles, were comprised such that *every single member had at least one Golden Linkage to every other member of the band.*

In this chapter, we will analyze the Golden Linkages of all of the Beatles, and the most successful incarnations of the Rolling Stones and Fleetwood Mac. The world will probably be amazed at the preciseness of these Golden Linkages.

We Can Acquire Super Aspects That We Do Not Have!

We can employ the principles of Magi Astrology that we have already discussed to maximize our chances of fulfilling our dreams. For example, if we want to succeed in the entertainment industry, perhaps in an acting or singing career, and we do not have highly charismatic aspects such as Gary Cooper and Clark Gable did, we can use Magi Astrology to help us attain the charisma we lack. This is because *we can acquire charismatic planetary geometry by becoming partners with someone whose chart, when combined with our own, will jointly have the planetary geometry needed for charismatic super success.* There are some linkages that provide charisma, and some that help attract fame, and we provide examples of both in this chapter.

In the past, astrology had a major drawback. It did not help us gain control of our lives! Magi Astrology now changes this limitation. Magi Astrology gives you the tools you need to not only analyze what you have, but *improve* what you have. With Magi Astrology, you can have more control over our life than ever before. You can even acquire Super Aspects that you may not already have.

We explained previously that a Super Aspect is a planetary aspect that provides a jump-start on success to anyone blessed enough to be born with one. Also, we have continually pointed out that every planetary aspect we are born with is a gift of a special talent or ability, and each such gift was given to us by a Benevolent Providence. Astrology is a Benevolent Design, but it would be cruel of astrology if we were all limited to achieving only what our natal aspects allow. Fortunately, astrology was designed in such a way so that if we were not born with an aspect we need, we can actually acquire it.

We can do so with Golden and Silver Linkages (collectively called Success Linkages). Every one of these Success Linkages is comprised of the same pairs of planets as a Super Aspect. The most important lesson from this chapter is not just that Success Linkages are helpful. It is that those of us who were *not* born with a desired exceptional talent do not have to be discouraged by that fact. With Magi Astrology, we can harness the power of the stars and acquire the aspect and the Planetary Geometry we need for maximum success. We can do so by becoming partners with those who make Success Linkages with us, and the three super-successful bands are all examples. We all should be greatly encouraged by what we read in this chapter. We will learn how we can best fulfill our dreams.

The Truly Incredible Saga of Fleetwood Mac

The story of the rise and fall and rise of Fleetwood Mac should teach all of us that perseverance and hard work will pay off once you find people with whom you make a lot of Golden Linkages. This is true even if a person is not all that talented.

In the 1960s, in England, Mick Fleetwood had a dream; he also had a problem. He wanted to form a band and be a superstar of popular music. The trouble was, he couldn't sing. As a matter of fact, neither was he all that good at writing songs or arranging music. To add to the problem, Mick Fleetwood wasn't even good at playing the all-important guitar. He had to make do with being a drummer and percussionist, the easiest instruments of popular music. So, if he was to fulfill his dream, he would have to find band members who could write moving lyrics, arrange fabulous music, have the great voices needed to create the necessary magical charisma—and who had a lot of Golden Linkages with him.

Mick got all of that and more. In the late '70s, his band, Fleetwood Mac, with Stevie Nicks and Lindsey Buckingham as the vocal anchors, eventually reached a level of stratospheric superstardom that has still never quite been equaled by any other band. The Beatles were superstars and so were the Rolling Stones, but none of them sold 25 million copies of any single album. Fleetwood Mac's most successful album, *Rumours*, sold that many copies, and is still selling. The band sold more than $800 million worth of records and albums in total. Some of the songs on their super album, *Rumours*, are still regularly played on soft-rock radio stations today, more than two decades later. That album even gave rise to Bill Clinton's successful 1992 presidential campaign theme song ("Don't Stop"...thinking about tomorrow)—and an invitation from the president to perform at his first inaugural ball.

How could Mick Fleetwood, a not-so-super-talented musician, become the founder and leader of such a supersuccessful band? You know the answer to that. When Mick was joined by Stevie Nicks and Lindsey Buckingham, they had the Golden Linkages needed to launch their rocket ship to superstardom.

However, we don't want to give you the idea that Mick Fleetwood's road to fame and fortune was smooth and easy. In fact, it was probably the most difficult of any founder of a superstar band—and really quite hilarious and comical.

We are going to tell you about Mick Fleetwood's rocky and often frustrating road to success because it is a good lesson for all of us. We should learn from his story that we should never ever give up on our dreams—no matter what. Too many of us look at ultrasuccessful people and think they had an easy road to the top. This is almost *never* the case. Nearly every fabulously successful person has had to work bone-crunchingly hard for what they achieved. The road to success is so torturous that it almost always passes through a town called Desperation. The common denominators of all supersuccessful individuals is that they never gave up—and that they had Golden Linkages. So our formula for success is: work hard, never give up, have big dreams, and attain Golden Linkages.

The actual Fleetwood Mac band was formed in 1967 (we would love to know the exact date . . . are you listening Mick Fleetwood?). From the very beginning, the nucleus of the band was Mick Fleetwood and John McVie; hence, the name Fleetwood Mac. And from the very beginning, there were problems because John McVie could not sing, write songs, or arrange music any better than Mick Fleetwood could. Well, John could sing a *little* better than Mick, but not well enough to carry a band. Luckily, John could play that all-important guitar, which was a start. Somehow, it seems these two were always able to find great talent in the areas where they needed help. The problem was that wherever they found great talent, there was also great turmoil and troubled souls.

The first successful lineup of the band was made up of Peter Green and Jeremy Spencer, along with Mick and John. Peter Green was the first of the band's tormented geniuses. With Greene's extraordinary musical talent, the band achieved number-one status in England. Their music was what was called the blues.

Trouble was, during the middle of a tour in Germany, Greene quit and became a gravedigger. Honest.

As Mick Fleetwood wrote in his autobiography years later, "Nothing ordinary ever happened to this band." (All the more reason that the Magi Society would love to know the exact date when the band was formed.)

Greene (the one who left to become a gravedigger) was replaced by

Danny Kirwan and Christine Perfect. Christine and John McVie hit it off so perfectly that they got married just a few weeks after they met. Forever after, she has been known as Christie McVie.

Christie was a great songwriter and filled one of the voids left by Greene's departure. The band was just about to reestablish itself when the next disaster hit. While on tour in California, Spencer disappeared without a word. He simply got up one morning, left his hotel one afternoon, and never returned. At least his predecessor, Greene, gave the band notice before he left.

With the help of the FBI, the band found Spencer under the influence of one of the many religious cults that seem to be as native to California as its famous weather. Somehow, the band convinced Spencer to temporarily return so that the band could finish its tour.

After settling back in England, the band eventually found Bob Weston to replace Spencer. Mick Fleetwood let Weston know that he really hoped he wouldn't leave the way Greene and Spencer did. Can't you just visualize Mick saying, "Bob, let me know if there is *anything* we can do to help you feel at home. This is not just a band, this is a family."

In Bob Weston, the Fleetwood Mac found someone who would not leave and really did feel like a permanent part of the band—and the family—so much so that Weston started having an affair with Mick's wife. Mick fired him.

By now, the band was so disrupted that it told its manager to cancel a U.S. tour. It was at this point that the band's manager made one of the biggest blunders in the history of popular music. Instead of cancelling the tour, he formed a group to impersonate Fleetwood Mac and sent them to America. Can you believe it? The lawsuits that followed this fiasco forced Mick and the McVies to leave England and return to California. Where else? After all, this was 1974, and California was the center of the music revolution.

It was in sunny California that Mick Fleetwood, John, and Christie had one of those chance encounters that would change many lives. They met Stevie Nicks and Lindsey Buckingham in a recording studio. These two musicians joined the band, and together they sold over three-quarters of a billion dollars' worth of records and albums.

So if you ever feel discouraged and think that your problems are unique, just remember the saga of Fleetwood Mac. Smile about it and get back to working toward your dream. Keep plugging. That's the only way that you can one day meet the person or persons who were dreaming about meeting you. When Mick Fleetwood and Christie and John McVie met Stevie Nicks and Lindsey Buckingham, they met the two individuals they needed to fulfill their dreams. It was these two persons who provided the perfect astrological fit, and a whole lot of Golden Linkages.

Here are the birth dates of the members of Fleetwood Mac (from now on, since we have so many examples, we're not providing charts for all individuals due to space limitations).

- Mick Fleetwood: drums, born 6/24/42
- John McVie: guitar, born 11/26/45
- Christie McVie: pianist, lyricist, composer, and vocalist, born 7/12/44
- Stevie Nicks: lyricist and vocalist extraordinaire, born 5/26/48
- Lindsey Buckingham: world-class guitarist, songwriter, vocalist, and the most extraordinarily talented composer of rock and blues music, born 10/3/47.

Together, these five band members produced songs that had a magical quality that one never tired of. Hence, their very first album went gold, and their second one sold 25 million copies, more by far than any other band up to that time.

There has been much that has been written about why Fleetwood Mac was so successful, but nothing, as far as we know, talked about the astrology of the band's super success. Of course, we think the astrology of it all is the most important part, as well as the most interesting.

For example, the Planetary Linkages show that once Stevie Nicks and Lindsey Buckingham joined the band, success for Fleetwood Mac was already destined in the stars. Stevie and Lindsey each formed at least one Golden Linkage with every other member of the band—and there were also a whole lot of Silver Linkages:

- Lindsey's Venus conjuncts John's Chiron—MAGIcal!
- Lindsey's Venus conjuncts John's Jupiter.
- Lindsey's Venus parallels John's Jupiter.
- Lindsey's Venus is trined by John's Uranus.

- Lindsey's Pluto is paralleled by Mick's Jupiter.
- Lindsey's Pluto is conjunct to Mick's Chiron.
- Lindsey's Uranus is paralleled by Mick's Jupiter.

- Lindsey's Chiron is contra-paralleled by Christie's Jupiter.
- Lindsey's Pluto parallels Christie's Venus.
- Lindsey's Jupiter trines Christie's Venus.

- Stevie's Chiron conjuncts John's Venus; more MAGIc.
- Stevie's Jupiter is contra-parallel John's Pluto.
- Stevie's Jupiter is contra-parallel John's Uranus.

- Stevie's Pluto conjuncts Mick's Chiron, exactly.
- Stevie's Jupiter is contra-parallel Mick's Pluto.
- Stevie's Pluto is paralleled by Mick's Jupiter (a Double Linkage).

- Stevie's Jupiter contra-parallels Christie's Pluto.
- Stevie's Jupiter is quincunx Christie's Venus.
- Stevie's Jupiter is contra-parallel Christie's Venus.
- Stevie's Jupiter is contra-parallel Christie's Uranus.

Stevie Nicks and Lindsey Buckingham formed a total of 11 Golden Linkages to the other three members of the band, plus another 9 Silver Linkages.

Interestingly enough, each band member had well-publicized emotional relationships with each other, and the Combined Planetary Geometry of each pair correctly predicted the particular relationship.

For example, only a few weeks after Christie and John McVie met, they got married. This usually requires a Romance Linkage as well as a Sexual Linkage plus a Chiron linkage. They had all three. The emotional attraction was generated by the Venus trine Sun (the Cupid Linkage, a Romance Linkage), and the sexual attraction by their Mars parallel Venus, which is a Sexual Linkage. And they have one wide Chiron linkage. This was the Neptune to Chiron contra-parallel, the Lifetime Linkage. The Cupid and Sexual Linkage can propel two persons to quickly get married, which they did. You might be thinking that this was really not enough to stay married. You're right, they got divorced.

Stevie and Lindsey also had a romantic relationship; they were living together when they first met Mick Fleetwood. This is expected because they have the Venus-Chiron Magical Linkage; Stevie's Venus is trine to Lindsey's Chiron. They did not ever get married, even though they reached superstardom together. Why? Perhaps because they did not have a Romantic Super Linkage. However, they were together because of the

Venus-Chiron Linkage, which is the MAGIcal Linkage. We think this linkage had a magical effect here even though they didn't get married. After all, by being together, they also joined Fleetwood Mac together, and that allowed them both to fulfill their career dreams.

Lindsey was the first to leave the band; then Stevie left, and so did Christie. They each went on to pursue a solo career, hoping to match the success they had as a member of the band. But none came close, not even Stevie Nicks and her spectacular voice. They needed each other and the Golden Linkages to have the success. *Talent does not equal success. Golden Linkages do.*

In 1997, the band reunited, cut a new album and went on tour in the U.S. Every concert was sold out, and they played to a standing ovation at that year's Grammys. Although they have not regained their status as the number-one band in the world, the reunited Fleetwood Mac was more successful than any of the individual musicians were alone. This is expected because Golden Linkages work very well.

Here are the Success Linkages for the other pairings of the band:

- Mick's Jupiter is parallel to John's Pluto.
- Mick's Chiron is conjunct John's Pluto.
- Mick's Jupiter parallels John's Uranus.

- Mick's Jupiter is parallel to Christie's Pluto.
- Mick's Jupiter parallels Christie's Venus.

More Golden and Silver Linkages!

The lesson that the Magi Society believes should be learned from this is that God, with His Benevolent Love, has designed astrology such that we can achieve with partners what we are unable to achieve by ourselves. Golden Linkages are signs that tell us a person can be the right partner. With Golden Linkages, the whole is always greater than the sum of the parts. We just have to find the right people and recognize them when we meet. With Magi Astrology, we can do that. It *is* a key to success in money matters!

Let's look at another superstar band, the Rolling Stones. Fleetwood Mac had their years of greatness as popular music's number-one band. However, over the long haul, the Rolling Stones have been the most successful band of all time.

The Rolling Stones All Had Golden Linkages to Each Other

In England, in 1962, while Mick Fleetwood was coming to the realization that he had a problem because he could not sing, write music or lyrics, or play an important instrument, Mick Jagger didn't think he had the same problem. You see, just like Fleetwood, Jagger wanted to be a rock superstar. Also, like Fleetwood, Jagger couldn't play a musical instrument very well, nor was he a great singer—at least not in the traditional sense of the word *sing*. But Mick Jagger thought, *So what?*

Remember, we're not talking about Mick Fleetwood. Jagger is a different Mick altogether, and he decided he would simply take the talents that he *did* have and remold popular music to showcase them. In doing so, Mick Jagger created an inimitable rock 'n' roll persona. Mick Jagger's rebellious and insouciant attitude has been his hallmark ever since. With it, he achieved his superstardom in a way that nobody else had before him—or since.

Mick Jagger, super icon of the 1960s and '70s, was luckier than Mick Fleetwood. Jagger met Keith Richards in Kent when they were both teenagers. As most rock music lovers know, these two lifetime partners are the fabulously successful founders of the Rolling Stones. They must have sensed destiny early on, because their Combined Planetary Geometry is as extraordinary as their success would indicate. Their CAC (Combined Alignment Chart) is Figure 11A on page 225. Here are their most powerful linkages:

- Keith's Jupiter conjuncts Mick's Chiron.
- Mick's Venus conjuncts Keith's Chiron: MAGIc!
- Mick's Jupiter conjunct's Keith's Pluto.

They have three Golden Linkages! When two people have three, they have the chance to make history together. In the case of all of the Rolling Stones, the whole band is exponentially greater than the sum of the individual members because they form a truckload of Golden Linkages to each other.

The other three original members of the Rolling Stones were Bill Wyman (bass, born 10/24/36), Charlie Watts (drums, born 6/2/41), and Brian Jones (guitar, born 2/28/42). This was the line-up of the Rolling Stones that accounted for each and every one of their number-one records, which began with "Satisfaction" and continued through "Honky Tonk Woman." The Rolling Stanes were not just a supersuccessful band—they dominated pop music and moved its boundaries to wherever they wanted them to be. Jagger and Richards wrote the songs; and of course Jagger was the key vocalist; while Richards, Jones, Wyman, and Watts provided instrumental innovations that would forever alter the landscape of popular music.

As a linked unit of five men, the Rolling Stones were able to redefine and reshape rock 'n' roll to their own liking and their own talents and make the public love it. This requires a whole lot of Golden Linkages, and the Rolling Stones had them. Every single one of them had at least one Golden Linkage to every one of the other four members of the band.

We have already given you the Golden Linkages between Mick and Keith. Here are all of the others, including the Silver Linkages:

- Mick's Jupiter conjuncts Brian's Pluto.
- Mick's Jupiter is parallel Brian's Uranus.
- Mick's Uranus trines Brian's Venus.

- Mick's Pluto is parallel Charlie's Venus.

- Mick's Pluto is contra-paralleled by Bill's Jupiter.
- Mick's Uranus is contra-parallel to Bill's Venus.

- Keith's Pluto is conjunct Brian's Chiron.
- Keith's Uranus is trine Brian's Venus.
- Keith's Uranus is paralleled by Brian's Jupiter.

- Keith's Pluto is contra-paralleled by Bill's Jupiter.
- Keith's Uranus is contra-parallel to Bill's Venus.
- Keith's Jupiter is parallel Bill's Uranus.

- Keith's Jupiter is parallel to Charlie's Chiron.
- Keith's Pluto is parallel to Charlie's Venus.
- Keith's Neptune is trined by Charlie's Jupiter.

- Brian's Pluto parallels Charlie's Venus.
- Brian's Uranus is paralleled by Charlie's Jupiter.

- Brian's Pluto trines Bill's Venus.
- Brian's Pluto is contra-paralleled by Bill's Jupiter.
- Brian's Jupiter is contra-parallel to Bill's Venus.
- Brian's Jupiter is parallel to Bill's Pluto.

- Charlie's Pluto is contra-paralleled by Bill's Jupiter.
- Charlie's Venus is conjunct to Bill's Chiron: MAGIc!
- Charlie's Pluto is trine Bill's Venus.
- Charlie's Chiron is conjunct Bill's Pluto.
- Charlie's Venus is contra-parallel to Bill's Jupiter.

No wonder the Rolling Stones were a super success! Even so, for a few years, the Rolling Stones were eclipsed by the Beatles. Like the most successful lineup of the Fleetwood Mac, the Beatles were not together that long, and we do not know what they would have done had they stayed together, but we do know what they did while they were a band.

The Beatles All Had Golden Linkages to Each Other

Paul McCartney and John Lennon first met in the summer of 1957, and they immediately became friends. Lennon was playing for a band called the Quarrymen, and Paul was soon invited to join. By 1960, George Harrison also became a member of the band, whose name was changed to the Beatles. The original lineup was comprised of Paul (born 6/18/42), John (born 10/9/40), George (born 2/25/43), Stu Sutcliffe (bass), and Pete Best on drums. The Beatles performed mainly in Liverpool and did a number of stints in Hamburg, Germany. Sutcliffe dropped out, and Paul McCartney took over on bass, so now the band was made up of just four young men. The dream of every band is a national recording contract, but the Beatles were turned down by Decca. Although they were very good, they lacked something—a certain something that Ringo Starr later provided. Before the Beatles made their first commercial recording, Ringo Starr had joined the Beatles and replaced Pete Best in the drummer's seat. And the rest is history.

The Beatles' situation is very similar to that of Fleetwood Mac, in that key members of the band were replaced by those who were a much better astrological fit than the original individuals. An analysis of the Combined Planetary Geometry using Magi Astrology will clearly explain why the underrated Ringo Starr (born 7/7/40) was a perfect fit astrologically to help the Beatles become what *Time* magazine called "the number-one band of the 20th century." Some drummers may have had more talent than Ringo, but the Golden Linkages he formed turned out to be irreplaceable.

Like Mick Jagger and Keith Richards, Ringo created three Golden Linkages to John Lennon. This is very rare. Also, he had a Golden Linkage with each of the other two Beatles. Here are all the Golden Linkages of the Beatles:

- Paul's Jupiter paralleled John's Pluto.
- Paul's Chiron was parallel to John's Venus: MAGIc!
- Paul's Venus was parallel to John's Jupiter.
- Paul's Jupiter is parallel to George's Pluto.
- Paul's Pluto is paralleled by George's Jupiter,
  a Double Linkage

- George's Jupiter was parallel to John's Pluto.
- George's Venus trined John's Chiron: more MAGIc!

- Ringo's Pluto is paralleled by Paul's Jupiter.
- Ringo's Pluto is paralleled by George's Jupiter.
- Ringo's Pluto is conjunct to John's Chiron.
- Ringo's Jupiter is parallel to John's Chiron.
- Ringo's Chiron was paralleled by John's Jupiter,
  a Super Double.
- Ringo's Venus was parallel to John's Uranus

Lessons We Have Learned

It's interesting to note that not a single member of any of these bands was truly successful as a solo artist or as a member of another band. Three members of Fleetwood Mac pursued solo careers. Stevie Nicks went furthest, but it was not that far, considering that she had the advantage of already being so famous from her success with the band. Each of the Beatles worked hard on individual careers, and Paul McCartney did the best through the band he formed called *Wings*. However, it did not fly anywhere close to the heights attained by the Beatles. Even Mick Jagger could not parlay his Rolling Stones success into a successful acting career or solo singing career.

We think all of these band members owed their success to hard work, talent, and Golden Linkages. So if you have a dream, keep working toward it and *never give up—no matter how much turmoil you might be going through*. The Fleetwood Mac story is a good lesson. During the entire time they were creating their hit album *Rumours*, every member of the band was going through some sort of major upheaval in their lives. Stevie and Lindsey were breaking up. John and Christie were breaking up. Mick was breaking up with his wife. It's hard to imagine how they were able to still work together, but they persevered, stayed focused, dug deep into their souls, and came up with super success.

And now that you've learned about Golden Linkages, you have the tools to fulfill your *own* dreams!

Symmetrical Combined Geometry Maximizes Success

Are you wondering what happened to Symmetrical Combined Geometry? It's alive and well, but it's rare enough so that of the three bands in this chapter, only one pair of partners formed it in a powerful way. In other chapters, we explained that Symmetrical Combined Geometry creates harmony and compatibility—it *lengthens* the lifetime of a relationship. So it would make sense that in all three of these bands, the two people who have been most successful and who have been together the longest are the two that have Symmetrical Combined Geometry. The pair is Jagger and Richards.

Mick Jagger and Keith Richards met when they were teenagers, and they've been partners and friends ever since. Like any two friends, their relationship has had its ups and downs, but the bottom line is that they are still together. A main reason for this supersuccessful long-term partnership is that there is a Grand Trine in their combined alignment chart. Although Golden Linkages are very powerful, they do not have the special added potency of a Grand Trine in a combined chart; it is this Grand Trine in the Mick Jagger/Keith Richards' combined chart that gives them that inimitable stage charisma. You can easily see that their CAC (Figure 11A) actually has a Double Grand Trine, with the conjunction formed by Chiron and Venus, the MAGIcal pair.

Symmetrical Combined Geometry works so well that the two persons who had the longest lasting supersuccessful entertainment partnership on television also had a Grand Trine in their combined charts, as well as Golden Linkages. Johnny Carson and Ed McMahon were teamed on the *Tonight* show from start to finish. These two had an ease and effortlessness about them that was unmatched. Their combined alignment chart is Figure 11B on page 226. They have a Double Grand Trine and also a third Grand Trine (essentially, they created a Star of David)! One of them includes a Venus-Chiron MAGIcal Linkage, just like Mick Jagger and Keith Richards. You're probably thinking that there's something magical about Chiron and Venus.

You're right.

Carson and McMahon did not have important linkages formed in the declinations, but they did not need any more than they already had in the longitudes. From time to time, there will be cases where the declinations will not have great significance. In such cases, we will not include the declinations in the charts.

Sean Connery Had Golden Linkages with the James Bond Producers

Sean Connery has had one of the most successful careers in Hollywood, but like almost all actors, he went through lean times during the early part of his career. For about nine years, he played small, unremarkable roles and was indistinguishable from the chorus. As a matter of fact, he *was* in the chorus of South Pacific! However, when Albert R. Broccoli and Harry Saltzman, co-producers of the first nine *James Bond* films, chose Sean Connery to play the lead role, Connery became an overnight superstar. There is a term for the circumstance where someone chooses a person for a role and the person becomes a superstar. It is called a Golden Handshake. Albert Broccoli and Harry Saltzman gave Sean Connery the Golden Handshake by choosing him to star as James Bond.

Even very prosperous people can use a Golden Handshake. Obviously, it is always helpful and it need not be as dramatic as 007's. How do you know when someone might give you such a handshake?

Golden Linkages are the signs of Golden Handshakes. Both Albert Broccoli and Harry Saltzman had Golden Linkages with Sean Connery. In fact, Broccoli had two, and Saltzman had three. Both of these men also had MAGIcal Linkages to Connery. The CAC's of Connery and each of these men are Figures 11C and 11D. Here are their Golden Linkages:

- Broccoli's Chiron and Connery's Venus are parallel: MAGIc.
- Broccoli's Pluto and Connery's Chiron are parallel.
- Saltzman's Venus and Connery's Chiron are contra-parallel: double MAGIc.
- Saltzman's Chiron is trine Connery's Pluto.
- Saltzman's Jupiter is trine Connery's Pluto.

Interestingly enough, Broccoli and Saltzman only had one Golden Linkage to each other. Astrologically speaking, the two of them did not really have anything else significant. Most supersuccessful partners have at least two Golden Linkages. Even though a single Golden Linkage is a passing grade, you really need two for real success. This explains why their partnership ended not long after Connery decided he would not do any more James Bond films. Without Connery, there just wasn't enough linkage between Broccoli and Saltzman. It was actually Connery who put the magic in the brew. Brocolli and Saltzman linked together through Connery.

If you have an entertainment career in your sights, we think mastery of Magi Astrology can be of immeasurable help to you. The birth dates of most producers and directors are obtainable. (We have most of the important ones.) The ones that you form Golden Linkages with are much more likely to hire you and maybe even make you a star.

George Lucas had three Golden Linkages with Mark Hamill and cast him in *Star Wars*. Lucas also had two Golden Linkages with Harrison Ford, whom he also made a star by casting him next to Hamill. Afterwards, Harrison Ford got another Golden Handshake from Steven Spielberg, with whom he has two Golden Linkages and great Super Linkages. Spielberg made Ford a superstar as *Indiana Jones*. This list can go on for a hundred pages.

As another example, Clint Eastwood got his biggest break in movies when he met a producer who formed three Golden Linkages with him.

Clint Eastwood and His Golden Linkages

Believe it or not, Clint Eastwood was not always superfamous and supersuccessful. Like almost all actors, he had worked at odd jobs such as pumping gas before he settled in Hollywood. He enjoyed modest success as the male lead in the TV series *Rawhide*. However, his career was stagnating until he met a little-known movie producer named Sergio Leone. Together, they created the three enormously popular "spaghetti Westerns" that catapulted Eastwood to worldwide stardom. These three movies were: *A Fistful of Dollars; For a Few Dollars More;* and *The Good, the Bad, and the Ugly.*

Eastwood and Leone had three Golden Linkages (their CAC is Figure 11E):

- Leone's Jupiter is trine Eastwood's Chiron.
- Eastwood's Venus conjuncts Leone's Pluto.
- Leone's Venus trines Eastwood's Pluto.

It is very rare for two persons to be so positively linked, and the result of such linkages can be spectacular success, as was the case with Clint Eastwood and Sergio Leone.

You probably know that Eastwood went on to become one of

Hollywood's most enduring superstars, but while his three films with Leone are still notable, Eastwood is most recognized for his leading role in the *Dirty Harry* films, which was a collaboration with Don Siegal (born 10/26/12), who directed this film. Eastwood and Siegal linked with four Golden Linkages:

- Eastwood's Venus is trine Siegal's Chiron—there's that MAGIc again.

- Siegal's Jupiter links with Eastwood's Chiron via a quincunx.

- Siegal's Jupiter links with Eastwood's Pluto through a contra-parallel.

- Siegal's Venus links with Eastwood's Pluto, also through a contra-parallel.

Neither Leone nor Siegal had any films that approached the popularity or financial rewards of the movies they did with Eastwood. Obviously, having Clint Eastwood in your film is a great advantage, but we think the Golden Linkages were the keys to the ultimate popularity of the films. They were also Eastwood's most successful roles.

Golden Linkages Create Combined Super Aspects

In chapter 4, we went to great lengths to explain that each aspect that anyone is born with is a sign of a gift endowing a special talent and ability. Our book *Astrology Really Works!* introduced and listed 12 Super Aspects that help anyone born with them to have a jump-start on success. The 12 Super Aspects work very well, but we did not include Chiron in our first book, so aspects with Chiron as a component were not considered when making up the list of Super Aspects for that book. Here, we add the enhancements of Jupiter-Chiron, Venus-Chiron, and Chiron-Pluto to the list of Super Aspects.

The power of Super Aspects and the validity of Magi Astrology is more convincing when we take into account the fact that every Golden Linkage is formed by a pairing of planets that forms a Super Aspect, and every Silver Linkage is formed by a pair of planets that is a Super Aspect. In other words, the component planets of Golden and Silver Linkages are also all the component planets of a Super Aspect. The reason that this makes Magi Astrology more convincing is that it means Magi Astrology is again consistent. What works in one part of Magi Astrology works just as well, and in the same way, as in another part of Magi Astrology. The rules for aspects and linkages are the same.

In our first book, we singled out the Jupiter-Pluto enhancement as the most powerful Super Aspect. The Jupiter-Pluto Linkage is also a Golden Linkage. We explained that the Venus-Pluto enhancement was the second most powerful money-making aspect of the Super Aspects that were revealed in the book. The Venus-Pluto linkage is also a Golden Linkage. This consistency is one of the most validating features of Magi Astrology. What we learned in this book reemphasizes and reconfirms the importance of Super Aspects.

However, one of the reasons we believe astrology is a Benevolent Design is that it gives all of us a chance for financial security. If someone was born without the Super Aspects that are so helpful to success, *the person can actually acquire Super Aspects in two ways:*

1. By becoming a partner with someone with whom the person forms Golden Linkages; such Golden Linkages then become COMBINED SUPER ASPECTS of both linked persons.

2. By beginning an endeavor on a day that has Super Aspects, thus creating a business chart, and having Golden Linkages to that chart. This utilizes some tools of Electional Astrology.

You Can Acquire Super Aspects Through Golden Linkages

If someone is not born with the Super Aspects required to become very successful, there is no need for the person to be discouraged. God designed astrology so that it is an invaluable aid to everyone, but we have to know how to use this tool. As we have seen already, you can be more successful by becoming a partner of someone with whom you make Golden and Silver Linkages. Every such linkage is really a Super Aspect for the two of you. When you have a linkage with someone else and the linkage meets the requirements of a Super Aspect, then you have a COMBINED SUPER ASPECT. They work just as well as a Super Aspect you are born with, so long as you're doing something *together* with the person you link with.

We saw that that was the case with Johnny Carson and Ed McMahon. Do you know what Carson and McMahon did before they were teamed together? Almost nobody does. But after they worked together and made a success of the *Tonight* show, just about everyone knew who they were.

Neither person had fabulous Super Aspects, but together, they had fabulous Golden and Silver Linkages and incredible Symmetrical Combined Planetary Geometry. Together, they actually have a Grand Trine and a Double Grand Trine. So they have three Grand Trines in their combined alignment chart—and five COMBINED SUPER ASPECTS.

A similar situation occurred with Broccoli and Saltzman. Neither of them had much in the way of Super Aspects, and they did not achieve super success until they picked Sean Connery to play James Bond. The partnership of these three men created all the Combined Super Aspects they needed. Before and after Connery, their success has been unremarkable. So in reality, Sean gave *them* Golden Handshakes just as he received such handshakes from them.

What if you have difficulty finding persons with whom you have Golden Linkages? And, what if you find that getting a Golden Handshake is not so easy? Well, don't give up. You can use the knowledge of Electional Astrology to acquire Golden Linkages and Combined Super Aspects. You can do what Bill Gates and Michael Dell did and form a company with Super Aspects that also makes Golden Linkages to you!

Of course, many of us are not so adventurous as to want to work for ourselves. For the most part, we just want to have a job we can enjoy and rely on so we can live comfortably and save money for retirement. What do we do then? We can choose an employer with whom we make Golden Linkages, and we can get married on a perfect astrological day.

We already discussed the power and importance of Marriage Charts. Now we add the advice that you must do your best to add Golden Linkages to the list of requirements of a Marriage Chart. A Marriage Chart has a profound influence on the careers of the spouses.

It can be very time-consuming to check to see if you have Golden Linkages with someone, but all of the Magi Society's computer software calculates such factors, and they are important enough that you do not want to miss any of them. (At the back of this book on page 435, we explain how you can obtain our unique software.)

Choosing Your Best Employer or Partner

There are many decisions that have to be made as we pursue our goals in regard to money, but very few of us realize how important it is to choose the right employer. Just as we can use Magi Astrology and Planetary Geometry to help us choose the right person as a lover and marriage partner, we can use the same principles of Magi Astrology to choose the right employer.

What most of us do not realize is that from the astrological point of view, our employer always has a birth chart. This is true in all cases, whether it is a person, partnership, company, institution, foundation, or government. This means we form Planetary Linkages and Super Linkages with the birth charts of whomever or whatever we work for. For example, the birth chart of the U.S. government is the same as the chart of the U.S., which is the chart for July 4, 1776. If you form Golden Linkages with this chart, you can do very well working for the federal government. Each U.S. government agency has its own chart; it is the chart of the day that the president signed the bill authorizing the creation of the agency.

Below is an example of how Success Linkages, and other linkages, helped one individual to become the CEO of the most valuable company in the world, General Electric.

General Electric and Jack Welch

For quite a while, Jack Welch has been CEO of General Electric Company, which is usually known simply as GE. GE is the most successful company in the world, as it owns NBC; makes most of Boeing's jet engines; has a giant market share of electric devices such as dishwashers, refrigerators, and light bulbs; builds the world's largest power plants; and is a major force in electrical equipment for medical diagnostics. The stock value of GE is greater than that of any other company in the whole world.

So let's see how astrology works on the linkages of GE to its CEO.

Jack Welch (born 11/19/35, chart not shown) joined GE (chart on page 115) when he was in his mid-20s and steadily rose up the ranks until he was the number-one person, becoming CEO shortly after his 20th year with the company. This is a very fast rise to the top. He does not have any Golden Linkages with GE, but he has three Silver Linkages to the company—and they are all very precise. Welch and GE form one Silver Linkage with a nearly exact contra-parallel of Jupiter and Neptune. However, his strongest linkages to GE are made by his natal Venus. GE has a very exact conjunction of Pluto and Neptune; Welch's Venus is trine to this conjunction, thus forming the Conjuncted Trine that we have explained is very powerful Combined Geometry. The Conjuncted Trine is just below the power of a Grand Trine in the hierarchy of Planetary Geometry.

There are also some other interesting interalignments. Welch's Mars is contra-parallel to GE's Venus, and Welch's Pluto is contra-parallel to GE's Mars. We are sure you will recall that when such linkages exist between two people, we call them Sexual Linkages. When the bonds are between a company and a person, they create attachments that prolong any relationship between the two, and create harmony. Bearing in mind that linkages can be interpreted by the range of the symbolisms of the planets that comprise the linkages, the Mars-Pluto linkage can lead to activities (Mars) and energy (Mars) directed at big business (Pluto) and making profits (Pluto), meaning the two can work together in business matters. The Venus-Mars linkage can mean the unification (Venus) of energies (Mars) for any purpose, not just sex, which is the normal channel. This is good news for all of us—especially those of us who are in a highly sexual relationship and who want to expand the relationship. It means that we can be business partners with those who are our best sexual partners—we just have to know how to do it.

The first step toward that goal is knowing that it is not only possible to do so, but it is also in the stars to be able to do so. This is all part of God's Benevolent Design; we *can* be business partners with our sex partners. That makes the world a much better place, don't you think?

An interesting thing we have learned is that for a person to be successful with a *company*, the Combined Geometry does not have to be as perfect as the ones needed in a love relationship. Usually, when it comes to two individuals, they cannot be successful together unless they have Golden Linkages. For the most part, in a personal relationship, the linkages have to be uncannily precise and numerous. But between an employee and a corporation, we have found that although there is a definitive need for linkages, they do not have to be as precise or as numerous for someone to be very successful with the company. We don't know why. Perhaps it is because God designed it this way since a company has to link with thousands of people, and a person only has to link with one spouse and a few close associates. Besides, you do not have to sleep with your company, meaning you don't have to be as close to your company as your lover.

So if you do not have great linkages with your employer, please do not walk out on your job or even feel depressed about it. In our research, we have found that a substantive portion of successful employees do not have great linkages with their employers, but they do have at least several linkages—and the rule is still the more the better.

The main reason that linkages between an employee and an employer is sometimes not absolutely crucial is that there is another astrological factor that has an equally strong influence on the success of an employee: the Planetary Geometry of the day a person becomes an employee, which is the

EMPLOYMENT CHART. We do not know the date when Welch started to work for GE. When Bill Gates and Michael Dell formed Microsoft and Dell, respectively, they became employees of the companies on the day of the formation of each company. Each such day was remarkably strong because it was the same as the chart of the corporation. This means they each had the same fabulous Golden Linkages to these Employment Charts as to the corporations' birth charts.

♋ ♋ ♋

Figure 11A: CAC of Mick Jagger (7/26/1943) with Keith Richards (12/18/1943) ♋

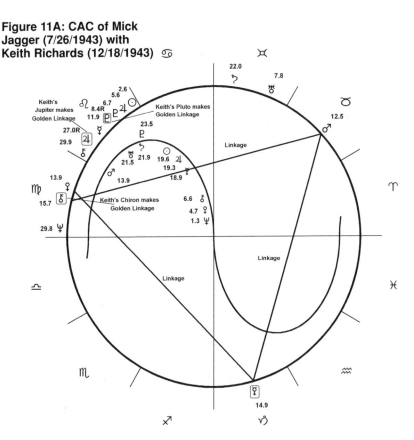

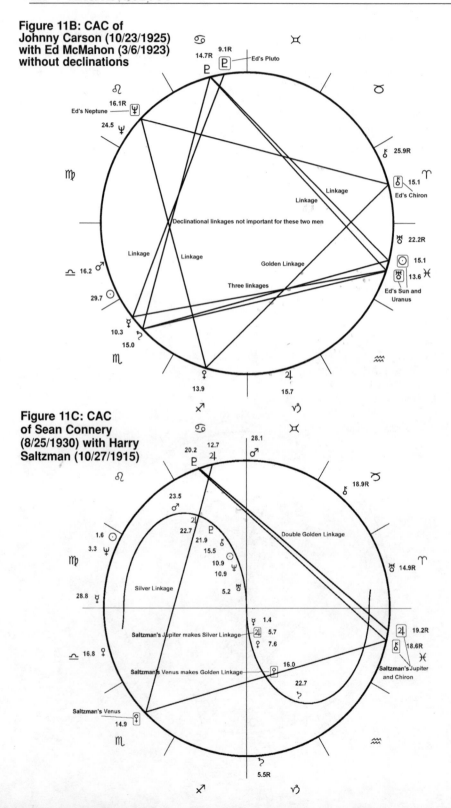

Figure 11B: CAC of Johnny Carson (10/23/1925) with Ed McMahon (3/6/1923) without declinations

Ed's Pluto

9.1R
14.7R P

Ed's Neptune — 16.1R Ψ

24.5 Ψ

25.9R

Ed's Chiron
15.1

Linkage

Linkage

Declinational linkages not important for these two men

22.2R

Linkage   Linkage

16.2

Golden Linkage

15.1

13.6

Ed's Sun and Uranus

Three linkages

29.7

10.3
15.0

13.9   15.7

Figure 11C: CAC of Sean Connery (8/25/1930) with Harry Saltzman (10/27/1915)

28.1

20.2 12.7
P ♃

23.5
♂

18.9R

1.6
3.3 Ψ

22.7 ♃ P
21.9
15.5
10.9
10.9
5.2

Double Golden Linkage

14.9R

28.8

Silver Linkage

Saltzman's Jupiter makes Silver Linkage

1.4
5.7
7.6

19.2R
18.6R

16.8

Saltzman's Venus makes Golden Linkage

16.0

22.7

Saltzman's Jupiter and Chiron

Saltzman's Venus
14.9

5.5R

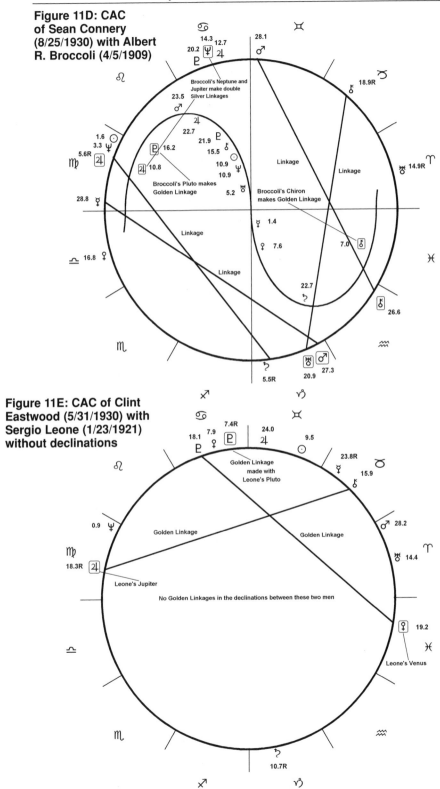

Figure 11D: CAC of Sean Connery (8/25/1930) with Albert R. Broccoli (4/5/1909)

Broccoli's Neptune and Jupiter make double Silver Linkages

Broccoli's Pluto makes Golden Linkage

Broccoli's Chiron makes Golden Linkage

Linkage

Figure 11E: CAC of Clint Eastwood (5/31/1930) with Sergio Leone (1/23/1921) without declinations

Golden Linkage made with Leone's Pluto

Golden Linkage

Golden Linkage

Leone's Jupiter

No Golden Linkages in the declinations between these two men

Leone's Venus

CHAPTER TWELVE

How to Choose the Best Days for Love and Money

There are two main ways we can use Magi Astrology to gain more control of our lives and to help us attain the highest degree of happiness and financial security that we are capable of. One of these ways is to utilize Success Linkages, especially the golden ones, to our best advantage in order to acquire Combined Super Aspects. The second way is to use Electional Astrology to choose the best times to begin a business or relationship chart.

We already learned the rationale behind Electional Astrology. In this chapter, we are going to learn more about how to select the most propitious times to begin any venture, or engage in any activity. We will learn about BI-DIRECTIONAL ASPECTS, APPLYING and SEPARATING ASPECTS, DOUBLE DIRECT ASPECTS, and TRANSITING ASPECTS. All of the above are criteria that will help us judge the Planetary Geometry of a day to determine if the day is good or bad for love and money. Some of the above criteria are unique precepts of Magi Astrology and all are such important astrological tools that one day, having such knowledge may save you from disaster. So it is worthwhile to learn them.

(*Please note:* In our first book, *Astrology Really Works!*, we went into great detail about much of the basics of Magi Astrology that we are about to learn in this chapter. If you plan to use Magi Astrology just to analyze your love and money relationships, you only need to master what is in *this* book. But if it is your intent to gain the maximum control of your life and learn how to best utilize the powers of astrology, we would recommend that you read our first book as well.)

Choosing a Perfect Day to Get Married

As we've mentioned, the stars give us signs to tell us the best time to do anything.

One set of criteria to be used in the choosing of a wedding date is Super Aspects. In *Astrology Really Works!*, we listed 12 aspects that we found to be SUPER ASPECTS. In chapter 5, we added three more. A Super Aspect is one that provides anyone or anything born with it the ability to get a jump-start on achieving super success and fame. Super Aspects work for people when we are born, and also for anything we natalize. In other words, Super Aspects work in Wedding Charts and business charts, but they are not all that are needed in these charts.

Super Aspects help us to make money and gain fame and power. We want marriages to have love and understanding, forgiveness, sharing, healthy and loving children, companionship we never get tired of, and a host of other wonderful attributes. Super Aspects do not necessarily help us attain any of this, but other aspects and certain Planetary Geometry do.

Similarly, in a business chart, in addition to profitability and success, we would hope for contented employees, a safe and tranquil work environment, the ability to be innovative and to lead, and many other positive things. Again, Super Aspects do not necessarily help us attain all of the above either, but other aspects and certain Planetary Geometry do.

For example, there is a particular aspect in a Wedding Chart that helps to bring healthy children to the marriage, and there is a particular aspect that helps a business to be humane and yet profitable. Believe it or not, there are even certain aspects under which you can begin a love affair and be almost certain that there will be no negative repercussions. (This is helpful if you only desire a fling.) There are also certain aspects that might lead you to a Fatal Attraction situation—the person will never go away. Obviously, you want to avoid those aspects. The reasons that some aspects have such influences is due to the angle of the aspects and the symbolisms of the planets that form the aspects. But there are other factors that weigh on how aspects are manifested. It is these other factors that we will discuss in this chapter.

Retrograde Motion and Bi-directional Aspects

A BI-DIRECTIONAL ASPECT is a planetary aspect that is formed by two planets that are moving in different directions. This distinction is most important in the longitudes, or Zodiac Sign Chart. Of course, most of us know that as the planets revolve around the Earth, they all move in the same direction around the Sun—always in the same direction. However, when viewed from the Earth, the planets can appear to be moving forwards or backwards. That's right—a planet can appear to be moving backwards. The apparent backward movement of a planet is caused by the same phenomenon that makes you think your car is going backwards when you stare at another car that has just passed you. When this occurs, that backward-"moving" planet is said to be in RETROGRADE MOTION. This condition is noted on all astrological charts with the letter *R*. Most of us have heard the familiar warning of astrologers: *Be careful, Mercury is in retrograde.*

When a planet is not in retrograde motion, it is said to be in DIRECT MOTION. In *Astrology Really Works!*, we explained that we do not have to be afraid of times when any planet is retrograde, including Mercury. In fact, even though planets spend less time in retrograde motion than in direct motion, there are more successful people with retrograde planets in their charts than those who do not have them—by a very wide margin. This is because an aspect that is formed by one planet in retrograde, and the other in direct motion, is more powerful than when both are direct—much more so.

To be able to refer to such aspects, the Magi Society has named them BI-DIRECTIONAL ASPECTS. Because of the way the planets move in the Earth sky, when there is a trine, it is usually a bi-directional aspect.

A bi-directional conjunction is very rare, but much more powerful than one that is not. Magic Johnson was born with a bi-directional conjunction of Mars and Venus signifying grace (Venus) of motion (Mars). He is the most graceful 6'9"-inch basketball player in history, so much so that he played the guard position, which needs the most grace.

There was a bi-directional conjunction of Mercury and Venus during the stock market crash of October 19, 1987. Guess what that was a sign of? It meant there would be news (Mercury) about money (Venus), and the world would be communicating (Mercury) about money (Venus). The crash was talked about all over the world. Astrology can be fascinating!

An aspect that is comprised of two planets that are both in direct motion is called a DOUBLE-DIRECT ASPECT, and an aspect that is comprised of two retrograde planets is called a DOUBLE RETROGRADE ASPECT. When the two planets that form an aspect are moving in the same direction, then we call the aspect a MONODIRECTIONAL ASPECT.

The main reason we explain this concept of bi-directional aspects is because for the purposes of Electional Astrology, it is an important criterion for judging if an aspect is favorable or unfavorable, and how strong it is. Bi-directional aspects are better than double-direct aspects if the aspect is turbulent (90 or 180 degrees) or quincunx (150 degrees), and a double-direct Turbulent Aspect is the worst type of aspect to include in a chart. So when you are looking for good days to begin something like a job or marriage, never choose a day that has a Turbulent Aspect that is double-direct. NEVER. Double-direct quincunxes are Turbulent Aspects.

What about the double retrograde aspects? When they are in enhancement, they are the best of all. But when they are turbulent, they are really turbulent; avoid these, also.

As an example of what we have been discussing, on October 1, 1907 (see page 244), a financial panic started that closed down some U.S. banks and started the depression of 1907–08. There were four turbulent monodirectional aspects on that day. It is very rare to have even two turbulent mono-direct aspects on a day. (When we say this, we are not including aspects to the Moon.)

If 1907 is too long ago for your memory, here is another example. There was a very unusual square of Uranus and Pluto that was a sign of the Great Depression—and the bottom of the U.S. stock market was only a few days from the formation of three double-direct squares. We are talking about July 15, 1932 (chart not shown), when the Sun and Pluto were in conjunction, and both were squared by Uranus, an obvious signal of the upcoming worldwide depression. In addition, this signification was reinforced by a Jupiter-Chiron square—all the squares were double-direct.

Where all of this becomes extremely helpful knowledge is when you are using Electional Astrology and choosing the best day to begin something important. Always avoid the monodirectional Turbulent Aspects. They usually do not last long, so you can wait for them to pass.

However, please bear in mind that all Personal Aspects are still gifts, even the monodirectional Turbulent Aspects. Thank God.

Applying Aspects and Separating Aspects

There is still another very important concept regarding aspects that we must now discuss. We have repeatedly emphasized that the more exact an aspect, the more powerful it is. This is always true. We just learned that double-direct aspects are also especially important. There is still another criterion that is useful in evaluating the relative power and importance of aspects. It is called APPLYING ASPECTS. Please look back at the chart of Hitler's birth on page 70 and focus on the most exact aspect, which was the Venus-Mars conjunction. Note the direction of movement of Hitler's natal

Venus and Mars. A planet that is retrograde moves clockwise on a chart, and a planet that is direct moves counterclockwise on a chart. When a planet is in direct motion, it moves from one degree to a *higher* degree. When a planet is in retrograde motion, it moves from one degree to a *lower* degree. When two planets form an aspect and both planets are moving toward each other, they are said to be APPLYING to each other. In describing Hitler's Venus-Mars aspect, astrologers refer to it by saying that Venus was APPLYING to natal Mars, meaning Venus was moving toward Mars. At the same time, Mars was applying to natal Venus. If Mars were moving away from the natal Venus, astrologers use the term SEPARATING and would say that Mars was separating from Venus.

In general, an applying aspect is more important than a separating one, but there is an important exception to this, and the exception is based on one of the many fascinating and unique concepts and tools of Magi Astrology. We are referring to the TIME ORB, which is a tool and concept that astrology has been in dire need of because it is an important step in advancing astrology to the New Age.

Time Orb

Before we explain *time orb,* we need to digress just a little and explain what astrologers mean when they use the term *"more exact aspect."* In the past, whenever astrologers have used that term, they always referred to the aspect that was closest to being exact when measured in degrees. For example, suppose astrologers are comparing two aspects, where aspect A is formed by a 117.5 degree angle, and aspect B is 118.5 degrees. In such a case, the orb of aspect A is 2.5 degrees (120 minus 117.5), and the orb of aspect B is 1.5 degrees (120 minus 118.5). In the past, astrologers have regarded the more exact aspect to be the aspect that has the smaller orb, as measured in *degrees.* In this case, it is aspect B.

This has been a useful criterion. There really is a hierarchy of the importance of aspects, and very exact aspects are usually more powerful than aspects with wide orbs. The smaller the orb of an aspect, the more powerful it is.

Usually. But not always.

At times, the exactness of an aspect has been a poor gauge of an aspect's level of influence. As it turns out, there are times when an aspect with a wider orb is actually more powerful than an aspect with a more exact orb. This happens most often when the two planetary aspects are formed by planets that move at very different speeds across the sky. All the planets

move at different speeds, and the speed of movement of the planets forming an aspect has an influence on the strength of the aspect.

There is a significant variation in the speed of the planets. The Moon
moves about 13 degrees each day and is by far the fastest-moving planet.
Mercury can move more than two degrees per day, whereas Pluto at its
fastest can barely move one degree in a month. Although the apparent
speeds of the movements of the planets vary from day to day, in general, the
FAST-MOVING PLANETS are the Moon, followed by Mercury, Venus,
Sun, and Mars. The SLOW-MOVING planets are Pluto, Neptune, Uranus,
Chiron, Saturn, and Jupiter. This variation in the speed of the planets
appeared to present itself for fruitful research, so the Magi Society concluded an extensive study that resulted in the following discovery:

***All planetary aspects are at their most powerful when
they are within three days of the time the aspect is exact,
regardless of the orb of the aspect.***

This means that besides the orb in degrees, there is another criterion to
judge the level of significance and power of an aspect. It means that an
aspect that is going to be exact three days from today is more powerful
today than an aspect that will be exact ten days from today, even if the second aspect has a more exact orb as measured in degrees. In this example,
we refer to the first aspect as having a TIME ORB of three days in terms of
DAYS UNTIL EXACTNESS. And the second aspect has a time orb of ten
days until exactness.

Whereas traditional astrology has limited its measurements of orbs to
only degrees, Magi Astrology has added the use of a time orb when analyzing which planetary aspects are the most important in any chart. The
time orb of a planetary aspect is the orb in time to exactness of the aspect;
it is not measured in degrees, but rather it is measured in time, so the parameters are days, hours, minutes, and so on. The orb that uses degrees is
specifically called the DISTANCE ORB because it is measured in degrees,
and a degree is a unit of space and distance. Since astrologers presently use
only the distance orb, we will just use the term *orb* when referring to it, and
the time orb will always include the word *time*.

The Magi Society's members' software has always included the time orb
of all aspects, and we have been researching time orbs since personal computers were first marketed in 1980. One result of this research is that we
now know that an aspect is at its most powerful when the time orb of the
aspect is within three days of time to exactness. (Aspects formed by the

Moon are an exception since the Moon moves so fast.) This means that an aspect formed by Neptune and Pluto is most powerful when the aspect is within a time orb of just three days, whether or not the aspect is applying or separating, and regardless of what the distance orb of the aspect is.

As another example, it also means that an aspect formed by the Sun and Pluto is at its most powerful when the aspect is within three days of being exact. This period of time from three days before an aspect is exact until three days after an aspect is exact is called the MAGICAL TIME of the aspect.

This is vital information for us to have and use when we are picking days to get married or to start a job or business. To maximize our chances of happiness and prosperity, we should choose days when the important aspects are in Magical Time, meaning within three days of time to exactness of the aspect. When an aspect is within its Magical Time, we simply refer to them as MAGICAL ASPECTS.

Aspects made by the slow-moving planets that are within Magical Time are the most powerful of the aspects. Such aspects foretell the highest level of athletic prowess. For example, Michael Jordan, Larry Bird, Julius Erving, Martina Navratilova, and Sergei Federov were all born with magical aspects formed by slow-moving planets.

We refer to our belief that all aspects are most powerful during its Magical Time as the THEORY OF MAGICAL TIME. This theory is so important that it is impossible to overstate its significance. This is because by applying this theory and other concepts of Magi Astrology, we have been able to formulate the earthshaking proof of the validity of astrology that is at the end of this book. Our next subject is TRANSITS.

Transits—a Fabulous Tool for Prediction

A TRANSIT is one of the most powerful tools available to astrologers. Transits and PROGRESSIONS are the two most important astrological methodologies for predicting the future. Have you ever wondered why:

- one day you're in love, but the next day you're about to kill each other? How could you have been so mistaken?

- sometimes your lover is so sweet that you are sure you're with the most caring and wonderful person in the world— you're perfect together. At other times, everything he or she does annoys you. How could you have been so mistaken?

- one day, the whole world loves you—life is fabulous. But the very next day, nothing is going right—*nothing!*

There is an astrological reason for all these wide swings in your life and relationships, and they are called TRANSITS. They influence our daily lives and impact the way we behave and the way people perceive us.

Have you ever wondered why nothing stays the same—*nothing!* It's because of transits.

As the planets move around and around in the Earth sky, they create transits and actually seem to have an effect on everything that happens on this planet. We know this is hard to accept. After all, Pluto is billions of miles away. How could it have any influence on our daily lives? Maybe they are just *signs* of another power or force or influence that we have no idea about. Let us explain what transits are.

Understanding Transits

To understand transits, please look at the Magi AstroChart of President Bill Clinton on page 165. He was born with the Sun at 26.1 degrees of Leo. This means that the natal position of his Sun is at 26.1 degrees of Leo. The natal positions of planets never change because they are the ones that existed at the time someone is born. But the planets keep moving in the sky. Whenever any planet in the sky makes one of the seven aspect-angles with the natal position of Bill's Sun, a TRANSIT of his Sun occurs and there will be a noticeable effect on him.

Transits can be so consequential that it is imperative to understand them. So let us go over this concept in more detail.

Since the actual planets in the sky are always in motion, all of the planets will move to a new position every hour, every minute, and every second. From time to time, on a regular basis, each planet in the sky will make an angle to the position of a natal planet such that the angle made will be considered meaningful by astrologers. Such an occurrence is called a TRANSIT. The angles that are considered meaningful angles by astrologers are the same angles as those that are interpreted to be meaningful because they form planetary aspects in a birth chart, and we are already familiar with these. For the longitudes, these angles are multiples of 30 degrees. These angles are 30 degrees, 60 degrees, 90 degrees, 120 degrees, 150 degrees, 180 degrees, and zero degrees. For declinations, transits occur when a planet in the sky is parallel or contra-parallel to any natal position of a planet.

Here is another example: If Venus is in two degrees Capricorn on a birth chart, then we say that the natal position of Venus is two degrees Capricorn. Then as Mars revolves around the Sun, every time Mars is in two degrees of any of the 12 signs, it is making a transit to the natal position of Venus in the birth chart, and Mars is creating a TRANSITING ASPECT to Venus. Mars is referred to as the TRANSITING PLANET or as TRANSITING Mars. Since any of the 11 moving planets can create a transit to any of the 11 natal positions of a birth chart, there can be quite a few transiting aspects at the same time.

That is how the transits work for the longitudes, but we also have transits for the declinations, and the principle is the same. A transit is made whenever a planet in motion is in the same degree as a natal planet's position. If Pluto is in eight degrees north declination at birth, then anytime one of the 11 moving planets passes eight degrees either north or south declination, a transit has occurred.

Astrologers believe that certain types of transiting aspects are good and helpful, while certain other types of transiting aspects are not so good and can be harmful. This is a subject that will be dealt with in detail in a subsequent book written by the Magi Society (entitled *Predict the Future Accurately Using Magi Astrology*). In this book, we will only briefly discuss the basics of transits.

Transits can be good or bad. The determining factors as to whether a particular transit is helpful or not include the angle of the transiting aspect, and which particular planet in the sky is creating the transit. Transits that are formed at enhancement angles are usually good, and transits that are created by the movement of Jupiter are also usually good. For example, when Jupiter makes an enhancement angle to one of our important natal planets, it cooperates with and helps that natal planet, and improves our lives in areas that are ruled by that natal planet. When Jupiter is trine to our Sun, everything that is ruled by the Sun is improved. The Sun rules the heart and our circulation system; our heart is stronger when Jupiter makes an enhancement angle to our Sun, and we are less susceptible to heart attacks during such transits. We also have more vitality.

On the other hand, *any* transit made by Saturn is a problem. It is a sign that the greatest care must be taken and that problems could come home to roost, particularly if the angle of the transiting aspect is a Turbulent Angle. Where this becomes critical information is in choosing a Wedding Chart or other crucial day to begin anything. ***Warning: You do not want to get married on a day when you have Saturn making any Turbulent Angles to any of your natal positions.*** If you do, you will preserve the negativity of

Saturn's influence into the Marriage Chart and feel it every day that you're married. The Theory of Natalization works with transiting aspects.

Another point to keep in mind when dealing with transits is that when Saturn is making Turbulent Angles to any person's critical natal positions, Saturn will put stress on that person and make the person show his/her bad side. So if you are in love with someone and cannot believe how inconsiderate your lover has been lately, check what the transits are to your lover's natal planets and see if that's the reason. It often is.

Transits at Work

Please take a look at the two charts on page 245. They show the second inaugurations of Presidents Nixon and Clinton. We have been saying all along that the first moment someone does something, the astrological chart of that moment is the chart of the activity. In the case of these two charts, they represent the second terms of both Nixon and Clinton and are the birth charts of those two presidencies. (Transits work on presidencies.)

In each chart, there is an extra symbol for Saturn, which is inside a box. This represents the position of transiting Saturn on a very critical day for the chart. In the case of Nixon's second term, the position of the transiting Saturn is where Saturn was on July 27, 1974, when the House Judiciary Committee approved two articles of impeachment against Nixon. In the case of Clinton's second term, the position of the transiting Saturn is that of Saturn on August 17, 1998, the day when Clinton had to make that speech admitting that he had an "inappropriate relationship" with Monica Lewinsky. Clinton apologized on national television, but the speech was a disaster and resulted in over 100 newspaper editorials across the country calling for his resignation.

As you can see, the position of transiting Saturn made three Turbulent Aspects in each chart. For Clinton's second term as president, Saturn was opposed to Chiron, quincunx to Pluto, and square to Sun. In the chart representing Nixon's second term, Saturn was opposed to Venus, square to Chiron, and quincunx to Mars. In both cases, the transiting Saturn was at the most critical weak point of the chart and was making the maximum number of Turbulent Aspects to crucial natal planets.

The point we are making is that we all need to be especially careful when transiting Saturn is making Turbulent Aspects to critical natal positions in our own charts. When this occurs, we call them TURBULENT TRANSITS BY SATURN. When we have them, even our friends will look at us through a microscope with inadequate light—they only see our worst side. During Turbulent Transits by Saturn, our judgment is at its worst, we are physically weakest, and any problems that have been looming come home to roost and are blown out of proportion. If we are in a good relationship with someone we love, Turbulent Transits by Saturn will put stress on that relationship. These are the times when you want to kill each other. Please do not do anything drastic during such times. Saturn is always moving and will move on.

So, we repeat, when the going gets tough, please check to see if you have Turbulent Transits by Saturn. If you do, please do your best to hold on to your love relationship, your job, and your friendships and wait for Saturn to pass—it *always* does. Afterwards, the Sun will shine again in your life. The way transits work, every bad period is always followed by a good one, so do not ever cave in. When you are having Turbulent Transits by Saturn, you will feel like your whole life has been turned upside down and nothing is going your way. But it will all pass. In the meantime, keep your head low, avoid confrontations, do not make any changes or major decisions, and grit it out. Then you will prevail. It's all in the stars. Everyone goes through such times—everyone. Even presidents, kings, and billionaires.

Most important: *When you have Turbulent Transits by Saturn to your natal planets, please do not get married or initiate any major project, such as a new job or business.* By initiating something, you natalize the Turbulent Transit, and it stays with you until you break what was initiated. Breaking off is sometimes a very difficult process. In the case of a marriage, breaking off requires a divorce.

So the next question is: When does a transit pass?

The Orb of a Transit

Astrologers generally use an orb for transits, just as they use an orb for aspects. The orb they use is plus or minus five degrees or so. In other words, astrologers tend to believe that if a planet is applying toward one of your natal planets (moving closer to an exact aspect-angle), the transiting planet's influence is able to be felt from the time the transiting planet is five degrees from your natal planet until the transiting planet has passed your natal planet by an angle of five degrees.

The Magi Society strongly disagrees with the plus and minus orb in transits. It has been our experience that a transit is active and effective only as the transiting planet is applying toward the natal planet up until the transiting angle is actually exact. The transit is not in effect very shortly after the passing of the transiting planet. Sometimes, if it is a negative transit, there will be what we will refer to as FALLOUT from the bad transit for a brief period, but we believe that all transits are complete, and peak at the time the transiting planet makes an exact aspect-angle to any natal planet. Once the transiting planet is moving away from an exact aspect-angle to a natal position, the transit itself no longer has any influence. So this means that usually you do not have to wait that long for a Turbulent Transit by Saturn to pass by.

Transits Can Help You Determine If You're About to Meet "the One"

When people are still single and dating, how many times do they say to themselves: *Tonight's the night—this will be different!*

Well, guess what? Transits can help us *know* if tonight is the night we will meet the *one*, or someone very significant in our lives.

Just as there are celestial signs of historical days of significance, there is also a sign for every major event in anyone's life, especially for the day we meet someone we're going to marry. Just as there are Romance Linkages and Cinderella Linkages, there are also ROMANCE TRANSITS and CINDERELLA TRANSITS. The Magi Society has done a great deal of research about this, and we were able to do so only because we have records of our members dating all the way back to 1625. Actual dates when two people meet are much harder to obtain than any other dates; the persons themselves often do not know the days they met. But of the ones that we know about, Romance and Cinderella Transits do work. In fact, Evita had both such transits when she met Peron. Bianca had both when she met Mick Jagger. Jacqueline had both when she met JFK. As usual, all such transits involve Chiron in one way or another.

For example, in Figure 12D on page 246, we gave you the natal chart of Evita, and added two planets in squares to the chart. These two planets represent the positions of Chiron and Pluto on the night she met Peron. Chiron was trine Evita's natal Sun, meaning that a marriage (Chiron) was coming to her (Sun); it was a sign that her destiny (Chiron) was coming to her (Sun). You can see how important it is for the planets to have consistent symbolisms. At the same time, Pluto was trine to her Chiron, meaning power (Pluto) would come to her by marriage (Chiron)! Transiting Pluto was also conjunct her natal Neptune, signifying that she would obtain powerful (Pluto) long-term security (Neptune). More important, Evita's

Neptune and Chiron form her Cinderella aspect, and Pluto was transiting the aspect, making her really a powerful (Pluto) Cinderella (the Chiron-Neptune aspect)!

Similar transits were occurring for Bianca when she met Mick Jagger. On page 246, Figure 12E, we have Bianca's natal chart with transiting Pluto, Chiron, and Mars for the day she met Mick. Again, we have transiting Pluto making an enhancement angle to natal Chiron, which is the same transit that occurred for Evita when she met Peron. In addition, Bianca's natal Pluto was transited by Chiron, which formed a trine foretelling of power from marriage and a powerful spouse! At the same time, transiting Mars was trine to Bianca's natal Sun, meaning a man (Mars represents the man in a relationship) was coming to her (Sun).

Unfortunately, this subject is more complicated than anything we have been dealing with in this book and will require over a hundred pages to properly teach it. Therefore, this subject will be one of the subjects of our next book. The reason such matters are more complex is that each person has different transits each day. Your transits for any time will be different from anyone else's transits for that same time, and your transits are constantly changing. There are also PROGRESSIONS (something we dealt with in *Astrology Really Works!*) which are even more powerful than transits. The transits and the progressions signal the ups and downs in everyone's life. Every up and down has a sign, and is predictable in the stars.

Transits Also Help You Discern When You're Most Sexual or Romantic

Learning about transits can be fabulously helpful in daily matters of love. Transits can be used to choose your best days to make love because they control the level of both your sexuality and your sensuality. As an example, when transiting Venus is trine to your natal Mars, your level of sexuality is very high. You will feel strong and energetic, and you will want to enjoy sex; you will also be capable of enjoying more repeated sessions of sex. As another example, when transiting Venus is trine someone's Neptune, that person's level of sensuality and romanticism will be very high. The person will be more romantic, and more capable of long-lasting, supersensual lovemaking. We know many of you want a chapter on this subject, but it is quite complex, and requires several new concepts, so we will deal with all of it in our next book.

We Have Tightened the Orb of Declinational Aspects

In our first book, we used a different orb for Super Aspects than the orb we have been using in this one. The orb in the longitudes has been the same in both books, but we tightened the orb in the declinations from 2.2 degrees to only 1.2 degrees.

We had always explained that the more exact any aspect is, the more powerful it is. By tightening the declinational orb, what we really did was raise the standards of qualification for an aspect. Even though a parallel or contra-parallel of two planets has an effect at 2.2 degrees (our original orb), the effect of the aspect is not very strong unless it is within the 1.2-degree orb. By now, you know that you can acquire Super Aspects that you were not born with, which is very encouraging to those who were not born with the Super Aspects that they wish they had. When we wrote our first book, we did not want readers to feel discouraged if they found out they were not born with Super Aspects, so the Magi Society decided that for the purposes of that first book, we would choose to use the widest possible valid orb. By doing so, it maximized the number of our readers who were born with Super Aspects. The result was that there would be the fewest number of people who would feel that they had no Super Aspects. We painstakingly explained in the book that astrology was a Benevolent Design and a gift, not a chain or albatross around anyone's neck.

But now, by revealing that you can acquire Super Aspects through linkages, nobody should be discouraged by a lack of Super Aspects in their birth chart. Everyone should realize that they have hope for enough success so that they can give their loved ones the financial security they need. They can always acquire Super Aspects that they do not have through partners and Golden Linkages, or an auspiciously chosen business or wedding day. For this reason, we have tightened the orb for declinational aspects for this book and now use the 1.2-degree orb, which has always been the one we preferred.

Multiple-Planet Aspects Are More Specific in Power

In our second book, the *Magi Society Ephemeris*, we introduced the astrological community to two of the many secrets of Magi Astrology: Magi Quads and Midpoint Crossings. Abbreviated MQs and MDXs, they are multiple-planet aspects. In the past, astrologers who used aspects focused their attention on aspects formed by just two planets, but we have seen in this book that Planetary Geometry of three or more planets, such as the Grand Trine and the Yod, deserve even more attention and have more power than aspects of just two planets. In the same way, multiple-planet aspects are more important than aspects of just two planets when it comes to defining a particular area of talent. In addition, multiple-planet aspects give us a more specific clue as to what our best talents and abilities are. An aspect of just two planets has a more general range of interpretation, but aspects comprised of three or more planets are able to pinpoint a very particular ability and talent.

Magi Quads and Midpoint Crossings are very powerful, but they are an esoteric and advanced part of astrology. If you plan to be a serious student of astrology, we advise you to learn about them. We will not go into them here because they are fully explained in the *Magi Society Ephemeris.* But it is MQs and MDXs that truly define why Microsoft is the leader in computer software and not other areas of computers, and why IBM is the leader in mainframe computers but not personal computers. They also explain why most supermodels are not successful in the acting field. MQs and MDXs are crucial when choosing a date to start a business.

ॐ   ॐ   ॐ

We have briefly touched upon some of the most important criteria that need to be taken into account in Electional Astrology and other areas as well. Ideally, we should take into account everything we discussed in this chapter when evaluating the strengths and weaknesses of any specific day that we select to commence something of great consequence, such as a marriage, job, or partnership. Some of you will think Electional Astrology is bewildering, and some will think it is a snap. We hope those of you who think it is simple will apply it and fulfill your dreams. But we hope that those of you who think Electional Astrology is too complicated will take the *time* to learn it because time is all that is needed. It is really not complicated, so please don't be discouraged. Astrology is a tool such that once we learn it, we can take it out at any time, use it, and apply it to our lives to better ourselves and our circumstances. It is worth every hour and day you devote to learning it.

We promise—it's in the stars.

ॐ   ॐ   ॐ

It Is Vital to Understand the Symbolisms of Magi Astrology

As the examples in this book would indicate, it's very important to master the symbolisms of Magi Astrology. Symbolisms are like definitions. Just as no one can understand a language without knowing the definitions of the words of the language, it is really not possible to interpret planetary aspects, linkages, transits, or Planetary Geometry without knowing the symbolisms of the planets. For this reason, we are going to devote the next few chapters to symbolisms. At the same time, we will be introducing new concepts and revisiting some we have already discussed in order to clarify them to make certain our readers understand them.

Figure 12A: Financial panic of 1907 began 10/1/1907

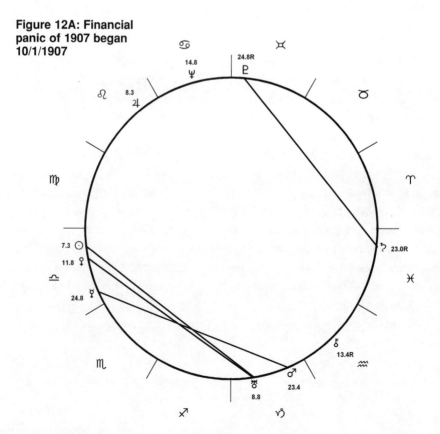

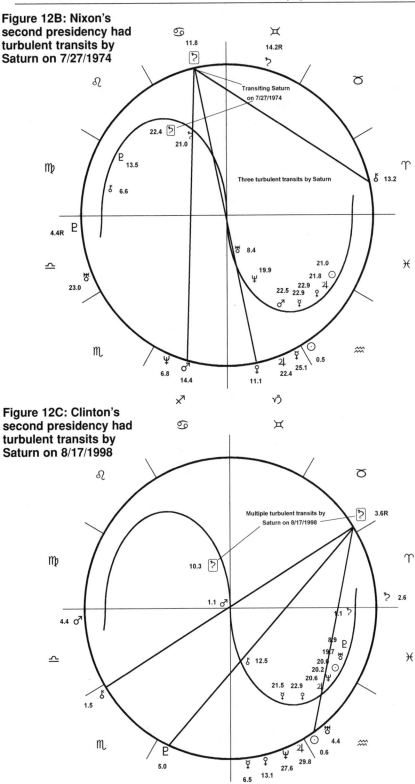

Figure 12B: Nixon's second presidency had turbulent transits by Saturn on 7/27/1974

Figure 12C: Clinton's second presidency had turbulent transits by Saturn on 8/17/1998

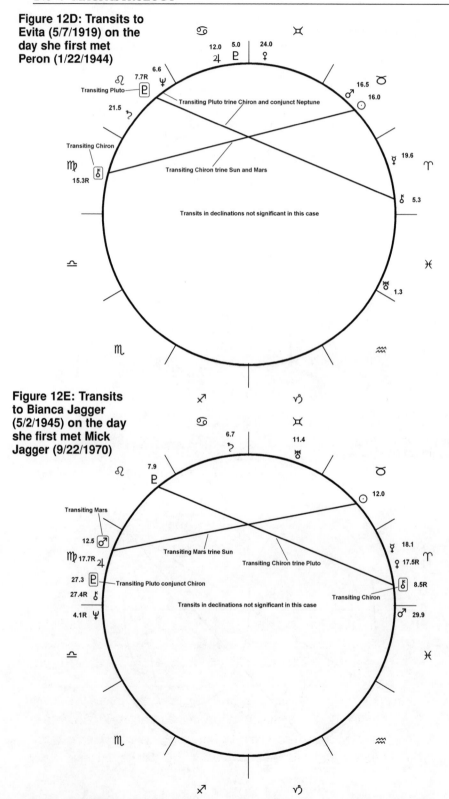

Figure 12D: Transits to Evita (5/7/1919) on the day she first met Peron (1/22/1944)

Transiting Pluto trine Chiron and conjunct Neptune

Transiting Chiron trine Sun and Mars

Transits in declinations not significant in this case

Transiting Pluto

Transiting Chiron

Figure 12E: Transits to Bianca Jagger (5/2/1945) on the day she first met Mick Jagger (9/22/1970)

Transiting Mars

Transiting Mars trine Sun

Transiting Chiron trine Pluto

Transiting Pluto conjunct Chiron

Transiting Chiron

Transits in declinations not significant in this case

CHAPTER THIRTEEN

Planets Have Personalities and Symbolisms

At one time or another, you may have wondered:

- Will this person be faithful to me, or will I be heartbroken beyond my ability to cope?

- Is this person the settle down-and-marry kind, or the play-the-field, game-playing type?

- Can I trust the person I'm with, or is there deception behind the smooth talk and charming smile?

- How can I tell if someone has a violent temper and can actually be a dangerous date to go out with?

- What are the chances that someone will act completely different once I know him or her better?

- Can this person truly love unselfishly, and is he or she capable of undying love?

These questions can be answered by mastering the symbolisms of Magi Astrology and using them to interpret the planetary aspects that someone is born with. Each aspect is a celestial mini-sign of what they were like in previous lives.

With Magi Astrology, we have the powerful keys that unlock the secrets of a person's probable true personality and inner tendencies. The basic tools of Magi Astrology that answer such questions are the planetary aspects that a person is born with, and appropriate symbolisms to interpret these aspects. Obviously, the precision of our interpretations is totally dependent on the accuracy of our symbolisms.

As we already mentioned, astrology is only as useful as the precision, consistency, and breadth of its symbolisms. After centuries of record keeping and analysis, and recent decades of intensive and devoted work, the Magi Society has developed a set of symbolisms that provide remarkably accurate interpretations. With these symbolisms, we can accurately assess the range of the probable manifestations of any planetary aspect.

Planets Have Personalities

The symbolisms of the planets are like the definition of words in that each has its own special connotation. However, symbolisms are much more complex than words and their definitions. Unlike words, each symbolism must always be applied in association with the character and nature of each planet. Every planet has its own PLANETARY PERSONALITY and puts its own spin or bias to everything it has rulership over. It is not possible to fully understand the significance of any symbolism without having mastery of the personalities of all of the planets. We have written these next few chapters to help you understand the personality of each planet. With this knowledge, you will be able to use each planet's symbolisms to obtain a much more elevated understanding and deeper insight into the natal planetary aspects of the important persons in you life, as well as anyone else you're interested in. Through knowledge of Planetary Personalities, you will also be much better equipped to use Electional Astrology to do something really significant, such as getting married or starting a job.

We explained previously that it's useful to view every planet as being masculine, feminine, or neutral. For example, Venus is feminine and rules seduction and lovemaking, whereas Pluto is masculine and rules the sex act itself. From this information, we should have more insight into why women often prefer seduction and foreplay over the sex act, whereas the man generally favors bypassing the seduction and foreplay process in order to get right into the sex act. However, there are men who have certain aspects that make them enjoy and prefer the slow approach just as much as a woman. For example, a man with a Venus-Neptune aspect is eager for long-lasting (Neptune) and sensual (Neptune) lovemaking (Venus). This aspect is made of two feminine planets! On the other hand, men with Mars-Pluto are quickest on the draw. This aspect is a sexual one, but its influence is sexual in terms of frequency of desire and the ability to perform frequently, rather than on the quality of lovemaking.

See how the personality of a planet can be a sign of the personality behind a planetary aspect? We will include personality traits in our discussion of the symbolisms of the planets.

Planets Have Symbolisms

There are thousands of things that need to have symbolisms, but there are only 11 planets. Therefore, as we explained in chapter 4, each planet has many symbolisms. We will be exploring the entire boundaries of the symbolisms that we believe are valid. Some symbolisms will relate to the character and nature of a person; others help us understand emotional and physical ties as used in Planetary Linkages. We will also include the important symbolisms of the planets, which will help you understand a person's capabilities and talents, and assist you in interpreting aspects in matters of financial and business astrology.

Once you master this knowledge and the techniques of combining and integrating the symbolisms of planets that form aspects, you will have a precise understanding of the true character and nature of anyone whose birth date is known to you. You will also be able to better harness the power of planetary aspects through natalization, and be able to choose days with the best aspects for initiating new endeavors.

But before we begin, it's important to realize that the symbolisms of the planets are not set in stone. The symbolisms we ascribe to each planet can, and probably will, change—but only a little. The Magi Society has been testing symbolisms since 1625, so we believe any future changes will not be substantive. We are highly confident that the symbolisms we are providing you are truly accurate, or at worst, will need only fine-tuning. Nevertheless, as we continue our research, we will discover new symbolisms of each planet and will reveal them to you in subsequent books.

Most astrology books deal with the symbolisms of the planets, but almost all of these books merely provide a long list of symbolisms, expecting the reader to accept the proposed symbolisms on faith. Generally, the authors seem to expect us to memorize tedious lists of unrelated words that they pass off as planetary symbolisms. They do not feel compelled to help us understand why any of the symbolisms were valid. We will take a different approach.

If a symbolism we ascribe to a planet is both a classic symbolism and accepted by the vast majority of astrologers, we may sometimes list it without comment, but at other times, we will comment on it in a way that will help you to understand why the symbolism makes sense and fits the planet. We will also be providing you with some symbolisms that are new, or ones that are quite different from those that are generally used by astrologers. When this occurs, we will usually give you some good reasons for accepting the symbolisms we're introducing. In addition, we will explain how each planet's personality reflects on its symbolisms.

We hope that this technique will be adopted by other astrologers when they write about symbolisms. Astrologers have taken too much liberty when drawing up lists of symbolisms, or what they sometimes call "key words." Too often, there is inconsistency, contradiction, and not enough backup. Symbolisms are too important to be dealt out like a deck of cards.

We will add one more twist to the way we are going to write these chapters on symbolisms. As we discuss the symbolisms of the planets, we will teach you how to use them to interpret planetary aspects and also teach you more about other related areas of astrology.

As you read the next few chapters about the planets' symbolisms, please keep in mind that some of the symbolisms we gave you earlier in chapter 4 will not be repeated here. There is no need for pure duplication. The following chapters on symbolisms are meant to provide you a depth of understanding about the personality of a planet, and how this influences the way symbolisms should be used in interpretations. It is with this added understanding of the symbolisms of the planets that you will also attain a deeper and clearer understanding of how each natal aspect influences those that are important to you. In the process, you will also have a much greater understanding of what someone is like, and how best to deal with the person on all issues of love and money.

Symbolisms of Mars, the Very Masculine Planet of the Warrior

Mars is the most masculine of the planets. It is aggressive and bold, brave and unflinching, action oriented rather than emotional or cerebral. It is also the most decisive planet. Mars is never short of initiative or the determination to carry through. Ancient Babylonian astrologers attributed the symbolisms of war and the warrior to the planet Mars; so did the Greeks and Romans. After all, in Roman mythology, Mars is the god of war. These ancient astrologers were amazingly accurate because Mars does actually rule war, has a temper, and a violent nature. Mars also symbolizes the intrinsic characteristics of war and the warrior, such as aggression, warlike behavior, anger, destruction, and brutality. And, Mars rules the tools of the warrior, such as guns, swords, armor, ammunition, tanks, and so on.

Going to war and doing battle is obviously dangerous and often results in sudden losses. Since accidents also result in sudden losses, Mars is attributed with the rulership of accidents, sudden losses due to accidents, war, and warlike behavior.

There are many other symbolisms for Mars, but it has the most limited range of symbolisms. So far, we have discussed the influences of Mars that can be the most problematic, but every planet is symbolic of some things that are very beneficial and essential to life. For instance, we already learned that Mars rules all forms of energy.

Mars rules muscles and energy and is therefore the most important planet for athletics—even more so since Mars also symbolizes competition, the competitive spirit, and competitiveness. It is Mars that provides the "never say die" attitude. As ruler of the muscles, Mars also imparts stamina; and Mars has dominion over motion, movement, and activities that require motion, such as dancing, ballet, gymnastics, and of course, all forms of athletics; Mars governs action, initiative, the willingness to take action, and the ability to resist intrusion (including emotional intrusions). In this regard, Mars represents the ability to defend, as well as the ability to attack and be offensive.

Because Mars rules muscles and energy, Mars is symbolic of the body and the use of the body. This means that Mars symbolizes physical work and professions that are body intensive, such as lumberjacking, bricklaying, carpentry, and construction. Along with Neptune, Mars co-rules farming. Neptune rules everything that grows from the ground, so Neptune's spin on farming is using the ground to grow food. Mars' spin on farming is the use of the body to perform the actual acts required to farm the land.

Mars Aspects Are a Sign of Possible Belligerence

Although Mars possesses symbolisms that are not related to aggression and war, we are going to focus on the belligerent nature of Mars for a few pages because we want to teach you what we believe could be a very important, possibly invaluable, lesson—especially for you readers who are single women. We want to help you figure out ahead of time if someone you just met might possess a tendency to become physically abusive and could have a violent temperament. After all, you would not want to become involved with an Adolf Hitler or Joseph Goebbels. In fact, we will use these two wretched men as examples, along with two of their equally evil accomplices: Heinrich Himmler and Hermann Göring. For those of you who have forgotten, Goebbels (born 10/29/1897) was Hitler's head of the Gestapo, Himmler (11/7/1900) was head of the SS, and Göring (1/12/1893) was the chief of staff of the German armed forces under Hitler's dictatorship. Göring also ran the infamous concentration camps.

All four of these despicable individuals were born with the very same planetary aspect, which was a sign of their tendency toward violence and war crimes, as well as their proclivity for belligerent behavior. (In the rest of this book, we will be referring to many examples of persons whose birth charts will not be provided due to space limitations. However, we will always give you the relevant details of their Planetary Geometry, and we will always provide their birth dates.)

All four of these men were born with an enhancement of Mars and Chiron. By using the rule of interpreting enhancement aspects, we can interpret this aspect to be representative of noteworthy (Chiron) belligerency (Mars) and brutality (Mars), or being noteworthy because of war—which they all were. It's also indicative of a career (Chiron) and destiny (Chiron) of war (Mars) and violence (Mars). Here are the precise angles of their Mars-Chiron enhancements:

- Hitler was born with an exact parallel of Mars and Chiron.

- Goebbels was born with both a parallel (0.9 degrees) and a wide conjunction. This is a planetary eclipse of Chiron and Mars and is the equivalent of one superstrong aspect of Chiron and Mars because of the principle of cumulative effects.

- Himmler has a strong, close-to-exact aspect of Mars trine Chiron.

- Göring has a strong, again close-to-exact aspect of Mars parallel to Chiron.

All of this is not a coincidence. The odds against any four persons randomly having such exact enhancement aspects of Mars and Chiron are higher than ten million to one.

We should emphasize the extreme significance of Hitler's exact parallel of Mars and Chiron. We have repeatedly explained that the more exact an aspect is, the more important the aspect. There are no exceptions to this rule. An exact parallel or conjunction is the strongest possible aspect. In chapter 4, we pointed out that Hitler had another almost exact aspect of Mars; his Venus was almost exactly conjunct to Mars. The Venus-Mars aspect can symbolize desire (Venus) for aggression (Mars) or love of war and brutality! So Hitler had two almost exact aspects involving Mars—the planet that rules war, aggression, brutality, belligerence, and weapons. How amazingly prescient astrology can be when you know how to apply it!

Even more amazing, all four of these warmongers were born with another aspect of Mars in addition to their Mars-Chiron enhancement.

- Goebbels had Mars quincunx Pluto (just 0.9 degrees from exact), which for him clearly signified his obsessive (Pluto) brutality (Mars).

- Himmler was born with Mars contra-parallel Sun; this aspect can represent a person (Sun) of war (Mars) and is only 0.7 degrees from exact.

- Göring was born with a nearly exact aspect of Mars quincunx Uranus; this aspect was a sign that Göring had the desire to bring war to the world (Uranus).

- We already know about Hitler's Venus-Mars conjunction.

The odds against any four persons randomly having such exact aspects of Mars and Chiron, and each such person also having another nearly exact aspect to Mars as they did, are higher than *100 billion* to one. The reason we point this out is to impress upon you that planetary aspects are accurate signs of the most significant aspects of the native's personality. It also means that the stated symbolisms of Mars are correct.

By the way, on the day Hitler became chancellor of Germany, there were also two exact aspects to Mars. Besides the Venus-Mars trine, there was a Mars-Uranus quincunx that was almost exact, and was symbolic of worldwide (Uranus) war! Both of these aspects also foretold that Hitler would plunge the world into a devastating war.

From what we've just discussed, we should all be convinced that every planetary aspect is a celestial sign of something uncommon about a person. We believe that God designed astrology such that the aspects are a reflection of what each of us has been in the most recent previous life. However, God designed the system of astrology so perfectly that it is also a way to help each of us improve ourselves. As we explained earlier, to the Magi Society, every single planetary aspect that we are born with is a divine gift of a special talent. Besides being a sign of the soul, God designed the aspects to give us a particular skill and ability. We can each improve ourselves by upgrading from one interpretation of an aspect to a better one.

Hitler certainly did not have to choose the abhorrent path of destruction, war, mass extermination, and infamy he took. There are innumerable other paths that he could have taken. The only limitation is that he was able to be most successful by being a person who would fit the symbolisms of his natal planetary aspects—but that gave him a very wide range of choices.

Hitler could not have been an opera singer or a scientist; he didn't have the planetary aspects (talents) for those professions. Nevertheless, Hitler could have chosen to promote the manifestation of his Venus conjunction of Mars by having love (Venus) of athletics (Mars) instead of war because Mars symbolizes athletics as well as war. He also could have made money (Venus) from sports (Mars). This same aspect could have made him a person with grace (Venus) of motion (Mars) so that he could have been successful at anything that requires this talent. This is because Venus symbolizes grace as well as desire, and one of the symbolisms of Mars is motion. Or, Hitler could have made his Venus-Mars aspect be manifested as beautiful (Venus) muscles (Mars), or succeed in a profession that required an attractive body.

The Venus-Mars conjunction also would be a helpful aspect to anyone who worked at a factory assembly line, of which there were many in Hitler's lifetime. This is because grace of motion gives a person the coordination and body grace needed to be a proficient assembly-line worker.

Another alternative for Hitler could have been to take advantage of the Venus-Mars conjunction ability to provide the native with boundless energy from which to draw vitality. This is because Venus is a benefic, like Jupiter, and as a benefic, Venus can simply provide bountifully and enhance the symbolisms of whatever planet matches degrees with itself. So the Venus-Mars aspect could mean bountiful (Venus) energy (Mars). In fact, this is the way most people born with the Venus-Mars aspect have chosen to use the aspect. Examples of this are Mick Jagger and Senator Bill Bradley. They were born just two days apart, and both have the Venus-Mars enhancement aspect. Mick Jagger uses it to provide him with the vitality to perform energetically on stage, as well as drawing from the aspect to obtain sexy (Venus) and eye-pleasing (also Venus) body movements (Mars). Bill Bradley used the aspect first to obtain great grace of motion and boundless energy to help him win two world championships as a basketball player. Then he drew on the energy the aspect provides to help him win three grueling campaigns for the U.S. Senate in New Jersey.

The most common results of the Venus-Mars enhancements are grace of motion and love of sex. In *Astrology Really Works!*, we devoted a whole chapter to the fact that a significant percentage of the best professional athletes were born with the Venus-Mars enhancement, including Michael Jordan, Magic Johnson, Nolan Ryan, Sandy Koufax, Mario Lemieux, and Bobby Orr. There is equally convincing data to support the belief that love of sex is also signified by the Venus-Mars aspect.

We hope that the above examples help you understand the range of interpretations that are both acceptable and correct in astrology, and the wide range of special abilities that a person can obtain with any one specific planetary aspect.

Our main point is that no one, not Hitler or anyone else, is limited or doomed to any particular manifestation of a planetary aspect. One of the many things that went wrong with Hitler is that he always took the easy route. He found that it was easy for him to be looked upon as a leader if he espoused hatred of Jews. It was horribly wrong, but he did not care about right or wrong, so Hitler chose to be immoral. Each time he made the wrong choice, he made it harder for himself to make the correct choice the next time.

This is one of the many reasons why moral teachings are important, and why Judeo-Christian values and ethics are essential to civilization. Too many people believe that ethics and morals are relative, but they are not. There is a right and a wrong way to do everything, and that never changes—no matter what alignments are in the stars.

God designed astrology to make each aspect both a reflection of our souls and a gift of a special talent and ability, so it is important that we make the most of each gift. In order to do so, we need to control any negative tendencies that we may have. The more we are able to suppress these tendencies, the better we can utilize the gift of the aspect and convert it into a special ability and talent. That is how we can become as successful as possible.

All of us go through periods in our lives when we find it is harder to overcome negative influences, but we can always succeed in doing so if we ask God for help.

In analyzing any chart, it is also necessary to understand the concept called ASPECT INTEGRATION, which is a Magi Astrology principle that states that no single aspect is so important that it dominates and controls the whole birth chart; instead, it is the sum total of the blending of all natal aspects that reflects the whole personality and character of the individual. This makes sense, because sometimes, one aspect cancels out another! Since all of us can use every aspect to help us obtain a special talent, and since we all have at least half a dozen aspects, we are all capable of greatness. What more could we ask for?

Symbolisms for Venus

Venus was the Roman goddess of beauty and seduction. How right those ancient Romans were. The planet Venus is very feminine and governs the female sex drive, intimacy, and the joyous exhilaration that comes with rapturous, slow lovemaking. Mars is too quick and impatient to enjoy it.

Two of the most important symbolisms of Venus are beauty and money. To the most idealistic of you, we apologize if linking money with beauty offends you a little. We know that some of you probably don't think that beauty and money should be tied together by the same planet. However, astrology's symbolisms are consistent and reflect the reality of life, and the fact is that a person who possesses great beauty is much more likely to also possess money than the hunchback of Notre Dame, Humpty Dumpty, or someone who looks like the wicked witch of the West. It is society, and not astrology, that has made beauty an accepted coin of the realm. Therefore, it makes sense that the planet that rules beauty also rules money.

But wait! One of the features about the symbolisms of Magi Astrology is how incredibly true-to-life Magi symbolisms are, especially when we dig deep into them. For example, just as the physical beauty that Venus symbolizes is not permanent, neither is the money that Venus rules! In other words, the possessions that are ruled by Venus are not of the more permanent variety, but rather, they are of the kind that can be lost, just like physical beauty. Venus does not rule assets that last for decades, such as land or property, minerals in the ground, patents or copyrights, or any artistic talent (something we usually have for a lifetime), which can provide us with money. This is because such assets have some longevity, and are therefore ruled by Neptune, which is the planet that rules long-term assets of all kinds. Neptune also rules long-term beauty (meaning the inner beauty of the soul), a charming personality, and the ability to be ageless in appearance. It is important to understand this.

Other important symbolisms of Venus include fashion and style, grace, and anything that is pleasing to the eye, such as jewelry.

But there are symbolisms of Venus that run deeper than the eye can see. On an emotional level, Venus is the ruler of desire and affections and infatuation and attraction (which is related to the beauty that Venus rules). Venus has dominion over adoration, emotional intimacy, attachment, desire, and infatuation, but in Magi Astrology, Venus does not rule love. This is because we at the Society are idealistic and think that love is forever. Nothing with Venus is forever, though. Venus is a very fast-moving planet and has a whimsical nature. Neptune rules love because love is long term, and

Neptune is ruler of everything that is long term.

However, because most of us have been mistaken about love, we will sometimes use the word *love* as a symbolism of Venus—but only when it comes to matters that have nothing to do with undying emotional love. For example, in Hitler's natal aspect of Venus conjunct to Mars, we will interpret this aspect to mean "love of war" even though it is not really *love*.

Venus also rules charm, enchantment, the ability to act seductively, allure, enticement. It is Venus that rules the actual act of making love, as opposed to the sex act, which is ruled by Pluto; and as opposed to the act of procreation, which is governed by Neptune. This is an example of how the planets' symbolisms look at the purpose and intent of an activity to determine which planet is ruler.

Venus has dominion over physical and sexual attraction, with the emphasis on the word *attraction*. Mars rules sexual attraction with the emphasis on the word *sexual*. This is an example of another important principle of Magi Astrology called FRATERNAL SYMBOLISMS.

Fraternal Symbolisms

No two planets have the same symbolism; and each and every symbolism of a planet is consistent with all of the other symbolisms of the same planet. However, since life is very complicated, and many parts of life overlap, the boundaries of a planet's symbolisms will also necessarily border the symbolisms of another planet, sometimes with a slight overlap. An example of this concept is that, as mentioned above, Venus rules sexual attraction with the emphasis on the word *attraction*, while Mars rules sexual attraction with the emphasis on the word *sexual*. This is a perfect example of how fraternal symbolisms play out. Two planets can actually have the same symbolism, as expressed in words. Both Mars and Venus rule "sexual attraction," but there is always a difference between the full meaning of the symbolisms of two different planets. And you can only understand this when you know the personality of the planets.

In Magi Astrology, we refer to this principle of symbolisms seemingly overlapping as FRATERNAL SYMBOLISMS, a term we borrowed from fraternal twins.

♉ ♉ ♉

Continuing on with the symbolisms of Venus: It also rules victory in war! At first glance, this is a strange symbolism to attribute to Venus. When we mentioned this in our first book, it raised the eyebrows of some noted astrologers, but when you think about it, it makes perfect sense. Can you guess why?

We have all heard the phrase "to the victor go the spoils." Such thinking goes back to the days when victorious armies plundered the riches of the kingdom that they just vanquished. So in those bad old days, victory in war meant acquiring riches and possessions—all of which are symbolisms of Venus. So, Venus is related to booty and what is gained from victory in war. Ah-ha! For that reason, Venus symbolizes victory in war. But remember, what an army wins can be lost in the next battle. That, too, is representative of Venus because of the fleeting nature of the "riches" that Venus rules.

✲ ✲ ✲

Along these same lines, there is a symbolism of Mars we did not want to introduce in the Mars section. We needed to wait until after the last few paragraphs. One of the worst symbolisms of Mars is that of rape. Unfortunately, everything—even the action of rape—has a planet that is symbolic of it. Besides the obvious association of rape to some of the other rulerships that Mars has, the reason Mars is symbolic of rape is also because in the bad old days, soldiers were the ones who perpetrated the most rapes—especially those soldiers who were victorious in war. We're sorry we have to bring this subject up, but knowing this information might one day help you female readers avoid such a horrifying and traumatic experience.

You see, men with strong aspects of Mars are the ones who are most susceptible to sexual urges, and they are the most aggressive men. Our advice to our female readers is to not invite such a man up for a nightcap unless you are willing to become intimate with him—or unless you have come to know him quite well and are sure that he has advanced beyond this part of the personality of a Mars aspect. The vast majority of men are trustworthy in this regard, but there are those who are not, and they usually have a strong Mars aspect. If you meet such a man, watch for signs and warnings as to whether or not he has learned to control and overcome overly aggressive impulses.

✲ ✲ ✲

Venus is ruler of the unification act in all manners of unifying—not just lovemaking, but also partnerships, mergers and acquisitions; and the uniting of countries, ideas, religions, and anything that can be united.

Because of Venus's rulership of the unification process, most astrologers have given Venus the symbolism of marriage and weddings. Although the boundaries appear blurry, nonetheless, there is no question from our research data that the unification of two people in a marriage is the dominion of Chiron, and not Venus. This is another example of fraternal symbolisms. However, astrologers had labored without Chiron for 10,000 years, so it is understandable to make this misjudgment. Here again, we have fraternal symbolisms. Chiron rules the unification of two persons in a marriage with the emphasis on marriage; Venus rules the unification of two persons in a marriage with the emphasis on unification.

Symbolisms of Jupiter

Jupiter represents wisdom, prayers answered, service to a higher order, morality, willingness to make sacrifices, unselfishness, and justice. It is neither feminine nor masculine, and prefers equality, helping the oppressed, and fighting for what it believes in.

Even a novice of astrology knows that the ancient Babylonian astrologers categorized Jupiter as a benefic, meaning that Jupiter brought good fortune, success, and the horn of plenty. The Babylonians were correct. Here are other symbolisms for Jupiter that are equally valid:

- Jupiter symbolizes forgiveness, compassion, benevolence, tolerance, hope, optimism, wisdom, knowledge, truth, success, good fortune, peace and peacemaking, help and the act of giving, and protection and the act of being both an ally and defender. Jupiter also bestows supremacy, superior talents, divine gifts, and in that vein, Jupiter symbolizes ELEVATED LEVELS of whatever is ruled by the planet that Jupiter makes an aspect with.

Quite a planet, but there's even more.

- Jupiter is representative of optimism, good judgment, wisdom, good old common sense, and true genius. It is also symbolic of divine revelations, the Judeo-Christian religions and the Providence represented by them, life-giving forces, protection and protectors of all kinds, morality, and the willingness to fulfill a promise or responsibility. Jupiter signifies banks and whatever is related to banking (such as the lending of money), foundations and charities, laws and judges—but not attorneys (which is symbolized by Saturn), publishing and knowledge, and the clergy.

Most astrology books attribute Jupiter with the symbolism of expansion, but we find that Jupiter is more discriminating than that. A lot can be learned about the planet from an analysis of transits by Jupiter. In transits, it is clear that Jupiter signifies expansion only when expansion is helpful, and Jupiter signifies contraction only when contraction is helpful. In other words, Jupiter is *helpful*. An enhancement transit of Jupiter to natal Sun brings blood pressure to normal; if the pressure is too high, Jupiter lowers it, and if the pressure is too low, it raises it. In such ways, each planet is actually intelligent. That is why astrology must be benevolently designed and maintained in that way by Providence. And that is another symbolism of Jupiter—it signifies God and Providence in the benevolent reality.

Symbolisms of the Sun

The Sun symbolizes the subject of the birth chart. Anything and everything has a birth chart, and the Sun represents it, whatever it is. Usually, the Sun represents the person, entity, event, or the day itself. The Sun can symbolize a marriage, a corporation, a country, or even a beginning and an end. The Sun can be symbolic of a relationship, too. The birth chart of the day you meet anyone is the birth chart of your relationship with that person, unless you marry the person or formalize a partnership in some other way, such as a legal partnership agreement, or making love. Once you do that, both birth charts are valid and work at the same time.

Like Jupiter, the Sun is neither feminine nor masculine; it is the most neutral of the planets and actually is the only planet that has no personality whatsoever because of its neutrality..

The Sun rules the heart, the circulation system, vitality, and the life force, but it does not rule life and death, which are ruled by Chiron.

Symbolisms of the Moon

The Moon deals primarily with emotions and is CO-RULER of emotions of most kinds. Side by side with some other planet, the Moon co-rules every emotion. For example, the Moon co-rules desire along with Venus;

the Moon co-rules greed along with Pluto; the Moon co-rules optimism along with Jupiter; and pessimism along with Saturn. The Moon is the ruler of fear, also along with Saturn. The Moon is sub-ruler of hatred where Saturn is ruler; and is sub-ruler of desire, where Venus is ruler. The Moon rules the maternal instinct, and is sub-ruler of procreation, which is ruled by Neptune. More than any other planet, the Moon is representative of the individual personality.

The Moon is feminine, instinctive, and emotional. It shares optimism with Jupiter, it shares greed and fear with Saturn, and shares desire with Venus. The Moon is not sexual, but because it is maternal, the Moon influences a woman's desire for conception and children. But it is Chiron that rules pregnancy and giving birth to children in a marriage.

The Symbolisms of Chiron

Chiron is neither feminine nor masculine, and it is the only planet that creates marriages; Chiron rules family ties, karmic bonds, spouses, and the soulmate. It also rules pregnancy, the birth of children in a family, motherhood, and fatherhood. However, Chiron also rules enduring relationships of all kinds, including ones that are strictly business. Chiron does not symbolize anything sexual—only the Sexual Planets and Sexual Linkages enhance sexuality between the linked persons. A Chiron relationship is platonic, without sexual overtones.

Because you cannot have a long-term relationship without trust, Chiron also rules this ideal in all of its many forms. Chiron rules not only the trust between two individuals, but also the trust between the public and individuals, such as politicians and entertainers. In this regard, Chiron rules image and appearance, reputation, charisma, noteworthiness, and public recognition, which are all components of super success and fame. We know this from the fact that the people who have a Jupiter-Chiron enhancement have the very best public images. For example, Franklin Delano Roosevelt had a very exact conjunction of Jupiter and Chiron. Here is a list of some others who were born with a Jupiter-Chiron enhancement:

- Bill Gates, Elvis Presley, Clark Gable, Sylvester Stallone, Madonna, Tom Cruise, Michael Jackson, Demi Moore, both Sonny and Cher (they should have stayed together—what a team they made), Barbara Walters, Connie Chung, Mother Teresa, and Frank Sinatra. Also, Bill Clinton—maybe it is his

Jupiter-Chiron enhancement that helped him get away with all that nonsense for so long.

The Venus-Chiron enhancement is another spectacular aspect that imparts the kind of charisma needed to hypnotize the crowds; it means charismatic (Chiron) appeal (Venus) and a beautiful (Venus) image (Chiron). It can also mean money from marriage or charismatic (Chiron) beauty (Venus)! Some examples:

- Richard Gere (talk about charisma), Gary Cooper (more charisma), Marilyn Monroe, Intel Corporation, Compaq, the Duchess of Windsor (talk about money through marriage!), Sir Laurence Olivier, and Walter Cronkite (who was once regarded as the most trusted person in America).

This is just a small sampling of charismatic and trusted people (and companies) with one of these two Super Aspects of Chiron. The most charismatic people usually have one or the other. Nobody has been more charismatic than Clark Gable, Gary Cooper, Marilyn Monroe, Elvis Presley, and Madonna. What a group—every one of them was or is an icon.

Okay, so now we know that Chiron rules charisma, and the Jupiter or Venus enhancement of Chiron imparts the most charisma. So does anyone have both the Jupiter-Chiron and the Venus-Chiron enhancement? Of course, the answer is yes.

Remember when we said that Hitler did not have a very strong astrological chart? He didn't. We explained that the reason he was able to push Germany into war was the strength of the chart of the day he came to power and became chancellor; that day had two Grand Trines. We do not know about you, but we still shudder when we see films of that monster speaking to thousands of Nazis and inciting them to cheer "Heil Hitler." That can only happen when there is enormous charisma—somewhere. It was not in Hitler's natal chart, but it was in the chart of the day Hitler took office. On that day, there was a Jupiter-Chiron trine and a Venus-Chiron trine; together they gave Hitler, as chancellor of Germany, the charisma he used to push Germany into the catastrophic war (see page 71). We get so upset when we think of this because Hitler could have used the charisma to do so much good rather than cause so much massive pain and grief.

So with the addition of Chiron as a new component of astrology, and knowing some of its symbolisms, we have answered a question that the world's greatest historians and psychologists have never been able to answer. Why did Germany follow Hitler almost blindly?

Astrology is amazing when you know how to use it. And so is Chiron. But the most amazing attribute of Chiron is that it is a celestial sign of the New Age. In the next chapter, we explain why.

CHAPTER FOURTEEN

᠙

Chiron Is the Sign of a New Age

The Babylonians constantly observed the stars, looking for a celestial sign that would foretell the coming of something momentous. Most astrologers seem to have forgotten this original goal, which led to the development of astrology in the first place. What is amazing is that one after the other, we have had four of the most important celestial signs of the last 2,000 years staring at us and waving flags—but we have not paid any attention to them.

The discovery of a new planet is a celestial sign!

Uranus was discovered in 1781, the year that the 13 colonies won their independence from England. It was also the very year that humankind learned how to build machines, leading to the onset of the Industrial Revolution. Uranus was a celestial sign of great importance and marked the year of these two mega-events.

In 1846, Neptune was discovered. It pointed to the commencement of the energy revolution as we learned how to harness the power of electricity and oil. It also marked the birth of the era of inventions, as humankind made the discoveries that led to modern-day conveniences such as light bulbs, refrigerators, automobiles, and airplanes.

In 1930, the coldest planet was discovered. Pluto marked the beginning of the worst period in the history of humankind. It started out with the Great Depression, followed by the world's most devastating and most far-reaching world war. Then we entered the Cold War, where the specter of nuclear holocaust hung over us each and every day. By 1977, when Chiron was discovered, the world had been on the brink of self-annihilation for over a quarter of a century and had gone through the worst 47 years of its history. The beginning of all of this was marked by the discovery of Pluto.

Next to a nova, a new planet appears to be the most important sign that we can have—foretelling an overpowering change in the course of history. The Magi Society believes that these changes are actually noticeable a few years before any planet is first discovered, and extend until a few years after another planet is discovered. If we examine these turning points in history, we can uncover and define some of the planet's symbolisms and personality by checking historic patterns after the planet's discovery. We refer to it as recognizing a planet's rulerships through HISTORIC SIGNIFICANCE. We will deal with each planet separately, and we will cover all four planets that have been discovered. If you do not understand our theory, read on and it will be clarified by examples.

Uranus was a celestial sign of the dawn of democracy, the birth of America, and the invention of the rotary steam engine, which helped humankind win its freedom from heavy manual labor. Thereafter, we made use of machines to do our work.

Neptune was a celestial sign of the dawn of modern times, and great inventions that would bring us to a level of existence that no one could have imagined beforehand.

Then there was Pluto, the celestial sign that was a portent of power-hungry dictators, fascism, oppression, depression, aggression, insurrection, the Holocaust, communism, and atheism. In 1977, the world was almost beyond the edge of self-annihilation. It was the time of the Looking Glass Plane, the name given to an American plane that was always in the air, loaded with electronic communications systems, capable of withstanding a nuclear attack and then signaling American military forces all around the world to launch a counterattack with nuclear weapons. We had over 10,000 of them—and we were building more. Russia had 20,000 nuclear weapons and was building more. Humankind was truly on the brink. There had never been a time of greater danger to the very survival of humankind.

But then God intervened. And Chiron was the sign of His intervention.

Chiron was discovered on November 1, 1977. Chiron marked the beginning of the fall of communism, the end of the Cold War, and a worldwide resurgence of the free enterprise economic system.

In China, communist leader Mao Zedong had died just the year before, which ended the Cultural Revolution, one of the most horrifying periods of Chinese history. At just about the time that Chiron was discovered, China began an experiment called "enterprise zones." What China did was to designate four small areas within the country's borders, giving citizens the right to conduct "capitalist" enterprises in those areas. Can you believe that? Just one year earlier, while Mao was still alive, anyone in China who would even suggest such a thing would have been shot, quite literally, quickly and without a trial. There were thousands who actually were shot just for that reason, but when Chiron was discovered in November of 1977, Mao had been dead for a little over a year, the Cultural Revolution was dead, and Mao's widow was being brought to trial for treason as part of the "gang of four."

In 1977, China—*communist* China—actually began to experiment with "enterprise zones" on its soil, and the mass hysteria of the Cultural Revolution had ended. Was all this the work of Chiron? Yes. Sort of. We believe all of this to be a divine gift, and the celestial sign of the gift is Chiron.

For the two decades before Chiron was discovered, there was a worldwide trend toward communist dictatorships. Not a single nation that had turned communist had ever reversed itself to become a democracy. Even major industrial countries that were far from being communist had began to experiment with socialism, which was a step in the direction of communism. Most of the world's industrial countries, including England, had socialized vast industries, meaning that the government took them over and ran them. After Chiron's discovery, the trend reversed.

About one and one-half years after Chiron was discovered, in the spring of 1979, Margaret Thatcher became prime minister of the United Kingdom. She was the most conservative prime minister that Great Britain had seen since the Victorian era, and the most anti-communist. During the several decades before Thatcher came to power, England's ruling Labor Party was nationalizing the country's basic industries. This was a step away from free enterprise and toward a communist economic system. However, Thatcher reversed all of it and privatized what the Labor Party's governments had socialized before her. In other words, she sold the industries that were nationalized and let them again be run by private companies. With Margaret Thatcher as prime minister, England put an end to its flirtation with socialism and fully embraced the free enterprise and free market economic system.

Across the Atlantic, in the United States, which has always been the most anti-communist and free enterprise country in the world, in the very year that Chiron was discovered, a revolution was occurring in how the massive U.S. national debt was being handled. Just months before Chiron was discovered, the Chicago Board of Trade began to trade T-Bond futures, a financial instrument that allowed investors to make money on the direction of interest rates. This was so successful that they soon created financial instruments that allowed anyone to invest in the direction of currencies. The reason this is important to free enterprise, the fall of communism, and the free market system is that it allowed companies to trade with those of another country without having to worry as much about the risk of currency fluctuations; the companies could hedge currency risks. It laid the foundation for a worldwide economy built on massive international trading, which is the main reason old-style communism is now on the verge of extinction.

Whereas the decades before Chiron saw leftists gaining more and more power around the world, the very first decade of Chiron saw conservatives gaining control of the most powerful democracies.

In 1980, the United States elected a president who was as conservative as Thatcher. Not very long after Chiron was first discovered, Ronald Reagan announced that he would run for the presidency, and almost immediately after he was elected, Reagan organized and held the first *Group of Seven* meetings. The purpose was to coordinate economic policy among the most powerful industrial democracies and enhance economic growth through free trade. The Group of Seven meetings became so successful that a decade later, even Russia asked to join them.

Was Chiron a sign of all this? Yes.

Also in 1980, less than three years after Chiron's entrance into world consciousness, Lech Walesa and Polish workers formed the Solidarity union. It turned out to be the first crack in the Iron Curtain of communism.

However, all of the above changes take a back seat to the most important change of all in the history of communism and free enterprise. Almost right on the heels of Chiron's discovery, in 1978, Mikhail Gorbachev became secretary of agriculture for the Soviet Union. From this position, he was able to become a full member of the Politburo in 1980, and from there he became premier. Gorbachev was the most important element in the fall of the Iron Curtain.

With more conservative governments firmly installed in all seven of the most industrialized democracies, the first decade of Chiron saw the most powerful and speedy move toward free enterprise that the world has ever seen. For the countries that adhered to free enterprise, there was also greater prosperity than they had ever known. Also, for the first time, satellite transmission of the economic success of the industrialized democracies was being received by the people living behind the Iron Curtain. This was what ultimately spurred the populace of those communist countries to throw out communism.

It seems that Chiron was a sign that God was putting into place the pieces that were needed to ultimately free the world of the lunacy of dictatorships. For these reasons, we believe that Chiron rules free enterprise, free trade, and freedom itself. Some astrologers have designated the symbolism of freedom to Uranus, but we believe that Uranus rules independence, the urge for independence, and also the urge for freedom—which is similar to freedom, but not freedom itself. This is another example of fraternal symbolisms.

The fact of the matter is, since the discovery of Chiron, a billion people have gained their freedom, or much of it. This is primarily a result of the fall of communism in Russia and their former satellite states. There has never been a period of time in the history of the world when a greater percentage of the world population has been freed—to say nothing of the fact that the whole world is free from the awful Cold War.

This also makes Chiron ruler of free will. Since we believe that when a person loses free will, the person virtually dies, we ascribe to Chiron the symbolism of being in control of one's life. This means Chiron has rulership over a part of life and death as well.

From our technique of searching for Chiron's symbolisms through its historic significance, we believe that Chiron rules progress; advancement in the form of innovation (as opposed to change in the form of innovation, which we believe is ruled by Uranus); and the ability to successfully blaze new frontiers of all kinds—including scientific, artistic, political and cultural ones. Therefore, Chiron rules pioneers and adventurers.

Chiron has helped to provide free will to a billion people who did not have it before, but to the world in general, we believe that the most important result of Chiron's work will be the *New Age,* and everything that is intrinsic to it.

Welcome, Chiron—Heavenly Sign of the New Age!

The Magi Society is cautiously optimistic that the present era is truly the opportunity for the dawn of the New Age, where democracy will be safe, all dictatorships will fall, and where all people will have the freedom to choose their own governments—ones that will be responsive and responsible to them. It will be a time where all of us can choose our professions and our religions; and where equality of race, gender, and sex will forever be each individual's inalienable birthright.

Of course, it is not really the planet Chiron that is behind all this. God created the astrological system as a Benevolent Design, and the planets ultimately answer to Him. So it is Divine Providence that has given us this unique opportunity to achieve all we could ask for. Now it is up to us to have the courage and wisdom to continue the course.

Symbolisms of Pluto

Before Chiron was discovered, Pluto was the most recently discovered planet, or what we call the CURRENT PLANET. Pluto was discovered in 1930, so the era between about that year, and about 1977, was the Plutonian era. The symbolisms of Pluto are diametrically opposed to those of Chiron, with the Plutonian era being the worst period in the recorded history of humankind.

Pluto's discovery marked the rise of fascism and the rise of Adolf Hitler. It was in 1930, the very year of Pluto's entrance into our consciousness, that Hitler and his Nazi party began to gain support from Germany's major industrialists. Hitler became chancellor just three years later.

The effect of Pluto was not limited to Europe and the Americas, though. In Asia, in 1930, Japan adopted an expansionist policy and decided to build up its armed forces and use them to gain territory and power. One year later, the Japanese invaded Manchuria in an egotistical and sadistic quest for power.

In China, Mao Zedong formed the beginnings of his communist army in 1930. In November of 1931, Mao Zedong founded the Chinese Soviet Republic, and three years later he led his army of communists on the Long March to try to gain power over all of China.

All of these events had a common denominator: Paranoid individuals were willing to do anything to seize *power*. For this reason, and about a million or so others, Pluto is the planet that symbolizes power, the desire for power, and the will to exert and exercise power that a person possesses. However, Pluto is always excessive (it rules excess).

Pluto also signifies dictatorships, oppression, greed, and a state of perpetual dissatisfaction. It also is representative of many of the components of power, such as nuclear weapons. It should come as no surprise that the birth years for nuclear weapons were the ones that began about the time Pluto was first discovered.

The personality of Pluto is very authoritarian, cold, power-hungry, selfish, and downright abusive—not anything like Chiron. As we explained earlier when discussing Chiron, during the Plutonian era, the world was first plunged into the Great Depression, then World War II, and that was followed by the Cold War and the specter of possible destruction of the human race. No period of time was quite as bad as the Plutonian era—and we have been through some real lulus.

Is it any wonder that Pluto symbolizes the ego and excessive high regard for oneself? In addition, since Pluto is the planet that rules power, which has a major impact on success, Pluto also then symbolizes big business, as well as the components of big business—such as acquisitions, the ability to successfully compete, the competitive edge, and even earning potential. In a similar vein, Pluto symbolizes debt and instruments of debt, such as bonds, mortgages, and all borrowings. Pluto has dominion over credit worthiness as well as credit itself, and profits obtained through competition and any form of investments—including trading of stocks, bonds, and commodities, as well as gambling. Because Pluto is related to competition, power, and business, it is also symbolic of lawsuits, which play a major role in big business.

As you can see, learning why astrologers assign symbolisms can be interesting and help you remember them.

Pluto's rulership of big business has the emphasis on the word *big*, whereas Chiron's rulership of free enterprise emphasizes the word *free*. Pluto's rulership of power directly causes it to symbolize the will and desire to exercise power, as well as all personages of power—such as politicians, film stars, and leaders of big business. It is Pluto that creates the people who love and thrive under competition, such as professional athletes. Here again, we have fraternal symbolisms. Mars rules the athlete and competitor with the emphasis on the athlete; Pluto rules the athlete and competitor with the emphasis on the competitor.

Pluto rules acquisitions and the urge to acquire. More precisely, Pluto signifies the unquenchable thirst for acquisitions of all kinds, including entire countries. It is the personality of Pluto to never be satisfied.

We now know one reason why there have been all too few examples of self-made billionaires who are generous. It seems, unfortunately, that self-made billionaires are those who are Plutonian, and they are never satisfied with what they have, so there is little room for generosity.

Since Pluto rules big business, some of the professionals that Pluto rules include entrepreneurs and businesspersons, and CEOs and marketing specialists. Together with Jupiter, Pluto rules venture capital and investment banking.

Because of the above and Pluto's rulership of power, a successful person in this society is one that is very Plutonian, and for this reason, Pluto rules success, which is a child of power; however, the emphasis is on power. Jupiter rules success with the emphasis on good fortune.

Since Pluto symbolizes the state of never being satisfied, we finally understand why those in power always seem to want more. They have Plutonian aspects.

Pluto is very masculine. It is also uncaring and abrasive, egotistical and abrupt, cold and power-hungry, and overbearing and sometimes unbearable.

It is sexual in the male way—forceful, pushy, and obsessive (but not as bad as Saturn). To Pluto, *love* is a word, and *feeling* is also a word, neither of which Pluto understands. It knows how to spell *sex*, but it misspells *PURSEnality* (with the emphasis on the "purse" strings).

Symbolisms of Uranus

Uranus was not discovered until 1781. To astrologers, the symbolisms of Uranus include inventions and inventors and man-made machines, among other things.

As is the case with all the New Planets, one of the reasons that Uranus symbolizes what it does is its history. In the year Uranus was discovered, James Watt invented the first steam engine that could convert steam power to rotary power. Prior to Watts's engine, people were essentially limited to using animals or their own muscles for power in virtually all of their daily needs. Because the steam engine so closely coincided with the discovery of Uranus, astrologers have always associated this planet with inventions and inventors. In fact, astrologers believe that the discovery of Uranus by human beings, and the influence of Uranus on such, was the actual impetus for the Industrial Revolution.

Although we agree that Uranus rules inventions, we believe that we have here another example of fraternal symbolisms. Uranus certainly rules inventions and the changes that inventions bring about, with the emphasis on change; whereas Neptune rules inventions and the changes that inventions bring about, with the emphasis on invention. This is because Neptune rules creative genius and new ideas.

The year of Uranus's discovery, 1781, was a very important time in history. The 13 colonies won their independence from England, and the French Revolution soon followed. From this, we believe that Uranus rules democratic forms of government and politics. Astrologers have also correctly assigned to Uranus the symbolism of revolutions, mass change, and the general public. By revolutions, astrologers are not just referring to revolts, but they include any broad-based change that affects an entire population. The revolution can be industrial, political, or scientific—or a revolution of ideas. Because revolutions also result in change, the symbolism of change for Uranus is reinforced.

Shortly after the discovery of Uranus, some Frenchmen successfully completed the first manned balloon flight on June 5, 1783. This meant that human beings could finally get off the ground after being able to merely dream about it since the dawn of humankind. This meant that humankind was independent enough to fly for the first time. For these reasons, astrologers have also used Uranus to symbolize flying and space travel.

Similarly, Uranus is the planet of whatever is worldwide or wide ranging. Uranus rules the general public, fame, and anything that has to do with fame. Because Uranus rules the general public, it also rules the businesses that are supported by the public, such as the entertainment industry, broadcasting, and any form of mass media, including the Internet.

Uranus's rulership of change gives it the symbolism of the need for change and what creates change, such as revolutions and revolutionaries. Uranus's dominion over change also makes it the planet that symbolizes astrology, which is really the study of the results of *changes* in the positions of the planets.

Uranus's rulership of change gives it another symbolism, but this one is new and will be surprising. It rules order and orderliness, meaning logical sequence as opposed to havoc. We will explain this later on when we talk about the symbolisms for Mercury. Uranus also rules adjustments, adaptation, and the ability and willingness to adapt and adjust.

The personality of Uranus is distinctive in affairs of love. Uranus is feminine, but only mildly so. There is an emotionalism about Uranus, but it is detached and flirtatious, noncommittal, difficult to satisfy, and always looking for greener pastures. It is coy, teasing, moody, changeable, and fun-loving. And it is always a challenge. If you have ever loved a Uranian, you know all this already.

Symbolisms of Neptune

We have discussed the symbolisms of Chiron, Pluto, and Uranus. Neptune is the only other planet that is not visible to the naked eye and had to be discovered.

The scientific discoveries that were made during the years immediately preceding and after Neptune's discovery in 1846 were more earthshaking than any others. During the few years preceding and shortly after its discovery, the most important events in the birth of humankind's capacity to harness electricity occurred. In 1831, Faraday discovered the principles of electromagnetic induction and the basis for the electric motor and generator. This led to a multitude of various electric motors being designed, tested, and produced in America and Europe. Essentially, the electric motor and generator were being perfected during the very year of Neptune's discovery.

Also during that year, Charles Goodyear began to reap the fruits of his 1839 discovery of the vulcanization of rubber, the process through which rubber became useful to humankind because it made rubber bounce back to its original form when stretched. Why is this so important? Well, no rubber means no electrical wiring, and without wiring, there can be no motors. No motors means no electrical machinery. No electrical machinery means no modern era.

It was also during this period of time that petroleum became truly significant to man. In 1848, James Young and Abraham Gesner, working independently, discovered the necessary ingredients for the kerosene lamp, which worked from by-products of petroleum. Prior to that, everyone used whale oil for lamps. Shortly afterwards, petroleum became the fuel on which electric generators eventually ran. It is amazing how all of this came together.

In the very year of Neptune's discovery, an American named George Westinghouse was born. His 400 or so patents made him one of the world's greatest inventors. Nearly all of his patents covered electrical devices, and he was instrumental in the development of massive electrical generators with the power and capacity to light whole cities.

Amazingly, the other great inventor of electrical devices, Thomas Edison, was born in 1847, just one year after Neptune was discovered. Edison invented the light bulb, which became the most important electrical device ever. Let there be light!

Guess what planet rules light from a source other than the Sun and fire? You're right if you said Neptune.

Is it any wonder, then, why the Magi Society has also assigned the symbolisms of electricity, electrical equipment, rubber and rubber products, oil and oil products—and most important—the symbolism of creative ideas, talent, and inventive and creative genius to Neptune?

Neptune rules creative genius with the emphasis on creativity. Jupiter rules creative genius with the emphasis on genius.

One year after Neptune's discovery, Louis Pasteur received his doctorate degree and was appointed professor of chemistry at the University of Strasbourg. Often called the father of modern medicine, his discovery of Pasteurization has saved untold millions of lives. He also discovered cures for anthrax, rabies, chicken cholera, and silkworm disease. Not surprisingly, Neptune symbolizes medicine and doctors.

All told, these events brought on the conveniences of modern times, which are almost all based on electricity or oil—the foundations for the most significant advances that shape our day-to-day lives. For this reason,

Neptune is also symbolic of being comfortable and secure, both in the physical and financial senses. Sometimes the comfort and well-being extends to the emotional and spiritual level as well, and it always extends to health.

As important as all such symbolisms are, Neptune's most important rulership is longevity and the ability to increase the lifetime of anything. As such, Neptune rules health, medicine, healing, and both the regeneration process and the regenerative capacity. Neptune is also ruler of youthfulness and being forever young. It is also the planet of everything that is long term. These are not traditional astrology's symbolisms for Neptune. But any astrologer who doubts them should examine the Magi AstroCharts of the women and men who have lived the longest. A listing of such people can be found in the *Guinness Book of Records,* and a significant number of them were born with enhancements of Neptune by Jupiter, Sun, or Chiron.

It is Neptune that rules all long-term assets such as real estate, stocks and bonds, patents, copyrights, and trust funds. For example, Queen Elizabeth, who has inherited more wealth than any other woman, has an exact enhancement of Jupiter and Neptune (massive amounts of inheritances). Prince Charles, who will inherit what Queen Elizabeth leaves behind, has two enhancements of Venus and Neptune (money from inheritances and long-term money).

Neptune also rules anything that a person was born with (and therefore is long term) that produces wealth. This includes creativity and originality in all areas, whether artistic or scientific. Since Neptune also signifies anything that prolongs life, such as medicine and drugs, Neptune must also rule doctors, hospitals, and medical equipment

The healing and regenerative nature of Neptune logically calls for Neptune to symbolize water, which is an absolute necessity for life on Earth. Neptune does rule water, and anything that comes from large bodies of water, such as oceans. This is an ancient symbolism of Neptune, who was also the Roman god of water and the seas.

Neptune's dominion over longevity also makes it ruler of anything that comes from the ground, because such things have longevity. We already know that Neptune rules oil, but it also symbolizes minerals, food, plants, and trees—most of which also have an effect on our health and longevity—or can provide us with long-term assets, both of which are symbolisms of Neptune.

Venus rules grace and beauty to the eye, but Neptune rules grace and beauty to the heart. In other words, Neptune rules grace and beauty of the *personality*, while Venus's influences are physical and impermanent in nature. Therefore, Neptune rules charm of personality, while Venus rules charm of the body. Venus also rules seduction, allure, and beguilement, which also have an impermanent quality about them. Neptune represents certain longer-lasting attributes of female charm, such as tenderness, sweetness, gentility, and receptiveness.

The most important feature of the personality of Neptune is that it rules femininity and manifests itself in providing the best of the female attributes, such as motherliness, the desire for the soft touch, and the ability to provide tenderness and softness in a relationship. In this regard, Neptune has several fraternal symbolisms with Venus.

Many astrologers associate Neptune with deceit and con artists. We strongly disagree. There is an idealistic genuineness about Neptune. Astrologers who believe Neptune is deceptive may think so because Neptune does symbolize immaturity, but this is a direct result of Neptune's representation of youthfulness and has nothing to do with deceit. Saturn rules deceitfulness and lies.

Along with Chiron, Neptune co-rules life and death, even though many astrology books ascribe all such important symbolisms to Pluto. But Neptune's rulership of healing, regeneration, and longevity necessarily extend its symbolisms to include life, in the sense of life and death. In addition, Neptune is also representative of safety, peace, and tranquility.

As if Neptune is not already complicated enough, it has still another important side to her. Neptune rules artistic talents of all kinds, including fashion design, musical and lyrical compositions, hairdressing and makeup, poetry, and absolutely anything that has to do with any art form whatsoever. Interestingly enough, this explains why so many men who have the greatest artistic talents are often gay. It is because Neptune is symbolic of both femininity and artistry. When a man has artistic talents, he usually has a very strong aspect of Neptune, which makes him prone to being more feminine than any other aspect because Neptune is the most feminine planet. But please do not jump the gun on this—all the aspects in the birth chart must be analyzed to obtain an overall picture.

Even though we have already provided more symbolisms for Neptune than any other planet, we're not finished. Neptune also rules food, water, drugs, and whatever can be normally ingested into the body. This includes alcoholic beverages and narcotics in every form. Here again, the rulerships of Neptune explain one of the heretofore inexplicable linkages between supercreative people and their often prolific use of drugs. These types of individuals often have aspects by Neptune, which is also a sign of susceptibility to drug use. It's important for such people to resist such urges because too many have ruined their lives with "recreational drugs."

There is no such thing. They will eventually kill you in one way or another. If drugs do not literally kill you, they will eventually kill your relationships, your career, and your family. People who take drugs think they can stop at any time, but nobody can really do so, because drugs are ruled by Neptune, and whatever is Neptunian is long-lasting. That's why drugs are so addictive.

The personality of Neptune is exquisitely charming. Impressionable, sweet, and gentle, Neptune is also the most loving; it rules long-term love. Neptune is guileless and does not know how to scheme. Open and frank, it is optimistic, forgets about problems, and hopes they will go away. There is a touch of irresponsibility about Neptune because of its youthfulness. But next to Jupiter, it is the best planet. Creative, original, poetic, and dramatic, Neptune represents some of the most wonderful attributes of humankind. Overall, Neptune does not get along well with Mars or Pluto, loves Jupiter, stays away from Saturn, and wants a family.

Symbolisms of Mercury

Mercury is the ruler of communications and all forms of communicating. It is also symbolic of the tools of communications, such as the voice, vocal chords, facial expressions; and all forms of expression, such as hand gestures. Therefore Mercury rules singing and acting, as well as singers and actors. Since Mercury rules all forms of communication, it also symbolizes writing and all those who make communication and writing their profession, such as authors, television and radio broadcasters, newspaper columnists, and so on.

Mercury has dominion over the instruments of communication, so it also rules the ears and the eyes; and their man-made substitutes and attachments, such as eyeglasses, cameras, lenses, copying machines, faxes, and the Internet (co-ruled by Uranus). Mercury is ruler of the mouth and throat, larynx, and of course, the vocal chords. It also rules the entire nervous and respiratory systems. Mercury signifies the mind and the intellect; and it rules the part of the body that is related to the mind and intellect, meaning the brain. Logically, then, Mercury also rules the professions associated with the mind, including psychology and psychiatry; as well as the professions that are associated with the eyes, such as photography and photographers.

Because Mercury rules the ears and nervous system, it also rules reflexes. Mercury's symbolisms of the brain and ear, including the inner ear, would naturally give it rulership over balance and coordination. But here again, there are fraternal symbolisms. Mercury rules balance in the sense of not falling, and the act of using visual perception to aid in coordination and movements. But Uranus is ruler of spatial positioning and the ability to adjust (change) the body's movements while in motion to accomplish a desired goal, such as getting a winning basket. You need both Mercury and Uranus to be the world's best basketball player, and that is why Michael Jordan has a nearly exact quincunx of Uranus and Mercury—perfect balance in both ways—which is one of the reasons he can fly to the basket.

Mercury also rules reflexes. One would think that Mercury would rule coordination, but if it does, it would be a fraternal symbolism with Uranus as the other ruler. Both reflexes and balance are a part of coordination, but the most important component of coordination is logical, sequential order; the ability to adjust to change; and speed of adaptation. A person has to do things in the correct sequence in order to be considered coordinated. Uranus is the ruler of logical sequences and adjusting to change. Interestingly enough, Uranus's power over sequence and order spills over to social order. Uranus rules democracy, which is the correct order and hierarchy for a form of government. A nation's people comes ahead of the government. That is the hallmark of democracy.

Mercury governs travel and the tools for traveling, including aircraft, automobiles, trains, motorcycles, and bicycles. It also symbolizes those who use such vehicles to make a living, such as travel agents, truck and taxi drivers, pilots and flight attendants; as well as the companies in any transportation-related businesses, such as airplane, automobile, and motorcycle manufacturers, airlines, delivery services, and companies such as FedEx.

Because Mercury is cerebral and devoid of emotions, it is masculine. Mercury has nothing to do with love or sex. It prefers the mind game, is happy with itself in its own cubbyhole, and thinks it is smarter than any other planet. It makes its own decisions and has a different perspective than any other planet. Mercury claims to be logical and has no taste for common sense, intuition, or emotions. Basically, it has the personality of a computer. Have you ever made love to a computer? You have if you've done it with a Mercurian.

Symbolisms of Saturn

Ancient astrologers regarded Saturn as a MALEFIC, which is the opposite of a benefic. They viewed Saturn as the antithesis of Jupiter. Ancient astrologers long believed that planetary aspects formed by Saturn were a sign of possible tragedies and disasters. Babylonian astrologers viewed Saturn aspects as signs of death, disease, plague, pestilence, floods, drought, evil, famine, and impending harm and doom. You get the picture.

As if all this was not bad enough, the Babylonians saw Saturn as the planet of limitation, obstruction, hindrance, loss, frustration, failure, undesirability, dissolution, tragedy, death, degradation, the lowering or negatization of anything, the aging process, confusion, recklessness, ineptitude, being lost, cruelty, revenge, immorality, temptation, and succumbing to temptation.

Interestingly enough, the ancient Babylonian astrologers were correct in ascribing such symbolisms to Saturn. Bearing in mind the fact that these astrologers did not know about the New Planets, we believe that astrology was nonetheless able to survive these last 4,000 years based in large measure on the accuracy of such symbolisms for Saturn.

However, during the last few decades, many astrologers have proposed and loudly supported the view that Saturn is not bad, and that it is even rather good. Astrologers who wish to revise the Saturn symbolisms in this way are the SATURN REVISIONISTS.

Some of the Saturn revisionists do not believe that there is a "bad" planet, and they do not like that idea. Saturn revisionists have sought to "cleanse" Saturn of its negative reputation, but the result has been confusion over Saturn. To Saturn revisionists, Saturn is symbolic of science and scientific thinking, discipline and being disciplined, long life, and in particular, the teacher and the learning process, reliability, steadiness of purpose, and faithfulness. We have a problem with such symbolisms. We know the Babylonian symbolisms worked for thousands of years, and these new symbolisms are inconsistent with the time-tested ones of the ancient Babylonians.

In many ways, Saturn is the most important planet to understand. In all ways, it is the most difficult. As we have said before, the symbolisms of the planets are the very heart and soul of astrology, and astrology is only as accurate as the symbolisms it employs.

To try to resolve the Saturn issue, the Magi Society concluded one of its most interesting research projects ever conducted in astrology. We examined the birth charts of the most powerful negative people that we know about, and every famous person who has a strong Saturn aspect. We also scrutinized the most tragic days that we know about, and every historic date that had a strong Saturn aspect. The purpose of the study was to see if a gentler, kinder Saturn might emerge from such a study. If so, then Saturn should be given a set of new clothes and a new set of symbolisms.

What we discovered was that the confusion that astrologers have had about Saturn seems to have stemmed from the fact that until Magi Astrology came along, all aspects were interpreted using the same rules. But in Magi Astrology, we have separated the aspects into Personal and Historic Aspects. We have already learned that Turbulent Aspects are interpreted differently depending upon which of these two types of aspects they are.

The Magi Society's research into Saturn's symbolisms resulted in our realization that the symbolisms of Saturn are different for Historic Aspects than Personal Aspects. It is the only planet that does this. From our research, we concluded that the evidence supported the view that a Saturn aspect is not bad when it is a Personal Aspect. Even Saturn aspects are gifts of special talents. Saturn revisionists should be very happy about this.

However, when it comes to Historic Aspects, Saturn is every bit as bad as the ancient Babylonians believed. The results of our study showed that the classic negative tone of the symbolisms for Saturn survived 4,000 years because they worked very well on Historic Aspects.

So we did give Saturn a new set of clothes—but only in a limited way. The clothes are made from the same type of fabric, but the style and colors are holographic and look different depending on the angle.

For anything other than Personal Aspects, the ancient Babylonian symbolisms of loss, tragedy, disaster, bad luck, and so on, have all been validated, confirmed, and actually even reinforced.

The Negative Symbolisms of Saturn Are Confirmed in Historic Aspects

Saturn is a bad boy in all Historic Aspects. Our research is very clear about this. There is an endless list of examples, so we will provide only a few from very recent history.

To start with, we will look at the two worst nuclear accidents in history: Chernobyl and Three Mile Island. These disasters occurred, respectively, on 4/26/86 and 3/28/79. In the case of Chernobyl, at least thousands were injured or killed by the worst nuclear accident in history. On Three Mile Island, one of the two nuclear reactors overheated, there was a partial meltdown, and radioactive material was released.

On both days, Saturn aspects were prominent. This was because the Sun is the essence of each day, and on both days, there was a quincunx of Sun and Saturn. A quincunx is a Turbulent Aspect for Historic Aspects. For the Chernobyl accident, the Sun-Saturn quincunx was part of a four-planet synchronization of Sun, Saturn, Pluto, and Chiron. We can interpret this as a long-lasting (Neptune), tragic (Saturn) day (Sun) for nuclear energy (Pluto). The area around Chernobyl was uninhabitable for years because of radioactive leakage. On the Chernobyl date, there was also a Mars-Chiron quincunx, which was double-direct. It means an accident (Mars) leading to deaths (Chiron in offset; this is because double-direct quincunxes are turbulent when they are also Historic Aspects).

On the day of the Three Mile Island accident, there was also a quincunx of Sun and Saturn, and a three-planet synchronization of Saturn, Sun, and Chiron. These aspects also foretold of a tragic (Saturn) day (Sun) for loss (Saturn) of life (Chiron). However, the synchronization of planets was not as bad on the day of the Chernobyl disaster. Chernobyl has a four-planet synchronization. The synchronization during the Three Mile Island accident had only three planets in it, and Neptune was not involved, so the accident at Three-Mile Island did not create a lasting effect (Neptune makes things lasting). The Chernobyl accident was by far the more tragic accident, and the aspects of its Planetary Geometry show that. Its effects are still felt.

There was a Sun-Saturn quincunx on both days of these nuclear accidents. Was Saturn the culprit—or do you believe in coincidence?

Now please look back at page 71, which has the chart for the day Adolf Hitler became chancellor of Germany (declinations not shown). There were three aspects to the Sun, which are the ones that define the essence, or true meaning, of the day. Two of them were Saturn aspects. On the day Hitler gained control of the German government, Saturn was both conjunct the Sun and parallel the Sun. Although both aspects are at the wide end of the allowable orb, the theory of cumulative effect would make the Saturn-Sun aspects very powerful. The aspects also easily qualify for a Sun-Saturn planetary eclipse, which is very powerful and very bad. It was, indeed, a tragic day, which caused an immeasurable amount of loss (Saturn). There was also a Neptune-Sun quincunx on that day. Unfortunately, this made Hitler's chancellorship long-lasting.

Remember the two Grand Trines of that day, and how we pointed out the awesome charisma created by the aspects of the Grand Trine? The Grand Trine was comprised of the two most charismatic aspects, the Jupiter-Chiron and Venus-Chiron enhancements. Well, please also look at the Grand Trine of Figure 14A on page 287. The chart shows the day that Saddam Hussein's party took over control of Iraq through a military coup, forming the new Iraq nation, which is the one that exists now. It is the chart of the Iraq that invaded Kuwait. It has the same Grand Trine!

When we interpret its aspects, we will finally understand why Iraq is such an outlaw nation. The birth chart of Iraq has one of the rarest of all possible Saturn aspects: There is a BI-LEVEL ASPECT of the Sun and Saturn. A bi-level aspect is a concept we first introduced in *Astrology Really Works!* It means that a planet is strongly aspected in both the Zodiac Sign Chart and the Declinations Chart. In Iraq's case, there is a Sun-Saturn quincunx and a Sun-Saturn contra-parallel. We judge the Sun-Saturn contra-parallel as the worst aspect in the declinations. We just learned that the Sun-Saturn quincunx is the worst of the Turbulent Aspects in the longitudes. It is the same aspect that existed on the two days of the worst nuclear accidents. When both of these Sun-Saturn aspects exist on the same day, you can imagine what they are a sign of.

There was also a bi-level aspect of the Sun and Saturn on the day that Hitler came to power in Germany. We think the day that started the existing Iraq government was an even worse day than the day Hitler became chancellor. This is very unfortunate, because what is represented by the Iraq chart is still alive.

Let us interpret all of the important aspects of the day Iraq was founded and see where we stand:

- Saturn contra-parallel Sun: a malevolent (Saturn) entity (Sun), which in this case is a country

- Saturn quincunx Sun: a malevolent country

- Jupiter square Sun: a malevolent country (this is a Turbulent Aspect, with *malevolence* being the antonym of the normal Jupiter symbolism of *benevolence*)

- Saturn opposition Venus: limitation (Saturn) of feelings (Venus)—in other words, heartless, cold, and cruel—this is a Turbulent Aspect, so the negative influences of Saturn are reinforced; we can add the word *very* and interpret this aspect as meaning "very heartless, cold, and cruel"

- A Yod of Saturn, Chiron, and Sun: infamous (the chaotic offset of Chiron's normal symbolism of noteworthy) country; also a country that has no freedom, or a country that is an enslaver (Chiron rules freedom, and the presence of Saturn represents the opposite of freedom)

- Venus parallel Pluto: desire (Venus) for nuclear weapons (Pluto) and love of power (Pluto)

- Saturn contra-parallel Pluto: uncontrollable (Saturn) risk taking (Pluto), meaning reckless and irresponsible; this means that Iraq is willing to use nuclear weapons if it ever acquired them

Iraq's love of war and ultrabelligerence is signified by its Chiron-Mars aspect (a contra-parallel), which is what Hitler, Goebbels, Himmler, and Göring were all born with. Normally, with a government or country such as Iraq, you do not have to worry, because they self-destruct. However, the Grand Trine of Jupiter, Venus, and Chiron is the same as the one in the chart of the day Hitler took power—and it was Hitler's most powerful astrological asset! In some ways, the Iraqi chart is even stronger than Hitler's chart. One reason is that Iraq also has a Jupiter parallel of Chiron, which means that it can fool people into thinking that it is really good, although it is not.

From all of the above aspects, we now know why Iraq attacked Kuwait. The Magi Society's advice to the U.S. government and the world is to never lower your guard when it comes to Iraq. Somehow, in some way, with help from Divine Providence, we need to cause the birth of a new nation in Iraq. Getting rid of Saddam Hussein would help, but it is not a final answer unless a new country is established, thus eradicating this most malevolent of charts.

The examples we have provided of prominent Historic Aspects with Saturn are representative of Saturn aspects and their impact on this world. As idealistic as we are, the fact is that a lot of bad things happen in this world, and there simply must be a planet that represents tragedy, loss, misfortune, and so on. Saturn is the one that does, but it is a sign, and not the cause.

How to Interpret Saturn in Personal Aspects

Okay, now we know how to interpret Saturn aspects when it comes to Historic Aspects. The next step is to understand how we should deal with Saturn aspects when we analyze the nature of a person who is born with Saturn aspects. Are these aspects malevolent and tragic? Ill-fated or unlucky? The answer to such questions is the most complicated one in astrology so far.

We explained before that the Magi Society believes that for a person, every aspect is a reflection of the soul, as lived in one's previous life. We also explained that God designed the system of astrology such that each aspect is also a gift from Providence; every personal aspect signifies a special talent and ability. That includes Saturn aspects; even they are gifts.

Good examples of very successful and admired persons with strong and exact aspects of the Sun and Saturn are John F. Kennedy (born 5/29/17), Martin Luther King, Jr. (1/15/29), and Gary Cooper (5/7/01). This is a stellar group of supersuccessful persons, each of whom has a very precise Sun-

Saturn aspect. Cooper had Saturn exactly trine Sun and exactly quincunx Pluto. JFK was born with a tight aspect of Saturn parallel Sun; his Saturn was also trine Chiron. Reverend King's Saturn was parallel his Sun, and contra-parallel his Pluto.

In contrast to such persons, men like Fidel Castro (8/13/26), Jim Jones (5/13/31), and Marshall Applewhite (5/17/31) also all were born with significant Saturn aspects.

Just to refresh your memory, on November 19, 1978, in Guyana, which is in South America, Jim Jones led a total of 908 Americans (who followed him from California) to commit mass suicide by drinking Kool-Aid laced with cyanide. Compared to Jones's body count, Applewhite is an amateur. Only 38 followed him when they committed group suicide in March 1997, in a San Diego suburb, in what has become known as the Heaven's Gate suicides. Jones and Applewhite were born only four days apart, each with a Sun-Saturn trine and a Venus-Saturn square.

As for Castro, he has a bi-level Sun-Saturn aspect, as was the case with Iraq and the day Hitler took power. (Isn't astrology amazing?)

Kennedy, Cooper, and King also all have Sun-Saturn aspects. How do we view Saturn in Personal Aspects and still be consistent? We actually think we have an answer—and we got it from the stars.

In our second book, the *Magi Society Ephemeris*, we were the first to propose the symbolism of "control" for Saturn. It appears that the one common denominator of people who have Sun-Saturn aspects is that they are themselves uncontrollable and have the skill of being able to control, and sometimes even dominate, others. We emphasize again that when it comes to natal aspects for an individual, every aspect is both a reflection of the soul and a gift from God that provides us with a special ability. How we use the gift is up to us because we have free will. Those with Saturn-Sun aspects can use them to lead others in a way that they believe will benefit the world, the way Martin Luther King did, and Kennedy tried. Others with the Saturn-Sun aspect will, unfortunately, lead others astray, the way Jones and Applewhite did. Still others with the Sun-Saturn aspect will use their ability to control and dominate others as a means of achieving career goals. We think Castro did that. As for Gary Cooper, we know one thing about him: No one was going to control him. Cooper was his own man and made his own decisions.

So when we interpret natal aspects for an individual, important symbolisms of Saturn are that of control, the will to control others, and the ability to do so.

Saturn Clashes

The controlling influence of Saturn is most evident when two persons have a Saturn interaspect. If the Saturn interaspect is a Turbulent Angle, it is what we call a SATURN CLASH, and it can create the type of relationship you would not want to be in, since such relationships are the ones that are most likely to end in bitterness and disaster. We will explain how to spot Saturn Clashes and how to evaluate them later in chapter 16.

But we have not yet finished with Saturn in this chapter.

Saturn Is Representative of Atheism

The symbolism of control is so pervasive and strong in Saturn that it shows up in other facets of Saturn's symbolisms. In other words, most Saturn aspects have that characteristic. As a result, people with Saturn aspects, particularly Sun-Saturn aspects, have an above-average inclination to be atheist or agnostic. This is because they despise the very idea of a higher power of any kind, since they themselves are the ones who want to be in control and not have to answer to, or even think about, a higher power. Obviously, Fidel Castro is an atheist, and he has the bi-level aspect of Sun and Saturn. Madalyn Murray O'Hair also has a Sun-Saturn aspect. She is the woman who founded an atheist group and filed the lawsuit that resulted in the U.S. Supreme Court decision that declared prayer in public schools unconstitutional. She eventually disappeared, and there are substantial funds missing from donations that she had collected through her atheist organization. Guess she lost control, even of herself. (O'Hair was born 4/13/19; her chart is not shown.)

Saturn also represents science, the scientist, and scientific thinking—all of which have been at odds with the belief in Providence.

Saturn Transits Are the Worst

The greatest significance of Saturn to most of us is how it influences us in TRANSITS. We already saw the influence of Turbulent Transits by Saturn in chapter 12. The effects of a transit by Saturn give us more symbolisms for it. When Saturn creates a transiting aspect to any of our planets, we are more susceptible to pessimism; bad judgment; selfishness; the will to do harm; and being immoral, selfish, and egotistical. We are also more likely to exhibit carelessness and harmful behavior, hatred and malice, intolerance and temper tantrums, emotional depression, coldness, selfishness, heartlessness, stubbornness, self-righteousness, and narrow-mindedness. In addition, we have less vitality and are more predisposed to become ill and make critical mistakes. We are also more likely to not believe in God.

The effect of Saturn transits leads the Magi Society to another new symbolism for Saturn. Besides control, Saturn signifies delusions. When Saturn makes a strong transiting aspect to one of our critical planets, it deludes us, or we delude ourselves. This results in our judgment going awry. Since we are less likely to believe in God when we have transits by Saturn, does that mean God is more than just a belief? We think so.

So Saturn is a problem in Historic Aspects, and it is a problem as a transit. But each of us can overcome the Saturn aspects in our charts by turning them into gifts. When we do so, we take a step toward greatness.

We Can Choose How Our Aspects Will Impact Us Most

We are finally at the end of our discussion on the symbolisms of the planets. We just want to emphasize one point and then we can go on to the next subject.

We have learned a lot of symbolisms for each planet, and we explained several times that we can use them to interpret planetary aspects and linkages, and that the valid range of interpretations is dependent on the range of valid symbolisms. We think this point needs additional emphasis.

Getting back to Jim Jones and Marshall Applewhite, they deluded themselves in a way that most of us will never understand. However, such people generally are not leaders and do not have the ability to lead others astray—but unfortunately, these two men did have that ability. They each had the Super Success Aspect of the Jupiter-Pluto conjunction. This aspect is the most common aspect among the giants of U.S. business. It can give the native superior (Jupiter) power (Pluto). Men such as Bill Gates and Warren Buffett use the aspect to help them gain power in the traditional manner and in the normal way. Jones and Applewhite used their Super Success Aspect to gain power over other people to maintain their own delusions. So every aspect can be misused and abused, and every aspect can be used wisely. The choice is ours.

☿ ☿ ☿

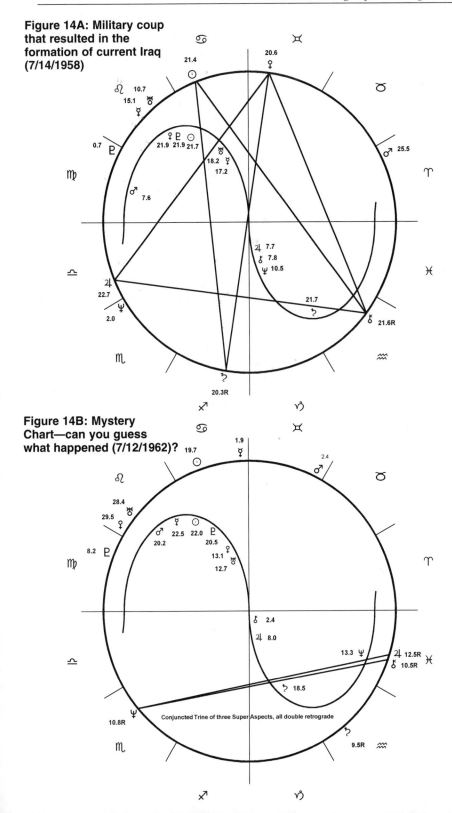

Figure 14A: Military coup that resulted in the formation of current Iraq (7/14/1958)

Figure 14B: Mystery Chart—can you guess what happened (7/12/1962)?

Conjuncted Trine of three Super Aspects, all double retrograde

CHAPTER FIFTEEN

♋

The Magi Society's Planetary Interpreter™— What Every Aspect and Linkage Means

We have now discussed how to analyze birth charts to help you check for linkages, activations, and Combined Planetary Geometry. You now also know how to interpret aspects and how important they are. Aspects are the basic building blocks of Planetary Geometry. They are the best clues to a person's personality because they are celestial signs of the essence of someone's nature.

We can also use the aspects of a day to evaluate if it is a good time to get married or begin anything consequential, and also to help us decide what activities are most suitable on that day. You now also possess an adequate working knowledge of interaspects and the symbolisms of the planets so you can understand the range of meanings of aspects, interaspects, and other forms of Planetary Geometry. You should be ready to put all this to work and improve your daily lives in all matters related to love and money.

However, the Magi Society has found that astrology is not helpful if the person using it is biased and wants to read things into something that is not there, or ignore something that *is* there. As a result, we are liable to make mistakes in the way we interpret the stars. For this reason, it is imperative that we have an objective guide to all the aspects and interaspects. To help you be as objective as possible, we have painstakingly prepared a PLANE-TARY INTERPRETER, which lists the most useful and valid interpretations for every aspect and interaspect as they apply to matters of love, sex, relationships, and money. In this way, you have a handy reference that allows you to analyze any individual chart or combined chart. You can sim-

289

ply check to see what aspects and interaspects exist, and use the interpretations listed in this chapter.

To help you learn how to use Magi Astrology to analyze relationships, we strongly advise that you first check the interaspects and Combined Planetary Geometry that you form with persons you know best. Your intimates, family members, and co-workers are good ones to start with. This exercise is usually eye-opening and always very instructive. You will find that the persons you have had the most enduring relationships with are those you have the strongest linkages with.

To begin to learn the importance of natal aspects and how well they indicate a person's character, you should also analyze the natal aspects of everyone you have an opinion about. This means not just friends, but also public figures such as celebrities, politicians, and so on. These people are all reflections of their natal aspects. You will soon realize what we meant when we said that with Magi Astrology, you will see the world with a clarity and perspective that will truly benefit your life.

One of the main purposes of this chapter is to provide you with predictions, interpretations, opinions, and analyses that are *objective* and not based on your own emotions and wishful thinking. Too many people look at interaspects that they have with someone, tilt the meanings a little, and then use them to justify the relationship. Please do not do that. We all have a blind spot in our judgment. No matter what precautions we take, nearly all of us at some point in our lives delude ourselves about someone, or are deluded by another person—and it is when we are deluded that we are most likely to get hurt.

We hope that this chapter, and this book as a whole, will help you protect yourself from being hurt. Delusion is one of the primary causes of heartbreak and emotional pain. It can also be the cause of significant financial losses. Unfortunately, we cannot promise that you will never again be misled or that your judgment will rival that of King Solomon, but we truly believe that if you master Magi Astrology, you will have an insight into love and money issues that you would not have had without it.

How to Use the Magi Society Planetary Interpreter

This chapter contains a condensed version of the Magi Society's Planetary Interpreter™, and it is written to help you in several crucial areas. First, we hope to help you better understand the true nature and potential of your relationship with any person. We do this by providing the most suitable and accurate interpretations for each interaspect as they relate to love relationships. All this information is derived from our mammoth research and is based on what we have found to be the most likely outcome of each linkage or activation.

Here are the steps to using the Planetary Interpreter: First, draw up the Combined Alignment Chart for yourself and the person you are interested in (such as your significant other), and list all of the interaspects the two of you make, both linkages and activations. Then check the Planetary Interpreter, and read each of our interpretations for every interaspect. That should give you a very solid basis for forming an initial assessment. The next step is to check to see if there are any important shapes of Planetary Geometry in the Combined Chart, such as Grand Trines or T-squares. If there are, they must be given added weight as far as the overall evaluation is concerned. (A blank Magi AstroChart is printed on page 433 so that you can make copies of it and use the copies for your charts.)

To understand any relationship, you also need to understand the other person. This requires an accurate interpretation of the person's aspects. The first step is to draw the chart of that other person and list all of the aspects of that chart. Then read all of the appropriate interpretations. With natal aspects, this Planetary Interpreter deals primarily with matters of love and lists the most salient characteristics that each natal aspect is likely to be a sign of as it relates to love relationships. You can then intertwine your judgments with our predictions to know the person better.

As a final step in your analysis, you should take into account the nature of your significant other, your interaspects and Combined Geometry, and look back at key incidents that have impacted your relationship to see if everything fits. For example, does the person have Romance Aspects, and do you have Romantic Super Linkages? Has your significant other ever talked about marriage with you? If the answer is yes to the first two questions, no to the last question, and you love the person and think this is "the one," you should pick a time to talk about your future together. You can use the Planetary Interpreter to choose which aspects you want to have on the day you decide to discuss the big question.

On the other hand, if the two of you have no Romantic Super Linkages and your significant other is talking marriage, maybe you should be careful. Do you have Sexual Linkages, and is your significant other confusing sex with love? Are *you*?

Love relationships are always very complicated, and there are no hard and fast rules. In the next chapter, we are going to analyze a number of very famous breakups, as well as some good marriages. The purpose is to help you learn what to look for in you own relationships, and to better understand them.

How We Categorize Linkages Versus Activations and Aspects

In the Planetary Interpreter, every possible interaspect and natal aspect is interpreted. We give separate meanings for planetary linkages, as opposed to activations. Activations are interaspects of 90 and 180 degrees; linkages are interaspects of 120, 0, 150 degrees, and parallels or contra-parallels. We've already explained that interaspects that are 30 or 60 degrees are too weak to warrant separate consideration.

There is an exception to the above rule, though. With an interaspect that is formed at the quincunx angle (150 degrees), if one of the planets is Saturn, the result is an activation, not a linkage. All Saturn activations are SATURN CLASHES. In the next chapter, we will give you examples of the effects of these Saturn Clashes.

All personal aspects, no matter what the angle of alignment, are interpreted in the same way, but we also give you useful meanings for election-al aspects. There are different meanings for enhancements and Turbulent Aspects because they are very different in Electional Astrology.

Connected Persons Feel the Effects of Interaspects Differently

When two persons form an interaspect, we have referred to these two individuals as connected persons. Throughout this book, we have assumed that the impact of an interaspect is the same on each connected person. Although this is true, the connected persons will differ on the level of the impact that they feel. This creates a complexity in the way every interaspect is interpreted, but there are good general rules that are usually applicable and helpful.

Once again, we need to create some terminology that has been missing from astrology, since astrology has never given a term to the person with whom you create an interaspect with. Depending on whether the interaspect is a Linkage or an Activation, we will refer to such a person as the LINKED PERSON or the ACTIVATED PERSON. In both cases, the two persons are also CONNECTED PERSONS, whether the interaspect is a linkage or acti-vation. Now that we have the terms we need, we can explain how to assess the different levels of influence of an interaspect.

Many of you have probably already thought about the fact that an interaspect usually has a stronger impact on one of the two Connected Persons depending on which person contributes which planet to the interaspect. For example, if two persons form a Venus-Sun linkage, the one that contributes the Venus (the Venus person of the linkage) is likely to feel more attachment than the Sun person (the one who contributes the Sun). *With all interaspects, one party is likely to feel the influence more strongly than the other.* The next questions would be: "How do you determine which connected person is impacted more? Who is more emotionally attached?" The Magi Society has discovered a way to accurately answer this interesting and often crucial question.

After a great amount of effort, we discovered that there is actually a specific hierarchy and order to the strength of the influence of the planets. Of all the planets, whenever a person contributes Chiron to an interaspect, that person is most impacted. In most cases, the person who is most involved emotionally is the one who contributes Chiron to the interaspect. For example, if two persons have a linkage of Chiron to any other planet, usually the Chiron person will feel the effects of the linkage more strongly than the other person, and will be more emotionally attached. You can see how vital this information is.

The planet that is second in level of interaspect influence is Venus, then Neptune, Mars, and the Sun. The following list shows the sequence:

1.	Chiron	7.	Pluto
2.	Venus	8.	Jupiter
3.	Neptune	9.	Uranus
4.	Mars	10.	Mercury
5.	Sun	11.	Saturn
6.	Moon		

You might have noticed that all three Romance Planets are at the top of the list. This is meaningful and consistent with all that we have learned.

You can use this list to analyze the relative and comparative effects of any interaspect. Each interaspect has a specific range of influences, but each person will feel the impact at a different level and intensity.

There is one other interesting and overwhelmingly important detail that affects which person is more influenced by an interaspect. Women are more influenced when there is a linkage that includes a Romance Planet, and men feel more attracted when there is an interaspect that includes a Sexual Planet. Why? C'est la vie. Life is more interesting that way, and you don't want to be bored, do you?

Saturn Clashes

There is an added twist to the rules we have just given you. It relates to Saturn and all interaspects that it is involved with.

We have said several times that Saturn is different from any other planet, but we have so far avoided a discussion of Saturn interaspects. This is because it was necessary for you to first have a feel for interaspects before we threw double curve balls, which is what Saturn interaspects are.

When two persons are connected by an interaspect of Saturn and another planet, the interaspect is never ever *by itself* a sign of love or affection. However, all Saturn interaspects are symbolic of strong bonds, because the Saturn person always has a measure of control over the other individual. If the interaspect is an enhancement angle, there can be a lasting relationship between the two connected persons, but much depends on the other interaspects that the couple has. However, if the angle of the Saturn interaspect is a Turbulent Angle (90, 180, 150), then the interaspect has the potential of being very disruptive. We call such interaspects Saturn Clashes, and they are often the most negative interaspects of any relationship. But, as in all matters of human relationships, look at the overall picture. All of the other interaspects and the Combined Planetary Geometry must always also be taken into account.

In the next chapter, we give you examples of how Saturn Clashes have influenced the outcome of the relationships of some very famous couples. That will give you a good grasp of how to properly weigh the impact of Saturn Clashes on your own relationships. Besides Chiron interaspects, the Saturn interaspects are the most important.

℧ ℧ ℧

MAGI ASTROLOGY PLANETARY INTERPRETER™

(The applicable orbs for all aspects and interaspects listed are the Magi Society's normal orb of 3 degrees for the longitudes and 1.2 degrees for the declinations.)

Please note: When we are referring to business charts, we include employment dates; thus, anything good for a business is good for starting a job or going on an initial job interview.

Chiron and Sun

Linkage: This is a special linkage and usually creates mutual trust, especially on the part of the Chiron person. For this reason, this is also called the Linkage of Trust. Another result of this linkage is great ease when the linked persons are in physical proximity or even just talking on the phone. Linked persons view each other as confidants, a part of the family, and long-term partners. Since the linkage creates a higher level of trust on the part of the Chiron individuals, they need to be alert to the possibility that they could be blind to the Sun person's faults.

Activation: This activation usually results in a lack of trust between the two connected persons. It is rare for two persons who form this activation to be able to sustain a relationship. This is one of the CLASSIC SCHISMS, meaning that when there is an interaspect that creates such a schism, it is very rare for the activated persons to overcome it.

Personal Aspect: This is one of the most powerful aspects that is not a Super Aspect. It helps the native to be noteworthy and/or charismatic. If the native also has a Super Aspect formed by Chiron, then he or she can have a hypnotic or mesmerizing influence on most of us. This is also a Female Romance Aspect where the native (person born with the aspect), if female, has an unusually intense desire for marriage and children. Such women often marry and have children when they are very young.

Electional Aspect in Matters of Love: *Enhancement*—one of the most favorable aspects under which to get married, because it is representative of marriage and family. This is singularly the very best aspect time to meet your prospective in-laws for the first time; the symbolisms of this aspect literally signify a person of the family, and you will be viewed as such. In love affairs, if your intention is to just have a fling, this aspect is not good for starting a love affair; affairs started under this aspect will likely be long-lasting and give rise to a desire for marriage or pregnancy.

Turbulent—one of the worst aspects under which to get married, as it signifies a day of divorce or a broken family. Avoid this aspect when getting married no matter what the other aspects are. This is a FLING ASPECT, so it is one of the best ones under which to commence a dalliance.

Electional Aspect in Matters of Money: *Enhancement*—a very helpful aspect when it comes to business; it is most helpful in technology, entertainment, and inventions. Dell Computer was incorporated with this aspect.

Turbulent—very bad, as it is likely to be tumultuous and unsuccessful. This is a highly destabilizing aspect. Do not choose such a day to start anything; the aspect creates disruption, especially for that which is ruled by Chiron—such as family values, children, marriages, and spouses. Bill Clinton's second inauguration occurred during this aspect; and look what has happened even though the inaugural date also has enhancements of Sun and Jupiter, Sun and Uranus, Sun and Neptune, Jupiter and Uranus, and Jupiter and Neptune.

Chiron and Moon

Linkage: This is a very strong linkage and creates the intuitive feeling of having known another person in a previous life—often a sign of "love at first sight"—especially for the Chiron person.

Activation: This is a very problematic activation and is a Classic Schism. One person, usually the Chiron person, sometimes feels a one-sided desire to make the relationship permanent, while the other person feels there is something very wrong with the relationship but cannot ascertain the reason. This activation is one of the HEARTBREAK ACTIVATIONS, and is indicative of a lack of compatible emotional outlooks.

Personal Aspect: This signifies a strong desire for marriage and children, someone who is highly intuitive and resourceful. It is a Female Romance Aspect, and if the native is a woman, all she thinks about is her Prince Charming or meeting one. She feels completely unfulfilled without one in her life.

Electional Aspect in Matters of Love: (Please keep in mind that the Moon moves very fast, about one degree every two hours. For this reason, all Moon aspects last only 12 hours.)

Enhancement—a good time to try to conceive and build a family, this is a FERTILITY ASPECT (if you are having a fling and want to remain uninvolved, be sure you take adequate birth-control precautions during this aspect). It is also a very good time to make amends with a loved one, as this aspect creates a very serene, peaceful, and loving mood. It is a good aspect under which to exchange vows or start a romance.

Turbulent—avoid this aspect in any important matters of love because it engenders the feeling of dissatisfaction and unfulfillment in a distraught manner. Romance tends to go awry during this aspect's time. It is a very bad aspect to have at the beginning of a marriage or romance, and creates an inability to feel comfortable with the relationship.

Electional Aspect in Matters of Money: *Enhancement*—a favorable aspect to start a business, especially one that is related to Chiron. It is also a very good aspect under which to start a job, because you will feel like part of a family. Employees who start working during this aspect will be more likely to feel loyal toward their employers.

Turbulent—whatever you start with the Moon-Chiron activation will be relentlessly problematic and emotionally draining. Don't do it—ever.

Chiron and Mercury

Linkage: This is the best linkage for improving the ability (and desire) for two persons to be able to effortlessly communicate with each other and to have mutual intuitive understanding. It is a very beneficial linkage, especially from the woman's point of view. In general, women need to be able to talk things over in a relationship, and this linkage creates the condition of being on the same wavelength, and helps to establish the condition of being of like mind—so much so that sometimes words are unnecessary.

Activation: This is bad to have with anyone important in your life, as it gives rise to a mental block against understanding each other on a verbal level; it is indicative of being worlds apart. This is a Classic Schism.

Personal Aspect: It is the most powerful aspect in helping someone to be a charismatic speaker (Evita Peron was born with this), writer, or singer. This aspect also promotes a New Age outlook and makes the native highly intelligent, adventuresome, and self-reliant.

Electional Aspect in Matters of Love: *Enhancement*—a particularly good time to discuss marital problems, family matters, children; and a good time for parents to talk over problems with their kids. It's also a favorable time to plan, think, or talk about the future and careers.

Turbulent—if you'd like to get engaged, don't bring up the question of marriage under this aspect, because if your lover is undecided, he/she will not want to discuss it now.

Electional Aspect in Matters of Money: Enhancement—a good time to commence a business in Mercury-related areas, including publishing anything, releasing an album, or starting a software and computer business.

Turbulent—impedes success in whatever is ruled by Mercury.

Chiron and Venus

Linkage: This is the MAGIcal Linkage and a Golden Linkage, and is singularly the most powerful and beneficial linkage that two persons can have. It is also a Romance Linkage and a Cinderella Linkage. Interpretation: COMBINED DESTINIES, the uniting of futures, becoming one family, money as partners, joining forces, a lifelong relationship, and a charismatic relationship. If you have this linkage with someone, chances are very high that you will be of great help to each other. This linkage also greatly improves the chances of a marriage with the linked person. This is the strongest of all linkages and helps form enduring bonds. It has almost mystical influences and seems to help the linked persons in anything that they do as a pair.

Activation: There is a very strong initial attraction, and it can be lasting, but somehow or other, a relationship with this activation very rarely results in a marriage. If it does, the marriage usually fails; therefore, we call this activation the IMPOSSIBLE DREAM. In the long run, this activation usually results in antagonistic viewpoints about the relationship and where it's going, and can be a cause of strident disharmony, with misleading, intermittent periods of ease. Such relationships are like yo-yos, but they spiral downward. You do not want this activation in any relationship because the odds of failure are very high, and it is highly destabilizing to all other areas of your life. It really is the impossible dream, yet you dream about it constantly.

Personal Aspect: This is a Super Aspect and the most significant Romance Aspect. Some interpretations: charismatic beauty, love of family and marriage, strong marriage and family orientation, a career involved with making money, love for the New Age and what is a part of the New Age, money from marriage and family, money from endeavors that are ruled by Chiron and what has to do with the public, and a charismatic amount of money. The native is almost always in love with being in love and therefore always needs to be in a love relationship, resulting in a tendency to fall in love too easily.

Electional Aspect in Matters of Love: *Enhancement*—singularly the best aspect to include in a love chart, as it greatly increases and nurtures mutual love; and gives birth to the desire, urge, and need to marry and build a family. It's also a great aspect time to first meet prospective in-laws. Whenever possible, include this aspect in selecting any relationship chart, unless you want only a fling (in which case, avoid this aspect or you'll end up with a serious relationship).

Turbulent—a Classic Schism, it has the opposite effect of the enhancement. This is a relationship breaker and must be avoided in a marriage chart under any circumstances; this activation creates a persistent barrier between the activated persons on most issues, especially family matters. We also advise that you do not conceive under the influence of this aspect; it can give birth to a child who somehow disrupts a marriage, even if the child is loving and helpful in other ways. Romantic affairs that begin with this aspect rarely result in a marriage, so if someone is a potential marriage partner, do not begin your love affair during this aspect. However, if you are looking for a mere dalliance, this is a great aspect to begin the fling. *Another warning:* If you want to get engaged, don't try to talk about marriage when this aspect exists, as an undecided person will decide not to wed during this aspect. Of course, this means that this aspect is a good time to break off a relationship!

Electional Aspect in Matters of Money: *Enhancement*—a very beneficial enhancement to have in any business chart, it is a Super Aspect. It is especially good for corporations that have anything to do with entertainment, and it is one of the three best aspects to have in the formation of an entertainment company (the others being Jupiter-Chiron and Jupiter-Uranus).

Turbulent—the worst Turbulent Aspects for business are Saturn aspects because they are *actively* negative, but this is one not far behind. It is especially bad for business endeavors in areas that are ruled by Chiron. One result of this aspect is an inability to obtain loyal employees; all the good ones leave and the bad ones stay.

Chiron and Mars

Linkage: This is a Sexual Linkage for the man, but the woman wants a family with the man of this linkage. In terms of attraction that leads to marriage, the Chiron-Mars linkage sometimes creates a level of attraction that is often impossible to ignore. For this reason, this is the one and only MARITAL SEXUAL LINKAGE. The man often will marry the linked woman.

Activation: Like other Chiron activations, this can create initial attraction but usually is ultimately disruptive of a relationship and is a sign of eventual incompatibility. In particular, this activation creates quarrelsomeness and even belligerence between the connected persons, especially about their relationship and marriage. Here, too, the man and woman react differently; the man just wants sex, and the woman wants marriage. But unlike the linkage, the man will not marry the activated woman.

Personal Aspect: One of the Male Sexual Aspects, it creates the ultimate high energy level, generates more pure energy than any other aspect, and rates as a Super Sports Champion Aspect (a term from *Astrology Really Works!*). But the Chiron-Mars aspect does not help coordination in the way the Venus-Mars aspect does. The native needs aspects that help coordination in order to most beneficially harness the energy this aspect provides. If this aspect is not well used and controlled through moral teachings, there can be constant moral slippage toward excessive aggressiveness, and even belligerency.

Electional Aspect in Matters of Love: Enhancement—choose this aspect to make love because this is one of the best times to do so, but if you do not want a pregnancy, you have to be especially careful and be absolutely certain to use effective contraception, because the conception rate is *highest* during this aspect, making it a FERTILITY ASPECT. On the other hand, if you have fertility problems and want a pregnancy, this is the best aspect under which to try to conceive; this aspect creates high energy that can be directed toward creating a family.

Turbulent—increased chance of fatal accidents; this is not a good time to try to conceive because there is a low fertility rate at this time, and conception is more likely to lead to miscarriages.

Electional Aspect in Matters of Money: Enhancement—a helpful aspect for any business chart because it provides vitality; the aspect improves competitiveness and helps attract good employees.

Activation: This creates an environment where employees are less likely to want to stay; therefore, it's a bad aspect for any business venture.

Chiron and Jupiter

Linkage: This is a Romance Linkage, a Golden Linkage, and also a Cinderella Linkage. Except for the Venus-Chiron linkage, it is the most beneficial and powerful linkage that you can have with anyone. Interpretations: combined super success, a blessed marriage and relationship, a fortunate family, success as partners, and mutual Golden Handshakes.

Activation: This is not always bad, but is still generally not helpful in that it usually reduces the chances of a long-term relationship. However, if the activation is a part of Combined Symmetrical Planetary Geometry, then the activation can often be very helpful. This is true of all Jupiter activations, but the Jupiter-Chiron activation is the most helpful activation when included in Combined Symmetrical Planetary Geometry.

Personal Aspect: This is one of the most powerful of all aspects, as this Super Aspect provides the native with a fabulous public image and a commanding presence, which instills confidence and wins trust. It foretells a great destiny and career and can result in noteworthy success, ultimate intuitive genius, and success through charisma in anything ruled by Chiron. No matter how powerful and helpful one aspect is, though, there is no substitute for hard work, determination, and tenacity.

Electional Aspect in Matters of Love: Enhancement—a Super Aspect, this is one of the very best aspects to include in a Wedding Chart and greatly enhances the chances of a successful marriage and *healthy* family. When this aspect exists, it is a great time to get engaged and to conceive. The Jupiter-Chiron enhancement is the *most blessed time* to conceive because it improves fertility and also provides the added benefit of increasing your chances of having a child that will be a pride and joy—one who will be loyal to the family.
Turbulent—avoid this aspect in Wedding Charts and any matters of love, as it usually destabilizes any relationship begun during the aspect's time.

Electional Aspect in Matters of Money: Enhancement—this Super Aspect is one of the best aspects when seeking success with the outside world, such as the entertainment industry or selling to the public. Interpretations: enormous power and a fabulous public image, super charisma, and a successful career and blessed future.
Turbulent—although this aspect can provide power and success, there is

an eventual downfall, making this the aspect of the Fallen Angel. Obviously, you do not want this aspect in a business chart.

Chiron and Saturn

Linkage: This creates a very strong bond; usually the Saturn person has a high level of control over the destiny of the Chiron person and has the upper hand in the overall relationship. This linkage itself does not have any negative or positive overtones. Marriage between the linkage persons is probable if there are also Romance Linkages.

Activation: This is a Classic Schism and a Heartbreak Activation. It is also a Saturn Clash—the worst one. Please remember that Saturn is different from any other planet in that it links only at an enhancement angle, and quincunxes are activations, not linkages. The Saturn person generally has control and dominance over the destiny of the Chiron person, but the chances of marriage are slim if the Saturn person is the man because he usually does not want to marry the Chiron woman. If there is a marriage, the marriage often ends in a divorce that is incredibly bitter. This activation usually results in heartbreak for the Chiron person. Princess Di and Prince Charles had this activation, and Princess Di was the Chiron woman.

Personal Aspect: This provides the native with the unusual ability to be a force against Judeo-Christian beliefs, morals and family values, and against marriage as an institution. This aspect also gives the native an ability to dominate the destinies of others, for better or worse. The native very often has a desire and ability to destroy marriages and break up families, and is often against the free enterprise economic system, preferring socialism or communism. Because this is a Saturn aspect, a turbulent angle can result in unconventionality. Especially in a woman, the turbulent Saturn-Chiron aspect is the SECLUSION ASPECT, with the native often living the last decades without a loved one. If a person has this aspect, there is far greater need to be much more careful about any involvements. In any relationship of love, a Romantic Super Linkage is required to offset this natal aspect. Please remember that all other natal aspects must be taken into account when analyzing a chart, and there could be offsetting aspects.

Electional Aspect in Matters of Love: Enhancement—this is a very complicated aspect to understand, and is disruptive of the status quo. It is called the MARRIAGE BREAKER. If you're married and you begin an affair with a new lover during this aspect time, the affair is likely to unbalance your marriage; you could become married to this new lover. However, if you're not married, then any affair begun under this aspect will break up some other relationship of yours, such as a job or close friendship. Basically, the aspect breaks up marriages, but if there is no marriage to break, it breaks up some other relationship. This makes this aspect the perfect one to include in a Love Chart if you are looking to displace someone's spouse. Does that give you any ideas? Also, if you want to break up your marriage, you may want to begin an affair under this aspect because it will help you get divorced. But in all cases, for the affair to have impact, the Sun must be enhanced.

Turbulent—also called a Marriage Breaker, one of the worst aspects to natalize into any Wedding Chart. It signifies destruction of families and relationships of all kinds, but in other ways, it works like the enhancement in that affairs started under this aspect break up existing marriages or other relationships. This is the worst aspect time to first meet your prospective in-laws.

Electional Aspect in Matters of Business: *Enhancement*—although there are a few successful businesses that have this aspect, we do not recommend it. It can help a business venture in Chiron areas, but there is a price to pay; the workplace of this business is not a happy environment, and employees are more likely to be disloyal.

Turbulent—this is one of the worst activations to have for business matters; avoid natalizing this aspect under any circumstances.

Chiron and Uranus

Linkage: This linkage is powerful in providing mutual respect and combined public acclaim and success. Interpretations: famous and charismatic partnership or career, and mutually magnified success.

Activation: This activation is an indication of stress and clashes that could become known to your friends, family, and business associates. It has a special power to propel you into harmful changes. In love affairs, this activation is particularly bad if you're only seeking a dalliance because it has a tendency to destroy whatever other relationships you already have.

Personal Aspect: This is a very powerful and helpful aspect, but unfortunately, it occurs too rarely (about every five years). It is most helpful when the native directs the aspect to achieve great fame and success in an area ruled by Chiron or Uranus. A person with this aspect has the ultimate in hypnotic charisma.

Electional Aspect for Matters of Love: Enhancement—a fabulous aspect to have in any love chart. It provides worldwide notability and acclaim to a marriage or romance.
Turbulent—problematic, and capable of shattering existing relationships. This is a very dangerous aspect to natalize in any love chart, especially an affair.

Electional Aspect for Matters of Money: Enhancement—one of the best; especially good for endeavors in entertainment, broadcasting, and any technology that improves our well-being.
Turbulent—It is powerful yet harmful. Because of the slow movements of these two planets, this aspect can last a while.

Chiron and Neptune

Linkage: The Lifetime Linkage, and a Cinderella Linkage, this is one of the linkages that creates very lasting relationships. This is also a Romance Linkage and the third most common linkage among married couples. Interpretations: lifelong togetherness, a lasting part of the family, security as a family, a secure family life, and long-term security through marriage and children.

Activation: It is still powerful but tumultuous and usually ends up being a disaster after a seemingly fruitful beginning. Be aware of these tendencies for this activation. We advise that you do not have your heart set on a long-term relationship with anyone with whom you form this activation, no matter how tempting; the activation is interpreted as a failed long-term relationship.

Personal Aspect: This is a CINDERELLA ASPECT. Interpretations: long-term financial security through marriage, long-term family ties, long-term charisma, lasting noteworthiness, New Age ideas and inspirations, and becoming a real live Cinderella. It works on men, also. Since Neptune is the most feminine planet, this aspect imparts a soft, feminine charisma that is very appealing. Princess Diana was born with this aspect. It is also a Romance Aspect. The native believes in real-life Cinderellas and dreams about marrying a form of royalty.

Electional Aspect in Matters of Love: *Enhancement*—a fabulous aspect to be able to incorporate into a wedding date. It signifies long-term marriage, family ties, and security as a family. It's also a very good aspect time to try to conceive.

Turbulent—one to avoid, this is destructive of harmony, the family, and emotions.

Electional Aspect in Matters of Money: *Enhancement*—one of the best aspects for any business, it provides the highest level of financial security, especially from Neptunian sources and endeavors.

Turbulent—bad, bad, and bad; no money, no resources, and no talent. It's not something you want in a business chart.

Chiron and Pluto

Linkage: This is a Golden Linkage. Interpretations: combined power and success, a prosperous and powerful partnership or marriage, noteworthy affluence, and compelling and effective family ties and emotional relationships.

Activation: It creates a persistent bond, but one that is often misleading because it has a very strong initial attachment but usually deteriorates at a slow pace. It can be highly disruptive of families and is a marriage breaker. If you are married and wish to remain so, do not have an affair with anyone who forms this activation unless you want to be tormented incessantly.

Personal Aspect: This is a Super Aspect. Interpretations: noteworthy success, a highly profitable career, power from marriage or the family, and a person of power and vision.

Electional Aspect in Matters of Love: *Enhancement*—one of the best aspects for a marriage chart, it is very rare. It signifies a powerful marriage and family or an unstoppable love affair. You must take advantage of this when it occurs because personal relationships commenced under this aspect have a formidable momentum, which greatly increases chances of marriage. A marriage with this aspect is extraordinarily powerful and financially strong, but has no influence on happiness, which must come from other aspects..

Turbulent—It makes a relationship tumultuous and self-destructive; it is a very bad aspect time under which to conduct anything to do with love.

Electional Aspect in Matters of Money: *Enhancement*—a Super Aspect; endows extraordinary profit-making power. This is a great enhancement to have in any electional chart. We call this enhancement the STAR WARS enhancement because the movie was released under such an enhancement.

Turbulent—provides charisma to a lesser degree than enhancement, but endeavors begun with such an aspect must weather very stormy times.

Venus and Sun

Linkage: This is the Cupid Linkage and gives birth to a very powerful mutual attraction. The Venus person usually feels the linkage more than the Sun person. This linkage is highly indicative of intimacy and seduction between the linked persons. Monica Lewinsky and Bill Clinton have two of these linkages.

Activation: It represents a result that is the opposite of the linkage; this is one of the few interaspects that create mutual dislike between the connected persons.

Personal Aspect: This is a Female Romance Aspect. The female native is highly romantic, believes in love at first sight and living happily ever after, and is very much in need of a husband and a family to fulfill her life. This is also the Glamor and Grace Aspect because it is indicative of great physical beauty of the face, the highest degree of social charm, and an irresistible smile. People with this aspect, especially bi-levels, are the most beautiful people in the world. This aspect also makes the native very fashion conscious and materialistic; money is usually very important to these people because they love luxury, which is ruled by Venus. When a beautiful woman is married to a millionaire who reminds you of Humpty Dumpty after his great fall, the woman often has this aspect, or the Venus-Pluto aspect. Women, especially, but also men who have this aspect, are the best seducers in the world. How do you think they get those millionaires? It is not just looks—it is seduction! When a Sun-Venus person seduces you, you will never forget it and will want it to be repeated every day of your life..

Electional Aspect for Matters of Love: *Enhancement*—a SEDUCTION ASPECT, it is the most romantic time, and it is one of the best times to seduce someone because your chances of success are greatly improved during this aspect. It is also a propitious time to start a romance or make love for the first time because the aspect often gives rise to a highly romantic relationship. Interpretation: a time for love and romance. The influence is strongest when the aspect is APPLYING (please see the glossary).

Turbulent—interestingly enough, this turbulent aspect never occurs because Venus is never far enough away from the Sun.

Electional Aspect for Matters of Money: *Enhancement*—although Venus rules money and movable possessions of all kinds, the Sun-Venus enhancement is not an especially good day for business and making money. This may be due to the fact that Venus and Sun work best for romantic endeavors, even though Venus does rule money. Nonetheless, the enhancement is mildly helpful in a business chart. The best use of this aspect is to form a business in fashion, makeup, or beauty.

Turbulent—does not occur.

Venus and Moon

Linkage: This is a strong karmic and intuitive bond. It creates elevated harmony and compatibility, with the feeling that this is the right person.

Activation: It eventually results in a sense of instability about the relationship. A couple with this activation is generally awkward when together, thus immobilizing any advancement of the relationship.

Personal Aspect: This is a female Romance Aspect; it is also indicative of a good memory and keen intuitive capabilities, being sensitive and sensible, and very steady emotionally. However, if this aspect is too exact, the native can have occasional bouts of hyper-emotionalism and think the sky is falling (caused by transits).

Electional Aspect for Matters of Love: *Enhancement*—a Seduction Aspect and an extremely romantic time; a great aspect to have on a date if you want to fall in love or you want someone to fall in love with you. If there is also an enhancement of the Sun, the love is likely to be long-lasting.

Turbulent—have you ever fallen out of love? This is one of the aspects that can begin the ball rolling in that direction; it lasts only an evening but is a very emotionally charged time. Do not get married, engaged, or initiate a romance during this aspect. Trying to make love now can be awkward.

Electional Aspect for Matters of Money: *Enhancement*—a good time for recruiting new employees or throwing an office party; also mildly helpful financially.

Turbulent—slightly diminishes the money-making ability of business, but good aspects in a chart can overpower this one.

Venus and Mercury

Linkage: This signifies ease of communication; the two linked persons could "talk forever." It is indicative of two persons who not only love to talk to each other, but who can make money together in areas ruled by Mercury, such as writing, teaching, and singing.

Activation: This impedes the ability to communicate with each other and is a problematic activation that usually leads to regular misunderstandings.

Personal Aspect: This is a very good aspect to have, as it signifies a highly intelligent person with great communication skills. Interpretations: an orderly and logical mind, a beautiful voice, money from, and love of, singing or writing; intelligent, articulate, and mentally adroit; good memory; especially well coordinated physically; elevated respiratory capacity; and a gracious and polite communicator.

Electional Aspect for Matters of Love: *Enhancement*—a good time to iron out misunderstandings and problems by talking things over. There is increased ease of communication under this aspect.

Turbulent—the oppositions and squares do not occur between Mercury and Venus. The semi-sextile is formed regularly, and this is the weakest of the activation angles, producing only a mild impediment to being able to express one's views and understand each other.

Electional Aspect for Matters of Money: *Enhancement*—a good time to negotiate and understand each other's perspective. This is a good aspect to incorporate into arbitration agreements, and it is helpful to have in business charts for commencing anything that is ruled by Mercury— especially computer software, singing, writing, transportation, and communications equipment.

Turbulent—this aspect makes it more difficult to come to agreement on anything; misunderstandings can arise that would not have normally occurred. Do not negotiate during this aspect, and do not disseminate office rules or procedures in this aspect time.

Venus and Mars

Linkage: This is one of the three SEXUAL LINKAGES and is therefore one of the three linkages that creates the highest levels of sexual attraction, desire for intimacy, and energy. This is the linkage of the male sex planet (Mars) with the female (Venus) sex planet. As such, it is almost irresistible when the Mars person is the man. However, the juxtaposed linkage is still very powerful. Interpretations: desire and lust for each other's body, love of sex, unified bodily movements, the joining of bodies, and bodies and sexual energies in synch.

Activation: This is one of those activations that has the same initial effect as the linkage. It burns out at a moderate pace, but it will fizzle out completely. An experience with someone with whom you form this interaspect can be exhilarating, but don't get your hopes up for many repeat performances or a real relationship; they usually do not last and can leave a pile of ashes. Don't get trapped into going back for more and more just to try to regain the highs you initially experienced; you will probably not ever reach them again with this person.

Personal Aspect: This is a Super Sexual Aspect for women and men; it creates a very elevated desire for, and ability to engage in, an abnormally high frequency of sexual activities. This person is also a great lover for you if body movements and being always willing and able are important to you. Interpretations: elevated energy level, including sexual energy; love of sex and love of the body; grace of motion and movement; great ability to make love with the body; highly coordinated; love of sports; love of aggressive activities; mercurial and quick tempered; beautiful body; and especially attractive muscles.

Electional Aspect in Matters of Love: Enhancement—a Seduction Aspect, whether you are a single person who is very much into dating or a very married grandparent, it is worthwhile to make a note in your calendar of every day that has any of the three Sexual Aspects when they form an enhancement. They are great times to make love and can produce a night you will not soon forget. When you make love during the time of such enhancements, you will harness the power of such aspects, and you will have greatly increased sexual capacity. Under this aspect, a normal man can be a tiger, and a normal woman can be like Aphrodite. These times are rare, so be certain to plan ahead and take advantage of each and every one of them. Obviously, if your marriage or relationship needs an added boost and extra spice, making love during such aspect times can do the trick.

Turbulent—can provide a burst of sexual energy, but does not last and is inconsistent. This aspect can cause great disappointment if you prefer the slow hand—you'd probably be better off having a great meal instead of trying to make love now.

Electional Aspect for Matters of Money: Enhancement—a helpful aspect for making money in Mars endeavors such as sports, munitions, and weapons; construction and labor-intensive work; dance, aerobics, and physical therapy; and farming.

Turbulent—not good for anything, and is negative for almost everything. The one exception: This is a good aspect in which to start the legal practice of divorce law.

Venus and Jupiter

Linkage: This is a Silver Linkage that promotes good fortune and success for the linked persons. It also greatly promotes a peaceful and harmonious relationship and significantly reduces the stress level in the relationship since it signifies a desire for peace and forgiveness. Arguments, when they do arise, will be settled quickly.

Activation: It creates disharmony and distrust of each other. It is rare for two persons with this activation to get married, and we would advise against it.

Personal Aspect: This is a Super Aspect and represents a born leader. This person often has truly extraordinary leadership skills and the ability to take command—for example, a champion in sports. Interpretation: love of peace; reliability; ethics, and honor. The emphasis is on reliability and honor; for this reason, the native often makes a great friend and can be counted on when the chips are down. This aspect is also a sign of selfless love (Jupiter rules selflessness), being unselfish and wanting to please, and being able to do so. Perhaps most important of all, this aspect is a sign of a person who is idealistic about love, and falls in love for a lifetime.

Electional Aspect in Matters of Love: *Enhancement*—an extremely good time to try to make amends for past wrongdoing in a relationship and ironing out differences. This is a good aspect time to ask for understanding and forgiveness or to convince someone of something that is true and fair. The truth is easier to see during this aspect. This is also a very good aspect for weddings, and engenders loyalty and honesty in the marriage. For these reasons, this is also an excellent aspect time to begin a romance you hope will lead to marriage.

Turbulent—the opposite effect of the enhancement, it is problematic for any relationship and leads to eventual mistrust and tormenting jealousy.

Electional Aspect in Matters of Money: *Enhancement*—very helpful in a business related to beauty, such as the fashion and makeup industries. It is a good day for starting anything where integrity and loyalty are of utmost importance, such as a law firm or a bank.

Turbulent—the Ruthless Aspect. Although there are successful businesses started with this aspect, we recommend avoiding it if you can. However, there is no need to go *much* out of your way to avert this aspect since it is somewhat passive and does not actively create problems for a business the way turbulent Saturn aspects do. This aspect deals more with the morality of the business rather than the profitability, and indicates that the business would be willing to straddle the line, and even cross it, to meet its objectives. It also signifies a lack of generosity and being willing to break agreements. For these reasons, this aspect is more important as an indication of the kind of company you are dealing with. In other words, do not trust a company that has this aspect; it can be ruthless.

Venus and Saturn

Linkage: This linkage symbolically represents the control of emotions and desires; it tends to reduce the intensity of emotional ties between the linked persons and replaces the emotion with a cool and calculating edge and a "What can you do for me?" attitude on the part of the Saturn person. The Saturn person has very strong control over the Venus person, who will find the relationship very hard to break off. We do not recommend that you be the Venus person in such a linkage, although if there are other very beneficial linkages, the disadvantages of this linkage can be overcome. It is useful if it is part of Combined Symmetrical Planetary Geometry.

Activation: This has the same influence as the linkage, but much stronger and much worse. It creates a highly one-sided control of the Venus person by the Saturn person, which is so overbearing that the Venus person will perpetually seek to break off the relationship. The Venus person will feel smothered, controlled, and stifled by the Saturn person. Definitely do not be the Venus person here.

Personal Aspect: This aspect makes the native very calculating and ambitious. It is indicative of love of money with the ability to make it. The aspect often indicates that the native has a reduced ability to love in a selfless manner, and is pushy.

Electional Aspect in Matters of Love: Enhancement—a very bad aspect to have in any marriage or relationship chart. This aspect usually restricts love from blossoming and engenders a coldly calculating relationship on the part of both connected persons.

Turbulent—same influence as the enhancement, but twice as bad. Avoid in Wedding Charts no matter what. Trying to seduce someone under this aspect is like trying to coax a bee to give up its honey; you will likely get stung. This is definitely not a good time to make love to someone for the first time, get engaged, or married.

Electional Aspect in Matters of Money: Enhancement—a good aspect to have when incorporating a company, since the company will be ambitious and move mountains to meet its objectives. Microsoft Corporation has this aspect.

Turbulent—not good for trying to make money because this aspect usually contracts money, and is interpreted as "contraction of money."

Venus and Chiron—the same as Chiron and Venus on page 298.

Venus and Uranus

Linkage: We find this to be one to avoid because it signifies love of change, including change of partners in a relationship. We call this the Swingers' Linkage, as it creates initial attraction but ultimately results in a desire for change and new partners. The Uranus person is the one who usually wants the change, while the Venus person may not. You can imagine the problems this will cause.

Activation: This is the activation that makes a couple less serious about having a permanent relationship; some even want to swing. When a couple has this activation, they often have a so-called open relationship, with no commitments. This is what some people want, but if you're looking for a lifelong marriage, this is one to avoid. With this activation, usually neither party regards the relationship seriously.

Personal Aspect: A SUPER ASPECT; the native is often a famous beauty who is photogenic, luminous, radiant, and glowing. There is a desire for change, including change of loved ones and the ever-present desire for excitement. This aspect appears often with swingers and those who have married more than several times, and deserves to be called the FLING ASPECT. For a man, this is the aspect of the eternal bachelor. For a woman, this indicates a girl who just wants to have fun; and who is adaptable, attractive, and often very successful in the entertainment industry. If the personal aspect is a Turbulent Angle, the native's love resembles the end of a bungee cord, and defines *long term* as the weekend.

Electional Aspect for Matters of Love: *Enhancement*—signifies a desire for change and excitement, this is a Fling Aspect and the perfect aspect to choose to natalize if you are looking for a quick affair with no commitments because an affair begun under this aspect does not last. In a Wedding Chart, this aspect creates dissatisfaction with the status quo and an urge to be with someone new, and the constant seeking of change and fame. Obviously, you do not want this aspect in your Wedding Chart because the marriage will personify love of fame and love of change; it creates a famous divorce.

Turbulent—if you do not want to stay up at night wondering where your spouse is, avoid this aspect in your marriage chart. It has the same influence as the enhancement, but is much worse. This is a very bad aspect under which to try to make love, because one party or the other can change moods before you get to second base.

Electional Aspect for Matters of Money: Enhancement—a Super Aspect that is very good for making money in a business chart, especially if the business is in a Uranian field such as technology, broadcasting, flying, and entertainment. But the aspect makes the business continually dissatisfied with its status quo and drains resources by pushing the business into a constant search for change and excitement.

Turbulent—this aspect can produce streaks of profits and streaks of heavy losses, where ultimately the losses exceed the gains. Obviously, it is not a good aspect for a business chart.

Venus and Neptune

Linkage: This is one of the Romance Linkages and is symbolic of long-term romance and union. It is the best Linkage that is not Chiron-based; and creates a very harmonious, peaceful, serenely romantic relationship. It will usually bind you long term to the linked person. This is also a Silver Linkage and is excellent for business partners.

Activation: It brings on enormous attraction at the onset, and then roller-coasters, sometimes fading away and sometimes orbiting into romantic exhilaration. However, we do not recommend it because the pain usually eventually outweighs the joy. For most people, such a relationship deteriorates into bitterness. This activation is often the sign of a very costly relationship (in the financial sense), and is a MONEY PIT ACTIVATION.

Personal Aspect: This is a Super Aspect. There's money, money, money—usually lots of it and often inherited. It is the aspect that is most indicative of significant inheritances. It also signifies money from other long-term sources, such as real estate, copyrights and patents, and health-related fields. This is also a Romance Aspect, with the native being generally a highly romantic and gentle person. The native is very idealistic in love, wants to have only one lover, and is very faithful. If you want to marry a millionaire, this is one of the aspects to look for in your prospect; once you find one, we hope the two of you have Romantic Super Linkages.

Electional Aspect for Matters of Love: Enhancement—one of the very best to have in a Marriage Chart, we call this the FOREVERMORE ASPECT, as it signifies long-term love and enduring financial security. It is a Super Aspect, and one you should do your best to include in your

Wedding Chart. If you are planning a first-time seduction of someone whom you may want to marry and are not sure when to do it, check your *Magi Society Ephemeris* and look to see when this enhancement will be here the next time. This is singularly the best Seduction Aspect if you want a long-term relationship.

Turbulent—do not get married in this aspect's time; it reduces the duration of a marriage. The same is true with regard to an affair, which will be short (of course, this may be what you want) and will be very financially draining to both of you (this is *not* what you want).

Electional Aspect for Matters of Money: *Enhancement*—one of the most powerful Super Aspects in terms of making money, especially from Neptune endeavors. By all means, maneuver your schedule and plans to try to include this aspect in all business charts, especially employment charts. This is a great aspect under which to start a job! It is even useful to initiate small business matters with this aspect, such as opening a bank or brokerage account (especially an IRA or pension account). It is also the very best aspect time to commit to any purchase over a period of time, such as buying a house on a mortgage or a car on credit. This aspect will help you make all the payments.

Turbulent—it is rare for a business or deal to succeed in this aspect time, so don't try to buck the trend; it means loss of money over the long term and persistent losses. It creates a money pit.

Venus and Pluto

Linkage: One of the three SEXUAL LINKAGES, this is the most obsessive and unforgettable Sexual Linkage and creates the most intense longing, but not necessarily the most attraction. You can't sleep without the person; you can't eat unless you're together. The downside is that for some, this linkage also creates jealousy, possessiveness, and even mistrust, so the couple's relationship can be highly problematic if the two are not together all the time. The jealousy that this linkage causes can destabilize a relationship if the linked persons are forced to be physically apart on a regular basis because of careers or other such circumstances. This is also a Golden Linkage and is great for making money together.

Activation: While this lasts, it creates the same obsessive desires as the linkage does, but it rarely has any longevity. Unlike the linkage, the activation causes costly disruptiveness. This activation is also one of the MONEY PIT ACTI-

VATIONS; it will drain financial resources in one way or another. If you thought dating or relationships are expensive, this is the worst, even if your date is considerate, because the stars have a way to make it very costly, such as your car breaking down during the date, or you lose your wallet or purse, etc.

Personal Aspect: This is a SEXUAL ASPECT for men and women, and it is the most powerful Sexual Aspect for a woman. It is therefore the Female Super Sexual Aspect—the sign of the insatiable woman. However, the insatiability extends beyond sex; this aspect is indicative of the most intense level of desire for success and power as well as sex, and also provides the ability to obtain them all. Women with this aspect are fabulous lovers, but remember that they also love money and power. If you are a man without money or power, avoid falling in love with a woman who has this aspect or you will be hurt so badly you could be tormented for life; she would leave you for someone who has the money and power and would not be nice in the way she does it. Interpretations: love of power, love of sex, obsessive love (but not the power to love), love of competition. This aspect creates very high energy levels and provides great money-making abilities. *Warning:* If you are a woman married to a man who is a boss, do not let him hire a woman with this aspect; such women do not care if a man is married, and will go after him even if she does not really want him.

Electional Aspect for Matters of Love: Enhancement—this is both a Sexual Aspect and a Seduction Aspect, so whatever you do, plan to be with a loved one in this aspect's time. If you do not have a loved one, when this aspect comes along, anyone will do; it helps to produce truly memorable sex, but unfortunately is less oriented to lovemaking.

Turbulent—the opposite of the enhancement, this aspect reduces lovemaking ability, and also minimizes sexuality and desire for sex. It is one of the worst times to make love. If a man has a problem that requires Viagra, the problem will be worse in this aspect time.

Electional Aspect for Matters of Money: Enhancement—as a Super Aspect, this is one of the best aspects for making money; do whatever you can to natalize this Super Aspect in business charts, including contracts. This aspect is also very helpful for starting dates of jobs, bank and brokerage accounts, and investments.

Turbulent—trying to make money in this aspect's time is like trying to swim up Niagara Falls; don't try to buck the odds. Almost no successful company has this aspect.

Mars and Sun

Linkage: This linkage has two faces, and they are always both present; there is attraction and cooperation between the linked persons, but there is also an edginess in the relationship because of the aggressive nature of Mars. Mars works well with Venus, Pluto, Jupiter, and Uranus, but not so well with the Sun, even in a linkage.

Activation: Since the linkage is not that great, the activation has to be worse; this is a very problematic activation, creating short-lived attraction and long-lasting strife. Avoid it at all costs.

Personal Aspect: The WARRIOR ASPECT, in a man, this is an indication of a man's man, the hard hat; in a woman, this is the sign of a very aggressive woman who will fight to the death for what she thinks she deserves. For both men and women, it signifies a self-willed and motivated person with initiative who holds nothing back and is a person of action. People with this aspect are never wallflowers; if they are interested in someone, they go right up to the person and strike up a conversation. You never have to seduce this person; Mars individuals do the seducing. Unfortunately, most such persons are not subtle, and lack the flair for romanticism and are also less sensitive than most. However, they are very active and aggressive lovers, and attack every aspect of their life with vigor and enthusiasm. Also, they stand up for whatever they believe in and are protective of those they love. The man of this aspect usually insists that his woman submit to him; the woman of this aspect submits to no one, and for this reason we call this aspect the YOU DON'T OWN ME ASPECT for women.

Electional Aspect for Matters of Love: Enhancement—a very bad aspect to include in a Wedding Chart, it creates a marriage that is a battleground. It is also a bad aspect time to begin an affair, because this is the aspect that signifies a time of war, not love. Although Mars rules male sexuality, the sexual nature of Mars is not strong under this aspect; instead, the belligerent nature of Mars dominates.

Turbulent—self-destructive (as in Jackie O's first engagement), and must be avoided in a Wedding Chart under any circumstance.

Electional Aspect for Matters of Money: Enhancement—this is a very bad aspect for any business chart. Although this enhancement occurs about 10 percent of the time, fewer than 2 percent of successful corporations have this enhancement as the only enhancement to the Sun, and most of them are in the business of making weapons of war, because Mars rules weapons.

Turbulent—even worse than the enhancement.

Mars and Moon

Linkage: This linkage creates sexual attraction and romantic attachment on both sides, which is very strong and just below the power of a Chiron or Sexual Linkage.

Activation: This has results similar to the linkage, but adds turbulence to the relationship because the Mars influence will oscillate from sexual attraction to warlike behavior. By itself, the roller-coaster nature of this activation can be overcome; but if there are other turbulent activations, then it would be very difficult to get past this highly volatile activation.

Personal Aspect: This aspect is representative of a person that is highly emotional, enthusiastic, never at a loss for initiative, can be susceptible to being hyper, and can't stay put. It is this aspect that is associated with a person who taps a table with the end of a pencil incessantly.

Electional Aspect for Matters of Love and Money: Enhancement and turbulent—neither the enhancement nor the turbulent version of this aspect is helpful in love or money. The enhancement is not harmful, but the turbulent version can be problematic, and it is better not to have either during any important activities, such as a wedding or an employment date. The Moon-Mars aspect is symbolic of hyper-emotionalism.

Mars and Mercury

Linkage: This linkage helps provide a desire for a communicative relationship, and promotes an ease in achieving it. As is the case with all Mercury linkages, this one is much more important and helpful to the woman than the man, because women are in greater need of being able to discuss problems and talk through issues that concern them. This linkage is best if the man is the Mercury person.

Activation: This activation hinders the ability of the two parties to discuss important issues without blowups. This does not bother the man as much as the woman, but it is a very bad activation to have with anyone, because sooner or later, every couple has to be able to understand each other's viewpoints, and that requires clarity and sensitivity during communication. However, this aspect hinders all of the above.

Personal Aspect: The EXPRESS YOURSELF ASPECT, this person holds nothing back and will not be silent; if there is a problem, you will know about it—fast. This individual is also highly intelligent, has great reflexes, is very coordinated, has a lightning mind with a natural ability to score high on aptitude and IQ tests, and is very communicative. Women with this aspect have a tendency to communicate in a masculine way, sometimes even in a vulgar fashion. Also, this aspect helps reduce the chances of respiratory ailments.

Electional Aspect for Matters of Love: Enhancement—this aspect's time increases everyone's need for discourse and discussion, but due to the combative nature of Mars, it is best to avoid trying to reconcile differences and talk over problems with a loved one. Just smile and say, "I love you" until the aspect passes.

Turbulent—strong negative influence that creates a belligerent background for any discourse; an impossible time to make up with a loved one.

Electional Aspect for Matters of Money: Enhancement—a good aspect time for a business chart involving anything ruled by Mercury, especially software and publishing. However, it is a very bad time to try to negotiate any agreement.

Turbulent—this aspect creates excessive aggressiveness in communication and is another aspect that you should avoid when trying to negotiate any business agreements. It is also not good to include it in a business chart because it restricts the business from being able to "get out the word."

Mars and Venus—the same as Venus and Mars on page 309.

Mars and Mars

The Mars-Mars interaspect is the only truly important interaspect formed by the same planet and warrants special discussion. The quincunx and linkage interaspects are very powerful sexually and are highly enduring in their influence. The Turbulent Interaspects are initially strong sexual stimulants, but then they wear out completely. However, they can take a year or so to wear out.

Mars and Jupiter

Linkage: This linkage improves and strengthens compatibility and can nurture harmony at a very high level. It is also helpful in providing overall good luck and often endows the relationship with a greater-than-average share of success, although in money matters, this linkage is not nearly as helpful as a Golden or Silver Linkage.

Activation: It is very problematic in that the Mars person inhibits and impairs the Jupiter person's judgment, causing bad decisions to be made. If two persons have other bad activations, this one will usually contribute to an eventual breakup, but often on friendly terms.

Personal Aspect: This aspect is very helpful, providing physical vitality, good health, and an optimistic outlook on life.

Electional Aspect in Matters of Love: Enhancement—helpful and moderately sexual in nature, it is a beneficial aspect time for love relationships. Try not to be away from your loved one in this aspect's time because it is very serene.
Turbulent—problematic for love charts because it impairs optimism; a wedding or affair begun under this aspect will usually suffer from excessive pessimism.

Electional Aspect in Matters of Money: Enhancement—helpful, but this enhancement's beneficial influences are not directed at success or money; instead, this aspect is most helpful in a selfless activity where you are serving others and is good to include if you are starting a charitable organization. It's also a particularly good aspect to have in an employment chart if you are beginning work at a foundation, church, or charity.
Turbulent—like all Turbulent Aspects, try to avoid this aspect, but it is not as bad as most others and is by no means a "deal breaker."

Mars and Saturn

Linkage: As a linkage, Mars and Saturn are essentially mildly helpful, or neutral and virtually powerless, but this linkage is very helpful if it forms part of Combined Symmetrical Planetary Geometry.

Activation: This usually creates a high level of mutual intolerance; Mars and Saturn are highly antagonistic at activation angles, so this is a very bad activation and is a Classic Schism. You usually don't see this aspect in your relationships because the connected persons often cannot stand each other. If you have this activation with a new boss, you might consider looking for a new job. But take into account all interaspects with the new boss.

Personal Aspect: All personal aspects are helpful, but this one ranks near the bottom of the list. It is helpful in providing above-average stamina and not much else.

Electional Aspect in Matters of Love: Enhancement—any aspect of Mars and Saturn reduces sexual energy; the enhancement does so to a lesser degree.
Turbulent—a very bad aspect for all matters of love, creates an excessively combative and tumultuous relationship. This aspect's time is also one of the worst times to make love. Men are more likely to be impotent during this aspect than during any other aspect. You might ask how we know. Well, the Magi Society has been keeping accurate records of such data since 1625.

Electional Aspect in Matters of Money: Enhancement—not helpful; not harmful.
Turbulent—harmful and must be avoided; a business begun under this aspect is very prone to internal strife and bickering among employees and partners. This is a sign of the workplace that resembles a battlefield.

Mars and Chiron—the same as Chiron and Mars on page 299.

Mars and Uranus

Linkage: This linkage indicates moderate physical attraction; it is not as helpful as most linkages are. If this linkage is part of Combined Symmetrical Planetary Geometry, it can be helpful in a general way.

Activation: This also creates mild physical attraction; the linkage is lasting, the activation is not, and usually deteriorates into bickering over minutiae.

Personal Aspect: This aspect signifies a great reservoir of physical energy and a special talent in Uranian endeavors and careers. In a man, this aspect is a Sexual Aspect, as well as often indicating a man who desires changes of sexual partners. Mars is the male sex planet, and the Uranian influence tends to cause Mars to fluctuate, thus changing the sexual attractions of the man. If the Personal Aspect is turbulent, the desire for a variation in sex partners is accentuated.

Electional Aspect for Matters of Love: Enhancement—a bad aspect to have in a Wedding Chart because the Uranian influence causes excessive desire for change, thus destabilizing emotional relationships. But this is a very good aspect under which to begin a fling; the aspect creates a sexual overtone, and the affair should end quickly without complications.

Turbulent—one to avoid, this is excessively destabilizing to any Wedding and Relationship Chart; it also increases the chances of unwanted fame, meaning the bad characteristics of the relationship become the talk of the town.

Electional Aspect in Matters of Money: Enhancement—this aspect is very helpful, specifically for any endeavor that is ruled by Uranus and Mars, such as sportscasting, but not much else. You do not want this aspect if you want to stay put and not travel; interestingly enough, sportscasting requires constant travel.

Turbulent—a harmful aspect to have in any business chart; this aspect creates sudden dramatic changes that are totally unexpected, and often includes an insurrection on the part of employees. If you are promoted, do not start your new position during this aspect's time.

Mars and Neptune

Linkage: This is a very strong linkage and creates sexual attraction that is only slightly less powerful than the three Sexual Linkages. However, the energy provided will vacillate from being sexual, to aggressiveness and anger, so we do not recommend this linkage. This is the LOVE/HATE LINKAGE.

Activation: It creates very strong sexual attraction that wears off quickly. After the attraction fades, the activation usually creates edginess, bickering, and belligerent attitudes between the activated persons. This is the activation that makes you say that "love is a battlefield."

Personal Aspect: This is a Male Super Sexual Aspect. President Clinton was born with a planetary eclipse of this aspect. In a woman, this aspect also increases sexuality, but not nearly as much, and is more directed toward conceiving rather than pure sex. Both men and women with this aspect are very aggressive and assertive, can have quite a temper, and have boundless energy. The energy can be most easily directed toward creative activities and other Neptunian areas.

Electional Aspect in Matters of Love: *Enhancement*—a very good aspect time in which to make love or conceive, but you do not want a love chart with this aspect because it creates very stressful relationships, with more than their share of strife.

Turbulent—the Mars-Neptune Turbulent Aspect is one that helps to justify the use of the term *turbulent* to describe an aspect. This is the most warlike and Turbulent Aspect you can have in an electional chart. You do not want it. Avoid at all costs unless you want to go to bed in a suit of armor. The hallmark of marriages with this aspect is a divorce proceeding characterized by unrelenting vengeance that is blown way out of proportion.

Electional Aspect in Matters of Money: *Enhancement*—helpful in Neptunian endeavors, but it has the side effect of overaggressiveness; it is better not to have it.

Turbulent—a very, very bad aspect to have in any business chart. Creates a "scorched Earth policy" and willingness to "cut off one's nose to spite the face."

Mars and Pluto

Linkage: One of the three Sexual Linkages, this is the one that makes lovemaking most urgently sexual in nature; foreplay is limited. However, this one can burn out and leave a pile of ashes after an extended period of fabulous sex. The other two Sexual Linkages are enduring.

Activation: This creates strong initial attraction that quickly disappears and turns to antagonism; this is very bad for an office romance because you have to work with the person after the sex disappears, and this activation often results in an open power struggle. Who needs that? Although the sex is good for a very short period of time, the disputes to follow make this activation not worth the trouble.

Personal Aspect: This is a Sexual Aspect and is a Male Super Sexual Aspect; it is the sign of the male sexual athlete and the most virile of men. It is also a sign of such high competitiveness that the natives often overreach. It provides a very high energy level, usually with extraordinary entrepreneurial desires; the aspect is representative of someone who is highly aggressive and cannot be pushed around.

Electional Aspect for Matters of Love: Enhancement—a Seduction Aspect, but more aptly labeled a Sex Time Aspect; this is the aspect that existed the night Evita met Juan Peron. It is singularly the best aspect time for the man to make love, or we suppose we should say, have sex. This is the most powerful time for sex, but not always so great for love; it depends on your needs. This is not a time to expect a slow hand; men feel very urgent under this aspect and are in no mood for a lot of foreplay, but are most capable of repeat performances during this aspect. If your relationship is flat and in the doldrums, and you want a night and morning to remember, do not miss this one. It can be magic, making the average man a tiger for the night. Getting married or beginning a sexual relationship under this aspect is very helpful in improving the quantity, if not quality, of sex in the relationship.

Turbulent—a very bad time to try to make love; during this aspect time, the man can have problems with impotency and/or will simply be disinterested. Obviously, a first-time seduction during this aspect time has a high risk of disaster. You do not want this Turbulent Aspect in any Love Chart.

Electional Aspect for Matters of Money: Enhancement—a very helpful aspect to have in any business chart; it helps provide the energy and drive needed for success. It also provides a special ability to be competitive in business.

Turbulent—not good. Avoid this; the aspect drains a business of its vitality and its will to compete.

Sun and Moon

Linkage: This is a very favorable and powerful linkage. It greatly enhances compatibility and mutual understanding and also creates nonsexual attraction and an affinity toward each other in a subtle manner, making both parties feel very comfortable together—sometimes even like soulmates.

Activation: This is not good to have with anyone important in your life; it instills the feeling in both parties that something is wrong with the other person, without being able to explain why (because it is in the stars!).

Personal Aspect: This aspect provides vitality and enhances motivation and drive.

Electional Aspect for Matters of Love and Money: Enhancement—helpful in a general way, but not powerful unless nearly exact.
Turbulent—harmful, but here, too, it is not powerful unless nearly exact, but it engenders self-destructiveness.

Sun and Mercury

Linkage: In a mild way, this linkage improves the ability to discuss issues and work out problems through communication and discourse.

Activation: This hinders the ability to understand each other through direct forms of communication, but does not hinder emotional and karmic ties.

Personal Aspect: This signifies a person who prefers to use the mind as opposed to the body; it is a good aspect for someone involved in Mercury activities, such as teaching, writing, journalism, computer programming, science, and research.

Electional Aspect in Matters of Love: Enhancement—means a communicative relationship, so if you are someone whose requirements in a relationship include discourse, communication, and exchanging viewpoints, then you should definitely include this aspect in selecting a relationship chart. This aspect does not add anything else to the relationship.
Turbulent—there cannot be a Turbulent Aspect made by the Sun and Mercury because Mercury never moves far enough away from the Sun.

Electional Aspect in Matters of Money: Enhancement—this aspect has helpful characteristics in a job or business related to Mercury; it is a great aspect under which to begin work as a writer, newscaster, or announcer. It's also good for releasing a book or recording; and starting a business in singing, book publishing, and developing and selling computer software.

Turbulent—there cannot be a Turbulent Aspect made by the Sun and Mercury because Mercury never moves far enough away from the Sun.

Sun and Venus—the same as Venus and Sun on page 306.

Sun and Mars—the same as Mars and Sun on page 317.

Sun and Jupiter

Linkage: This is the LINKAGE OF FORGIVENESS, so for relationships, this is obviously very helpful, especially for the Sun person. The Jupiter person will often forgive the Sun person unquestioningly and will help the Sun person as much as possible; the reverse can also be true. This can be a very strong linkage for friendships; if lovers have this linkage, they can be best friends as well as lovers, and will usually have a very peaceful and blessed relationship.

Activation: This often indicates a clash of wills and personalities, and the condition of being miles apart in viewpoints.

Personal Aspect: This is a Super Aspect and the WISDOM ASPECT; the native is attracted to seeking the truth. When the aspect is an enhancement, the native usually finds truth in Judeo-Christian values. When the aspect is not an enhancement, the native is usually attracted to non-Judeo-Christian ideas. Generally, the native is highly responsible, faithful, and peace-loving, but willing to fight and die for a cause.

Electional Aspect in Matters of Love: Enhancement—a Super Aspect, this is the single best aspect time to get married, as it strengthens the marriage in whatever way is needed. It also helps to promote a marriage of harmony, forgiveness, and understanding; and promotes good fortune. This is also a good aspect time to begin a romance, but not a fling. Interestingly enough, flings don't start under the Sun-Jupiter enhancement; affairs started under this aspect become serious and, therefore, are not flings.

Turbulent—a bad aspect to have in any electional chart, it fosters misunderstandings and intolerance.

Electional Aspect in Matters of Money: *Enhancement*—corporations born under this aspect are very fair and generous employers, with the workplace being a great place to be because it is a sea of tranquility. Employees will be most loyal to businesses with this aspect, but try to add a Venus- and Pluto-based Super Aspect as well.

Turbulent—very harmful in business charts, this aspect creates overspending and overexpansion, eventually leading to financial disaster.

Sun and Saturn

Linkage: This is a very powerful linkage even though no attraction is created by this linkage; instead of attraction, this creates a bond and provides the Saturn person with a high degree of control over the Sun person in every area of the person's life. The Sun person could feel tied down and controlled unless there is a SATURN BALANCE, which exists if there are two Saturn linkages, and each person is the Saturn person of one of the linkages.

Activation: Like the linkage, the Saturn person has control over the Sun person, but with an activation, the result is usually unbearable for the Sun person, who will seek to break off the relationship—sooner rather than later.

Personal Aspect: This signifies a determined, strong-willed person with enormous drive. It is the sign of the bulldozer who will run over anyone in sight to meet an objective, but who is often successful because of this drive and determination. Generally unorthodox, the native neither seeks nor accepts advice from others, and is happiest when being the boss in all relationships. This is the IMMOVABLE ASPECT, and the natives usually are the most self-willed and controlling persons in the zodiac. The upside is that they are very often genuinely faithful, are good providers, and are responsible to their family.

Electional Aspect in Matters of Love and Money: Both the enhancement and the Turbulent Aspects are among the worst aspect times for anything to do with love and money; fortunately, they do not last long, so it is easy to bide your time and bypass such aspects. Both aspects are a sign of self-destructiveness unique to the Saturn-Sun aspect. Marriages and businesses with any Sun-Saturn aspect are most likely to blow up from internal causes. *This is singularly the worst aspect to have for any endeavor.* Success can come, but at a great price and is rarely enduring. The more likely outcome is that Saturn somehow makes a relationship or business highly susceptible to disruptions and crises that are rooted primarily from within.

Sun and Chiron—the same as Chiron and Sun on page 295.

Sun and Uranus

Linkage: This linkage greatly increases compatibility and helps two people to be on the same wavelength, especially in terms of working together in an attempt to advance their lives together. This linkage is also extraordinarily helpful in achieving combined fame and success in Uranian endeavors. It has no sexual overtones, but it does heighten attraction.

Activation: From time to time, this activation causes dramatic differences in perspectives and outlooks that will overshadow the entire relationship; one partner wants to go to the left and the other to the right. The accumulation of these differences over time will often create an irreparable rift between the two activated persons; this is a Classic Schism.

Personal Aspect: A Super Aspect, this is very helpful in achieving fame and success in Uranian endeavors. It can also be the mark of a person who is charismatic, prefers to be very different from the norm, who maintains an unusual or extreme outlook, has a keen sense of drama, and is a seeker of excitement. Often, the natives are not content with the status quo. They long for change, are persuasive, and can convince others to follow them. Some have the determination and the wherewithal to change those around them— and sometimes the entire world. This is the DON QUIXOTE ASPECT.

Electional Aspect for Matters of Love: Enhancement—a Super Aspect, it can help bring about both fame and recognition, but there is quite a substantial downside. Because Uranus rules change and unconventionality, this is not an auspicious aspect under which to tie the knot, since it creates a marriage with a desire for an unusual type of relationship and for change, including a change of spouses. But this makes this aspect perfect for a fling.

If you are single and wish to stay that way, and you're looking for a love affair, this is a good aspect time to begin such a dalliance. The affair will be exciting but will not lead to marriage. The relationship will ease off naturally without complications or acrimony.

Turbulent—due to the fact that Uranus is the ruler of freedom and independence, this is a horrible aspect under which to say "I do" because you will want to say, "I do . . . change my mind" right afterwards. The Uranian influence will immediately make both partners worry about losing their independence and freedom, even if they did not feel that way before the vows. If you are married and want to remain so, do not start an affair under this aspect time; the affair could disrupt your marriage due to the tumultuous nature of Uranus when at an activation angle.

Electional Aspect for Money Matters: *Enhancement*—a good aspect for a business chart related to Uranian endeavors, such as entertainment, broadcasting, and technology or innovations.

Turbulent—very bad aspect under which to begin anything regarding business, as it creates incessant upheavals. Be certain to avoid this aspect.

Sun and Neptune

Linkage: A romantic linkage, this is one of the most beneficial linkages that you can have with anyone other than the Chiron or Venus linkages. Sun-Neptune creates a karmic bond and the feeling that you were close to this person in a previous life. It is also indicative of immediate attraction on a nonsexual level. The effects of this linkage are long-lasting.

Activation: This is a very problematic activation that reduces the duration of the relationship and engenders discord and incompatibility in a subtle way. Both sides look at each other through cracked glasses and are uncomfortable in each other's presence. This is a Classic Schism.

Personal Aspect: A Super Aspect and a very blessed aspect to be born with, it imparts a blissful and optimistic attitude toward life, high levels of artistic and creative talent, long-term good health, and helps the native not take anything too seriously. The downside is that sometimes the native lacks determination and focus.

Electional Aspect for Matters of Love: Enhancement—one of the very best aspect times to say "I do," because once you're married with this aspect, you are likely to want to say "I do" over and over, till death do you part. The serene and long-term nature of Neptune imparts onto a marriage the longevity, peace, and happiness that every marriage needs. Any Love Chart begun with this aspect will be lasting. If you are looking for a fling, avoid this aspect; if you want a marriage, this is a great aspect under which to begin a romance.

Turbulent—the Sun-Neptune activation angles reverse the pleasantness and longevity that the enhancement creates; therefore, it is imperative that this aspect be avoided in a Wedding Chart. If you're looking for a very quick affair that is not likely to harm anyone or any relationship, this is a good aspect under which to begin such an affair. The affair will usually discreetly ease out of existence without complications because Neptune has no harshness to it.

Electional Aspect for Matters of Money: Enhancement—the Sun-Neptune enhancement is a Super Aspect, and is one of the most helpful aspects under which to start a job. Neptune will help the job be peaceful and long-lasting. This makes this aspect good for starting bank and brokerage accounts. But this aspect is not really helpful for other business charts, such as an incorporation date. Neptune is the most impressionable and least competitive planet, and a corporation born under a Sun-Neptune enhancement will be less willing and less able to compete in the dog-eat-dog world of big business—or even small business.

Turbulent—one to avoid at all costs, Sun and Neptune at turbulent angles create significant problems in any business project and job. You do not want this aspect, as it causes friction, misunderstandings, and turns minor problems into irreconcilable differences. The aspect also has a way of sapping vitality from what is begun during its aspect time. Do not begin a job during this aspect; you could be fired after receiving the first paycheck.

Sun and Pluto

Linkage: This is a strong bond that greatly improves compatibility and the ability to work together, especially on Plutonian matters such as business issues and the attainment of power. This linkage has sexual overtones and would greatly increase sexual attraction if there is also a Sexual Linkage involved. This linkage amplifies other linkages of sexuality in a relationship and can create obsessiveness.

Activation: This is a strong activation; sometimes there is initial attraction, but inevitably, the activation influence creates an intolerable clash of wills between the activated persons. This is a highly problematic activation and will always have an impact on a relationship, no matter what other interaspects there are. This is a Classic Schism.

Personal Aspect: A Super Aspect, it is especially helpful in making money and greatly increases competitive skills and the desire and willingness to duel to the death. Such natives are driven, resourceful, and hate to lose, even when the stakes are low. The aspect also provides remarkably judicious business and investing acumen; therefore, the natives are often highly successful and consider themselves masters of the universe. The downside is that the native is often overly self-centered and uncompromising, with an ego too big to fit into some relationships.

Electional Aspect for Matters of Love: *Enhancement*—this is the best aspect under which to begin an affair if you want the affair to end in a marriage. When an *initial* seduction occurs with this aspect, the seduced person is likely to become willing to sacrifice everything for the seducer; the reverse is also often true. This is the CLEOPATRA ASPECT. If you get married with this aspect, the marriage will be all-encompassing and will be the focal point of both your lives. The downside of this aspect is that the marriage will lack ease and serenity, bliss and tenderness, forgiveness, and is less likely to sustain mutual love; the focus of the marriage is likely to be power and success.

Turbulent—a very bad aspect that you should avoid under all circumstances for a Wedding Chart because the aspect will quickly push the marriage to the breaking point—and usually beyond it. Pluto and Sun are very incompatible at turbulent angles, and most of the time give birth to an unending string of crises. It's also bad for beginning affairs, as this is the aspect of the one-night stand that comes back to haunt you. For this reason, when it comes to affairs, we call this the FATAL ATTRACTION ASPECT.

Electional Aspect for Matters of Money: *Enhancement*—a Super Aspect and one of the best ones to have when it comes to a business chart. Do your best to harness the power of this aspect in any business chart, including starting jobs and starting businesses; it has a magical quality when it comes to making money. Half of the most successful companies in the world have this aspect, including Microsoft, AT&T, GE, Merck, and Boeing.

Turbulent—very few business charts with this Turbulent Aspect have noteworthy success. It tends to create an inability to compete, along with unwitting self-destruction. Under no circumstances should you initiate a business endeavor with this aspect.

Jupiter and Sun—the same as Sun and Jupiter on page 326.

Jupiter and Moon

This combination is in all ways very similar to Jupiter and Sun, but with a magnified level of emotional intensity, which is the case with any alignment involving the Moon.

Jupiter and Mercury

Linkage: This is a great linkage to have with anyone, and you will find it to be the most powerful one in enhancing your ability to communicate peacefully and intelligently, exchange viewpoints, and reach fair compromises and overcome differences. We call this the FAIR HEARING LINKAGE.

Activation: This activation has the opposite effect of the linkage.

Personal Aspect: The TRUE GENIUS ASPECT, it signifies a brilliant mind, both logical and wise, with ample common sense. The native is remarkably gifted at writing and has great communication skills. He or she may not be as quick to grasp a new concept as some others, but possesses the ability to delve deeper into any theory than anyone without this aspect.

Electional Aspect for Matters of Love: Enhancement—this is a very auspicious time to secure a better understanding of your loved one through discourse and exchange of views; this enhancement reduces the possibility of misunderstandings and argumentativeness. It's good for all Relationship Charts.
Turbulent—restricts mutual empathy, but not very much.

Electional Aspect for Matters of Money: Enhancement—helpful, especially for achieving success in business endeavors involving anything ruled by Mercury, such as publishing, software, writing, communications, and the Internet.
Turbulent—slightly impedes success in areas ruled by Mercury.

Jupiter and Venus—the same as Venus and Jupiter on page 310.

Jupiter and Mars—the same as Mars and Jupiter on page 320.

Jupiter and Saturn

Linkage: This is the most complicated and difficult linkage to interpret; Jupiter and Saturn are such opposites that they do not link well together. Sometimes the Saturn person is greatly helped by the Jupiter person, but sometimes the Jupiter person is led astray by the Saturn person. If you are the Jupiter person, the best thing to do is simply avoid a relationship with this linkage because it is unpredictable, and the negatives can overwhelm the positives.

Activation: This is usually highly stressful and creates a clash of wills and different outlooks, with little room for accommodation or compromise. It could be the worst of all activations.

Personal Aspect: This is the most complicated aspect to interpret; the native is sometimes enormously successful but is usually unable to handle the power the success brings. So, this aspect ends up making the native a Fallen Angel. We will deal more thoroughly with this aspect in a future book, but for now, let us say that this is the most complex of aspects because its influences have the strongest of spiritual overtones.

Electional Aspect for Matters of Love and Money: Enhancement—if Saturn is not APPLYING toward Jupiter, this is a very helpful aspect. If Saturn is applying toward Jupiter, this aspect is a problem and you should make certain to avoid it in any electional chart.
Turbulent—no matter which planet is applying, this is bad. It creates immorality and failure and is not good for any chart.

Jupiter and Chiron—the same as Chiron and Jupiter on page 301.

Jupiter and Uranus

Linkage: This is a very helpful linkage that benefits the relationship in a broad, generalized way. It helps the linked persons to become famous and achieve success, particularly in Uranian areas of endeavor.

Activation: This weakens ties and creates intermittent periods of enormous stress, but is not usually by itself a relationship breaker.

Personal Aspect: A Super Aspect, it is the Super Fame Aspect and most helpful in the Uranian areas, such as the entertainment and broadcasting industry, publicity, politics, engineering, and aeronautics. This aspect often gives the native a commanding presence, with a special ability to gain acclaim and fame. This aspect is also helpful in astrological endeavors, which the natives often have an aptitude for.

Electional Aspect for Matters of Love: Enhancement—if you're looking for a discreet affair that nobody will notice, don't begin an affair under this aspect, since it has the ability to make an affair very public. (Bill Clinton and Monica Lewinsky's affair began with this aspect.) For a Wedding Chart, this is a great aspect to have. It helps to make the marriage well known, causing you to be envied by others; the downside is that you may prefer your privacy.
Turbulent—this is a horrible aspect because it imparts infamy. What is done under this aspect will be well known, but for the wrong reasons.

Electional Aspect for Matters of Money: Enhancement—a Super Aspect, this is one of the best aspects to have in a chart of a business that is involved in Uranian affairs, including entertainment, broadcasting, aerospace, and astrology.
Turbulent—most Turbulent Aspects impede success, and so does this one, but it does so in the mildest way and can be overcome if there are good aspects elsewhere in the chart, or if the aspect forms part of Symmetrical Planetary Geometry.

Jupiter and Neptune

Linkage: One of the most beneficial and powerful linkages to have. It provides lasting ease, understanding, and a karmic attachment to the relationship, as well as financial security to the linked persons.

Activation: This activation is not helpful, but also is not actively harmful, except in the mildest of ways. So, although this activation can be mildly detrimental to a relationship, it can be readily overcome if the connected persons also have strong linkages.

Personal Aspect: A Super Aspect, this signifies a person who has artistic and creative talents, as well as the ability to achieve the highest levels of accomplishment using them. The native is also usually extraordinarily healthy and blessed with longevity.

Electional Aspect in Matters of Love: Enhancement—a very helpful and powerful aspect to have in any chart, it is one of the best for any Marriage Chart, as it improves the chances of long-term financial security and also strengthens the marriage itself by engendering a high level of peacefulness and understanding. This is a Super Aspect and is also a very favorable aspect under which to begin a romance that you want to advance to marriage. Not right for flings.
Turbulent—moderately stressful for unions of all kinds because the aspect will often impede the general well-being of any relationship.

Electional Aspect in Matters of Money: Enhancement—this Super Aspect is one of the best aspects for maximizing money-making potential, especially in areas ruled by Neptune. A rare aspect, take advantage of it when it occurs, even if it is just to open a bank or brokerage account.
Turbulent—in business charts, sidestep this aspect because it greatly hinders financial prospects.

Jupiter and Pluto

Linkage: This is a Golden Linkage, meaning the linked persons should be able to work fabulously well together to attain shared dreams. The power of this linkage is so potent that it has a nearly mystical quality. This linkage also promotes the highest level of general harmony and compatibility between the linked persons and can be mildly helpful with sexual compatibility, but it does not have any direct effect on love and marriage.

Activation: Like almost all activations, this is an impediment to long-term relationships but is one of the least onerous. It is a sign that the activated persons will have disagreements about ambitions and how to achieve their dreams. However, this activation can be overcome if the persons also have strong linkages.

Personal Aspect: This is the most powerful Super Aspect when it comes to helping the native achieve success in Pluto matters, such as big business and power. The native is never satisfied and will always push to accumulate more wealth and power.

Electional Aspect in Matters of Love: Enhancement—if wealth or power is important to you, make certain that you include this in your Wedding Chart. It will help you become as successful as possible.

Turbulent—Avoid this aspect in Wedding Charts unless you and your spouse believe love is all that matters because the aspect will reduce the ability of both spouses from achieving career ambitions. But this is not as bad as some other aspects, such as Saturn-Neptune and Saturn-Pluto.

Electional Aspect in Matters of Money: Enhancement—one of the best aspects to include in any Business Chart, especially when starting a new job, business, or corporation.

Turbulent—Reduces ability to make money but can be overcome if there are also other very powerful money-making aspects such as Venus-Pluto and Venus-Neptune enhancements.

Jupiter and Chiron—the same as Chiron and Jupiter on page 301.

Saturn and Sun—the same as Sun and Saturn on page 327.

Saturn and Moon

This pairing is in all ways the same as Sun and Saturn, but all the linkages and aspects are more emotionally charged.

Saturn and Mercury

Linkage: Linkages are almost always helpful, but in this case, the restrictive nature of Saturn is such that we have found this linkage to be actually more harmful than helpful, with the Saturn person often impeding the Mercury person's judgment.

Activation: This inhibits the activated persons from understanding each other. Sometimes this activation can be an intangible, yet powerful, roadblock to any progress in the relationship, especially in the ability to exchange viewpoints. This inability to discuss problems eventually has a snowball effect, making some small problem turn into an avalanche.

Personal Aspect: Most of the time, the native has the ability to focus attention on a project and bring to bear scientific thinking; the native is naturally inclined to the empirical ways of science, as opposed to using intuitive skills or seeking spiritual guidance. The native often has a disdain for the arts and creative pursuits.

Electional Aspect in Matters of Love: Enhancement—Mercury-Saturn has a limited influence on matters of love, but we advise you not to get married or begin an affair under this aspect because it restricts both emotional and intuitive bonds from developing. The cold and empirical nature of Saturn is the cause of this problem.

Turbulent—a very bad aspect to have in any Relationship Chart, it will normally be relentless in blocking the free exchange of viewpoints and will prevent a strong mutual understanding from ever developing.

Electional Aspect in Matters of Money: Enhancement—a good aspect to natalize when beginning a business, job, or project that will require scientific thinking—such as a scientific research position or the writing and publication of science articles.

Turbulent—this is a bad aspect to have for any business chart, especially for almost anything ruled by Mercury; therefore, this aspect would be particularly bad for businesses involving publishing, the Internet, and computer software.

Saturn and Venus—the same as Venus and Saturn on page 311.

Saturn and Mars—the same as Mars and Saturn on page 321.

Saturn and Jupiter—the same as Jupiter and Saturn on page 333.

Saturn and Chiron—the same as Chiron and Saturn on page 302.

Saturn and Uranus

Linkage: This linkage is essentially neutral and helpful only if it forms a part of Symmetrical Combined Planetary Geometry. The Saturn person has the ability to inflict change upon the Uranus person; how such changes work out usually depends on the wisdom and judgment of the Saturn person.

Activation: This interaspect can be quite harmful to the Uranus person; the Saturn person has the tendency to rearrange the Uranus person's life, with most such changes leading to problems for the Uranus person.

Personal Aspect: This aspect signifies the ability to command attention from others and to control others. The native is often endowed with the ability to move the masses and mold public opinion. The downside is that there is an inclination toward extremely unconventional viewpoints.

Electional Aspect in Matters of Love: Enhancement—not a good aspect for a Wedding Chart; it can give your relationship a notoriety that you may not want because this aspect often makes public any problems you have. If you begin an affair under this aspect, you risk having everyone gossip about the affair in a critical way.

Turbulent—awful for Wedding Charts, the aspect will often create a problem that will result in infamy for the marriage. An affair begun with this aspect often becomes indiscreet and highly public, as well as highly inflammatory and destabilizing to the lives of both persons.

Electional Aspect in Matters of Money: Enhancement—can be helpful in achieving dominance in areas ruled by Uranus, but not as good as the Jupiter-Uranus enhancement.

Turbulent—a very bad aspect to have in a business chart, it is unsettling and persistently creates upheavals, both from within and through outside forces. Do not start a job or business during this aspect time.

Saturn and Neptune

Linkage: Any interaspect of Saturn and Neptune is problematic, even a linkage. This linkage usually creates an overall negative tone to the relationship, even if the linkage is a component of Symmetrical Combined Planetary Geometry.

Activation: This activation can be devastatingly harmful to both activated persons and is especially bad for the Neptune person, who is likely to suffer financially and emotionally. This is one of the worst activations and is a Saturn Clash. But this is similar to the Saturn-Pluto clash, so please read what we wrote about that activation.

Personal Aspect: This aspect provides the native with an unusually high level of attachment to scientific thinking. More often than not, the native is agnostic, an atheist, or attracted to Buddhism..

Electional Aspect for Matters of Love: Both the enhancement and the turbulent angles of the Saturn-Neptune aspect are highly restrictive of the development of love and long-term relationships. Obviously, this is not an aspect you would want in your Wedding Chart, or in any Relationship Chart. The aspect also signifies financial problems and ill health; people who wed under this aspect's time are more prone to life-threatening illnesses and poverty.

Electional Aspect for Matters of Money: *Enhancement*—a favorable aspect to incorporate into a business chart of an endeavor requiring scientific research, such as a biotech company or a job as a scientific researcher.

Turbulent—a very bad aspect for any business chart, it reduces financial wherewithal, inhibits creativity, and shortens lifespan.

Saturn and Pluto

Linkage and ***Activation:*** This is one of the most complex of the interaspects. Even the linkage version does not improve harmony between the connected persons. The Saturn person has a high degree of control over the Pluto person, and the effect of this interaspect on the relationship will in large measure depend on how the Saturn person exercises this control. If the Saturn person is benevolent, wise, and has a selfless love of the Pluto person, then the Saturn person can use this control to help the Pluto person. An example of this is Meg Ryan and Dennis Quaid (please refer to pages 359–361). However, such cases are rare and can only occur when the connected persons also have very powerful and beneficial linkages and the Saturn person is remarkably loving and giving, similar to the way Meg Ryan and Dennis Quaid are.

Personal Aspect: This aspect is indicative of persons who are very drawn to big business and power, and dream about being masters of the universe. Great success can be achieved by such persons, but they are not suited for the business world or the power game and will most likely find success in another area, such as teaching or research.

Electional Aspect in Matters of Love: Both the enhancement and the turbulent versions of this aspect are ones that must be avoided in any Love Chart, especially a Wedding Chart. The aspect tends to create a relationship that is tumultuous, with unexpected severe downturns.

Electional Aspect in Matters of Money: Both the enhancement and the turbulent versions of this aspect are nearly insurmountable blocks to the ability to be profitable, and must be avoided in any Business Chart. These aspects are also horrible to have on days when beginning a new job because under Saturn-Pluto, promotions and salary increases are very hard to attain.

Uranus and Neptune, Uranus and Pluto, Neptune and Pluto

Interaspects between these three pairings of planets are rare and have few specific meanings, but any linkage of these three pairings is helpful to any relationship, and any activation is problematic unless it forms a component of Symmetrical Combined Planetary Geometry.

The aspects involving these three pairings are rare because of the slow movement of these planets. But when the enhancements occur, they are very powerful and can be a great asset to any Business or Love Chart. The turbulent aspects must be avoided.

Ascendant and the Planets

The ascendant interacts with the planets in a way that is very similar to the Sun. Please refer to the equivalent Sun-planet combinations. In other words, to know what the ascendant and Mars combinations represent, see the Sun and Mars, and so on.

CHAPTER SIXTEEN

℘

Recognizing the Astrological Signs of Heartbreak

Sometimes, it is more helpful to recognize a prospective heartbreak than a soulmate. To those who have gone through them, heartbreaks are the most traumatic emotional experiences that anyone can go through. They mean shattered dreams, emotional paralysis, sleepless nights, having no purpose in life, and often an inability to want to go on. They are always unbearable. Millions of people have used astrology to help them answer the question:

- What is it that leads to heartbreak situations? And how can you avoid them?

With Magi Astrology, we finally have a reliable solution to this dilemma.

Saturn Clashes

No matter how strong we are, and no matter how prepared we think we are, if a love relationship falls apart, we are always devastated. This may never change, but we can help both women and men learn the early warning signs of a prospective breakup in order to avoid pain, and also to effect a smooth transition into a relationship that will be more fruitful.

The Magi Society's research has discovered that there are some SIGNS that are clear warnings of possible traumatic breakups. Like all signs, these warnings are not foolproof, but they are generally reliable indications of mismatches and ultimate failures in love relationships. There is one particular sign that we need to pay special attention to. It is a SATURN CLASH, which is a specific type of interaspect involving Saturn.

Please always keep in mind that Saturn is different—it is the deception planet, the planet of control and dominance. When a couple has a Saturn Interaspect, the Saturn person tends to have a measurable degree of control over the destiny and future of the other individual. Depending on many factors, this can either be good or bad for a long-term relationship. Some people don't mind if their love partner has some control over their lives, and others can't stand it. The latter will usually seek to break off the relationship sooner or later, but a good percentage of happy marriages have Saturn Interaspects. In fact, sometimes it's even necessary to have a Saturn interaspect, or else one or both individuals will be too free and will not feel compelled to marry or stay married.

Saturn interaspects are very complicated; they are the most complex of any interaspects. The result of having one depends in large measure on the nature of the two persons involved. For example, if the Saturn person does not like to exercise control over the other, and the other does not mind giving in a little more than normal, then the Saturn interaspect is not a problem.

Whether or not Saturn interaspects are tolerable also depends on the actual angle of the interaspect, and which planet is connected to Saturn. There are some Saturn interaspects that are much worse than others.

A few specific Saturn Interaspects are so intolerable that we call them CLASHES. If one person's natal Saturn forms a quincunx, opposition, or square to any other person's natal planet, especially Chiron, Pluto, Neptune, Venus, Jupiter, Uranus, or Sun, the result is a Saturn Clash, which is one of the most reliable signs of an eventual breakup in any relationship. But please remember, in human relationships, nothing is a certainty.

In this chapter, we will learn how to detect and interpret Saturn Clashes. This is the last chapter in this book where we show how to use Magi Astrology in matters of love and money. For this reason, besides learning about Saturn Clashes, we will use the examples in this chapter so we can master the use of all of the tools of Magi Astrology that we have already learned. We will analyze Combined Charts, Wedding Charts, individual charts. and whatever else we need to round out and complete our education in the Magi Astrology of love and money.

Saturn Clashes Are Signs of Traumatic Breakups

Mia Farrow and Woody Allen—Mia Farrow was outraged. You would be too under the same circumstances. Before she and Woody Allen broke up, they had been lovers and partners for over ten years. Allen produced films and television shows, and Mia starred in them. Even though they never married, she bore him a natural son, and they adopted two children together. There were times when the relationship seemed like it would be lifelong. But then Mia discovered that Woody was having an affair with Soon-Yi, a teenager whom Mia had adopted as a baby during her earlier marriage to Andre Previn. (Proof, once again, that truth is stranger than fiction. This story would be almost too unbelievable to be written into a daytime soap opera!)

Woody and Mia ended their relationship on one of the most bitter notes in the history of Hollywood—even though, to be exact, this all took place in the New York area. Mia even went to court to ask for a restraining order preventing Woody from attempting to visit their children. The court gave it to her. On his part, Woody Allen did not deny he was having an affair with her adopted daughter. In fact, he eventually married Soon-Yi.

Can any of this be explained through the stars? We think much of it can. See if you agree with us. Mia and Woody's CAC is Figure 16A.

From the standpoint of Magi Astrology, it makes sense that Mia and Woody never got married, because they had no Romantic Super Linkage and no Chiron linkage—you know, the kind that all the other couples in this book have had. We've learned that such linkages are crucial in creating the love, trust, and circumstances needed for two persons to exchange vows.

What did Mia and Woody have? They had Romance Linkages, a Sexual Linkage, and Symmetrical Combined Planetary Geometry. When two people are together for a long time and don't have a Romantic Super Linkage, the odds are extraordinarily strong that there is at least one Romance Linkage and probably also a Sexual Linkage. Mia's Mars is contra-parallel Woody's Pluto, forming a powerful Sexual Linkage. Also, Mia and Woody form two Romance Linkages with a Double Linkage of Sun-Venus. In addition, Woody's Jupiter and Sun align in a Double Grand Trine with Mia's Venus and Pluto. This forms Super Linkages, but there is no Chiron, so there are no Romantic Super Linkages. What these interaspects do create is very powerful Planetary Geometry that greatly promotes harmony and long-term relationships. But the magical ingredient, Chiron, is not a component of this Planetary Geometry. As we have repeatedly stressed in this book, Chiron creates marriages. Without Chiron, even the Double Grand Trine does not create the mystical mutual desire and opportunity for a marriage.

However, this did not mean that Woody and Mia weren't in love. There is often a difference between loving someone and wanting to commit to a marriage with that person. One reason we know they were in love is that they were together ten years, which is certainly longer than a lot of marriages. Another reason is that there was a Double Linkage of the Cupid Linkage (Sun-Venus), which is a Romance Linkage and a sign of probable love.

So there was no Chiron in the brew, and that explains why they did not marry. But what went so wrong that they came to such a bitter end? And could a proficient Magi Astrologer have predicted the outcome of the relationship?

We honestly believe we could have warned Mia that there was a time bomb with Woody, had we been asked. Using the rules of Magi Astrology, we would have strongly suspected a bitter end to the relationship because Allen's Saturn was quincunx to Farrow's conjunction of Chiron and Neptune. This is an unusually bad interalignment; it creates two SATURN CLASHES.

A Saturn Clash is formed whenever someone's Saturn makes a CLASH ANGLE to anyone else's natal planets. The clash angles are the opposition and square, as well as the quincunx. We discussed earlier how different the symbolisms of Saturn are from that of any other planet. Now we are about to learn how distinctive Saturn interaspects are, and how crucial they are to the outcome of any relationship.

The Chiron-Neptune conjunction is representative of Farrow's long-term (Neptune) family (Chiron), as well as the security (Neptune) of her family (Chiron). Woody's Saturn being at a clash angle to this conjunction creates two Saturn Clashes, or a DOUBLE SATURN CLASH. Unfortunately for them, this unusually bad interalignment signified impending doom, revealing the possibility that Allen would destroy (Saturn) and harm (Saturn) Farrow's long-term family (Neptune conjunct Chiron), as well as the tranquility and stability (Neptune) of her family (Chiron).

Mia and Woody's story can be very instructive with respect to the astrology of love relationships that are bound together by Symmetrical Combined Geometry and Sexual Linkages but which lack Chiron Linkages. Since Chiron is the key ingredient for marriage, most such relationships result in breakups, but the breakups are usually not as tumultuous. The sign of the volcanic breakup is the Saturn Clash.

Saturn Clashes are a crucial factor to consider. With Mia and Woody, there were two Saturn Clashes that we believe contributed a great deal to the unhappy ending of their relationship. Beware of Saturn Clashes. Whenever there are any, it is necessary to have overwhelming positive linkages to counterbalance them. The best counterbalance to Saturn Clashes are Chiron Linkages. For a love relationship to survive Saturn Clashes, you generally need at least an equal number of Chiron linkages. This is a good guideline to follow, but there are no absolutes when dealing with the astrology of relationships because our souls and psyches are too complex and variable. However, when there is a Double Saturn Clash the way there was with Mia and Woody, the odds are that the ending will be a very sad one.

Princess Diana and Prince Charles—This royal couple also had a Double Saturn Clash. Prince Charles's Saturn is opposed to Diana's Chiron and quincunx to her Jupiter. (Please see their charts on page180.) This Double Saturn Clash is representative of the destruction (Saturn) of a royal (Jupiter) family (Chiron), or something harmful (Saturn) to a peaceful (Jupiter) marriage (Chiron).

We already discussed how incompatible this royal couple was from the sexual point of view. It is an unfortunate fact of life that if a man has a Sexual Aspect and he is not getting what he wants at home, he is very likely to wander. This means that the downside with men who do have Sexual Aspects is that they are less likely to be faithful husbands. But the upside is that men with Sexual Aspects are more energetic lovers. Is this a matter of a woman having to choose her poison? No. There are men who have Sexual Aspects and are faithful because they have another aspect that helps them be faithful. The Sun-Jupiter and Venus-Jupiter aspects are indications of fidelity.

Christie Brinkley and Billy Joel—We did their charts in chapter 9. Remember how great their Combined Planetary Geometry is? They have Romantic Super Linkages, Chiron Linkages, Romance Linkages, Symmetrical Planetary Geometry that is a Double Grand Trine, and a Sexual Linkage. They got married, had a child, and then got divorced. What went wrong? Their relationship had great joy, but ended in sorrow (however, they are now friends). It's a shame the relationship ended, because we believe the breakup could have been avoided if Christie and Billy had exchanged their vows on a much better astrological day. Their marriage was an example of how imperative it is to be married on a day with the most favorable Planetary Geometry.

Christie and Billy were married on March 23, 1985 (Figure 16B). On that day, there was a nearly exact Turbulent Aspect of Sun and Neptune that was double direct. As you can see from our Planetary Interpreter in the last chapter, this aspect is indicative of a marriage that results in divorce. The most important aspects of a Wedding Chart are the aspects to the Sun, because the Sun represents the essence and vitality of the marriage. Earlier, we discussed bi-directional aspects and double-direct aspects. We explained that a Turbulent Aspect that is also double-direct is the worst aspect to have in any electional chart such as a Marriage Chart.

Unfortunately, this famous couple got married on a day with a double-direct Turbulent Aspect that involved the Sun—there was a square of Sun and Neptune. Normally, such an aspect would have separated the couple within a few years, but their Wedding Chart had other Planetary Geometry that helped to offset the Sun-Neptune square. (The Wedding Chart also had a symmetrical pattern of Sun, Neptune, Pluto, and Chiron.) As a result of this, the marriage produced a daughter, and Christie and Billy were not divorced until nine years later, on August 24, 1994.

The Joels' Wedding Chart also had the worst aspect any marriage can have. There was a contra-parallel of Saturn to Chiron, meaning destructive (Saturn) and restrictive (Saturn) of marriage (Chiron) and family (Chiron). This is another example of how consistent astrology is. The Saturn-Chiron Clash is bad, and the Saturn-Chiron aspect isn't good for the same reasons.

We have been saying over and over that marriages will take on the characteristics of the Planetary Geometry of the wedding date. This includes the careers of the spouses. Billy Joel's success in music was foretold by the Wedding Chart, which had a trine of Venus and Uranus with Mercury in conjunction to Venus. He was already very popular before the marriage, but the Conjuncted Trine supercharged his career, providing extra ability to earn money (Venus) from singing (Mercury) to the world (Uranus). Please recall that Uranus signifies globalization, so the Uranus trine to Venus and Mercury molded a hallmark of the marriage. Billy Joel was the first American artist to go on tour in Russia. He performed to sell-out crowds in half a dozen cities there. Later, Joel went on tour all over the globe, setting attendance records in several cities.

The Joel Marriage Chart also had a yod of Chiron to Neptune and Pluto. We learned how powerful yods could be when we introduced them earlier. Baryshnikov, Turner, GE, and Exxon were examples of this awesome shape of Planetary Geometry. The original Microsoft and Dell Computer companies also had the exact same Chiron to Neptune-Pluto yod! Here we see it again, in the chart of Billy Joel's wedding to Christie Brinkley. During their marriage, Billy Joel became the world's bestselling male recording artist. Both the eventual divorce and the super success in music were predictable from the Planetary Geometry of their Wedding Chart.

The marriage of Christie and Billy is a good example of how important the Wedding Chart always is to the career of both spouses. Evidence in support of this is the fact that prior to the marriage, Billy was already very prosperous and popular, but he never had a number-one song, although he came close. But after the wedding, Billy Joel had a string of number-one songs, the last one hitting big in 1993. Billy and Christie were divorced about a year later, effectively eradicating the Wedding Chart and the help that it provided to Billy's career. Since the divorce, he has not had a real hit song, in spite of his worldwide fame. But we just love Billy Joel no matter what; he is a man with real soul, and he is fabulously talented (he writes and composes all of his own songs). We wish him the best and hope he will find happiness and super success married to someone else. He deserves both.

We can learn a lot from this example. For one thing, if you have a good thing going (like a marriage with success), do not tinker with it too much. Sometimes, a Marriage Chart is irreplaceable. The Wedding Chart is often the key to someone's career and how much earning power the spouses have. This should be good news because it reaffirms that we can acquire Super Aspects and other helpful Planetary Geometry by harnessing the power of the stars and choosing a highly propitious Wedding Chart.

Brigitte Nielsen and Sylvester Stallone—She came into his life like Cleopatra unto Caesar. Legend tells us that Cleopatra entered Julius Caesar's bedroom hidden in a rolled-up carpet and seduced him into helping her defeat her brother and maintain her crown of Egypt. Brigitte sent Sly a provocative picture of herself; he invited her to a get-together (and they got together), and the rest is *their*-story.

Okay, Brigitte was not a Cleopatra, and Sly was not a Caesar. But he was Hollywood royalty as a result of his enormously popular starring roles in the *Rocky* and *Rambo* series of films. Sly's superstardom was foretold by his Conjuncted Trine of Jupiter conjunct Chiron trine to Uranus, which is a sign of a great (Jupiter) career (Chiron) in entertainment (Uranus).

Brigitte was a little-known Danish actress. Marrying Stallone made her life Cinderella-like. Most Cinderellas have the Planetary Geometry needed to be a Cinderella. Guess what? Brigitte was born with the Cinderella aspect of Chiron trine Neptune! (Brigitte was born 7/15/63; Sly was born 7/4/46.)

Cinderellas also usually make Cinderella Linkages with their "royal" spouses. Brigitte and Sly have that, also. The most important linkage that Nielsen and Stallone have is the Cinderella Linkage of Jupiter and Chiron; they have two of them. His Jupiter is quincunx her Chiron, and her Jupiter is contra-parallel his Chiron. How amazing can astrology get?

Apparently, they immediately fell in love. This was predictable from their very strong Symmetrical Combined Planetary Geometry: Brigitte has a Grand Trine of Venus, Neptune, and Chiron, while Sly's Sun is conjunct to her Venus (Cupid Linkage) and forms a Double Grand Trine in the com-

348 ❦ MAGI ASTROLOGY

bined chart. This also created Romantic Super Linkages.

They probably fell in lust immediately, too. This was easily predictable from their Sexual Linkage of his Mars conjunct her Pluto.

So what went wrong?

The main problem arose from a clash of personalities that could have been foreseen in their CONFLICTING Planetary Geometry. Brigitte (chart not shown) has a Synchronization of Sun, Saturn, and Mars. This is a sign of a person (Sun) who is controlling (Saturn) and aggressive (Mars). Her aggressiveness is one reason she was able to meet Sly in the first place. How many women would dare to actually send a provocative photo of themselves to a superstar? Many dream of it, but few actually do it.

Brigitte is strong-willed, and there is nothing wrong with that. Everyone knows that the most successful people on Earth are people with iron wills. Sly is also one of those people. You cannot imagine him giving in, can you? He has a triple parallel of Sun, Pluto, and Uranus (chart not shown). This is indicative of a person (Sun) who is massively (Uranus) competitive (Pluto), and one who has a great desire for command of his own destiny—so much so that before he became a star, and while he was broke, he turned down an offer of over $200,000 for his *Rocky* screenplay unless he himself could star in it. It was an incredible gamble, but he has the ability to win the big bets because he is helped by the Sun-Pluto Super Aspect (signifying a good risk taker because Pluto rules risk).

So both Stallone and Nielsen are iron-willed, which resulted in a struggle of those wills. But that's not all. The confrontation of wills was exacerbated by three Saturn interaspects, one of which was a Saturn Clash. Brigitte's Saturn is opposed to Stallone's Venus, a sign that she had some influence over (Saturn) his desires (Venus). He had Saturn conjunct her Mercury and parallel her Sun, giving him command over her (Sun) and her ability to communicate (Mercury) and deliberate (also Mercury). When Saturn creates an enhancement angle such as a parallel or conjunction, the resulting interaspect is not a clash. It is a linkage, but because Saturn is different from any other planet, it means that Saturn Linkages are also not like other linkages. They are usually a little oppressive to the non-Saturn person. When there are several Saturn interaspects, even when someone is not controlling, the other person will feel restricted and will want to break free. This problem is compounded when the connected persons are strong-willed. In the case of Brigitte and Sly, you can see how the conflicting Planetary Geometry between them would get out of hand. Disastrous incompatibility resulted, and then . . . divorce.

Loni Anderson and Burt Reynolds—This couple is another great example of a clash of wills and conflicting Planetary Geometry. Like two of the other three couples we have analyzed in this chapter, the initial love and attraction was the result of a Double Grand Trine that is the focus in their combined chart (Figure 16C). Loni Anderson was born with a Conjuncted Trine with Jupiter conjunct Chiron, and these two planets are in trine to Uranus. Burt Reynolds's Sun is trine to all three of these planets, creating a Double Grand Trine, which includes Chiron. Of course, this means they have Romantic Super Linkages. This is the main astrological reason why they got married. Things were good for a while, but the marriage ended after five years in a divorce that was so acrimonious that the tabloids were calling it the most hostile Hollywood divorce in decades. When we see the Saturn Clashes, we understand why.

Loni was born with a Sun-Pluto aspect (like Sly). She has a conjunction; this aspect is the mark of a person who has an iron will. You do not push her around. Burt is an easygoing guy, but he was born with Saturn located such that it makes a quincunx to Loni's Sun-Pluto conjunction, creating a Double Saturn Clash. Even though Burt is not pushy, these two Saturn Clashes made Loni feel that he was; that can happen with Saturn Clashes. Saturn causes misunderstandings and delusions.

To make matters worse, Loni's Saturn is square to Burt's Uranus and opposed to Burt's Mercury, creating a dreadful T-square that made Burt feel that Loni was imposing her will on him. Such exact Saturn Clashes almost always eventually takes their toll on a relationship. Again: disastrous incompatibility and divorce. (T-square not shown in CAC we provided.)

Pamela Anderson and Tommy Lee—Burt and Loni had a very ugly divorce, but neither of them ended up in jail. On the other hand, Tommy Lee pushed Pamela around while she was pregnant and holding their little son in her arms. He was sentenced to six months in jail (and served four) for felony spouse abuse, and she divorced him. There is never any excuse for a man to abuse a woman—never! But a look at their Combined Planetary Geometry will explain how the tensions of Saturn Clashes could generate belligerency.

Pamela Andersen is one of the original beauties that helped make the television series *Baywatch* the most watched, gawked-over show in the world. Tommy Lee has been called one of the greatest lovers in the history of rock 'n' roll. Before marrying Pamela, he was married to Heather Locklear, the very talented, incredibly beautiful star of Aaron Spelling's hit TV series *Melrose Place*. (She also starred in Spelling's *Dynasty*—Locklear and Spelling have a MAGIcal Linkage which is a Golden Linkage.)

What does Tommy Lee (Figure 16D) have that made two of Hollywood's most beautiful female stars say "I do" to him? He has two natal aspects that are particularly appealing and attractive to women. These aspects are a parallel of Sun and Chiron and a conjunction of Jupiter and Chiron. Chiron rules spouses and marriages, and these two aspects signify success (Jupiter) at getting married (Chiron) and having the image of a good husband (Sun parallel Chiron). These two aspects give a man that mystical allure that makes him almost irresistible to some women.

With regard to the relationship between Pamela and Tommy, they have some very powerful linkages that inspired them to fall in love (Pamela was born 7/1/67; her planets that form crucial interaspects to Lee's natal planets are drawn on Lee's chart):

- Tommy's Venus is contra-parallel Pamela's Sun; this is the Cupid Linkage.

- Tommy's Venus is conjunct Pamela's Neptune. One of the strongest Romance Linkages; this is usually long-lasting, signifies undeniable attraction, and is emphasized in their charts because this linkage occurs a second time in the declinations, creating a Double Linkage.

- Tommy's Neptune trines Pamela's Sun, helping to give rise to a long-term relationship. (Not shown in the CAC.)

- Pamela's Chiron links with Tommy's Sun through a contra-parallel, this is the Linkage of Trust.

Note that they do not have any Sexual Linkages, and neither of them was born with any Sexual Aspects. This is an example that helps to confirm that Sexual Linkages are not a necessity in a relationship except for those who have Sexual Aspects. It also means that their marriage was born out of love, not sex. We believe they had genuine love for each other.

What went wrong here?

To put it simply, they had Saturn Clashes—*three* of them. There was also STRESSFUL COMBINED Planetary Geometry; the two of them formed a T-square.

Pamela's Saturn is opposed to Tommy's Sun, and quincunx to both his Pluto and Neptune! Her Saturn clashes with three of Tommy's planets.

Their two charts also form a T-square. Pamela was born with a square of Sun and Saturn; Tommy's Sun's position completes a T-square formation since it is square her Sun and opposed by her Saturn. (Not shown.)

Together, the Saturn Clashes and very Stressful Combined Planetary Geometry resulted in a very sad divorce. As we have been saying, Saturn Clashes are bad, especially for the non-Saturn person.

Heather Locklear, Richie Sambora, and Tommy Lee—Before marrying Pamela, Tommy Lee was married to Heather Locklear. Although she also divorced him, he was luckier with Heather, since he did not have to worry about serving jail time. It is instructive to look at their astrological match-up. It wasn't great, but was not as bad as the mismatch with Pamela.

Heather was born with a Venus-Chiron opposition (Figure 16E). Chiron and Venus are the most important Romance Planets. When a woman is born with any Venus-Chiron aspect, Magi Astrology tells us that she would be most likely to marry those who have important planets that form linkages with these two planets. This is another example of how well the rules of Magi Astrology work. *Both* of the men Heather married form important linkages to her Chiron and Venus.

Heather's first husband, Tommy Lee, had his Jupiter conjunct her Chiron and his Uranus was conjunct her Venus. This formed a Romantic Super Linkage and a Cinderella Linkage. We regard Lee as the male Cinderella in this relationship since Heather has been part of the royalty of television actors.

But the conjunction of Heather's Venus and Tommy's Uranus created a problem. If you check with the Planetary Interpreter in the last chapter, you will see that this linkage makes the linked persons have "love of change, including change of partners in a relationship." Along comes Richie Sambora born with a conjunction of Venus and Pluto, which sits right on top of (is conjunct to) Heather's Venus, resulting in a Super Linkage anchored by the Venus-Pluto Sexual Linkage. Adding fuel to the fire, Richie and Heather also have the Venus-Neptune Romance Linkage signifying a long-term relationship between Heather and Ritchie. Heather divorced Tommy to marry Richie. Another male Cinderella? Yes. Amazingly, it was also foretold by a Cinderella Linkage. Heather's Chiron forms a trine to Richie's Neptune, resulting in a Romantic Super Linkage.

With Heather and Richie, there are other linkages that greatly enrich a relationship. One such linkage is that his Chiron trines her Mercury and Mars, providing both ease of communication (Mercury) and enhanced sexual attraction (Mars).

The tabloids tell us that Richie and Tommy used to be friends, and Heather met Richie because of their friendship. Heather and Richie were so attracted to each other that Heather divorced Tommy to marry Richie. This example should serve as a warning to all of us. We should not introduce anyone to someone we love if we suspect that our loved one might be more attracted to this other person than to us. And we can use Magi Astrology to warn us of such a possibility.

Melanie Griffith, Antonio Banderas, and Don Johnson— Unfortunately, society has become used to couples divorcing. Even one person divorcing two or more times is not uncommon. However, it *is* rare for someone to marry and divorce the same person twice. We can probably learn something from analyzing the Combined Planetary Geometry of such cases.

Melanie Griffith was married to Don Johnson twice, and they divorced twice. She is now happily married to Antonio Banderas. The tabloids tell us that these two fell madly in love the moment they met. Magi Astrology reveals the astrological reasons why.

Melanie and Antonio have the MAGIcal Linkage, Romantic Super Linkages, and three Sexual Linkages. (Their CAC is Figure 16F.)

Melanie was born with a Sexual Aspect—she has Mars conjunct Pluto. Women who are born with Sexual Aspects are rarely happy with a man who does not have one. But Antonio does! In fact, he has a Male Super Sexual Aspect. This should surprise no one. When you look at Antonio, he exudes masculinity and magnetic sex appeal. We think a major reason for all this is that he has Mars parallel Pluto.

Melanie and Antonio have extraordinarily precise linkages. His Venus is conjunct to her conjunction of Mars and Pluto, making Multiple Sexual Linkages. In addition, her Mars is parallel his Venus, making a third Sexual Linkage. Guess what they do when they're alone together?

But Melanie and Antonio also have a multidimensional relationship and are genuinely in love. This is obvious from the Combined Planetary Geometry of their Romance Planets. Antonio has a Romance Aspect of Venus-Chiron in opposition. Melanie's Neptune is trine to his Chiron, creating a Romance Linkage, as well as an all-important Romantic Super Linkage.

We have never seen Melanie happier than she is now. We wish them both the very best. Hopefully, they got married on a great day. (We do not have the date.) We notice that Melanie's Saturn is square to Antonio's Pluto and opposed to his Mars. This is not good and can cause them to have fights that resemble a world war, but they have so many good linkages, combined with a deep love, that they should each be willing to compromise enough to make their marriage work. No two people ever match perfectly, but that makes life and the relationship more interesting. As a result, there will always be a need for compromise and understanding in any relationship.

Compromise and forgiveness are the keys to lasting marriages.

Long before Melanie married Antonio, Melanie met Don Johnson (born 12/15/49, chart not shown) and married him. She was only 14 when they first met. They fell in love, lived together, and were married after she turned 18. This marriage lasted only two years. After their first divorce, Don was a good friend (he is that kind of guy, as indicated by his Venus-Jupiter parallel) and helped her through a tough period when she was fighting off alcohol and drug abuse. They married a second time in 1989 and were divorced again a few years later.

Here again, the rules of Magi Astrology help us understand what happened. When you get married, you usually wed someone with whom you form Romantic Super Linkages. Looking at their Combined Planetary Geometry, we can see that they do indeed form such a Super Linkage. Don's Chiron links to Melanie's Sun-Chiron aspect. They also have two important Chiron Linkages: his Chiron trines her Sun, and her Chiron is trine to his Neptune. One is the Lifetime Linkage, and the other is the Linkage of Trust. Since the Chiron-Neptune linkage is the Lifetime Linkage, it can inspire two people to try marriage again.

Melanie and Don got married and divorced twice. Why? They obviously had genuine love, but we think that their relationship had several astrologically predictable deficiencies. They had two problems that were astrologically related. The first involves Sexual Aspects. Remember when we said that Melanie has a Sexual Aspect? Well, Don does not. (Antonio does.) Most women who have Sexual Aspects seem to end up with a man with a Sexual Aspect. This does not mean Don is not a good lover. We are sure he is; Venus-Jupiter aspects are signs of very considerate, sensitive, and caring people, and such persons make the best lovers. After all, there is much more to making love than sex. Nonetheless, there is usually a gap between the people who have sexual aspects and those who do not. We refer to such a problem as the SEXUAL ASPECT MISMATCH.

The second crucial astrological problem between Don and Melanie is that they have an activation of Venus opposed to Uranus, which has the effect of making the activated persons seek new horizons, greener pastures, and different love partners. (We already saw this problem between Heather Locklear and Tommy Lee.) If it were not for Don's Venus-Jupiter parallel, they would not have remarried. But Venus-Jupiter people, like Don, fall in love for a lifetime, and are the most loyal and responsible persons in the zodiac.

Bill Clinton, Gennifer Flowers, Paula Jones, Monica Lewinsky, and Hillary Clinton—Bill, what is it with you? Are you unhappy at home? Or just oversexed?

Probably both. And it shows in the stars.

You see, Bill Clinton has a Mars-Neptune PLANETARY ECLIPSE (we already saw his chart on page165). A planetary eclipse is a conjunction and parallel formed by the same two planets. As common sense would tell us, such alignments greatly intensify the influences of the conjunction and parallel. (We mentioned this in our first book.) The Mars-Neptune enhancement is a male Sexual Aspect, and Bill Clinton has two of them in a planetary eclipse. It means that sex is a focal point of his life. But this is not news. Everyone in the world knows it. However, the rest of what we have to say is news.

Bill Clinton has a Sexual Linkage with Monica Lewinsky (born 7/23/73), Gennifer Flowers (born 1/24/50), Paula Jones (born 9/17/66), and his wife, Hillary:

- Bill's Venus is contra-parallel Monica's Mars.
- Bill's Venus is conjunct Gennifer's Mars.
- Bill's Pluto conjuncts Paula's Mars.
- Bill's Pluto conjuncts Hillary's Mars.

Note that Paula's Mars and Hillary's Mars are in the same sign and the same degree; also, they both have an enhancement of Mars and Pluto. Hillary has the conjunction, Paula the parallel. People with the same aspect have similar Personal Energy. Paula and Hillary have this similarity, and Bill could have been attracted to Paula for this reason—and also because they have a Sexual Linkage.

Of all the women whom Bill Clinton has met, it is Paula Jones who has caused him the most grief (since she initiated the sexual harassment lawsuit that eventually involved Monica and the gang). This is because Paula Jones's Saturn is quincunx to Bill's Sun, and it is a Saturn Clash. This clash is a celestial sign that she could harm (Saturn) Clinton (Sun). What an understatement! It was Jones's lawyers who first found out about Monica and asked Clinton about her in their deposition. The press found out about this, and the rest is public knowledge.

The stars have a sense of humor, and we can see the twists that they can take. Bill's Jupiter is quincunx to Paula's Chiron, and this is normally a very good linkage because it is a Cinderella Linkage. But there are so many clashes between the two of them that the result of this Cinderella Linkage was definitely not fairy tale-like. However, the linkage did raise Paula's social station, since she became the darling of the ultra right wing, which is a significant elevation from her position as an obscure state government employee. So the Cinderella Linkage did not have the effect we would have expected, yet the result is still within the consistent and valid interpretations of the linkage. Besides, how many Cinderellas are there, anyway?

Paula and Bill also have Venus and Chiron contra-parallel to each other, the sign of linked destinies. Again, the stars played a joke on both of them. This linkage resulted in the two of them having linked destinies in the sense that from now until forever, Paula Jones's name will always be linked to Bill Clinton—always. Again, there was an unexpected twist in the result of the linkage, but it was still consistent with the valid interpretations of the linkage. You might find twists in interpretations of the linkages in your own relationships. There usually are. But the twists are always within the valid range of interpretations.

The Combined Planetary Geometry of Bill and Gennifer is also a mirror of their relationship. Bill Clinton's Saturn is opposed to Gennifer's Sun, indicative of his ability to have some control over her and to also create problems for her. She insists that she had a 12-year affair with him and didn't get much out of it, except being ridiculed by most of the media—that is, until Clinton's admission under oath in the Paula Jones deposition. (He claimed, though, that he only engaged in one sexual act with Gennifer—and not 12 years' worth!)

We believe Gennifer's statements that she had such a long affair with Clinton. For one thing, they have the Chiron-Neptune conjunction, which is the Lifetime Linkage. For another thing, Gennifer believes in making her love relationships long term as opposed to flings; she was born with Venus trine Neptune.

What about Monica? Monica and Bill have the Cupid Linkage; her Venus conjuncts his Sun, so she fell for him hard—even more understandable when we see that Monica's Venus is parallel to Bill's Sun. In each case, it is Monica who is the Venus person, so she is the one most likely to have the emotional attachment, which was certainly the case. Since Venus rules intimacy, these two linkages help us understand why the two became intimate. In many ways, oral sex is more intimate than sexual intercourse.

Monica was born with a Venus-Pluto parallel, the Female Super Sexual Aspect, which also signifies love of power. Who has more power than the President of the United States?

Clinton has his Saturn conjunct Monica's Sun, a sign that he could use Monica for his own purposes. Hmmm. But Monica's Saturn is parallel to both Bill's Pluto and Uranus, indicating the possibility that she could reduce (Saturn) his power (Pluto) and political standing (Uranus).

Believe it or not, Hillary and Bill do not have much in the way of linkages other than one Sexual Linkage. They do have a Venus-Neptune conjunction, a sign of long-term relationships, but why they got married is hard to understand. The fact that they are so poorly matched makes it easy to explain all those other women.

Our analysis of Bill Clinton and those women tells us one thing: Bill could use a good lesson in Magi Astrology. With this knowledge, he would have known who to fool around with and who not to fool around with. If you are a Democratic congressman or senator, you might want to consider giving the president a copy of this book. Seriously. And you might think about reading it yourself!

Jack Nicholson and Anjelica Huston—After a very long relationship, these two Hollywood actors broke up because Jack had an affair. However, if you read the tabloids, you would have expected that to happen because Jack is a known womanizer. You would have also expected the worst to happen once you checked out the Combined Planetary Geometry of their planets, because Anjelica and Jack have the worst of all Saturn Clashes. It is the same one Mia and Woody had. Jack's Saturn is square to Anjelica's Chiron. This breaks up marriages, families, and relationships. Anyway, after more than 16 years with Anjelica, Nicholson had an affair with Rebecca Broussard, who was, get this, Jack's daughter's best friend. She got pregnant, and they decided to keep the baby. Guess this means that at some point Jack would have to fess up to the affair and tell Anjelica. She didn't take it too well, but can you blame her? End of relationship. By that time, their "union" had lasted 17 years.

When we analyze the Combined Planetary Geometry of these two individuals, we find that there were remarkable similarities between them and Mia and Woody. Both couples had the Mars-Pluto Sexual Linkage in their declinations. Jack's Pluto is parallel to Anjelica's Mars, and Jack and Anjelica also have the Cupid Linkage (Anjelica was born 7/8/51 and Jack was born 4/22/37), just like Mia and Woody. Anjelica's Venus is trine to Jack's Sun. Also, like Mia, Anjelica, the woman in the relationship, is the Venus person of this linkage. Jack and Anjelica have no Symmetrical Combined Planetary Geometry, but the two of them actually do have a Romantic Super Linkage. Anjelica's Chiron links with Jack's Jupiter-Pluto opposition, and they almost have the MAGIcal Linkage. Anjelica's Chiron is four degrees from a trine to Jack's Venus, but a near linkage is a

DECEIVING LINKAGE. It had just enough influence to make them think that their relationship would work, but it wasn't strong enough to create a marriage (although they were together 17 years, which is longer than a lot of marriages).

However, the overriding reason Jack and Anjelica never married is that there was a one-two punch that prevented it. The first blow was Jack's Saturn being square to Anjelica's Chiron, thus forming a Saturn Clash. The second punch was Anjelica also being born with a square of Saturn and Chiron. This aspect can signify restriction (Saturn) in marriage (Chiron) and family (Chiron). There is something about women who are born with the Saturn-Chiron Turbulent Aspect that makes them more likely to have long relationships that end without marriage. Mia Farrow has the same aspect. It doesn't mean that such women never marry. After all, Mia married Frank Sinatra and Andre Previn, and you can't do too much better than that. However, it does mean that those who were born with such an aspect must be especially careful in choosing partners to become involved with. Such women are more susceptible to self-delusion in matters regarding love relationships. To remember such an aspect, we call it the SECLUSION ASPECT, because when it comes to spouses, the native tends to live a more secluded life than most.

Incidentally, for decades, Jack Nicholson and Warren Beatty were the most noteworthy Lotharios of Hollywood, carving so many notches on their bedposts that the beds probably fell apart. They both have the Venus-Uranus natal aspect, which we have pointed out is a mark of an incurable womanizer. If a woman has this aspect, she is often a girl who just wants to have fun.

Priscilla and Elvis Presley—When we first looked at the Combined Planetary Geometry of the king of rock 'n' roll and Priscilla, we saw how perfectly they were linked, but we commented that they got divorced because their Wedding Chart was weak. We promised to explain why later on, and we will do that now. (Chart not shown.)

We have discussed the rule of Magi Astrology that says that the most important aspects in a Wedding Chart are the aspects to the Sun, because the Sun represents the marriage itself. How strong the Sun is depends on the aspects to the Sun. Priscilla and Elvis were married when there were no enhancement aspects to the Sun (5/1/67). We call such a Sun an UNEN-HANCED SUN. An unenhanced Sun means that the Sun (in this case, the marriage) is not strong enough to withstand trauma and outside influences. A Marriage Chart needs an enhancement to the Sun. The best enhancements for the Sun in a Wedding Chart are by Jupiter, Chiron, or Neptune.

Another problem in Priscilla and Elvis's Wedding Chart was the Venus-Pluto and Venus-Uranus squares. They are horrible for marriages. In particular, the Venus-Uranus square is very similar to the Venus-Uranus activation that Melanie Griffith has with Don Johnson, and that Heather Locklear has with Tommy Lee. It is also similar to the Venus-Uranus natal aspect that Liz Taylor, Warren Beatty, and Jack Nicholson were all born with. The Venus-Uranus square in a Marriage Chart signifies a marriage where one or both spouses really wants to roam freely on the range. In other words, no commitments—hence, no marriage. We hope you are beginning to realize that the Venus-Uranus pairing of planets spells trouble for love relationships.

The Planetary Geometry of his Wedding Chart did help Elvis to sustain his career. Like the other Wedding Charts we've seen, the Planetary Geometry of Elvis's Wedding Chart was a clue to the career potential of the husband and wife. Jupiter and Chiron were synchronized with Mercury, representing Elvis's ability to have charismatic (Chiron) success (Jupiter) from singing (Mercury). The synchronization of Venus, Pluto, Uranus, and Mars is symbolic of grace (Venus) of motion (Mars) that is sexy (Pluto) and revolutionary (Uranus) and known worldwide (also Uranus). Has anyone ever been able to truly duplicate Elvis's sexy gyrations?

Of course, Elvis had all of these attributes before the marriage, but this tells us that astrology is consistent and knows what will work.

Bo and John Derek—John met Bo when she was only 16 years old. To avoid controversy, we are told that John whisked Bo off to Europe and married her as soon as she turned 18. That would mean that they were married November 20, or November 21, 1974 (chart not shown). Both days were fabulous as a Wedding Chart because there was a triple parallel of Sun, Neptune, and Venus, which is symbolic of a long-term (Neptune) union (Sun parallel Venus). This unusual triple parallel was maintained for four days, so if they were married four days after she became 18, the triple parallel was still in place. We believe that this was a reason they remained happily married until John's death in 1998. As we have been saying, an enhancement of the Sun by Jupiter, Neptune, or Chiron provides the best aspects for a wedding.

Lauren Holly and Jim Carrey—Lauren Holly, one of Hollywood's most charming actresses, married Jim Carrey, one of the most talented and best-paid actors in the world, on September 23, 1996 (chart not shown). We were really pulling for them, but we were worried the moment we looked at the Planetary Geometry of that day.

The Sun was opposed by Saturn and also parallel to Saturn, so there were two Sun-Saturn aspects! How horrible for a marriage. There was an enhancement of the Sun. It was a trine to the Sun by Uranus, but Uranus is not friendly to marriages. There is that Uranus again causing problems with a marriage. It brings fame, publicity, and too often also brings a desire for independence and perpetual change, which is not what marriage is about. Lauren Holly filed for divorce on July 29, 1997, before their first anniversary. After their divorce, the pair remained good friends, and were even seen out and about together. This is indicative of the fact that it was the weakness of their Wedding Chart that made the marriage so short-lived.

Meg Ryan and Dennis Quaid—Meg and Dennis were married in 1991. Their zodiac sign charts do not have much in the way of Combined Planetary Geometry, but they do have a spectacular set of linkages in the Declinations Charts (please see their CAC, which is Figure 16G). They each have a Romance Aspect in the declinations, and their Romance Aspects are linked, thus creating four linkages in the declinations. Meg has Venus parallel Neptune, and Dennis has Venus contra-parallel Chiron. All four of these planets are in degree 13 of the declinations. Therefore, these two aspects link to each other, creating a very strong Romantic Super Linkage, a MAGIcal Linkage, as well as the Chiron-Neptune Lifetime Linkage.

It is interesting to note that the position of Meg's Saturn creates a double clash with Dennis's Pluto and Neptune. This brings us to our final lesson on compatibility. We have been saying that double Saturn Clashes are very tough, but Meg and Dennis are very much in love, and we think there is an excellent chance they will remain that way—even with Saturn clashes. We mentioned before that you must have very strong linkages to overcome Saturn Clashes. Meg and Dennis have the MAGIcal Linkage and the Lifetime Linkage, which is a very powerful Romance Linkage. They also have an all-important Romantic Super Linkage. So they have what is needed to overcome Saturn Clashes. As crucial as such great linkages are, they do not match the importance of that most wondrous gift of all: truly selfless love.

Throughout this book, we have looked at the astrology of relationships. From time to time, we have mentioned that the nature of a person is also important, but we've never emphasized it. After all, this is an astrology book showing how the alignment of the planets may have a bearing on relationships. But now we're near the end of this book, and it's time to emphasize the human element, which is what love is really about.

We are confident about everything we've told you so far. We just want to add something. We've told you several times that astrology is a Benevolent Design and that we all have free will. Each aspect we're born with is a reflection of our soul, and we can all improve ourselves and convert all of our natal aspects into special talents. What we haven't yet discussed is that we can do the same sort of thing with linkages, activations, and even Saturn Clashes. It is not easy, but if we truly love someone in a selfless way, and we are the Saturn person in a Saturn Clash, we can use the control we have over the individual to help him or her. It takes selflessness and a very deep love, and it takes patience and uncommon understanding, but it is always within our power to help those whom we have a measure of control over. It is up to us to use this power for better rather than worse.

Meg Ryan chose to use her little bit of control over Dennis in a most loving and giving way. Dennis had a cocaine problem, and Meg helped him to overcome it when she was his girlfriend. We don't think she would have been able to do so if her Saturn did not interaspect with Dennis's Neptune. Neptune rules drugs and addictions to drugs, and Dennis was born with Neptune quincunx Mercury, a sign of drugs (Neptune) that are inhaled (Mercury rules the respiratory system). Since every aspect is a gift from God, the Mercury-Neptune quincunx can also be utilized to provide the most artistic (Neptune) singing (Mercury) and acting (Mercury). Dennis harnessed this aspect and used it to achieve a valid claim to fame in his outstanding performance in *The Big Easy*. But he also became susceptible to cocaine, which is understandable since it is passed around so freely in Hollywood.

One reason Meg was able to help Dennis is that they were able to engage in loving discourse; they have two Mercury linkages. His Chiron parallels her Mercury, and his Mercury trines her Sun. No two people can ever resolve their problems without a profound level of communication.

Meg also has another Saturn Clash with Dennis. Her Saturn is quincunx to his Pluto, which rules beginnings, endings, and also the ego. Meg helped Dennis end his cocaine addiction, curb his ego, and forge a new beginning—she married him. That is the kind of woman Meg is. She has a planetary eclipse of Venus and Neptune, signifying that her love (Venus) is long term (Neptune) and feminine (Neptune). Meg's love is true and selfless, and that allowed her to help Dennis.

We use Meg and Dennis as our last example because, more than any of the other couples we've discussed, they illustrate our point that in any love relationship, what will make the union work is selfless love, understanding, forgiveness, and compromise, as well as doing one's best to help the other person improve his or her life. Together, those characteristics are more important than everything else.

To love selflessly, and be loved in that same way in return, is a feeling that is incomparably exhilarating. We all need love, and we all need to *be* loved. It is part of God's Benevolent Design. Whether we are princes or paupers, rock stars or groupies, we all need love. Whether it is parents, lovers, spouses, children, grandchildren or just friends, life in this world was designed in such a way that we all have ample opportunities to learn how to truly love in a selfless way. The beauty of the Benevolent Design is that it is through the exchange of selfless love that we can all enhance our own lives and upgrade our natal aspects to a higher level of talents and abilities. We can even acquire Super Aspects through marriage.

If you are undecided about a relationship, or have crucial choices to make, you can apply Magi Astrology to help you make your decisions. All the techniques explained this book are valuable tools to help you discern if you're deceiving yourself about someone, or being deceived by someone else. The techniques we have given you are a fabulous reality check; they are the most unbiased and objective criteria there is. However, the final decision about whom to love should and must be made from the heart. Besides, no one can love an astrological chart, and a chart cannot love us in return.

Once you've made the choice about whom to love, you can use Magi Astrology to help you take advantage of the stars and harness the power of the planets to maximize both your happiness and prosperity by choosing the best Planetary Geometry for your important electional charts—which brings us to our final lesson on money. It is a lesson filled with hope and dreams.

The Rolling Stones' First Gig Occurred on a Dream Day

We are almost at the conclusion of this book. All that's left is a chapter in which we present our proof of astrology, the Love Calendar, and the glossary. However, we *will* write other books. As we mentioned, the next one is on predicting the future and will be called *Predict the Future Accurately Using Magi Astrology.* You can actually predict the major trends in your life and in anyone else's life through the techniques and methodologies of Magi Astrology. You can even predict the trends of nations, corporations, and marriages—basically anything that has a chart.

Our final example in this book should leave you with the hope of greater prosperity for yourself and your family and should encourage you to dream big dreams because you *can* fulfill them. We are going to use the Rolling Stones as our case study. See our "mystery chart," Figure 14B on page 287, for their first gig. It is the first time that Mick Jagger, Keith Richards, and the original members of the band performed together in front of a live audience. It happened on July 12, 1962 at a place in London called the Marquee Jazz Club. It was Mick and Keith's baptismal gig and essentially the chart of the birth of the Rolling Stones (although they used to call the band the "Rollin' Stones").

As you can see from this chart, there is a Conjuncted Trine; Jupiter and Chiron are conjunct, and both are trine to Neptune. We have repeatedly pointed out that this is a shape of Planetary Geometry that is immensely powerful and is just below the power of a Grand Trine. The Conjuncted Trine helps to explain the unparalleled success of the Rolling Stones, but if you take a closer look, you will see that this is not an ordinary Conjuncted Trine. All three planets are in retrograde motion. We explained in chapter 12 that we consider retrograde planets to be better than those that are in direct motion. We said the same thing in our previous books. The chart of the Rolling Stones' first performance is an example. The chart has one of the rarest of all shapes of Planetary Geometry—and one of the most powerful. It has a Conjuncted Trine with all three planets in retrograde. It almost never happens. Remember when we explained that double retrograde enhancements are the best of all? There were three of them that day.

The actual shape of Planetary Geometry by itself was enough of a sign of extraordinary and ultimate success. On top of that, the symbolisms of the planets that make the shape are perfect for the type of success the Rolling Stones needed. The Jupiter-Chiron conjunction gave them charisma and a fabulous public image, and Neptune made certain it was long term. They are the longest-lasting rock music superstars.

There was also a planetary eclipse of Venus and Uranus, meaning that the Stones would be adored (Venus) worldwide (Uranus). Also, the parallel of Mercury and Sun coincides with the fact they are musicians (Mercury) and singers (Mercury). Even the Stones' macho, sexually charged, and energetic style is foretold by the Mars-Pluto parallel.

We Can All Fulfill Our Dreams

When Mick Jagger and Keith Richards were young boys, they had a dream, a very big dream. By having their first gig on the day that had such extraordinary Planetary Geometry, they were able to fulfill their dreams.

With help from Magi Astrology, so can *you*.

We wrote this book to help you learn how to fulfill your own dreams. The examples and information in this book should give all of you the hope that you can indeed do so. Now you know how to take advantage of the principles behind Magi Astrology to help you achieve your goals.

You *will* make it.

Remember, the stars are there not to limit you or hurt you. They are there to give you signs, to guide you, and to help you achieve your dreams. It's the way astrology was designed.

And you can see it all in the stars!

TO BE CONTINUED . . .

Figure 16A: CAC of Mia Farrow (2/9/1945) with Woody Allen (12/1/1935)

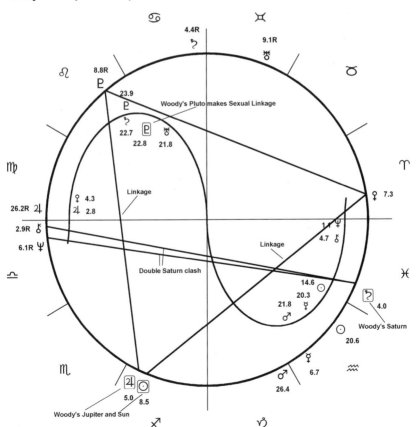

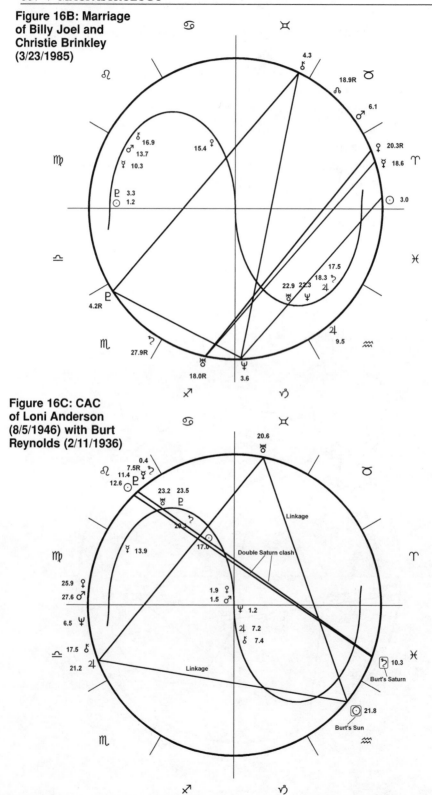

Figure 16B: Marriage of Billy Joel and Christie Brinkley (3/23/1985)

Figure 16C: CAC of Loni Anderson (8/5/1946) with Burt Reynolds (2/11/1936)

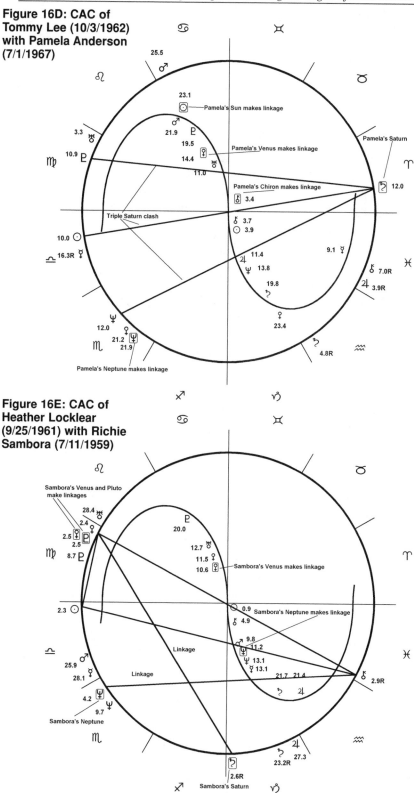

Figure 16D: CAC of Tommy Lee (10/3/1962) with Pamela Anderson (7/1/1967)

Pamela's Sun makes linkage

Pamela's Venus makes linkage

Pamela's Saturn

Pamela's Chiron makes linkage

Triple Saturn clash

Pamela's Neptune makes linkage

Figure 16E: CAC of Heather Locklear (9/25/1961) with Richie Sambora (7/11/1959)

Sambora's Venus and Pluto make linkages

Sambora's Venus makes linkage

Sambora's Neptune makes linkage

Linkage

Linkage

Sambora's Neptune

Sambora's Saturn

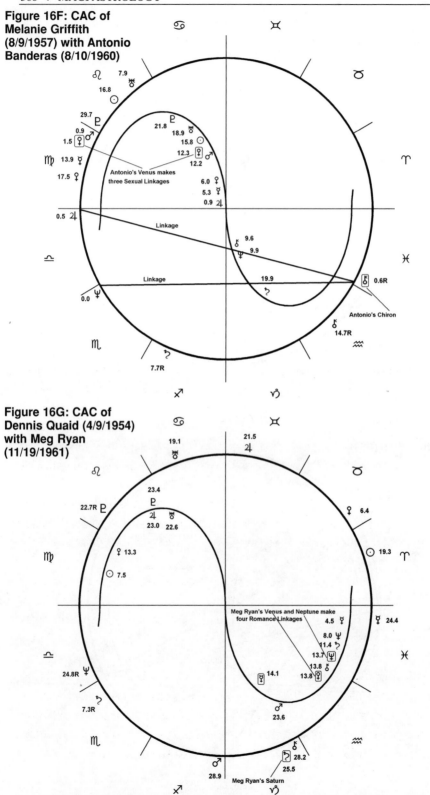

Figure 16F: CAC of Melanie Griffith (8/9/1957) with Antonio Banderas (8/10/1960)

Antonio's Venus makes three Sexual Linkages

Linkage

Linkage

Antonio's Chiron

Figure 16G: CAC of Dennis Quaid (4/9/1954) with Meg Ryan (11/19/1961)

Meg Ryan's Venus and Neptune make four Romance Linkages

Meg Ryan's Saturn

Editor's Note: We have concluded our discussions on the astrology of love and money, except for the Love Calendar that follows this chapter. It is not necessary that you understand the contents of this chapter because it is written strictly for the most advanced reseachers in astrology.

CHAPTER SEVENTEEN

Astounding Proof of the Validity of Planetary Geometry

In this chapter, we will present some new concepts in astrology that we call PLANETARY BALANCE, MID-DEGREE, HIGH BALANCE, and MAXIMUM BALANCE. These concepts all relate to Planetary Geometry. We will apply these new concepts to analyze the birth charts of great athletes and artists. What we will find is that the Planetary Geometry of all great athletes have the same features, and their Planetary Geometry is very different from that of great artists. All of this will result in proving that Planetary Geometry is a reliable sign of the types of talents and skills we are born with. In other words, astrology really works.

We believe we already proved the validity of astrology in *Astrology Really Works!* Like much of scientific research, our proofs ultimately relied on statistics. Unfortunately, skeptics of astrology can usually muddy the waters whenever statistics is used to prove astrology.

Fortunately, it is not always necessary for a proof of a theory to require statistical analysis. Statistics is required only when there isn't a 100 percent fit or correlation. In other words, if something does not work all the time, you need statistics to verify that it actually works often enough to have validity. In the past, there has never been a way to prove astrology without statistical analysis because nothing in astrology worked 100 percent of the time. For example, some Virgos are neat and orderly, but others are not. Or, most supersuccessful entrepreneurs have enhancements of Pluto, but some do not. What astrology has always needed was a correlation that worked nearly all the time. But no one could ever find one.

Until now.

Lo and behold, because we are about to enter the dawn of a New Age, the Magi Society actually has discovered an astrologically based correlation that essentially always works, and therefore cannot be dismissed or disproved. The Magi Society has discovered that just about all great athletes are born on days when there is MAXIMUM OVERALL PLANETARY BALANCE, even though such days occur less than one-third of the time. This new validation of astrology is based on a rule of Magi Astrology that the Magi Society first introduced on page 145 of *Astrology Really Works!* On that page, we wrote that "the tighter the synchronization of planets, the better the athlete." This rule is a part of the criteria for Maximum Overall Planetary Balance. To understand Maximum Overall Planetary Balance, we must first understand PLANETARY BALANCE.

Planetary Balance

Planetary Balance is a type of Planetary Synchronization. We have already explained that when at least three planets match degrees, they are SYNCHRONIZED and form what we call Planetary Synchronization. This is a very powerful and useful concept, but is not as important as Planetary Balance.

**Planetary Balance is the special type of
Planetary Synchronization of just three planets that exists
when the Pivot Planet is within 31/2 days of being in perfect
balance to the mid-degree of the other two planets.**

Let us explain all this: Two examples of Planetary Balance can be found in Figures 17C and 17F at the end of this chapter. They are the birth charts of Wayne Gretzky and Michael Jordan, two of the greatest athletes that ever lived. In Gretzky's chart, Venus, Saturn, and Uranus are synchronized. Venus is said to be IN BALANCE to Saturn and Uranus because it is at the MID-DEGREE of Saturn and Uranus. Similarly, on Jordan's birth date, Venus is in balance to Saturn and Pluto because it is at the mid-degree of Saturn and Pluto. The mid-degree is not to be confused with MIDPOINTS, which is a different concept. The mid-degree of two planets is calculated by obtaining the mathematical average of the degrees that those two planets are in, regardless of the signs that the planets are in. This mid-degree is then projected to the same degree of each of the 12 signs so that there are 12 locations for each mid-degree, and each such location is positioned in the same degree of each of the 12 signs.

In Gretzky's birth chart, the mid-degree of Saturn and Uranus is (22.6 + 24.5)/2, which is 23.55 degrees. Gretzky's Venus is at 23.5 degrees and is therefore almost exactly at the mid-degree of Saturn-Uranus. If Venus were exactly at the mid-degree of Saturn-Uranus, Venus would be in PERFECT BALANCE to the Saturn-Uranus mid-degree. Although Venus was not exactly at the mid-degree, as is the case in most astrological criteria, we allow an orb, and Venus is close enough here to be judged to be in balance since it is only a mere 0.05 degrees from perfect balance.

Similarly, the mid-degree of Jordan's Saturn and Pluto is (15.5 + 11.2)/2, which is 13.35, and his Venus is within 0.15 degrees of being exactly at the Saturn-Pluto mid-degree. Jordan's Venus is close enough to this mid-degree to be regarded as being in balance to Saturn-Pluto, because of the orb that we use. Almost all astrological criteria employs an orb.

But when it comes to Planetary Balance, the orb that we use is a TIME ORB and not a DISTANCE ORB. Remember we had explained what a time orb is on page 233. The time orb for planetary balance is 3 1/2 days. If a planet is within 3 1/2 days of being in perfect balance with any two planets' mid-degree, it qualifies as being in balance. The day that a planet is in highest balance is called the HIGH BALANCE DAY. The day before the High Balance Day is called the PRE-HIGH DAY, and the day after is the POST-HIGH DAY.

In general, when someone in born on a High Balance Day, the person is endowed by the planets with more energy, stamina, respiratory capacity, and a higher degree of coordination than someone who is born on a day that is not a High Balance Day. Such a person also is less likely to be physically injured, and will recover more quickly and more completely than a normal person. These hypotheses are all part of our Theory of PLANETARY BALANCE. A day is a High Balance Day if there is a Planetary Balance that is more perfect than the day before, and the day after. This means that when we examine birth charts to see if there is High Balance on any day, we must also look at the charts of the day before and day after and compare the charts to determine which day has High Balance.

As our first example of exactly how we determine if a day has High Balance, we will quite naturally use the birth chart of Wayne Gretzky, who holds almost every scoring record in hockey and is considered by almost all hockey authorities to be the greatest hockey player of all time. That is why they simply refer to him as "the Great One."

On pages 383 and 384, we have provided you with the Magi AstroCharts for Gretzky's birth date, and also for the day before and the day after he was born. These three days are collectively referred to as the three RANGE DAYS. We already learned that on Gretzky's birth date, Venus was almost exactly in balance with the mid-degree of Saturn-Uranus. As we mentioned above, a High Balance Day is defined as a day when three planets form a Planetary Balance, and a planet is more balanced than either the day before and the day after. To help us refer to the other two range days, we will refer to the day before someone's birth date as the MINUS ONE DAY, and the day after someone's birth date as the PLUS ONE DAY.

By comparing the position of Venus on the three range days, we can easily see that Gretzky was born on the High Balance Day. To both verify and understand our criteria, please look at the Magi AstroChart for the day after Gretzky was born, which is the Plus One Day (Figure 17D). On that day, Venus was about a degree away from the Saturn-Uranus mid-degree. Venus was not at High Balance because it was not as close to the mid-degree of Saturn-Uranus as it was on Gretzky's actual birth date.

Similarly, the Minus One Day is also not the High Balance Day because Venus was not as close to the mid-degree of Saturn-Uranus as the next day, which was the actual day Gretzky was born.

Therefore, Gretzky was born on the day of High Balance of Venus to Saturn-Uranus. His birth date was more balanced than either the Minus One Day or the Plus One Day.

As always, when we have new concepts in astrology, we need new terms to help us discuss the details of the concept. In Gretzky's example, Venus is called the PIVOT PLANET, because it is pivotal in determining if there is High Balance. Saturn and Uranus are the PAIRED PLANETS and form the mid-degree. The rule of High Balance is as follows:

A day has High Balance if that day has three planets that form a Planetary Balance, and the Pivot Planet is more balanced than on both the Minus One Day and the Plus One Day.

Except for the Moon, any three planets can form a Planetary Balance and a High Balance Day. Below, we drew up a very simple diagram to help illustrate the level of balance that existed on the day Gretzky was born, as well as the day before and after he was born.

Figure 17A

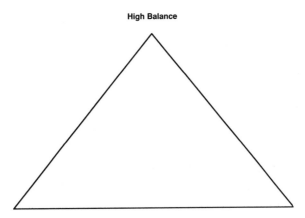

High Balance

Minus One Day has less balance   Plus One Day has less balance

Although this diagram appears to be far too simplistic to really work, in actuality, it clearly and precisely illustrates the type of Planetary Geometry that almost every superstar athlete has in common. The Michael Jordans and Wayne Gretzkys of the world are almost always born on a High Balance day.

Obviously, our next example should be Michael Jordan.

The Magi AstroCharts of the three Range Days for Jordan are on pages 385 and 386. In all three charts, if you examine the varying positions of Venus relative to the more stable positions of Saturn and Pluto, it is obvious that Venus reached High Balance on Jordan's birth date. The position of Venus on the Minus One Day was not as balanced as the day Jordan was born. The same is true of the position of Venus on the Plus One Day. In this sense, the similarities between Jordan and Gretzky are uncanny; and both are the best that ever played their sports.

As our third example of High Balance, we chose Mark McGwire, who set a record by hitting 70 home runs during the 1998 baseball season. He also was born on a day when Venus was at High Balance. On his birth date, Venus was at High Balance with Jupiter and Saturn, even though if we only look at the chart of the birth date, we might think that Venus is too close to the degree that Saturn is in. But Venus is indeed at High Balance on McGwire's birth date because Venus was more balanced (closest to the mid-degree of Saturn and Jupiter) on that day than on the Minus One and Plus One days. On the Minus One Day, Venus was in a degree that was lower than both Jupiter and Saturn; on the Plus One Day, Venus was in a degree that was higher than both Jupiter and Saturn. For ease of writing, we will refer to the Minus One Day and the Plus One Day collectively as the two OUTER RANGE DAYS.

So far, we have seen three examples of superstar athletes who were born on days of High Balance. In each case, it was Venus that was in High Balance, but Venus is not the only planet that can be at High Balance.

Pivot Planets Determine High Balance

For Jordan, Gretzky, and McGwire, each was born on a day with a Planetary Balance where Venus was the PIVOT PLANET; sometimes we just call such a planet the PIVOT.

A Planetary Balance is always comprised of three planets. The PIVOT PLANET of a Planetary Balance is the planet that is at or close to the mid-degree of the other two planets. The planets that form the mid-degree are called the PAIRED PLANETS. (The Moon is disregarded in the determination of a High Balance Day because it moves too quickly to be useful in this concept.) Although any planet except the Moon can act as the Pivot Planet, the Pivot Planet is usually one of the four fastest-moving planets. They are the Sun, Mercury, Venus, and Mars. They are the fastest-moving planets because they are the closest to the Sun. On average, these four planets move about a degree each day; therefore, their movements are tailor-made for creating Planetary Balance and High Balance Days. This is because High Balance Days are most easily detectable when there is a discernible difference between the Planetary Geometry patterns of each of the three Range Days. In Magi Astrology, when we are referring to Planetary Balance, the Sun, Mercury, Venus, and Mars are collectively called the PIN-POINT PLANETS. So to speak, it is usually the movement of these four planets that pinpoint the day of High Balance.

Jupiter, Saturn, Chiron, Uranus, Neptune, and Pluto are referred to as the STABLE PLANETS. They are divided into two groups. Jupiter, Saturn, and Chiron are the MODERATELY STABLE PLANETS because they move moderately. Uranus, Neptune, and Pluto are the HIGHLY STABLE PLANETS because they move so slowly from day to day.

The three planets that are aligned such that they form a Planetary Balance are called the BALANCED PLANETS.

So far, all of our examples have Venus as the Pivot Planet. Let us give you examples of High Balance Days when each of the other three Pinpoint Planets is the Pivot Planet. (In these next three examples, charts are provided only for the birth dates and not for the Outer Range Days.)

Emmitt Smith is the Dallas Cowboy football player who holds the record for the most touchdowns scored by a running back in a single season; he scored 25 touchdowns in 1995. He was born with High Balance of the Sun with Jupiter and Pluto (see figures 17K-17M.)

As an example of High Balance of Mercury, we will use another football running back, Barry Sanders. Sanders and Smith have been rivals for a decade because they have alternated as the best at their position in terms of rushing yards gained. Sanders has Mercury synchronized with Jupiter and Chiron, and Mercury was at High Balance on the day Sanders was born.

Evander Holyfield is our example of someone born with High Balance of Mars. Holyfield is the dominant boxer of the 1990s and has held the title of Heavyweight Champion of the World through much of the decade in spite of the fact that he is older than most boxers. His Mars is synchronized with Jupiter and Saturn and was at High Balance on the day he was born. The mid-degree of Jupiter and Saturn is 3.4, and his Mars was at 3.5 at noon of his birth date.

Interpreting Planetary Balances

A Planetary Balance is a form of Planetary Geometry; so are aspects. Just like an aspect, Planetary Balance endows the native with a gift of a special talent. The talent can be related to any field of endeavor, whether it is sports or not. We can accurately foretell the most likely outcome of Planetary Balances by combining and integrating the symbolisms of the planets that create the balance. But we give the most weight to the symbolisms of the Pivot Planet. For example, if Mercury is the Pivot Planet (called Mercury balance), the native will be most likely to be supergifted in an area that is ruled by Mercury. When it comes to sports, Mercury is most symbolic of coordination and reflexes. An athlete with a balance of Mercury will have the highest degree of coordination and the most superlative reflexes.

But Planetary Balance also endows talents unrelated to sports. For example, with Mercury balance, the native could be remarkably endowed with Mercury's artistic talents, such as singing, writing, music, and song composition. Mercury also rules design and engineering; someone with a Mercury Balance can be remarkably skilled in these ways as well.

Some Days Have More Than One High Balance

It only requires three planets to form a Planetary Balance. Since there are ten astrological planets that can align in balance, it is possible for a day to have more than just one group of Balanced Planets. For example, Jordan, McGwire, Smith, and Sanders were all born on days when there was DOUBLE HIGH BALANCE, meaning that there were two groups of Balanced Planets, and both such groups were forming High Balance on the same day..

In McGwire's case, in addition to Venus being at High Balance, Mars was also at High Balance with Chiron and Neptune. Michael Jordan's Venus was at High Balance to not just Saturn-Pluto, but also to Saturn-Neptune. Smith's Sun forms a second High Balance with Pluto and Neptune. Sanders's Sun is at a second High Balance with Saturn and Neptune.

As you might logically expect, the more sets of planets that are at High Balance on a day, the better the athlete is who is born on that day.

Another Type of High Balance

There are other ways to form Planetary Balance and High Balance. So far we have only dealt with the type of Planetary Balance that has a Pivot Planet and is therefore referred to specifically as PIVOTED PLANETARY BALANCE. There is also a type of Planetary Balance called BALANCE OF ASPECTS. This refers to the alignment of planets that occurs when a single aspect is most exact. On the day that any aspect is most exact, that day has High Balance because both the Minus One Day and the Plus One Day is less balanced with regard to that aspect. In such instances. the mid-degree is simply the mathematical average of the positions of the two planets that form the aspect. When the aspect is exact, both of the planets are at the mid-degree, thus creating perfect balance.

An example of a great athlete born on High Balance of Aspects is Roger Clemens. The charts for his three Range Days are at the end of this chapter. Note that Mars and Mercury were clearly most balanced on the day he was born. The Mercury-Mars aspect was not nearly as balanced on the Minus One Day or on the Plus One Day.

High Balance of Aspects works like Pivoted High Balance in that it greatly enhances the athletic abilities of the native (person born with the balance). Any two planets that form an aspect can form a High Balance of Aspects, but there are only two special pairs of planets that create a strong enough High Balance of Aspects to give birth to a superstar *athlete*. One of them is the Mercury-Mars pairing that Clemens was born with. The other is the Venus-Mars pairing that was the main subject of chapter 10 of *Astrology Really Works!*

When someone has a High Balance of either Mercury-Mars or Venus-Mars, that person is born with the astrological help necessary to be empowered enough to become a superstar athlete. Almost always, someone born with a High Balance of just an aspect of any other two planets is only good enough to be a star in high school or a college athlete, but is not talented enough to be a great professional athlete. This is consistent with all that we have written in each of our books, because Mars rules athletics, energy, and the muscles. Both the Mercury-Mars and Venus-Mars aspects are expected to be the most important for athletic prowess based on Magi Astrology's rules and symbolisms. The aspects that would be the next most important in this regard would be the other Mars aspects, such as Mars-Chiron, Mars-Pluto; and Mars-Neptune. However, the Venus-Mars and Mercury-Mars aspects are the ULTIMATE SPORTS CHAMPION ASPECTS.

Multiple High Balance of Aspects

Since the average day has about six aspects, it would make sense that there can be High Balance of more than one aspect, and that this type of High Balance is more powerful than High Balance of only one aspect. When two or more planetary aspects are exact on any given day, then there is MULTIPLE HIGH BALANCE OF ASPECTS.

Whenever there is Multiple High Balance of Aspects, there are four factors that influence the athletic potential of the native (person born). They are defined in the following four RULES OF BALANCE:

1. The more aspects that are in Multiple High Balance, the better the athlete.

2. The closer together in time that two or more balanced aspects are exact, the better the athlete.

3. The more the aspects in High Balance are formed by planets associated with athleticism, the better the athlete.

4. Applying aspects are in higher balance than separating ones of equal time orb.

Maximum Overall Planetary Balance

We are now finally ready to understand what Maximum Overall Planetary Balance is.

A day of Maximum Overall Planetary Balance is a day that has more High Balance alignments than both the day before and the day after.

All of the athletes who we have used as examples in this chapter were born on a Day of Maximum Overall Planetary Balance. For ease of writing, we will simply refer to such days as Maximum Balance Days. By definition, there cannot be two consecutive days of Maximum Balance because there cannot be a Maximum Balance Day unless the day is more balanced than the two Outer Range Days. Therefore, by definition, there are more days *without* Maximum Balance than *with*. In fact, days of Maximum Balance occur less often than one out of three days. Yet essentially every great athlete was born on a day of Maximum Balance.

Take, for example, the case of Michael Jordan. His birth date was the Maximum Balance Day because there were more High Balance alignments on that day than the two Outer Range Days. Not only was Venus at Double High Balance, but there was also Multiple High Balance of Aspects. Both the Mars-Chiron and Mercury-Uranus aspects of that day were in High Balance. They also were exact within 45 minutes of each other, which is an example of the second of the four Rules of Balance. On both Outer Range Days, there were fewer High Balance alignments.

The same type of Planetary Geometry existed on the day Gretzky was born. Not only was there a High Balance of Venus, but there was also a Multiple High Balance of Aspects created by the Mars-Chiron and Sun-Pluto aspects. In Gretzky's case, also, both aspects were exact within 75 minutes of each other. In addition, on both Outer Range Days, there were fewer High Balance alignments.

Alternate High Balance Days

When there are only two planets that form any type of Planetary Balance, there can never be any doubt as to which day is the Maximum Balance Day. However, because of the way the planets move in alignment in the sky, when there is a Planetary Balance of three planets (Pivoted Planetary Balance), sometimes there can be two consecutive days that could both be considered to be the High Balance Day, in which case we call such days ALTERNATE HIGH BALANCE DAYS. This happens usually under one of the following two conditions:

1. A group of three planets are in balance, and the actual perfect balance occurs at about midnight. Since we are using mainly noontime charts, there will be two days when the pivot planet will be at about equally high balance, about 12 hours from the actual perfect balance; both those days qualify as Alternate High Balance Days.

2. There are two different groups of planets forming Pivoted Planetary Balance. One group forms Pivoted High Balance on a particular day, and the other group forms its Pivoted High Balance on the next day. This results in the two consecutive days both being Alternate High Balance Days. This condition is called CONSECUTIVE HIGH BALANCE.

In both such circumstances, a great athlete could be born on either of the Alternate High Balance Days because each such day is essentially a High Balance Day. But our research has found that it is very rare for a great athlete to be born on an Alternate High Balance Day. This is because most superstar athletes who are born with Pivoted High Balance are born on days that also have what we call a MARKER.

Markers

We have explained that almost all great athletes are born on a Maximum Balance Day. Such a day can have one or more High Balance alignments. Although it is possible for a great athlete to be born with only one High Balance alignment, they are usually born with at least two of them, where one is a Pivoted High Balance, and the other is an aspect that is in High Balance. Such an aspect is called a marker. A marker is an aspect that is in High Balance (exact), and on the same day, there is a Pivoted High Balance. So to speak, the marker marks the day that a Pivoted Planetary Balance reaches High Balance, and a great athlete can be born.

Essentially Every Great Athlete Was Born on a Day of Maximum Balance

In *Astrology Really Works!*, we detailed how every basketball player who ever won the award for the Most Valuable Player (MVP) in the National Basketball Association (NBA) was born on a day when there was at least one Super Aspect and also one Sports Champion Aspect. *We can now reveal that each such player was also born on a day with Maximum Balance.* Ninety percent of them were born with a Pivoted High Balance and an aspect in High Balance (a marker). Since the publication of our first book, there have been two new athletes who have received the award. These two also fit the criteria! Here are all 20 of the NBA's MVPs and how each forms their Maximum Balance.

Bob Petit: Born December 12, 1932
High Balance of Sun to Jupiter and Uranus, with marker of Venus-Uranus

Bob Cousy: Born August 9, 1928
High Balance of Mercury to Jupiter and Chiron with marker of Venus-Neptune

Bill Russell: Born February 12, 1934
High Balance of Sun to Jupiter and Pluto with marker of Venus-Neptune

Wilt Chamberlain: Born August 21, 1936
High Balance of Mercury to Saturn and Chiron with marker of Sun-Pluto

Oscar Robertson: Born November 24, 1938
High Balance of Mercury to Jupiter and Neptune with marker of Sun-Pluto

Wes Unseld: Born March 14, 1946
High Balance of Sun to Jupiter and Chiron with marker of Mercury-Pluto

Willis Reed: Born June 25, 1942
High Balance of Sun to Jupiter and Pluto with marker of Venus-Neptune

Kareem Abdul-Jabbar: Born April 16, 1947
High Balance of Mars to Saturn and Chiron with marker of Sun-Jupiter

Dave Cowens: Born October 25, 1948
High Balance of Sun to Saturn and Uranus with marker of Mercury-Venus

Bob McAdoo: Born September 15, 1951
High Balance of Mercury to Saturn and Venus with marker of Mars-Neptune

Bill Walton: Born November 5, 1952
High Balance of Mars to Jupiter and Uranus with marker of Venus-Mars

Moses Malone: Born March 23, 1955
High Balance of Venus to Jupiter and Uranus with marker of Venus-Saturn

Julius Erving: Born February 22, 1950
High Balance of the Mercury-Mars aspect with marker of Sun-Venus

Larry Bird: Born December 7, 1956
High Balance of Mercury to Jupiter and Pluto with marker of Mars-Pluto

Magic Johnson: Born August 14, 1959
High Balance of the Venus-Mars aspect; no marker, but this is Ultimate Sports Champion Aspect

Michael Jordan: Born February 17, 1963
High Balance of Venus to Saturn and Pluto with marker of Mars-Chiron

Charles Barkley: Born February 20, 1963
High Balance of Mercury to Mars and Uranus with marker of Venus-Neptune

Akeem Olajuwan: Born January 21, 1963
High Balance of Venus to Saturn and Neptune; no marker

David Robinson: Born August 6, 1965
High Balance of Sun to Saturn and Uranus with marker of Mars-Chiron

Karl Malone: Born July 24, 1963
High Balance of Mercury to Chiron and Neptune with marker of Venus-Saturn

You have them all—every MVP in the NBA. All 20 of them, and each of them was born on a day of Maximum Balance, and not the day before or after such a day. The odds against this happening by chance are over a billion to one!

The Level of Planetary Balance Is Also Crucial to Athletic Ability

All but one of the above great athletes not only have Maximum Balance, they also have very high levels of Planetary Balance because they have Multiple High Balances. All except Magic Johnson and Julius Erving have Pivoted High Balance plus High Balance of at least one aspect, which is the marker. But Magic Johnson and Julius Erving each have High Balance of one of the two Ultimate Sports Champion Aspects, which are the most helpful balances for athletes.

The more High Balances that there are on a day, the greater the potential of any athlete born on that day. You cannot become a great athlete unless your Planetary Geometry is similar to that of the great athletes. They essentially all have Maximum Balance. Most also have high levels of overall Planetary Balance or an Ultimate Sports Champion Aspect in High Balance.

The Greatest Artists Are Not Born with Unusual Maximum Balance

Let us compare the Planetary Geometry of our group of superstar basketball players with a group of very successful people who are not great athletes. An obviously perfect contrast would be to great artists, since artistic individuals would not be expected to have the same type of Planetary Geometry as superstar athletes. We wanted to make such a comparison when we wrote our first book, but at that time there was no listing of great artists that would be comparable to the MVPs in basketball. However, after our first book was published, *Time* magazine wrote a cover article about the artists who the magazine's editors believe have been the greatest artists of this century. In their June 8, 1998 issue, they provided a short biography of each of their top 20 artists. It actually turned out that there were 22 such artists, including all 4 members of the Beatles. We were excited when we heard about this list and were anxious to test Maximum Balance on the birth dates of the great artists. We had already tested over 10,000 artists, so we knew what the results would be. But we were delighted to have a simple list of super artists to compare with our list of super athletes.

Of the 22 artists that *Time* magazine chose as the greatest artists of this century, only half were born on days of Pivoted High Balance; and only five had Planetary Geometry that had a similarity to that of the superstar basketball players, even though a closer scrutiny would result in the conclusion that only two or three were somewhat similar. We chose three of these great artists' charts as examples of charts without the type of High Balance that great athletes have. Their Magi AstroCharts are at the end of this chapter.

The three we chose are Pablo Picasso, Ringo Starr, and Jim Henson. Clearly, none of these great artistic geniuses were born on a day of Maximum Balance, and the Planetary Geometry of each of their charts bears no true parallels to that of the superstar athletes.

Please recall that Pivoted High Balance can endow the native with a gift of a talent other than athletic ability. Of great interest is the fact that the artists who had Pivoted High Balance were born with the Pivot Planet that you would expect from the way they achieved their success. For example, Frank Sinatra and Bob Dylan were great singers and both had Mercury (ruler of singing) as the Pivot of a Planetary Balance.

Conclusion

So now you have more reasons to believe that what you read in this book about Planetary Geometry is based on scientific truths and validated principles.

We do not expect you to understand what we have written until you analyze quite a few charts by yourself. You should find that there is simply a discernible difference in the Planetary Geometry of differently talented individuals. If your mind and heart are open to the beauty of astrology, you will also understand that astrology has been designed, just for us, and Planetary Geometry is a sign of the gifts God gave us when we came into this world. If you run into a skeptic of astrology, ask the person to come up with a list of superstar athletes who were born without Maximum Planetary Balance. It would be a very short list.

ॐ ॐ ॐ

If you are a serious astrologer or scientist and wish to conduct independent research into Maximum Balance, we have prepared the following summary of additional parameters related to Maximum Balance and/or the level of influence of Planetary Geometry and how it influences athletic capabilities. These were not explained above because they are intricate and boring details of how the Maximum Balance Day is determined under various planetary conditions, as well as other astrological factors that are indications of extraordinary athletic abilities. These details are in addition to those presented in *Astrology Really Works!,* in particular on page 145.

1. When there is Consecutive High Balance where each High Balance is formed by a Pinpoint Planet, then we determine the Maximum Balance Day by applying the following hierarchy of Pivot Planets: Mercury, Mars, Sun, and Venus. For example, a Pivoted High Balance of Mercury is more important as a determinant than one of the Sun. There is also a hierarchy of the order of value of High Balances. Pivoted High Balance creates a higher level of balance than High Balance of Aspects.

2. Three planets can be synchronized and yet not form a Planetary Balance. If the Pivot Planet is a Pinpoint Planet, then there is no Planetary Balance unless the Pivot Planet is within Magical time of an aspect with each of the paired planets. Since we are using only birth times of noon, this means that both aspects made by the Pivot must be within 3.5 days of exact.

3. The Theory of Maximum Balance works also in the declinations (see Sandy Koufax, which is last chart of this chapter), but the longitudes are more important. Balance in the declinations occurs much less frequently than in the longitudes. If there are two consecutive days that could be the Maximum Balance Day in the longitudes and there is no other way to distinguish between them, then the declinations will be the deciding factor.

4. There is also SUPER BALANCE, which is a balance formed by only the Stable Planets. When a balance is formed by three Stable Planets, the level of enhancement is so high that it overrides the requirement of High Balance. Anyone born within 3.5 days of the perfect balance has the capacity for super success in sports. An aspect formed by the Stable Planets has similar power when within 3.5 days of exact.

5. Certain planetary combinations are not allowed in Planetary Balance when determining Maximum Overall Planetary Balance for athletes. For example, the two Paired Planets cannot both be Highly Stable Planets.

6. Only two planets that are in aspect to each other can form a mid-degree. Here again, we use our standard orb of three degrees for the longitudes. When two planets form an aspect and the two planets are close to the cusps of the signs, the calcu-

lation of their mid-degree can be different from the one we have been using, which is the mathematical average of the degree-values of the two planets (degree-value is the position of the planet in degrees). If the difference between the degree-values of the two planets is greater than 3 (the orb), then the mid-degree is 15 plus or minus the mathematical average of the degree-values of the two planets. Whether we add or subtract 15 depends on whether the result would exceed 30 or be less than 0; the mid-degree must have a value of 0 to just below 30. As an example, if Saturn is at 28 degrees Scorpio, and Jupiter is at 1 degree Scorpio, their mid-degree is 29.5; it is not 14.5 or -0.5.

We welcome and encourage scientists and serious researchers of astrology to conduct independent studies of Planetary Balance. If you are such a person, please feel free to contact us at the address or telephone number listed on page 437.

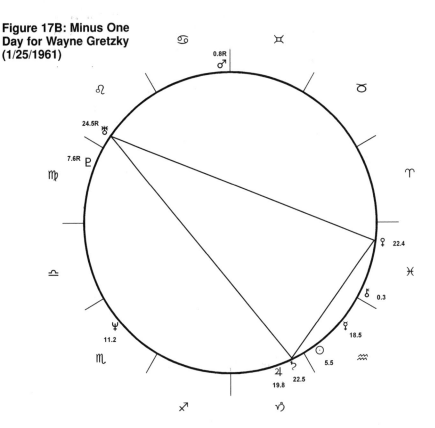

Figure 17B: Minus One Day for Wayne Gretzky (1/25/1961)

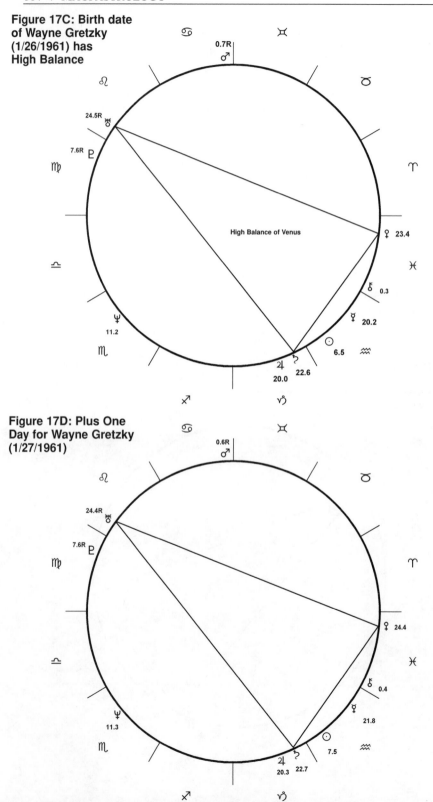

Figure 17C: Birth date of Wayne Gretzky (1/26/1961) has High Balance

High Balance of Venus

Figure 17D: Plus One Day for Wayne Gretzky (1/27/1961)

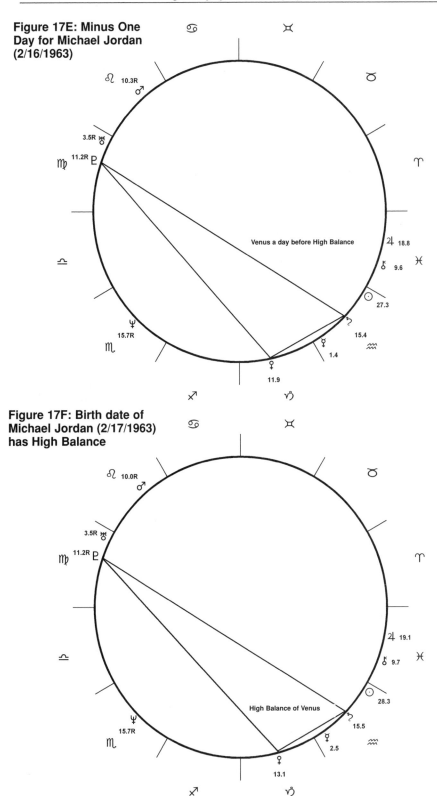

Figure 17E: Minus One Day for Michael Jordan (2/16/1963)

Venus a day before High Balance

Figure 17F: Birth date of Michael Jordan (2/17/1963) has High Balance

High Balance of Venus

Figure 17G: Plus One Day for Michael Jordan (2/18/1963)

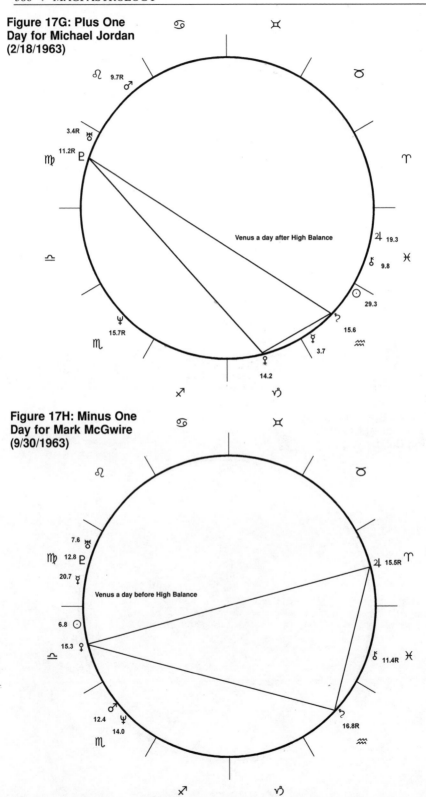

Venus a day after High Balance

Figure 17H: Minus One Day for Mark McGwire (9/30/1963)

Venus a day before High Balance

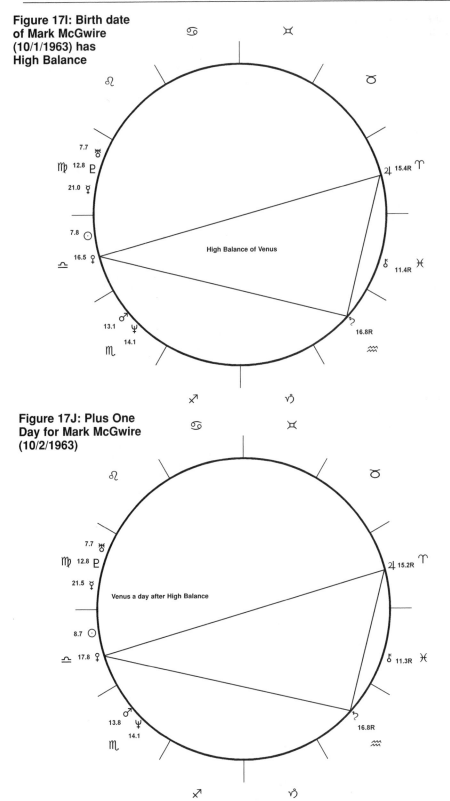

Figure 17I: Birth date of Mark McGwire (10/1/1963) has High Balance

High Balance of Venus

Figure 17J: Plus One Day for Mark McGwire (10/2/1963)

Venus a day after High Balance

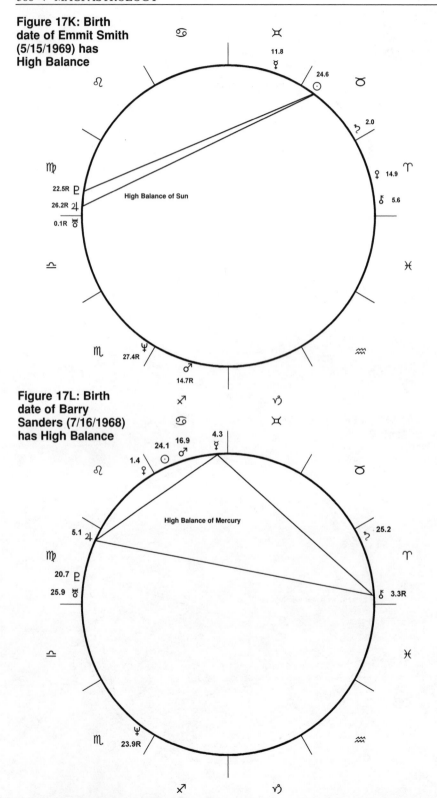

Figure 17K: Birth date of Emmit Smith (5/15/1969) has High Balance

High Balance of Sun

Figure 17L: Birth date of Barry Sanders (7/16/1968) has High Balance

High Balance of Mercury

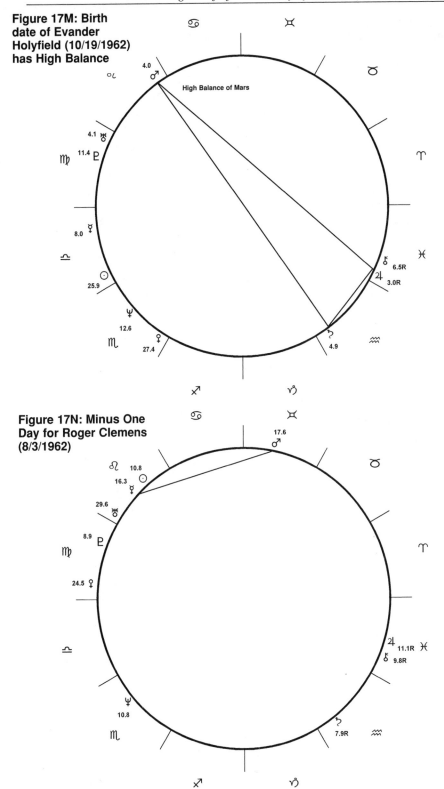

Figure 17M: Birth date of Evander Holyfield (10/19/1962) has High Balance

High Balance of Mars

Figure 17N: Minus One Day for Roger Clemens (8/3/1962)

Figure 17O: Birth date of Roger Clemens (8/4/1962) has High Balance of aspect

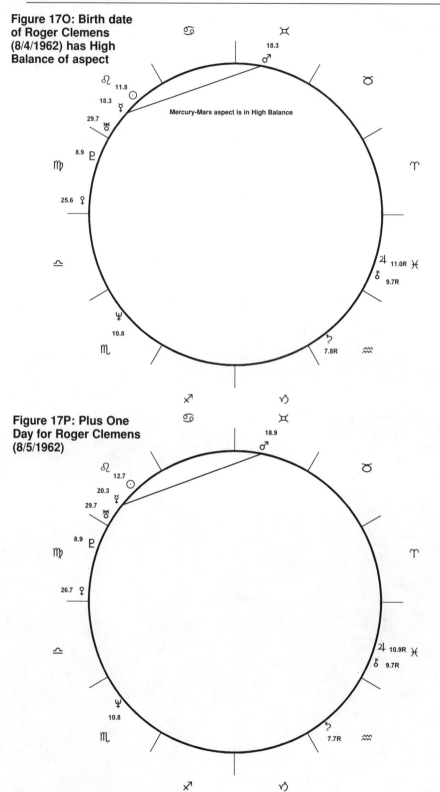

Mercury-Mars aspect is in High Balance

Figure 17P: Plus One Day for Roger Clemens (8/5/1962)

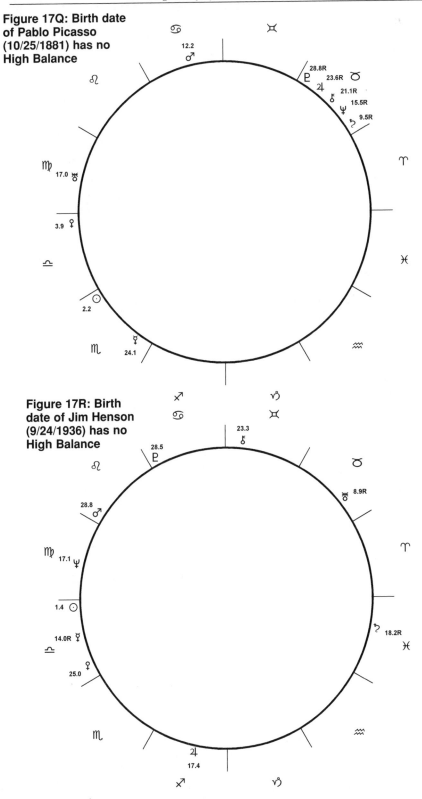

Figure 17Q: Birth date of Pablo Picasso (10/25/1881) has no High Balance

Figure 17R: Birth date of Jim Henson (9/24/1936) has no High Balance

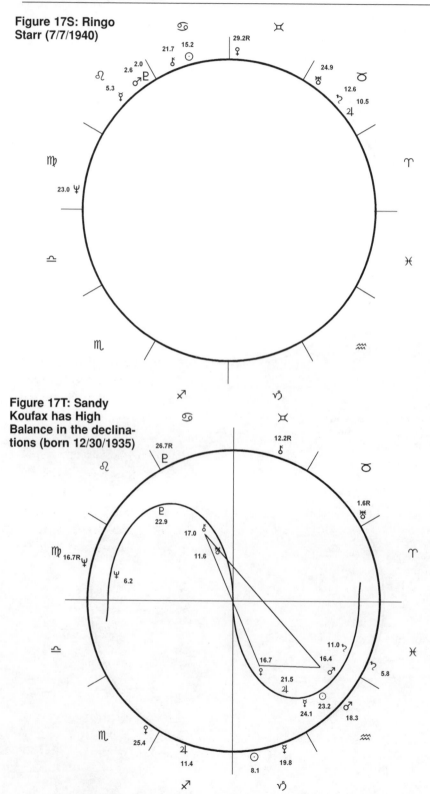

Figure 17S: Ringo Starr (7/7/1940)

Figure 17T: Sandy Koufax has High Balance in the declinations (born 12/30/1935)

The Magi Society's Love Calendar

The following is the Magi Society's Love Calendar for the five years 1999–2003. You can rely on it as your guide for determining which days are best in matters of love, such as the ideal days for making love and for seductions. We also let you know the worst days for both.

This is a condensed version of our Love Calendar. We use the word *condensed* because lunar aspects are not noted, and only the sure-fire dates are given, not the 80 percent types. We also leave out favorable and unfavorable days for getting married and for meeting someone new. Such matters would require a customized calendar specifically for you alone, because your individual transits would need to be taken into consideration. But the Love Calendar we do provide in this chapter will work for everyone. Try it! You will find that lovemaking will simply be on a higher level during the days we suggest! Also, you will learn that a seduction will be much more rewarding if it is carried out on the days we choose as being good for love. You will also see that on the bad days that we point out, love could go awry and you will be better prepared to handle such times because you are forewarned.

Go ahead and take the plunge. Enjoy life more fully and use the Love Calendar to your advantage. With it, you will know what is in the stars!

(Please read a few samplings of our Love Calendar. You will notice that we provide the time when an aspect peaks; the times given are for Pacific Standard Time, so if you are on the East Coast, you have three more hours. If we say that an aspect occurs "all day," it means until midnight. We should also note that days that are good for love are also good for seductions, whether or not these activities are being engaged in for the first time.)

YEAR 1999

1/4	Venus conjunct Neptune until dawn; enjoy an all-night love fest
1/10	Venus parallel Neptune until dawn; another all-night love fest
1/16	Venus parallel Chiron until dawn; ask for a commitment
1/29	Venus square Chiron until midnight; a time to say good-bye to someone
2/1	Venus parallel Pluto until late evening; love is in the air—take advantage of it
2/2	Mars parallel Pluto until dawn; a night you cannot miss
2/4	Venus square Pluto until next morning; trouble could lurk—but just stay cool
2/23	Venus trine Chiron until next morning, plus a Conjuncted Trine, make this a fabulous time to talk about marriage or commitment
3/1	Venus trine Pluto until next morning; tonight's the night . . . seduction
3/20	Venus square Neptune until dawn; do not count on love today
3/27	Venus opposition Mars until evening; no loving today either
4/14	Venus opposition Chiron until early evening; good time to say good-bye to someone and end a relationship if that is what you want
4/15	Venus trine Neptune until 8 P.M.—take the day off and make love—it will be worthwhile; this is a very sensuous time
4/20	Venus opposed to Pluto until 9 P.M.; not the right time for love or money
5/6	Venus trine Mars until next afternoon; find time to make love now; the Sun-Uranus square makes this a great time to have a fling or any affair without commitment
5/12	Mars parallel Pluto until 8 P.M.; take the afternoon off and make love
5/30	Venus square Mars until late night; a time for books, not love-making
6/4	A Romance Aspect plus a Sexual Aspect until morning; this Friday is the best day all year to seduce someone

6/5–6/6   Mars parallel Pluto and Sun-Uranus trine make this an ideal time to have a tryst or begin a fling

6/14   Venus trine Pluto until early P.M.; why not have an A.M. love session before work?

7/8   Venus square Chiron until early evening; breaking up is easy over lunch

8/15   Venus square Chiron until next morning; another time to break up

9/14   Mars conjunct Pluto until 8 P.M.; take day off and make love

10/8   Venus square Chiron until next morning; all day to say good-bye

10/17   Venus square Pluto all day; no love today

11/9   Venus trine Neptune until next morning, plus other factors, make tonight the night; very romantic time and should bring an enchanted evening of lovemaking

12/10   Venus parallel Pluto until early P.M.; great lunch break of lovemaking

12/22   Venus parallel Mars until 10 P.M.; make love early and eat out later

12/23   Venus square Mars; finish Christmas shopping—love is not in the air

12/30   Venus parallel Chiron all day; good time to build a relationship

YEAR 2000

1/3   Venus parallel Neptune all day; celebrate the New Year again—all day long in bed

1/6   Mars parallel Pluto until dawn; plan a seduction and it will last all night long

1/8   Venus conjunct Pluto until next late morning; business or pleasure, your choice

1/18   Mars square Pluto until next morning; everyone is too pooped to pop; get rest

2/21   Venus trine Neptune, all day; begin love session early, order food in

2/23   Venus parallel Neptune, until 9 P.M.; take the afternoon off and play in bed

2/28	Mars trine Pluto until 3 P.M.; switch schedules and make love early, work in P.M.
3/15	Venus parallel Pluto late P.M.; make early date, make love before dinner
3/22	Venus square Pluto through next morning; bad for love and work; catch up on sleep
3/26	Venus square Chiron all day; all day to say good-bye to someone
4/16	Venus trine Pluto till 4 P.M.; this one is best for money, work hard
4/19	Venus trine Chiron until next morning; you can make someone commit tonight
5/5	Venus square Neptune till morning; be careful not to lose anyone
5/19	Mars square Pluto till next morning; everyone has a headache, so wait for better times
5/29	Venus trine Neptune till morning; great seduction time, or catch someone new
6/2	Venus opposition Pluto till morning; go slow, very bad time for love and work
6/4	Venus opposition Chiron till next noon; breakup time; take care it is not you
6/9– 6/10	Sun-Venus planetary eclipse; romance is in the air; good time to start one
6/20	Venus square Mars till next noon; time to sleep and wait for better stars
7/16	Venus opposition Neptune till morning; the slow hand replaced by Mr. Speedy
7/20	Venus trine Pluto till morning; do not miss this one; solidifies relationship
7/21	Venus trine Chiron till dawn; great time to ask for commitment
8/14– 8/15	Double trouble for love, take special care; Venus square Chiron and Pluto
8/16	Mars trine Pluto only in morning; make love in A.M. and make up for last two days

9/1–

9/2   Horrible T-square makes these very troublesome days for relationships; be super careful and do not get into arguments; keep your head low and wait for stars to change

9/24   Venus parallel Pluto till 4 P.M.; good for love or work—make your choice

9/26   Venus square Neptune till next morning; bad time for love and money

10/3   Mars square Pluto till 4 P.M.; no energy

10/12   Venus parallel Neptune till 5 P.M.; good for love or money—do what you need most

10/27   Venus conjunct Pluto till dawn; another good time for love or money

10/31   Venus conjunct Chiron till 8 P.M.; push for commitment

11/21   Venus squares Mars till dawn; not good for love, it is a workday anyway

12/11   Venus conjunct Neptune all day; great day to spend all day making love, especially if you like extended foreplay

12/18   Venus parallel Neptune till morning; spend the entire evening falling deeper in love

12/20   Venus parallel Chiron till dawn; have candlelight dinner and talk about marriage, family, having children

12/31   Mars parallel Pluto till next afternoon; very rare occurrence of when New Year's and super Seduction Aspect occur at same time—Happy New Year! Find a partner and you will never forget it. Also fabulous for a new affair (see next day).

YEAR 2001

1/1–1/3 Year starts with a string of Sexual Aspects; a great time to start a new affair

1/27   Venus square Chiron till dawn; if your New Year's lover did not work out, you can use this time to make a break; also good time to say good-bye to anyone else

2/24   Venus trine Pluto all day; another good day for money or love

3/17–

3/18   Best days of the year to make love; Conjuncted Trine of Sexual Planets; do not miss them

3/29–

4/2   *Warning:* an affair begun now will break your existing relationship

5/18   Venus trine Pluto and other factors make this an unusually good day to start a Love Chart

6/1–6/2 Venus trine Mars and Chiron; supercharged for love; highest chances of pregnancy

6/14   Venus square Neptune and other factors make this the very best time to end a relationship for good; perfect time to say good-bye

7/11   Venus trine Neptune till next noon; elevated sensuality makes this a time for love

7/17–

7/19   Two oppositions make this another sure-fire time to break off an affair

7/25   Venus opposition Chiron till next noon; avoid confrontations, they could snowball

8/31   Venus opposition Neptune till dawn; not good for love or money

9/5   Venus trine Pluto till dawn; good time for love and money

9/14   Venus trine Chiron with unusual synch makes this a Friday night to seek excitement and new romance

10/9   Venus square Chiron till next noon; guard against arguments with your loved one

10/20   Venus trine Neptune all day; nice Saturday to spend all day with lover for love's sake

11/12   Venus square Neptune and other factors make this a bad time for any romantic pursuits

11/13   A sudden change in the stars makes loving fun again! Go for it— lasts all day

11/22   Venus square Mars and other factors make this a trying time; stay cool and let it pass; lasts till next morning

11/28   Venus parallel Neptune till dawn; perfect midweek break for supersensual lovemaking

12/13   Venus conjunct Pluto till dawn; work hard in day and be with your love at night

12/26   Venus conjunct Chiron till dawn; the most romantic time of this holiday season

12/29   Mars square Pluto till next morning; avoid disappointment by not trying to make love

YEAR 2002

1/28   Venus parallel Neptune and Sun make today a romantic time of month; lasts till next morning

2/10   Two Sexual Aspects make today the best day for making love the whole year; lasts all day

2/25   Venus square Pluto till 4 P.M.; stay out of trouble and do not look for adventures

3/13   Venus square Chiron till next morning; a time to say bye-bye

3/21   Venus trine Pluto till 10 P.M.; work hard but go home early to enjoy love till 10

4/7   Stars favor seeking of a commitment; you can push for it now

4/9   Sudden change in the stars now makes love difficult; hibernate till 3 P.M.

5/3   Venus trine Neptune makes this a romantic time until next morning

5/6   Venus parallel Mars in high declinations make this supercharged time for sex; lasts till dawn; take full advantage and go to work late; make arrangements with office early

5/7–
5/8   Two oppositions make love impossible; work hard and make up for 5/6

5/9   From noon to next noon, Venus conjunction of Mars revives your sexual desires and everyone else's. You worked hard last two days, right? Take a 24-hour love break!

5/26   Venus opposition Chiron all day, makes it tough on all relationships; hang in there

5/31   Through 6/1 all day, superb stars for romance and lovemaking; enchantment is in the air

6/22	Venus opposition Neptune till next noon with Sun-Mars parallel make this a super dangerous time for love relationships; just smile and be as understanding as possible
6/28	After the morning, a good time for love and money the rest of the day
7/14	Venus trine Chiron all day with Sun-Jupiter planetary eclipse; great wedding day and also a time to push for commitment
7/23	Venus square Pluto with Mars parallel Sun; care must be taken to keep the peace
8/5	Mars trine Pluto till 6 P.M.; leave work early and have afternoon of fabulous lovemaking
8/9	Venus Square Chiron and other factors make this a dangerous time for relationships and lasts until next afternoon
8/15	Venus trine Neptune with Jupiter-Chiron quincunx makes this a romantic time all day
8/31– 9/2	Venus parallel Pluto with Venus-Uranus and Mars-Chiron trine make this a perfect weekend for short affair; starts on Saturday and ends Monday
9/15	Tonight till dawn is last chance for good love session before stars turn negative
9/18– 9/21	Stars aligned to impede romance and sex; very bad time for love relationships
11/3– 11/5	Parallels of Romance Planets make this a romantic time
12/13	Venus and Mars square Neptune all day; very trying time for lovers
12/23	Venus parallel Pluto till next noon, best time of these holidays for making love

YEAR 2003

1/7	Venus parallel Chiron till dawn; good time for romantic interlude
1/11	Venus parallel Neptune till dawn; very good time for romance and lovemaking
1/24	Venus conjunct Pluto till next morning; this one is for satisfying love
2/15– 2/16	A Sexual conjunction plus a Romantic conjunction make this the best time for love and sex all year; it even falls on a weekend and lasts until Monday noon—don't miss it!
3/11	Venus parallel Neptune only till 6 P.M.; treat yourself to an afternoon love fest; followed by Venus conjunct Neptune, but the Sun-Saturn square offsets it entirely
5/5	Venus square Chiron till dawn; creates friction between lovers
5/6	Venus trine Pluto and Sun trine Chiron gives you opportunity to make up and make love with loved one; lasts till dawn
5/25– 5/26	Bad stars can create havoc with a relationship; do not do anything drastic
5/29	Venus trine Chiron till next morning is romantic time and good for rebuilding or enhancing love
6/19	Venus trine Neptune till dawn with Mercury enhancements; rare alignment makes this one of best times for sensual lovemaking and clear discourse; you can solidify your relationship today
6/22	Super rare Yod of Venus, Jupiter, and Chiron make this day highly romantic all day
6/23– 6/24	Sudden shift of alignments creates a time of stress in love relationships
7/1	Mars parallel Pluto until dawn; a night of lovemaking to remember; every man will be a tiger
7/10	Venus trine Mars till 11:30 P.M.; leave work early to make love; you will not regret it
7/15	Venus opposed to Chiron till dawn; an opportunity to end a relationship

8/1   Mars parallel Pluto till dawn; best aspect for repeat performance in sex

8/6–8/7 Misalignments create havoc with relationships; just grit your teeth and let them pass

8/11   Venus trine Pluto till 9 P.M.; work hard, leave work early, and seduce your love

8/30–
8/31   Venus trine Chiron; plan a romantic weekend to remember

9/23   Venus trine Neptune till 9 P.M.; work hard, leave work real early and enjoy highly romantic time

9/24   Venus square Chiron till dawn; another good time to end a relationship

10/13   Pluto parallel Mars all day; too bad it is Monday, but leave work early to make love

10/17–
10/23   Saturn opposed to Chiron; trouble in Romanceland; great understanding is needed

10/24   Venus parallel Neptune till dawn; chance to rebuild with loved one after last week

11/11   Venus, Mars, and Saturn all misaligned; be calm and hold on to your relationships

11/25   Mars square Pluto till next afternoon; too pooped to pop; be understanding

12/9   Very Conjuncted Trine of Venus conjunct Chiron trine Jupiter all day; push for commitment, and also enjoy highly romantic time

12/29   Venus conjunct Neptune till dawn

❦ ❦ ❦

APPENDIX

Glossary

ACTIVATED PERSONS: The two persons who are connected by an activation (interaspects of 90 and 180 degrees).

ACTIVATION: An interaspect formed between two persons that is either 90 or 180 degrees. Activations are stressful interaspects although they can initially cause attraction.

ACTIVATION ANGLES: The two angles that form activations, which are 90 and 180 degrees.

ALIGNMENT CHART: An astrological chart that employs the use of a circle, and where the positions of the planets are placed on the circle in a proportional manner relative to their actual positions in the sky, as opposed to relative to the houses.

ALIGNMENTS: The relative positioning of the planets as they are seen in the earth sky.

APPARENT: The way that the planets look like they are moving, as opposed to what their actual motions are; in other words, what the eye sees rather than what is actually happening.

APPLYING: A term referring to the condition where a planet is moving toward another planet; but if, for example, Jupiter is moving away from another planet, Jupiter is separating. The term *applying* may also be used to describe an aspect where the two planets making the aspect are moving closer to each other.

ASCENDANT: The degree and sign of the zodiac that is just rising at the eastern horizon at the time of a birth chart. The ascendant is one of the calculated points and is considered by most astrologers to be very significant.

ASPECT: Please see PLANETARY ASPECT.

ASPECT ANGLE: An angle that forms a planetary aspect. In the longitudes, there are seven of them. They are 0, 30, 60, 90, 120, 150, and 180 degrees.

ASPECT INTEGRATION: A term in Magi Astrology referring to the process of blending and combining all the astrological aspects of a birth chart to create an integrated whole analysis that takes into account the force of all the aspects working simultaneously and continuously.

ASPECT TIME: The time period during which an aspect is within orb.

ASTROLOGICAL ASPECT: An alignment between two planets that is considered meaningful by astrologers. In the case of longitudes, all alignments between any two planets that create an angle that is a multiple of 30 degrees is an astrological aspect. There are also other angles that are considered to be meaningful by most astrologers but are not dealt with in this book because there is no proof at this time that they work. In the case of the declinations, an astrological aspect is an alignment between two planets where the two planets are in the same degree of declination, regardless of whether they are both in north or south declination, or one planet is in north declination while the other is in south declination.

ASTROLOGICAL CHART: The birth chart or natal chart of a person, event, time, country, any entity or occurrence, or commencement of an activity.

BABYLONIAN ALIGNMENT CHART: An astrological chart that does not include the houses, and is based on a circle divided into 12 equal parts for the 12 signs. Such a chart is designed to allow the user to easily see the alignments of the planets.

BENEFIC: A planet that is considered by astrologers to provide beneficial influences; the influences can be either as a planet in aspect to another planet or as a planet in transit to a natal planet.

BIDIRECTIONAL ASPECT: A Magi Astrology term referring to any longitudinal aspect that is comprised of one planet in retrograde, while the other planet is in direct motion.

BI-LEVEL ASPECT: A Magi Astrology term referring to the condition where a natal planet is aspected in both the declinations and the longitudes. An example would be if the Sun is contra-parallel Neptune, and at the same time Neptune is quincunx to the Sun. Bi-levels are superpowerful.

BIRTH CHART: An astrological chart of the day someone or something is born; the chart always includes the positions of the planets for the birth date.

BUSINESS CHART: The astrological chart of the day someone begins a job or the day a corporation, partnership, or business is founded.

CAC: Abbreviation for Combined Alignment Chart.

CELESTIAL EQUATOR: The imaginary circle created by projecting the Earth's equator onto the backdrop of the sky.

CHIRON: A cometlike planetoid that orbits the Sun between Saturn and Uranus, and which has the most profound astrological significance.

CHIRON ASPECT: An aspect that is formed by Chiron and another planet.

CHIRON LINKAGE: A linkage formed by one person's Chiron to any natal planet of another person.

CINDERELLA ASPECT: One of the two aspects that are most often found in Cinderellas (Venus-Chiron and Chiron-Neptune).

CINDERELLA LINKAGE: One of the three linkages most often found in Cinderellas (Venus- Chiron, Jupiter-Chiron, and Neptune-Chiron).

CLASSIC SCHISM: One of a number of interaspects that prevent two persons from having similar outlooks or mutual destinies. These interaspects create enormous tension and friction between the connected persons.

COMBINED ALIGNMENT CHART: An astrological chart that is comprised of all the natal planets of one person, and some or all of the natal planets of another person.

COMBINED PLANETARY GEOMETRY: (also called COMBINED GEOMETRY). The Planetary Geometry that is created by overlaying some or all of the natal planets from one chart on top of some or all of the natal planets of another chart.

COMBINED SUPER ASPECTS: Super Aspects that are attained through linkages; the pairs of planets that form them are the same as those that form Super Aspects.

COMBINED SYMMETRY: Symmetrical pattern that is formed by the natal planets of two individuals.

COMPANIONSHIP CHART: The astrological chart of the time that two persons first look into each other's eyes. It is the chart of the relationship between the two persons unless they make love or get married.

COMPLEX PLANETARY GEOMETRY: Planetary Geometry that is formed by more than two planets.

CONFIGURATION: A pattern created by three or more planets.

CONJUNCT: Forming a conjunction.

CONJUNCTED TRINE: The second most powerful shape of Planetary Geometry that three planets can form in the longitudes; it is a conjunction of two planets where both planets are in trine to a third planet.

CONJUNCTION: An aspect formed by two planets that are in the same sign and the same degree of longitude.

CONNECTED PERSONS: The two persons who are astrologically associated by virtue of their forming an interaspect.

CONTRA-PARALLEL: An aspect in the declinations made between two planets that are in the same degree of declinations, but with the two planets on different sides of the celestial equator.

CUMULATIVE EFFECT: In a single astrological chart, when two aspects are comprised of the same two planets and one or both of the aspects are just wide of the normal orb, then the two aspects are said to add to each other's level of power, and accumulate, with the result that the two aspects together have more power than just either one.

CUPID LINKAGE: The linkage formed by one person's Venus and the other person's Sun.

DECEIVING LINKAGE: A linkage that is actually beyond the standard orb and is therefore not really strong enough to be a linkage.

DECLINATIONS: The vertical coordinate (or location) of the planets. The declination of a planet is the distance, in degrees, north or south of the Celestial Equator. The Sun's declination varies between about 23.5 degrees north to 23.5 degrees south declination. The change in declination is caused by the tilt of the Earth as it revolves around the Sun.

DIRECT MOTION: Unlike retrograde motion, direct motion refers to the condition that exists when a planet appears to be moving forward.

DISTANCE ORB: The standard orb in degrees as opposed to a time orb.

DOUBLE DIRECT ASPECT: An aspect formed by two planets, both of which are in direct motion.

DOUBLE LINKAGE: A condition that exists when two persons have two linkages made of the same combination of planets.

DYNAMIC: A term in Magi Astrology to describe a condition where all the planets of a pattern match degrees with each other.

DYNAMIC SYMMETRICAL PATTERN: A symmetrical pattern where all the planets that form the pattern match degrees.

ECLIPTIC: The apparent path of the Sun in the sky.

ELECTIONAL ASTROLOGY: That part of astrology that deals with the selection of favorable days and times to begin an endeavor or a relationship. The theory is that every activity has a natal chart, and the astrological chart of a relationship or an endeavor is the chart of the commencement date of the activity. Just as is the case for natal charts of people, the natal charts of electional dates have aspects, progressions, and transits. The more favorable the natal chart of the time and date elected to begin the activity, the more successful the results will be.

ENHANCED SUN: A natal Sun that is enhanced by virtue of having any of the planets make an enhancement angle to it.

ENHANCEMENT ANGLE: One of four angles: a conjunction, or trine, or parallel or contra- parallel.

ENHANCEMENT ASPECT: A term in Magi Astrology referring to a condition where any of the following four aspects exist: conjunction, trine, parallel, or contra-parallel.

EPHEMERIS: A book of astrological data that includes the astrological locations (at least the longitudes) of the planets on a periodic (usually daily) basis.

EQUAL DEGREE ASPECT: A term in Magi Astrology referring to a longitudinal astrological aspect formed by two planets such that the angle between the two planets is a multiple of 30 degrees. Examples are the 90-degree square aspect or the 180-degree opposition aspect.

FALLOUT: A term in Magi Astrology referring to residual negative influences existing for a short duration after an exact negative transit or progression peaked and began to separate.

FOCUS: The most important Planetary Geometry of a birth chart.

FOUNTAIN-OF-YOUTH ASPECT: A Magi Society discovery, this aspect is an enhancement of the Sun by Neptune; the aspect bestows youth and longevity to the native.

FOUR STRONGEST PLUTO ENHANCEMENTS: In Magi Astrology, this refers to the four enhancements to Pluto that are most helpful.

FRATERNAL SYMBOLISMS: Symbolisms that are very close in meaning but which are nonetheless different and ruled by two different planets.

GOLDEN LINKAGE: One of five linkages most favorable to have with anyone in terms of achieving success together.

GRAND CROSS: A configuration of four planets aligned to each other in such a way that each is square to two of the other planets, and each planet is opposed to another.

GRAND TRINE: A configuration of three planets where each of the three are 120 degrees apart from the other two planets.

HISTORIC ASPECT: An aspect that occurs in the chart of an event, as opposed to a living being. An aspect in the chart of a living being is a Personal Aspect, and the two are interpreted differently in Magi Astrology.

HOROSCOPE CHART: An astrological chart using a circle that includes divisions for the 12 houses; it always has the ascendant at the nine o'clock position, but emphasizes the positions of the planets in the houses, as opposed to the alignment of the planets.

HOUSES: There are 12 houses in the usual horoscope chart; each of the houses are said to rule different things. There are dozens of different ways to divide the 360-degree longitudinal horoscope into 12 houses, but all these different ways of calculating the house do have one parameter in common—they all have six houses on each side of the horizon.

INTERASPECT: An aspect that is formed between two charts, as opposed to one. An interaspect is the result of any alignment of two natal planets where two persons each contribute one natal planet, and the two planets are at an aspect angle to each other.

LINK: To form a linkage.

LINKAGE: An interaspect that is formed by any enhancement angle or a quincunx.

LINKAGE ANGLE: An angle that forms a linkage, which is any of the four enhancement angles or the quincunx.

LINKED PERSONS: The two persons who form a linkage.

LONGITUDES: The commonly used dimension of astrology. When an astrologer says that the Sun is in 15 degrees Cancer, it means the longitude of the Sun is 15 degrees Cancer. The longitudes are the horizontal coordinate (or location) of a planet. It is measured in degrees eastward from 0 degrees of Aries.

LOVE CHART: The astrological chart of any love relationship, such as that of a marriage or that of the first time two persons make love.

LUNAR CYCLE: The cycle of one full moon to the next full moon.

MAGI ASTROCHART: A birth chart drawn the Magi Astrology way. Normal birth charts depict the locations of only the longitudes of the planets. A Magi AstroChart includes the declinations. All planets that are in significant declinational aspect to each other are highlighted by connecting lines. The lines may directly connect the aspecting planets, or the lines may first touch at the S-curve, or at either the horizontal or vertical lines, which run the length of the diameter and create a cross-hair.

MAGI ASTROLOGY: A branch of astrology with astrological principles and rules of interpretation developed by the Magi Society in 1625. In Magi Astrology, Chiron and the declinations are always included, and unique analytical tools of Planetary Geometry are applied to obtain a more complete analysis than the standard methods in general use.

MAGICAL ASPECTS: Aspects that are in the Magical Time.

MAGICAL TIME: The time period when an aspect is most powerful; in Magi Astrology, these are the three days before and after an aspect is exact.

MALEFIC: A planet that is considered by astrologers to have negative influences; these influences can be either as a planet in aspect to another planet or as a planet in transit to a natal planet.

MATCH DEGREES: When two planets match degrees, they are in the same degree of either the same sign, or the same degree of two different signs. They can also be in the same degree north or south declinations.

MEGA-EVENT: An historic event of significance.

MIDHEAVEN: A calculated point in a natal chart, it refers to the degree and sign of the zodiac that is at the most elevated point at the instant of birth.

MIDPOINT: Usually refers to the unoccupied point in the zodiac that is exactly equidistant in longitudinal degrees to two planets. In Magi Astrology, the midpoint may be occupied and may be in the declinations.

MINI-EVENT: An uncommon event, but not historic. It could just be the birth of someone with an uncommon ability.

MONODIRECTIONAL ASPECT: A Magi term for an aspect that has both planets in retrograde, or both planets in direct motion.

NATAL: Refers to the planet at birth. The position of the natal Sun is the astrological position of the Sun at birth. In Magi Astrology, there are always two natal positions for each planet—one in the longitudes and the other in the declinations.

NATAL ASPECT: An aspect that existed at the time that someone was born.

NATALIZATION: The concept wherein an action creates a birth chart, and the Planetary Geometry of the moment of the action is preserved in the birth chart, which then has all of the properties of astrological charts.

NATAL PLANETS: The planets as represented in a natal chart.

NATAL POSITION: The position in longitude or declination of a planet at the time of birth.

NATIVE: The subject of the birth chart or the subject that has a particular aspect. For example, if we say that a Mars-Venus parallel provides the native with boundless energy, we mean that the person who has the Mars-Venus parallel aspect will have boundless energy.

NUPTIAL PLANETARY GEOMETRY: One of four types of Combined Planetary Geometry deemed to be conducive to a marriage. They are: Romantic Super Linkages, Symmetrical Combined Planetary Geometry, Romance Linkages, and Sexual Linkages

OFFSET: A technique of interpreting an aspect by reversing the symbolism of one of the two planets that form the aspect. This is done in Magi Astrology when interpreting a Turbulent Aspect that is also an Historic Aspect.

ORB: The number of degrees within which an aspect is regarded as active and effective.

PARALLEL: An aspect in the declinations made between two planets that are in the same degree declination, and also on the same side of the celestial equator.

PERSONAL ASPECT: An aspect that exists in the chart of a person or other living entity. In Magi Astrology, these aspects are interpreted differently than Historic Aspects.

PERSONAL ENERGY: The mystical and metaphysical energy that defines the individual soul.

PLANETARY ACTIVATION: See **ACTIVATION.**

PLANETARY ASPECT: Any meaningful alignment formed by two planets. A planetary aspect is formed whenever two planets form any of the seven aspect angles in the longitudes (match degrees). In the declinations, a planetary aspect is formed when two planets are parallel or contraparallel.

PLANETARY ECLIPSE: The Magi term for *occultation.*

PLANETARY GEOMETRY: Any line (or lines), shape, or pattern that is formed when connecting lines are drawn between the planets. Besides the planets, Planetary Geometry can include the ascendant, midheaven, asteroids, and comets and any other astrologically significant factor, whether real or calculated.

PLANETARY LINKAGE: See **LINKAGE.**

PLANETARY PERSONALITY: In Magi Astrology, it is believed that each planet has a personality, just like each of the 12 signs.

PLANETARY SYNCHRONIZATION: A concept of Magi Astrology, it refers to the condition where at least three planets are within orb to all make aspects to each other. This can occur in the longitudes or declinations.

PROGRESSION: In this book, and in Magi Astrology, progressions are transits that begin occurring immediately after birth and which are projected to influence the native in the future on the basis of a whole year of influence for each day of transit. For example, the transits that occur on the 50th day after birth will influence the native for the entire 50th year of the native's life.

RELATIONSHIP CHART: An astrological chart of a relationship, such as that of a marriage or love relationship. If two persons are not married, the relationship chart of two persons who are intimate is that of the first time they made love.

RETROGRADE MOTION: A visual phenomenon where a planet appears to be moving backwards in the sky from day to day; a planet does not actually move backwards, but will appear to do so from time to time because of the rate of change of the angular relationship of the Earth and the planet.

ROMANCE ASPECT: An aspect formed by two Romance Planets.

ROMANCE LINKAGE: A linkage formed by at least one Romance Planet.

ROMANCE PLANET: Chiron, Venus, or Neptune, based on the belief that these planets have rulerships that govern matters of romance and love.

ROMANCE TRANSIT: A transit by or to a Romance Planet.

ROMANTIC SUPER LINKAGE: A Super Linkage where at least one of the interaspects is a Chiron Linkage.

RULED BY: Influenced and controlled by. Each part of our body is ruled by a different planet. Each type of profession is ruled by a different planet. Everything has a planet as the ruler and another planet as a sub-ruler.

RULER: The planet or sign that has primary control and influence over a particular thing; for example, Chiron is the ruler of marriage; Mars is the ruler of energy.

RULERSHIPS: What a planet or sign has dominion over or control over. The same as SYMBOLISMS.

SATURN ASPECT: An aspect where Saturn is one of the two planets that form the aspect.

SATURN CLASH: A Turbulent Interaspect formed by Saturn to any planet, especially Chiron, Neptune, Pluto, Venus, Sun, Uranus, Moon, or Jupiter.

SEDUCTION ASPECT: An aspect in the sky such that when it occurs, most people are more disposed to seduction, and more susceptible to seduction.

SEPARATING: A term referring to the condition where a planet is moving away from another planet; but if, for example, Jupiter is moving toward another planet, Jupiter is applying rather than separating. The term *separating* may also be used in reference to an aspect where the two planets making the aspect are moving farther apart.

SEXUAL PLANETS: A term in Magi Astrology that refers to Venus, Mars, and Pluto because it is believed that their symbolisms are the ones that relate to sex.

SEXUAL LINKAGE: A linkage between any two of the sexual planets.

SILVER LINKAGE: One of the five linkages that are Success Linkages, but which is not as strong as a Golden Linkage.

SQUARE: An angle of 90 degrees between two planets in the longitudes.

STATISTICALLY VALID: A scientific term referring to validation through the use of statistical testing procedures.

SUCCESS LINKAGE: One of ten linkages that are either Golden Linkages or Silver Linkages.

SUN-SIGN ASTROLOGY: The branch of astrology that deals with Sun Signs. A Sun Sign is the zodiac sign that the Sun is in at the time of birth, or at the time an event occurred.

SUPER ASPECT: In Magi Astrology, one of 15 aspects discovered by the Magi Society that bestows to the native a significant advantage in achieving fame and fortune, or success in general.

SUPER LINKAGE: A Super Linkage exists between two persons if one person has an aspect and the second person has a natal planet that matches degrees with both planets that create the aspect, thus forming two interaspects to the first person. At least one of the interaspects must be a linkage.

SUPER SUCCESS ASPECT: An enhancement of Jupiter and Pluto.

SYMBOLISMS: The symbolisms of a planet are what the planet signifies, rules, represents, governs, or has influence over. They are derived from the astrological principle that different planets have different influences; and each planet represents, or rules, different things, professions, disciplines, ideas, parts of the body, etc.

SYMMETRICAL PLANETARY GEOMETRY: A symmetrical pattern in the sky or on an alignment chart that is formed by connecting lines between the positions of at least three planets.

THIRTY-DEGREE TYPE ANGLE: One of seven angles between 0 and 180 that is divisible by 30. When two planets are aligned at any such angle, they form an aspect.

TIME ORB: An orb measure in time to exactness rather than degrees to exactness.

TIME TO EXACTNESS: The time in days, hours, etc., before an aspect will be exact, or the time after an aspect was exact.

TRANSIT: The passage of a planet in motion over a position, such that the passing planet is in aspect to a natal planet.

TRANSITING ASPECT: The aspect made by a planet making a transit to a natal planet.

TRINE: An aspect between two planets where the planets are 120 degrees apart in longitude.

T-SQUARE: A symmetrical triangle of three planets where two planets form an opposition and the third planet is in between the other two and is therefore square to both. A T-square is a form of Turbulent Planetary Geometry.

TURBULENT ASPECT: An aspect that is made by the 90- or 180-degree angles. If the aspect is a Saturn aspect, then it could also be 150 degrees.

TURBULENT PLANETARY GEOMETRY: Planetary Geometry that is formed by only Turbulent Aspects.

TURBULENT TRANSIT BY SATURN: A transit by Saturn in the sky where Saturn makes a Turbulent Angle (or a quincunx) to a natal planet. When this occurs, the native's judgment and health are impaired.

VALID RANGE OF INTERPRETATIONS: The range of interpretations that an aspect or interaspect can be reasonably ascribed; the range depends on the breadth and the scope of the numerous validated symbolisms of the planets comprising the aspect or interaspect.

YOD: A triangular shape of symmetrical Planetary Geometry formed by three planets, where one planet is in quincunx to the other two planets, which in turn are sextile to each other.

ZODIAC SIGN CHART: An astrological chart that utilizes the circle with the 12 zodiac signs placed around the circle. Such a chart is designed to provide only the longitudes of the planets.

CHIRON EPHEMERIS 1920-2015
Including Declinations

DATE	1920 ♈	1920 ♈ Decl	1921 ♈	1921 ♈ Decl	1922 ♈	1922 ♈ Decl	1923 ♈	1923 ♈ Decl	1924 ♈	1924 ♈ Decl	1925 ♈	1925 ♈ Decl
01/01	02.62♈	03.51N	06.07♈	04.53N	09.51♈	05.53N	12.99♈	06.52N	16.52♈	07.51N	20.10♈	08.47N
01/11	02.83♈	03.56N	06.25♈	04.57N	09.66♈	05.56N	13.11♈	06.55N	16.59♈	07.52N	20.15♈	08.48N
01/21	03.11♈	03.64N	06.51♈	04.65N	09.90♈	05.63N	13.31♈	06.60N	16.76♈	07.56N	20.31♈	08.52N
01/31	03.47♈	03.76N	06.86♈	04.76N	10.22♈	05.74N	13.60♈	06.69N	17.02♈	07.64N	20.55♈	08.59N
02/10	03.90♈	03.91N	07.28♈	04.90N	10.61♈	05.87N	13.96♈	06.81N	17.37♈	07.76N	20.87♈	08.70N
02/20	04.39♈	04.08N	07.75♈	05.07N	11.06♈	06.02N	14.39♈	06.96N	17.78♈	07.90N	21.26♈	08.83N
03/01	04.92♈	04.27N	08.21♈	05.23N	11.51♈	06.18N	14.83♈	07.12N	18.25♈	08.06N	21.67♈	08.97N
03/11	05.48♈	04.48N	08.76♈	05.43N	12.05♈	06.38N	15.36♈	07.31N	18.77♈	08.24N	22.18♈	09.15N
03/21	06.06♈	04.69N	09.34♈	05.65N	12.62♈	06.59N	15.92♈	07.51N	19.32♈	08.44N	22.73♈	09.34N
03/31	06.65♈	04.92N	09.92♈	05.87N	13.20♈	06.80N	16.51♈	07.72N	19.91♈	08.65N	23.31♈	09.54N
04/10	07.23♈	05.14N	10.51♈	06.09N	13.79♈	07.02N	17.10♈	07.94N	20.50♈	08.86N	23.91♈	09.75N
04/20	07.80♈	05.36N	11.08♈	06.31N	14.37♈	07.24N	17.68♈	08.16N	21.10♈	09.08N	24.51♈	09.96N
04/30	08.34♈	05.57N	11.63♈	06.52N	14.93♈	07.45N	18.26♈	08.37N	21.68♈	09.29N	25.10♈	10.17N
05/10	08.83♈	05.77N	12.15♈	06.72N	15.46♈	07.65N	18.80♈	08.57N	22.24♈	09.49N	25.68♈	10.37N
05/20	09.28♈	05.95N	12.61♈	06.91N	15.95♈	07.84N	19.31♈	08.76N	22.76♈	09.68N	26.22♈	10.56N
05/30	09.67♈	06.11N	13.02♈	07.07N	16.38♈	08.01N	19.77♈	08.93N	23.24♈	09.85N	26.73♈	10.74N
06/09	09.99♈	06.25N	13.37♈	07.21N	16.76♈	08.15N	20.17♈	09.08N	23.66♈	10.00N	27.18♈	10.89N
06/19	10.23♈	06.35N	13.64♈	07.32N	17.07♈	08.27N	20.51♈	09.20N	24.02♈	10.13N	27.57♈	11.02N
06/29	10.39♈	06.42N	13.84♈	07.40N	17.29♈	08.36N	20.76♈	09.30N	24.31♈	10.23N	27.89♈	11.13N
07/09	10.47♈	06.47N	13.95♈	07.45N	17.43♈	08.42N	20.94♈	09.38N	24.52♈	10.30N	28.14♈	11.21N
07/19	10.47♈	06.47N	13.98♈	07.47N	17.49♈	08.45N	21.04♈	09.41N	24.64♈	10.34N	28.29♈	11.26N
07/29	10.37♈	06.45N	13.91♈	07.45N	17.46♈	08.44N	21.05♈	09.40N	24.67♈	10.35N	28.36♈	11.28N
08/08	10.19♈	06.38N	13.76♈	07.40N	17.35♈	08.40N	20.97♈	09.38N	24.62♈	10.33N	28.35♈	11.26N
08/18	09.94♈	06.29N	13.54♈	07.32N	17.16♈	08.33N	20.80♈	09.31N	24.47♈	10.27N	28.25♈	11.22N
08/28	09.61♈	06.17N	13.24♈	07.21N	16.88♈	08.22N	20.56♈	09.22N	24.25♈	10.18N	28.05♈	11.14N
09/07	09.23♈	06.02N	12.88♈	07.06N	16.55♈	08.09N	20.24♈	09.10N	23.96♈	10.07N	27.78♈	11.03N
09/17	08.81♈	05.85N	12.48♈	06.90N	16.16♈	07.94N	19.86♈	08.95N	23.60♈	09.93N	27.44♈	10.90N
09/27	08.37♈	05.67N	12.04♈	06.73N	15.72♈	07.76N	19.45♈	08.78N	23.19♈	09.77N	27.05♈	10.75N
10/07	07.92♈	05.48N	11.59♈	06.54N	15.27♈	07.58N	19.00♈	08.60N	22.75♈	09.59N	26.60♈	10.58N
10/17	07.49♈	05.29N	11.13♈	06.35N	14.82♈	07.39N	18.55♈	08.42N	22.27♈	09.41N	26.14♈	10.40N
10/27	07.07♈	05.10N	10.71♈	06.16N	14.38♈	07.21N	18.10♈	08.24N	21.82♈	09.22N	25.68♈	10.22N
11/06	06.70♈	04.94N	10.33♈	05.99N	13.98♈	07.03N	17.67♈	08.05N	21.39♈	09.05N	25.24♈	10.04N
11/16	06.40♈	04.79N	10.00♈	05.84N	13.62♈	06.87N	17.29♈	07.89N	21.00♈	08.89N	24.82♈	09.88N
11/26	06.17♈	04.68N	09.74♈	05.72N	13.33♈	06.74N	16.98♈	07.75N	20.66♈	08.74N	24.45♈	09.73N
12/06	06.03♈	04.59N	09.56♈	05.62N	13.12♈	06.64N	16.74♈	07.64N	20.39♈	08.63N	24.15♈	09.60N
12/16	05.97♈	04.54N	09.47♈	05.56N	13.00♈	06.56N	16.58♈	07.56N	20.21♈	08.54N	23.93♈	09.51N
12/26	06.01♈	04.52N	09.47♈	05.53N	12.96♈	06.53N	16.51♈	07.52N	20.11♈	08.49N	23.80♈	09.45N

DATE	1926 ♅	1926 ♅ Decl	1927 ♅	1927 ♅ Decl	1928 ♅	1928 ♅ Decl	1929 ♅	1929 ♅ Decl	1930 ♅	1930 ♅ Decl	1931 ♅	1931 ♅ Decl
01/01	23.77♈	09.43N	27.55♉	10.38N	01.45♉	11.30N	05.51♉	12.21N	09.77♉	13.10N	14.25♉	13.94N
01/11	23.79♈	09.43N	27.53♉	10.36N	01.40♉	11.28N	05.43♉	12.18N	09.64♉	13.06N	14.07♉	13.90N
01/21	23.91♈	09.45N	27.61♉	10.38N	01.44♉	11.29N	05.44♉	12.18N	09.61♉	13.05N	14.00♉	13.88N
01/31	24.11♈	09.52N	27.78♉	10.43N	01.59♉	11.33N	05.55♉	12.22N	09.68♉	13.08N	14.04♉	13.91N
02/10	24.40♈	09.61N	28.05♉	10.52N	01.82♉	11.41N	05.76♉	12.29N	09.85♉	13.13N	14.17♉	13.95N
02/20	24.78♈	09.74N	28.40♉	10.63N	02.14♉	11.51N	06.06♉	12.38N	10.13♉	13.22N	14.40♉	14.03N
03/02	25.22♈	09.89N	28.82♉	10.77N	02.58♉	11.66N	06.45♉	12.51N	10.49♉	13.34N	14.73♉	14.13N
03/12	25.72♈	10.06N	29.31♉	10.93N	03.06♉	11.81N	06.91♉	12.66N	10.93♉	13.47N	15.14♉	14.26N
03/22	26.27♈	10.24N	29.84♉	11.11N	03.59♉	11.99N	07.43♉	12.82N	11.43♉	13.63N	15.64♉	14.40N
04/01	26.84♈	10.44N	00.42♊	11.31N	04.17♉	12.17N	08.00♉	13.00N	11.99♉	13.80N	16.19♉	14.56N
04/11	27.45♈	10.65N	01.02♊	11.51N	04.77♉	12.37N	08.61♉	13.18N	12.60♉	13.98N	16.80♉	14.73N
04/21	28.05♈	10.85N	01.64♊	11.71N	05.40♉	12.57N	09.24♉	13.38N	13.24♉	14.16N	17.44♉	14.91N
05/01	28.66♈	11.06N	02.26♊	11.91N	06.03♉	12.76N	09.88♉	13.57N	13.90♉	14.35N	18.11♉	15.08N
05/11	29.25♈	11.26N	02.87♊	12.11N	06.66♉	12.95N	10.53♉	13.76N	14.56♉	14.53N	18.79♉	15.26N
05/21	29.82♈	11.45N	03.45♊	12.29N	07.26♉	13.14N	11.16♉	13.94N	15.22♉	14.70N	19.47♉	15.43N
05/31	00.34♉	11.62N	04.00♊	12.47N	07.84♉	13.31N	11.77♉	14.11N	15.85♉	14.87N	20.14♉	15.59N
06/10	00.82♉	11.78N	04.51♊	12.63N	08.38♉	13.47N	12.33♉	14.26N	16.46♉	15.02N	20.78♉	15.74N
06/20	01.24♉	11.91N	04.96♊	12.76N	08.86♉	13.60N	12.85♉	14.40N	17.02♉	15.16N	21.39♉	15.87N
06/30	01.58♉	12.02N	05.35♊	12.88N	09.28♉	13.72N	13.32♉	14.52N	17.52♉	15.27N	21.94♉	15.98N
07/10	01.86♉	12.10N	05.67♊	12.97N	09.63♉	13.81N	13.71♉	14.61N	17.97♉	15.37N	22.43♉	16.07N
07/20	02.05♉	12.16N	05.90♊	13.03N	09.89♉	13.87N	14.02♉	14.68N	18.33♉	15.44N	22.85♉	16.15N
07/30	02.16♉	12.18N	06.04♊	13.06N	10.07♉	13.89N	14.26♉	14.72N	18.61♉	15.49N	23.19♉	16.19N
08/09	02.17♉	12.17N	06.10♊	13.07N	10.16♉	13.90N	14.40♉	14.73N	18.80♉	15.51N	23.44♉	16.22N
08/19	02.09♉	12.13N	06.06♊	13.03N	10.17♉	13.87N	14.44♉	14.72N	18.89♉	15.50N	23.59♉	16.22N
08/29	01.92♉	12.06N	05.93♊	12.97N	10.07♉	13.81N	14.38♉	14.68N	18.89♉	15.46N	23.64♉	16.19N
09/08	01.67♉	11.96N	05.72♊	12.88N	09.88♉	13.76N	14.23♉	14.60N	18.79♉	15.40N	23.59♉	16.14N
09/18	01.35♉	11.84N	05.42♊	12.77N	09.60♉	13.66N	13.99♉	14.51N	18.60♉	15.32N	23.43♉	16.06N
09/28	00.96♉	11.69N	05.06♊	12.63N	09.25♉	13.52N	13.67♉	14.39N	18.31♉	15.21N	23.19♉	15.96N
10/08	00.54♉	11.53N	04.64♊	12.48N	08.84♉	13.37N	13.29♉	14.25N	17.94♉	15.08N	22.85♉	15.84N
10/18	00.08♉	11.36N	04.17♊	12.30N	08.39♉	13.21N	12.84♉	14.10N	17.51♉	14.94N	22.44♉	15.71N
10/28	29.61♈	11.18N	03.69♊	12.13N	07.91♉	13.04N	12.37♉	13.94N	17.03♉	14.78N	21.98♉	15.57N
11/07	29.13♈	11.00N	03.22♊	11.96N	07.43♉	12.87N	11.86♉	13.77N	16.53♉	14.62N	21.48♉	15.42N
11/17	28.70♈	10.83N	02.77♊	11.79N	06.96♉	12.71N	11.37♉	13.61N	16.03♉	14.47N	20.97♉	15.27N
11/27	28.32♈	10.69N	02.36♊	11.64N	06.51♉	12.56N	10.91♉	13.46N	15.54♉	14.32N	20.44♉	15.12N
12/07	28.00♈	10.56N	02.00♊	11.51N	06.13♉	12.42N	10.49♉	13.32N	15.10♉	14.19N	19.95♉	14.99N
12/17	27.75♈	10.46N	01.72♊	11.40N	05.82♉	12.32N	10.15♉	13.21N	14.70♉	14.07N	19.52♉	14.88N
12/27	27.59♈	10.40N	01.52♊	11.33N	05.59♉	12.24N	09.87♉	13.13N	14.38♉	13.98N	19.16♉	14.79N

DATE	1932 ⚷	1932 ⚷ Decl	1933 ⚷	1933 ⚷ Decl	1934 ⚷	1934 ⚷ Decl	1935 ⚷	1935 ⚷ Decl	1936 ⚷	1936 ⚷ Decl	1937 ⚷	1937 ⚷ Decl
01/01	19.02♉	14.75N	24.08♉	15.48N	29.56♉	16.13N	05.54♊	16.67N	12.13♊	17.03N	19.36♊	17.14N
01/11	18.79♉	14.70N	23.80♉	15.43N	29.23♉	16.08N	05.15♊	16.62N	11.65♊	16.99N	18.84♊	17.12N
01/21	18.67♉	14.68N	23.63♉	15.41N	29.00♉	16.06N	04.85♊	16.59N	11.27♊	16.97N	18.39♊	17.12N
01/31	18.64♉	14.69N	23.56♉	15.41N	28.87♉	16.06N	04.66♊	16.59N	11.00♊	16.97N	18.05♊	17.14N
02/10	18.73♉	14.73N	23.61♉	15.45N	28.87♉	16.09N	04.58♊	16.62N	10.85♊	17.00N	17.83♊	17.17N
02/20	18.92♉	14.79N	23.78♉	15.51N	28.98♉	16.14N	04.62♊	16.66N	10.83♊	17.04N	17.73♊	17.22N
03/01	19.22♉	14.88N	24.02♉	15.58N	29.17♉	16.20N	04.76♊	16.72N	10.94♊	17.10N	17.75♊	17.27N
03/11	19.61♉	15.00N	24.37♉	15.69N	29.49♉	16.30N	05.05♊	16.81N	11.17♊	17.18N	17.90♊	17.34N
03/21	20.08♉	15.14N	24.82♉	15.81N	29.90♉	16.41N	05.43♊	16.91N	11.50♊	17.27N	18.18♊	17.42N
03/31	20.63♉	15.28N	25.34♉	15.95N	00.42♊	16.53N	05.90♊	17.02N	11.95♊	17.37N	18.60♊	17.51N
04/10	21.23♉	15.44N	25.94♉	16.09N	01.00♊	16.67N	06.47♊	17.13N	12.50♊	17.47N	19.11♊	17.60N
04/20	21.88♉	15.61N	26.59♉	16.25N	01.65♊	16.81N	07.11♊	17.26N	13.14♊	17.58N	19.72♊	17.69N
04/30	22.55♉	15.77N	27.28♉	16.40N	02.34♊	16.95N	07.81♊	17.38N	13.85♊	17.68N	20.41♊	17.77N
05/10	23.26♉	15.94N	28.00♉	16.56N	03.08♊	17.09N	08.56♊	17.50N	14.61♊	17.78N	21.18♊	17.85N
05/20	23.96♉	16.10N	28.73♉	16.70N	03.83♊	17.22N	09.34♊	17.62N	15.41♊	17.88N	22.00♊	17.92N
05/30	24.66♉	16.25N	29.46♉	16.84N	04.60♊	17.34N	10.14♊	17.73N	16.25♊	17.96N	22.86♊	17.97N
06/09	25.35♉	16.39N	00.18♊	16.97N	05.36♊	17.46N	10.95♊	17.82N	17.09♊	18.03N	23.75♊	18.01N
06/19	25.99♉	16.52N	00.88♊	17.09N	06.11♊	17.56N	11.74♊	17.91N	17.94♊	18.09N	24.65♊	18.04N
06/29	26.59♉	16.62N	01.53♊	17.19N	06.82♊	17.65N	12.51♊	17.97N	18.77♊	18.14N	25.55♊	18.05N
07/09	27.14♉	16.71N	02.14♊	17.27N	07.49♊	17.72N	13.24♊	18.03N	19.58♊	18.16N	26.43♊	18.05N
07/19	27.62♉	16.78N	02.68♊	17.33N	08.10♊	17.77N	13.93♊	18.06N	20.34♊	18.17N	27.27♊	18.03N
07/29	28.02♉	16.83N	03.15♊	17.38N	08.64♊	17.80N	14.55♊	18.08N	21.04♊	18.16N	28.08♊	17.99N
08/08	28.33♉	16.86N	03.53♊	17.40N	09.09♊	17.82N	15.10♊	18.09N	21.67♊	18.14N	28.82♊	17.94N
08/18	28.55♉	16.86N	03.81♊	17.40N	09.46♊	17.82N	15.56♊	18.08N	22.22♊	18.11N	29.48♊	17.88N
08/28	28.66♉	16.84N	04.00♊	17.38N	09.74♊	17.80N	15.91♊	18.06N	22.67♊	18.06N	00.06♋	17.80N
09/07	28.66♉	16.79N	04.09♊	17.34N	09.89♊	17.76N	16.16♊	18.04N	23.02♊	18.00N	00.31♋	17.72N
09/17	28.57♉	16.72N	04.05♊	17.28N	09.93♊	17.70N	16.29♊	18.00N	23.26♊	17.93N	00.72♋	17.63N
09/27	28.37♉	16.63N	03.91♊	17.20N	09.86♊	17.62N	16.32♊	17.94N	23.37♊	17.85N	01.01♋	17.54N
10/07	28.08♉	16.53N	03.66♊	17.10N	09.67♊	17.53N	16.21♊	17.86N	23.34♊	17.77N	01.18♋	17.44N
10/17	27.70♉	16.41N	03.32♊	16.99N	09.39♊	17.44N	15.99♊	17.78N	23.19♊	17.68N	01.20♋	17.35N
10/27	27.25♉	16.27N	02.89♊	16.87N	09.00♊	17.33N	15.66♊	17.69N	22.92♊	17.59N	01.10♋	17.26N
11/06	26.76♉	16.13N	02.40♊	16.74N	08.54♊	17.21N	15.23♊	17.59N	22.54♊	17.50N	00.88♋	17.18N
11/16	26.21♉	15.99N	01.88♊	16.62N	08.02♊	17.10N	14.71♊	17.49N	22.07♊	17.42N	00.53♋	17.10N
11/26	25.68♉	15.85N	01.33♊	16.49N	07.47♊	16.99N	14.16♊	17.39N	21.53♊	17.34N	00.06♋	17.04N
12/06	25.17♉	15.73N	00.79♊	16.37N	06.87♊	16.88N	13.58♊	17.29N	20.95♊	17.27N	29.20♊	16.99N
12/16	24.70♉	15.62N	00.26♊	16.26N	06.32♊	16.78N	13.00♊	17.20N	20.33♊	17.21N	28.58♊	16.96N
12/26	24.29♉	15.53N	29.80♉	16.18N	05.82♊	16.70N	12.44♊	17.06N	19.70♊	17.16N	27.95♊	16.93N

DATE	1938 ♂	1938 ♂ Decl	1939 ♂	1939 ♂ Decl	1940 ♂	1940 ♂ Decl	1941 ♂	1941 ♂ Decl	1942 ♂	1942 ♂ Decl	1943 ♂	1943 ♂ Decl
01/01	27.58♊	16.93N	06.90♋	16.25N	17.50♋	14.93N	29.64♋	12.79N	13.52♌	09.66N	29.02♌	05.49N
01/11	26.99♊	16.93N	06.21♋	16.28N	16.81♋	15.00N	28.96♋	12.89N	12.91♌	09.77N	28.60♌	05.57N
01/21	26.46♊	16.95N	05.60♋	16.33N	16.14♋	15.09N	28.24♋	13.02N	12.18♌	09.93N	28.05♌	05.71N
01/31	26.01♊	16.99N	05.06♋	16.40N	15.51♋	15.19N	27.49♋	13.19N	11.45♌	10.12N	27.38♌	05.91N
02/10	25.68♊	17.03N	04.62♋	16.47N	14.95♋	15.31N	26.82♋	13.35N	10.72♌	10.33N	26.64♌	06.15N
02/20	25.47♊	17.09N	04.31♋	16.55N	14.48♋	15.43N	26.24♋	13.52N	10.02♌	10.56N	25.82♌	06.44N
03/02	25.41♊	17.16N	04.14♋	16.64N	14.13♋	15.56N	25.78♋	13.69N	09.40♌	10.79N	25.07♌	06.73N
03/12	25.48♊	17.23N	04.14♋	16.72N	13.97♋	15.67N	25.45♋	13.84N	08.86♌	11.02N	24.39♌	07.02N
03/22	25.72♊	17.31N	04.20♋	16.81N	13.95♋	15.77N	25.29♋	13.98N	08.47♌	11.22N	23.81♌	07.30N
04/01	26.06♊	17.39N	04.45♋	16.88N	14.10♋	15.85N	25.27♋	14.09N	08.25♌	11.39N	23.37♌	07.55N
04/11	26.53♊	17.47N	04.85♋	16.95N	14.43♋	15.92N	25.42♋	14.18N	08.20♌	11.53N	23.08♌	07.76N
04/21	27.11♊	17.54N	05.38♋	17.01N	14.87♋	15.97N	25.73♋	14.24N	08.32♌	11.63N	22.96♌	07.92N
05/01	27.79♊	17.60N	06.02♋	17.05N	15.45♋	16.00N	26.19♋	14.27N	08.65♌	11.67N	23.02♌	08.04N
05/11	28.56♊	17.65N	06.77♋	17.07N	16.15♋	15.99N	26.82♋	14.26N	09.11♌	11.66N	23.25♌	08.09N
05/21	29.39♊	17.69N	07.59♋	17.08N	16.96♋	15.97N	27.56♋	14.21N	09.73♌	11.63N	23.67♌	08.08N
05/31	00.29♋	17.71N	08.50♋	17.06N	17.86♋	15.92N	28.42♋	14.13N	10.49♌	11.54N	24.28♌	08.01N
06/10	01.22♋	17.71N	09.45♋	17.03N	18.84♋	15.84N	29.38♋	14.01N	11.37♌	11.40N	25.02♌	07.88N
06/20	02.17♋	17.70N	10.45♋	16.97N	19.87♋	15.73N	00.41♌	13.86N	12.37♌	11.21N	25.90♌	07.69N
06/30	03.13♋	17.67N	11.48♋	16.90N	20.95♋	15.60N	01.51♌	13.68N	13.46♌	10.99N	26.91♌	07.45N
07/10	04.09♋	17.62N	12.51♋	16.80N	22.06♋	15.44N	02.67♌	13.46N	14.62♌	10.72N	28.02♌	07.17N
07/20	05.02♋	17.56N	13.54♋	16.68N	23.16♋	15.27N	03.85♌	13.22N	15.85♌	10.42N	29.21♌	06.83N
07/30	05.92♋	17.48N	14.54♋	16.55N	24.27♋	15.07N	05.06♌	12.95N	17.11♌	10.09N	00.48♍	06.46N
08/09	06.77♋	17.38N	15.51♋	16.40N	25.37♋	14.85N	06.26♌	12.66N	18.39♌	09.73N	01.80♍	06.05N
08/19	07.55♋	17.28N	16.43♋	16.24N	26.42♋	14.62N	07.44♌	12.35N	19.69♌	09.35N	03.16♍	05.61N
08/29	08.25♋	17.16N	17.27♋	16.07N	27.41♋	14.38N	08.59♌	12.03N	20.98♌	08.95N	04.54♍	05.14N
09/08	08.85♋	17.04N	18.04♋	15.90N	28.34♋	14.14N	09.69♌	11.71N	22.24♌	08.54N	05.91♍	04.67N
09/18	09.34♋	16.92N	18.71♋	15.72N	29.17♋	13.90N	10.73♌	11.38N	23.46♌	08.12N	07.27♍	04.18N
09/28	09.70♋	16.80N	19.25♋	15.55N	29.90♋	13.66N	11.67♌	11.06N	24.60♌	07.71N	08.60♍	03.68N
10/08	09.96♋	16.68N	19.65♋	15.39N	00.51♌	13.44N	12.52♌	10.75N	25.67♌	07.31N	09.87♍	03.20N
10/18	10.05♋	16.57N	19.92♋	15.25N	00.98♌	13.24N	13.23♌	10.47N	26.64♌	06.93N	11.07♍	02.72N
10/28	09.99♋	16.47N	20.04♋	15.12N	01.32♌	13.05N	13.80♌	10.21N	27.49♌	06.57N	12.18♍	02.27N
11/07	09.80♋	16.39N	20.03♋	15.01N	01.47♌	12.91N	14.21♌	09.99N	28.20♌	06.25N	13.17♍	01.86N
11/17	09.47♋	16.32N	19.85♋	14.93N	01.48♌	12.80N	14.46♌	09.82N	28.77♌	05.97N	14.03♍	01.48N
11/27	09.03♋	16.27N	19.52♋	14.88N	01.30♌	12.73N	14.57♌	09.68N	29.14♌	05.76N	14.73♍	01.16N
12/07	08.49♋	16.24N	19.07♋	14.86N	00.98♌	12.70N	14.46♌	09.60N	29.33♌	05.60N	15.26♍	00.89N
12/17	07.88♋	16.23N	18.51♋	14.87N	00.52♌	12.70N	14.21♌	09.58N	29.34♌	05.51N	15.65♍	00.68N
12/27	07.23♋	16.24N	17.84♋	14.91N	29.96♋	12.75N	13.78♌	09.62N	29.16♌	05.48N	15.80♍	00.56N

DATE	1944 ⚷	1944 ⚷ Decl	1945 ⚷	1945 ⚷ Decl	1946 ⚷	1946 ⚷ Decl	1947 ⚷	1947 ⚷ Decl	1948 ⚷	1948 ⚷ Decl	1949 ⚷	1949 ⚷ Decl
01/01	15.81♍	00.52N	03.14♎	04.71S	20.23♎	09.56S	06.28♏	13.43S	20.94♏	16.11S	04.19♐	17.65S
01/11	15.67♍	00.52N	03.34♎	04.82S	20.78♎	09.75S	07.10♏	13.65S	21.95♏	16.30S	05.27♐	17.77S
01/21	15.35♍	00.60N	03.38♎	04.86S	21.14♎	09.87S	07.77♏	13.81S	22.83♏	16.44S	06.25♐	17.86S
01/31	14.87♍	00.75N	03.19♎	04.80S	21.30♎	09.91S	08.25♏	13.91S	23.55♏	16.54S	07.10♐	17.91S
02/10	14.24♍	00.97N	02.82♎	04.66S	21.26♎	09.87S	08.58♏	13.95S	24.11♏	16.59S	07.82♐	17.93S
02/20	13.54♍	01.25N	02.30♎	04.44S	21.04♎	09.76S	08.68♏	13.92S	24.48♏	16.60S	08.38♐	17.92S
03/01	12.78♍	01.55N	01.72♎	04.19S	20.69♎	09.60S	08.61♏	13.84S	24.68♏	16.55S	08.78♐	17.89S
03/11	12.01♍	01.88N	00.94♎	03.86S	20.17♎	09.36S	08.35♏	13.69S	24.70♏	16.47S	09.02♐	17.82S
03/21	11.27♍	02.22N	00.16♎	03.50S	19.52♎	09.07S	07.93♏	13.49S	24.54♏	16.34S	09.09♐	17.73S
03/31	10.57♍	02.57N	29.40♍	03.14S	18.79♎	08.74S	07.34♏	13.24S	24.21♏	16.17S	08.99♐	17.60S
04/10	10.02♍	02.87N	28.68♍	02.79S	18.01♎	08.39S	06.66♏	12.96S	23.73♏	15.97S	08.72♐	17.46S
04/20	09.62♍	03.13N	28.05♍	02.46S	17.20♎	08.02S	05.96♏	12.67S	23.13♏	15.75S	08.31♐	17.30S
04/30	09.39♍	03.33N	27.52♍	02.15S	16.49♎	07.68S	05.21♏	12.36S	22.41♏	15.50S	07.78♐	17.14S
05/10	09.35♍	03.47N	27.16♍	01.91S	15.88♎	07.38S	04.47♏	12.06S	21.68♏	15.26S	07.16♐	16.97S
05/20	09.52♍	03.53N	26.97♍	01.73S	15.40♎	07.12S	03.76♏	11.77S	20.95♏	15.03S	06.47♐	16.80S
05/30	09.85♍	03.53N	26.96♍	01.63S	15.07♎	06.92S	03.17♏	11.53S	20.25♏	14.82S	05.76♐	16.64S
06/09	10.35♍	03.46N	27.15♍	01.60S	14.93♎	06.79S	02.72♏	11.33S	19.63♏	14.63S	05.03♐	16.49S
06/19	11.02♍	03.32N	27.56♍	01.66S	14.95♎	06.73S	02.42♏	11.20S	19.10♏	14.47S	04.38♐	16.36S
06/29	11.85♍	03.12N	28.11♍	01.79S	15.16♎	06.74S	02.29♏	11.12S	18.71♏	14.36S	03.81♐	16.25S
07/09	12.82♍	02.85N	28.83♍	01.98S	15.55♎	06.83S	02.36♏	11.10S	18.47♏	14.30S	03.34♐	16.22S
07/19	13.91♍	02.52N	29.70♍	02.24S	16.12♎	06.98S	02.59♏	11.17S	18.40♏	14.29S	03.03♐	16.18S
07/29	15.10♍	02.15N	00.71♎	02.56S	16.87♎	07.21S	03.00♏	11.28S	18.47♏	14.32S	02.88♐	16.17S
08/08	16.38♍	01.73N	01.83♎	02.93S	17.75♎	07.52S	03.57♏	11.44S	18.79♏	14.42S	02.89♐	16.20S
08/18	17.72♍	01.27N	03.06♎	03.35S	18.77♎	07.82S	04.29♏	11.66S	19.23♏	14.55S	03.04♐	16.29S
08/28	19.10♍	00.79N	04.37♎	03.81S	19.90♎	08.20S	05.17♏	11.93S	19.82♏	14.71S	03.34♐	16.39S
09/07	20.52♍	00.28N	05.75♎	04.30S	21.12♎	08.61S	06.17♏	12.24S	20.56♏	14.92S	03.81♐	16.52S
09/17	21.96♍	00.25S	07.17♎	04.81S	22.42♎	09.04S	07.28♏	12.57S	21.43♏	15.15S	04.43♐	16.67S
09/27	23.40♍	00.79S	08.61♎	05.33S	23.79♎	09.50S	08.47♏	12.93S	22.41♏	15.40S	05.18♐	16.83S
10/07	24.81♍	01.33S	10.07♎	05.86S	25.20♎	09.97S	09.74♏	13.30S	23.50♏	15.66S	06.05♐	17.01S
10/17	26.18♍	01.85S	11.53♎	06.39S	26.63♎	10.45S	11.06♏	13.67S	24.66♏	15.94S	07.02♐	17.19S
10/27	27.49♍	02.37S	12.95♎	06.92S	28.07♎	10.92S	12.42♏	14.05S	25.89♏	16.21S	08.07♐	17.37S
11/06	28.72♍	02.86S	14.33♎	07.42S	29.49♎	11.38S	13.81♏	14.42S	27.16♏	16.48S	09.18♐	17.54S
11/16	29.84♍	03.31S	15.64♎	07.90S	00.88♏	11.82S	15.19♏	14.78S	28.45♏	16.73S	10.36♐	17.70S
11/26	00.85♎	03.73S	16.86♎	08.35S	02.22♏	12.24S	16.54♏	15.12S	29.75♏	16.97S	11.56♐	17.85S
12/06	01.72♎	04.09S	17.97♎	08.75S	03.48♏	12.62S	17.86♏	15.44S	01.04♐	17.20S	12.78♐	17.98S
12/16	02.41♎	04.39S	18.95♎	09.11S	04.65♏	12.97S	19.11♏	15.72S	02.30♐	17.39S	13.98♐	18.09S
12/26	02.92♎	04.61S	19.78♎	09.40S	05.71♏	13.27S	20.28♏	15.98S	03.50♐	17.56S	15.16♐	18.18S

DATE	1950 °	1950 ° Decl	1951 °	1951 ° Decl	1952 °	1952 ° Decl	1953 °	1953 ° Decl	1954 °	1954 ° Decl	1955 °	1955 ° Decl
01/01	15.85♐	18.22S	26.18♐	18.10S	05.36♑	17.50S	13.67♑	16.57S	21.05♑	15.47S	27.76♑	14.25S
01/11	16.95♐	18.27S	27.26♐	18.08S	06.40♑	17.43S	14.65♑	16.47S	21.97♑	15.34S	28.61♑	14.11S
01/21	17.98♐	18.29S	28.30♐	18.04S	07.41♑	17.34S	15.61♑	16.34S	22.89♑	15.18S	29.48♑	13.94S
01/31	18.91♐	18.29S	29.26♐	17.98S	08.36♑	17.23S	16.54♑	16.20S	23.79♑	15.02S	00.34♒	13.76S
02/10	19.75♐	18.26S	00.13♑	17.91S	09.26♑	17.12S	17.43♑	16.05S	24.65♑	14.84S	01.18♒	13.56S
02/20	20.44♐	18.22S	00.90♑	17.82S	10.07♑	16.99S	18.25♑	15.88S	25.47♑	14.66S	01.99♒	13.36S
03/02	21.00♐	18.15S	01.56♑	17.72S	10.86♑	16.84S	18.98♑	15.72S	26.22♑	14.47S	02.74♒	13.15S
03/12	21.40♐	18.07S	02.08♑	17.61S	11.44♑	16.70S	19.62♑	15.56S	26.89♑	14.28S	03.43♒	12.95S
03/22	21.64♐	17.97S	02.48♑	17.50S	11.91♑	16.57S	20.15♑	15.40S	27.47♑	14.10S	04.03♒	12.75S
04/01	21.73♐	17.87S	02.71♑	17.38S	12.24♑	16.43S	20.56♑	15.25S	27.94♑	13.93S	04.55♒	12.57S
04/11	21.65♐	17.75S	02.79♑	17.27S	12.42♑	16.31S	20.86♑	15.11S	28.30♑	13.78S	04.96♒	12.40S
04/21	21.42♐	17.63S	02.71♑	17.16S	12.48♑	16.20S	21.01♑	14.99S	28.53♑	13.64S	05.26♒	12.25S
05/01	21.05♐	17.51S	02.50♑	17.07S	12.39♑	16.11S	21.03♑	14.89S	28.64♑	13.53S	05.45♒	12.12S
05/11	20.55♐	17.39S	02.15♑	16.98S	12.16♑	16.03S	20.91♑	14.81S	28.63♑	13.45S	05.51♒	12.03S
05/21	19.93♐	17.28S	01.69♑	16.90S	11.81♑	15.98S	20.67♑	14.76S	28.49♑	13.39S	05.45♒	11.96S
05/31	19.28♐	17.18S	01.13♑	16.84S	11.35♑	15.94S	20.32♑	14.73S	28.23♑	13.36S	05.27♒	11.93S
06/10	18.60♐	17.09S	00.52♑	16.80S	10.79♑	15.93S	19.87♑	14.73S	27.87♑	13.36S	04.99♒	11.93S
06/20	17.93♐	17.02S	29.86♐	16.77S	10.19♑	15.93S	19.34♑	14.75S	27.42♑	13.39S	04.61♒	11.95S
06/30	17.29♐	16.96S	29.18♐	16.76S	09.57♑	15.96S	18.77♑	14.80S	26.88♑	13.45S	04.15♒	12.01S
07/10	16.71♐	16.93S	28.55♐	16.76S	08.94♑	16.00S	18.16♑	14.86S	26.32♑	13.53S	03.64♒	12.10S
07/20	16.24♐	16.92S	27.99♐	16.78S	08.35♑	16.05S	17.53♑	14.94S	25.73♑	13.63S	03.09♒	12.20S
07/30	15.88♐	16.93S	27.51♐	16.82S	07.79♑	16.12S	16.96♑	15.04S	25.16♑	13.74S	02.52♒	12.33S
08/09	15.66♐	16.96S	27.14♐	16.87S	07.33♑	16.20S	16.44♑	15.14S	24.61♑	13.86S	01.95♒	12.47S
08/19	15.60♐	17.02S	26.91♐	16.93S	06.97♑	16.28S	16.00♑	15.25S	24.11♑	13.99S	01.43♒	12.61S
08/29	15.70♐	17.09S	26.80♐	17.00S	06.73♑	16.37S	15.66♑	15.35S	23.70♑	14.12S	00.98♒	12.76S
09/08	15.94♐	17.18S	26.83♐	17.08S	06.62♑	16.45S	15.46♑	15.46S	23.38♑	14.24S	00.60♒	12.90S
09/18	16.33♐	17.28S	27.02♐	17.16S	06.67♑	16.54S	15.33♑	15.55S	23.17♑	14.35S	00.31♒	13.03S
09/28	16.86♐	17.39S	27.34♐	17.25S	06.84♑	16.61S	15.36♑	15.64S	23.08♑	14.45S	00.14♒	13.14S
10/08	17.52♐	17.51S	27.82♐	17.33S	07.14♑	16.68S	15.51♑	15.71S	23.13♑	14.53S	00.07♒	13.24S
10/18	18.30♐	17.62S	28.41♐	17.41S	07.57♑	16.74S	15.80♑	15.77S	23.29♑	14.59S	00.13♒	13.31S
10/28	19.18♐	17.73S	29.11♐	17.47S	08.12♑	16.78S	16.22♑	15.80S	23.58♑	14.63S	00.31♒	13.36S
11/07	20.15♐	17.83S	29.91♐	17.52S	08.78♑	16.80S	16.74♑	15.81S	23.98♑	14.64S	00.60♒	13.38S
11/17	21.18♐	17.92S	00.80♑	17.56S	09.54♑	16.81S	17.36♑	15.80S	24.48♑	14.63S	01.01♒	13.37S
11/27	22.26♐	17.99S	01.75♑	17.58S	10.37♑	16.79S	18.08♑	15.78S	25.09♑	14.59S	01.52♒	13.33S
12/07	23.37♐	18.05S	02.75♑	17.58S	11.27♑	16.76S	18.86♑	15.71S	25.78♑	14.53S	02.11♒	13.27S
12/17	24.50♐	18.08S	03.79♑	17.56S	12.21♑	16.70S	19.71♑	15.63S	26.53♑	14.44S	02.78♒	13.17S
12/27	25.63♐	18.10S	04.84♑	17.52S	13.18♑	16.62S	20.60♑	15.53S	27.34♑	14.32S	03.51♒	13.05S

DATE	1956 ☌	1956 ☌ Decl	1957 ☌	1957 ☌ Decl	1958 ☌	1958 ☌ Decl	1959 ☌	1959 ☌ Decl	1960 ☌	1960 ☌ Decl	1961 ☌	1961 ☌ Decl
01/01	03.89≈	12.98S	09.63≈	11.67S	14.88≈	10.38S	19.81≈	09.09S	24.45≈	07.83S	28.91≈	06.57S
01/11	04.69≈	12.83S	10.36≈	11.51S	15.57≈	10.22S	20.44≈	08.94S	25.03≈	07.68S	29.44≈	06.43S
01/21	05.50≈	12.65S	11.13≈	11.33S	16.28≈	10.04S	21.11≈	08.76S	25.66≈	07.51S	00.03✶	06.26S
01/31	06.32≈	12.46S	11.91≈	11.13S	17.03≈	09.84S	21.81≈	08.56S	26.32≈	07.31S	00.67✶	06.07S
02/10	07.14≈	12.25S	12.69≈	10.92S	17.78≈	09.62S	22.53≈	08.35S	27.01≈	07.10S	01.33✶	05.86S
02/20	07.92≈	12.04S	13.46≈	10.70S	18.52≈	09.40S	23.26≈	08.12S	27.71≈	06.87S	02.01✶	05.63S
03/01	08.67≈	11.82S	14.12≈	10.50S	19.17≈	09.19S	23.89≈	07.91S	28.40≈	06.64S	02.61✶	05.43S
03/11	09.36≈	11.61S	14.81≈	10.27S	19.86≈	08.96S	24.57≈	07.68S	29.07≈	06.40S	03.27✶	05.19S
03/21	09.99≈	11.40S	15.45≈	10.05S	20.50≈	08.73S	25.21≈	07.44S	29.70≈	06.17S	03.90✶	04.95S
03/31	10.53≈	11.20S	16.01≈	09.84S	21.08≈	08.51S	25.80≈	07.22S	00.29✶	05.94S	04.50✶	04.72S
04/10	10.99≈	11.01S	16.50≈	09.65S	21.58≈	08.31S	26.32≈	07.01S	00.83✶	05.73S	05.04✶	04.50S
04/20	11.34≈	10.85S	16.88≈	09.47S	22.00≈	08.13S	26.77≈	06.82S	01.29✶	05.53S	05.52✶	04.30S
04/30	11.58≈	10.71S	17.17≈	09.32S	22.34≈	07.96S	27.14≈	06.65S	01.67✶	05.35S	05.93✶	04.11S
05/10	11.70≈	10.61S	17.36≈	09.20S	22.57≈	07.83S	27.41≈	06.50S	01.97✶	05.20S	06.26✶	03.95S
05/20	11.72≈	10.53S	17.44≈	09.11S	22.70≈	07.73S	27.58≈	06.39S	02.18✶	05.08S	06.50✶	03.82S
05/30	11.62≈	10.48S	17.40≈	09.05S	22.72≈	07.66S	27.65≈	06.31S	02.28✶	04.99S	06.64✶	03.72S
06/09	11.41≈	10.47S	17.26≈	09.03S	22.63≈	07.63S	27.62≈	06.26S	02.29✶	04.94S	06.69✶	03.66S
06/19	11.11≈	10.49S	17.01≈	09.05S	22.45≈	07.63S	27.49≈	06.26S	02.19✶	04.92S	06.64✶	03.63S
06/29	10.71≈	10.55S	16.68≈	09.10S	22.17≈	07.67S	27.27≈	06.29S	02.00✶	04.95S	06.51✶	03.63S
07/09	10.25≈	10.63S	16.26≈	09.18S	21.81≈	07.74S	26.95≈	06.35S	01.73✶	05.00S	06.28✶	03.66S
07/19	09.72≈	10.75S	15.79≈	09.29S	21.38≈	07.85S	26.57≈	06.45S	01.38✶	05.08S	05.97✶	03.72S
07/29	09.18≈	10.88S	15.28≈	09.42S	20.91≈	07.98S	26.12≈	06.57S	00.97✶	05.21S	05.59✶	03.82S
08/08	08.63≈	11.03S	14.76≈	09.57S	20.38≈	08.13S	25.64≈	06.72S	00.52✶	05.36S	05.16✶	03.95S
08/18	08.11≈	11.18S	14.23≈	09.73S	19.87≈	08.30S	25.14≈	06.89S	00.03✶	05.52S	04.68✶	04.11S
08/28	07.62≈	11.34S	13.71≈	09.90S	19.36≈	08.47S	24.64≈	07.06S	29.52≈	05.71S	04.20✶	04.36S
09/07	07.19≈	11.50S	13.26≈	10.07S	18.89≈	08.65S	24.16≈	07.25S	29.04≈	05.89S	03.73✶	04.55S
09/17	06.85≈	11.64S	12.87≈	10.23S	18.48≈	08.82S	23.71≈	07.43S	28.59≈	06.08S	03.27✶	04.74S
09/27	06.60≈	11.77S	12.57≈	10.38S	18.13≈	08.98S	23.33≈	07.60S	28.20≈	06.25S	02.85✶	04.92S
10/07	06.45≈	11.88S	12.37≈	10.50S	17.87≈	09.12S	23.03≈	07.75S	27.87≈	06.41S	02.49✶	05.09S
10/17	06.43≈	11.97S	12.27≈	10.60S	17.70≈	09.24S	22.81≈	07.88S	27.62≈	06.55S	02.20✶	05.24S
10/27	06.52≈	12.03S	12.27≈	10.68S	17.64≈	09.33S	22.70≈	07.98S	27.47≈	06.67S	02.00✶	05.37S
11/06	06.72≈	12.06S	12.39≈	10.72S	17.69≈	09.38S	22.69≈	08.05S	27.45≈	06.75S	01.90✶	05.46S
11/16	07.03≈	12.06S	12.62≈	10.74S	17.86≈	09.41S	22.78≈	08.10S	27.60≈	06.80S	01.89✶	05.52S
11/26	07.45≈	12.05S	12.95≈	10.72S	18.12≈	09.40S	22.98≈	08.09S	27.85≈	06.81S	01.99✶	05.55S
12/06	07.95≈	11.97S	13.39≈	10.66S	18.48≈	09.36S	23.27≈	08.07S	28.19≈	06.79S	02.18✶	05.52S
12/16	08.55≈	11.88S	13.91≈	10.58S	18.93≈	09.28S	23.66≈	08.00S	28.62≈	06.73S	02.47✶	05.50S
12/26	09.20≈	11.76S	14.50≈	10.46S	19.46≈	09.17S	24.14≈	07.90S	29.08≈	06.64S	02.84✶	05.42S

DATE	1962 ☿	1962 ☿ Decl	1963 ☿	1963 ☿ Decl	1964 ☿	1964 ☿ Decl	1965 ☿	1965 ☿ Decl	1966 ☿	1966 ☿ Decl	1967 ☿	1967 ☿ Decl
01/01	03.10✶	05.35S	07.14✶	04.16S	11.02✶	02.99S	14.82✶	01.84S	18.49✶	00.72S	22.07✶	00.37N
01/11	03.60✶	05.22S	07.59✶	04.04S	11.43✶	02.88S	15.20✶	01.73S	18.83✶	00.63S	22.37✶	00.45N
01/21	04.15✶	05.06S	08.10✶	03.88S	11.91✶	02.74S	15.65✶	01.60S	19.24✶	00.50S	22.75✶	00.57N
01/31	04.75✶	04.87S	08.66✶	03.71S	12.44✶	02.57S	16.16✶	01.44S	19.72✶	00.35S	23.20✶	00.72N
02/10	05.38✶	04.67S	09.27✶	03.51S	13.02✶	02.37S	16.71✶	01.25S	20.25✶	00.17S	23.71✶	00.89N
02/20	06.03✶	04.45S	09.90✶	03.29S	13.63✶	02.16S	17.30✶	01.04S	20.81✶	00.03N	24.25✶	01.08N
03/02	06.69✶	04.22S	10.54✶	03.06S	14.31✶	01.92S	17.91✶	00.82S	21.41✶	00.25N	24.83✶	01.29N
03/12	07.33✶	03.98S	11.18✶	02.83S	14.94✶	01.68S	18.52✶	00.59S	22.01✶	00.47N	25.43✶	01.51N
03/22	07.96✶	03.74S	11.80✶	02.59S	15.55✶	01.45S	19.13✶	00.36S	22.62✶	00.70N	26.02✶	01.74N
04/01	08.56✶	03.51S	12.39✶	02.36S	16.15✶	01.22S	19.73✶	00.12S	23.21✶	00.94N	26.62✶	01.97N
04/11	09.10✶	03.29S	12.95✶	02.13S	16.71✶	00.99S	20.29✶	00.10N	23.78✶	01.16N	27.19✶	02.20N
04/21	09.60✶	03.08S	13.45✶	01.92S	17.22✶	00.78S	20.81✶	00.32N	24.31✶	01.38N	27.73✶	02.42N
05/01	10.02✶	02.89S	13.89✶	01.73S	17.67✶	00.58S	21.28✶	00.52N	24.80✶	01.59N	28.23✶	02.63N
05/11	10.36✶	02.73S	14.27✶	01.56S	18.06✶	00.40S	21.69✶	00.70N	25.22✶	01.77N	28.68✶	02.82N
05/21	10.63✶	02.59S	14.56✶	01.41S	18.37✶	00.25S	22.03✶	00.86N	25.58✶	01.93N	29.06✶	02.98N
05/31	10.80✶	02.49S	14.77✶	01.30S	18.60✶	00.13S	22.29✶	00.98N	25.87✶	02.07N	29.37✶	03.12N
06/10	10.88✶	02.41S	14.88✶	01.22S	18.74✶	00.05S	22.47✶	01.08N	26.08✶	02.18N	29.61✶	03.24N
06/20	10.87✶	02.38S	14.91✶	01.17S	18.79✶	00.01N	22.55✶	01.15N	26.20✶	02.25N	29.76✶	03.32N
06/30	10.76✶	02.38S	14.84✶	01.16S	18.76✶	00.03N	22.55✶	01.17N	26.23✶	02.29N	29.83✶	03.37N
07/10	10.56✶	02.42S	14.68✶	01.19S	18.63✶	00.01N	22.46✶	01.16N	26.17✶	02.29N	29.81✶	03.38N
07/20	10.28✶	02.50S	14.44✶	01.25S	18.42✶	00.05S	22.28✶	01.12N	26.03✶	02.26N	29.70✶	03.36N
07/30	09.93✶	02.60S	14.13✶	01.35S	18.13✶	00.14S	22.02✶	01.04N	25.81✶	02.19N	29.50✶	03.30N
08/09	09.53✶	02.74S	13.75✶	01.47S	17.77✶	00.26S	21.70✶	00.93N	25.51✶	02.08N	29.23✶	03.21N
08/19	09.08✶	02.89S	13.33✶	01.63S	17.36✶	00.41S	21.32✶	00.79N	25.15✶	01.95N	28.90✶	03.08N
08/29	08.61✶	03.07S	12.87✶	01.80S	16.92✶	00.58S	20.89✶	00.63N	24.75✶	01.80N	28.51✶	02.94N
09/08	08.14✶	03.26S	12.39✶	01.99S	16.46✶	00.76S	20.44✶	00.45N	24.30✶	01.62N	28.09✶	02.77N
09/18	07.66✶	03.45S	11.93✶	02.18S	16.00✶	00.95S	19.97✶	00.25N	23.85✶	01.43N	27.64✶	02.58N
09/28	07.24✶	03.64S	11.50✶	02.37S	15.56✶	01.14S	19.52✶	00.06N	23.40✶	01.24N	27.19✶	02.39N
10/08	06.86✶	03.81S	11.10✶	02.55S	15.14✶	01.33S	19.10✶	00.06S	22.97✶	01.05N	26.74✶	02.20N
10/18	06.56✶	03.97S	10.77✶	02.71S	14.79✶	01.50S	18.73✶	00.25S	22.58✶	00.87N	26.33✶	02.01N
10/28	06.33✶	04.10S	10.50✶	02.86S	14.51✶	01.65S	18.42✶	00.46S	22.24✶	00.70N	25.98✶	01.84N
11/07	06.19✶	04.21S	10.32✶	02.97S	14.30✶	01.77S	18.18✶	00.59S	21.97✶	00.56N	25.69✶	01.70N
11/17	06.15✶	04.28S	10.23✶	03.06S	14.19✶	01.87S	18.03✶	00.70S	21.78✶	00.45N	25.47✶	01.57N
11/27	06.20✶	04.32S	10.24✶	03.11S	14.17✶	01.92S	17.97✶	00.77S	21.68✶	00.37N	25.34✶	01.48N
12/07	06.35✶	04.32S	10.35✶	03.12S	14.24✶	01.95S	18.00✶	00.80S	21.68✶	00.32N	25.29✶	01.43N
12/17	06.60✶	04.28S	10.56✶	03.09S	14.40✶	01.93S	18.12✶	00.80S	21.77✶	00.32N	25.34✶	01.41N
12/27	06.94✶	04.21S	10.85✶	03.03S	14.66✶	01.88S	18.35✶	00.75S	21.95✶	00.35N	25.48✶	01.42N

DATE	1968 ⚷	1968 ⚷ Decl	1969 ⚷	1969 ⚷ Decl	1970 ⚷	1970 ⚷ Decl	1971 ⚷	1971 ⚷ Decl	1972 ⚷	1972 ⚷ Decl	1973 ⚷	1973 ⚷ Decl
01/01	25.58♓	01.44N	29.09♓	02.50N	02.53♈	03.54N	05.97♈	04.56N	09.41♈	05.56N	12.89♈	06.55N
01/11	25.86♓	01.52N	29.33♓	02.57N	02.74♈	03.59N	06.14♈	04.60N	09.56♈	05.59N	13.01♈	06.58N
01/21	26.21♓	01.62N	29.66♓	02.67N	03.04♈	03.68N	06.42♈	04.68N	09.80♈	05.66N	13.22♈	06.64N
01/31	26.63♓	01.76N	00.06♈	02.79N	03.41♈	03.80N	06.76♈	04.79N	10.11♈	05.76N	13.52♈	06.73N
02/10	27.11♓	01.92N	00.51♈	02.95N	03.85♈	03.95N	07.17♈	04.93N	10.50♈	05.89N	13.89♈	06.85N
02/20	27.63♓	02.11N	01.03♈	03.13N	04.34♈	04.12N	07.64♈	05.09N	10.95♈	06.04N	14.33♈	07.00N
03/01	28.19♓	02.31N	01.52♈	03.31N	04.82♈	04.29N	08.10♈	05.26N	11.45♈	06.22N	14.77♈	07.16N
03/11	28.78♓	02.53N	02.09♈	03.52N	05.38♈	04.50N	08.65♈	05.46N	11.99♈	06.42N	15.29♈	07.35N
03/21	29.37♓	02.75N	02.67♈	03.74N	05.96♈	04.72N	09.23♈	05.67N	12.56♈	06.63N	15.86♈	07.55N
03/31	29.96♓	02.98N	03.27♈	03.97N	06.54♈	04.94N	09.81♈	05.89N	13.15♈	06.85N	16.44♈	07.76N
04/10	00.54♈	03.21N	03.85♈	04.20N	07.13♈	05.16N	10.40♈	06.11N	13.73♈	07.06N	17.03♈	07.98N
04/20	01.09♈	03.43N	04.40♈	04.42N	07.69♈	05.38N	10.97♈	06.33N	14.31♈	07.28N	17.61♈	08.20N
04/30	01.60♈	03.64N	04.93♈	04.63N	08.23♈	05.59N	11.52♈	06.54N	14.87♈	07.49N	18.18♈	08.41N
05/10	02.06♈	03.83N	05.41♈	04.82N	08.73♈	05.79N	12.03♈	06.74N	15.39♈	07.69N	18.72♈	08.61N
05/20	02.47♈	04.00N	05.83♈	05.00N	09.17♈	05.97N	12.50♈	06.93N	15.87♈	07.88N	19.22♈	08.79N
05/30	02.81♈	04.15N	06.20♈	05.16N	09.56♈	06.13N	12.91♈	07.09N	16.30♈	08.04N	19.67♈	08.96N
06/09	03.07♈	04.27N	06.49♈	05.28N	09.88♈	06.27N	13.25♈	07.23N	16.67♈	08.19N	20.07♈	09.11N
06/19	03.26♈	04.37N	06.70♈	05.38N	10.12♈	06.37N	13.53♈	07.34N	16.96♈	08.30N	20.39♈	09.23N
06/29	03.35♈	04.42N	06.83♈	05.45N	10.28♈	06.45N	13.72♈	07.43N	17.18♈	08.39N	20.64♈	09.32N
07/09	03.36♈	04.44N	06.87♈	05.48N	10.36♈	06.49N	13.83♈	07.48N	17.31♈	08.45N	20.82♈	09.39N
07/19	03.29♈	04.43N	06.84♈	05.48N	10.35♈	06.50N	13.85♈	07.49N	17.36♈	08.47N	20.90♈	09.42N
07/29	03.13♈	04.38N	06.71♈	05.44N	10.26♈	06.47N	13.79♈	07.48N	17.33♈	08.46N	20.90♈	09.43N
08/08	02.89♈	04.30N	06.50♈	05.37N	10.08♈	06.41N	13.65♈	07.43N	17.21♈	08.42N	20.80♈	09.39N
08/18	02.58♈	04.19N	06.22♈	05.27N	09.82♈	06.32N	13.42♈	07.34N	17.00♈	08.34N	20.63♈	09.32N
08/28	02.22♈	04.05N	05.88♈	05.13N	09.50♈	06.19N	13.13♈	07.23N	16.72♈	08.23N	20.38♈	09.23N
09/07	01.81♈	03.89N	05.48♈	04.98N	09.13♈	06.04N	12.77♈	07.09N	16.38♈	08.10N	20.06♈	09.10N
09/17	01.37♈	03.71N	05.04♈	04.80N	08.71♈	05.88N	12.37♈	06.93N	15.98♈	07.94N	19.68♈	08.96N
09/27	00.91♈	03.51N	04.60♈	04.62N	08.27♈	05.70N	11.92♈	06.75N	15.55♈	07.77N	19.27♈	08.79N
10/07	00.46♈	03.32N	04.15♈	04.43N	07.82♈	05.51N	11.47♈	06.56N	15.11♈	07.59N	18.82♈	08.61N
10/17	00.05♈	03.14N	03.73♈	04.24N	07.37♈	05.31N	11.03♈	06.38N	14.66♈	07.40N	18.35♈	08.42N
10/27	29.67♓	02.96N	03.32♈	04.06N	06.96♈	05.13N	10.61♈	06.19N	14.23♈	07.22N	17.91♈	08.24N
11/06	29.36♓	02.81N	02.98♈	03.90N	06.60♈	04.97N	10.22♈	06.02N	13.82♈	07.04N	17.50♈	08.06N
11/16	29.10♓	02.68N	02.71♈	03.76N	06.30♈	04.82N	09.89♈	05.87N	13.47♈	06.89N	17.13♈	07.91N
11/26	28.94♓	02.57N	02.51♈	03.65N	06.07♈	04.71N	09.63♈	05.74N	13.20♈	06.76N	16.83♈	07.77N
12/06	28.86♓	02.51N	02.39♈	03.57N	05.93♈	04.62N	09.46♈	05.65N	13.00♈	06.66N	16.59♈	07.66N
12/16	28.87♓	02.48N	02.38♈	03.53N	05.87♈	04.57N	09.36♈	05.59N	12.88♈	06.59N	16.44♈	07.58N
12/26	28.97♓	02.48N	02.45♈	03.52N	05.90♈	04.55N	09.36♈	05.56N	12.86♈	06.56N	16.38♈	07.54N

DATE	1974 ⚷	1974 ⚷ Decl	1975 ⚷	1975 ⚷ Decl	1976 ⚷	1976 ⚷ Decl	1977 ⚷	1977 ⚷ Decl	1978 ⚷	1978 ⚷ Decl	1979 ⚷	1979 ⚷ Decl
01/01	16.39♈	07.53N	19.95♈	08.49N	23.59♈	09.45N	27.31♈	10.38N	01.15♉	11.30N	05.14♉	12.19N
01/11	16.48♈	07.54N	20.01♈	08.50N	23.61♈	09.44N	27.30♈	10.37N	01.11♉	11.27N	05.05♉	12.16N
01/21	16.66♈	07.59N	20.16♈	08.54N	23.72♈	09.47N	27.39♈	10.39N	01.17♉	11.29N	05.06♉	12.16N
01/31	16.93♈	07.68N	20.40♈	08.61N	23.93♈	09.53N	27.58♈	10.45N	01.31♉	11.33N	05.17♉	12.20N
02/10	17.28♈	07.79N	20.71♈	08.72N	24.22♈	09.62N	27.85♈	10.53N	01.55♉	11.41N	05.38♉	12.26N
02/20	17.69♈	07.93N	21.10♈	08.85N	24.60♈	09.75N	28.21♈	10.65N	01.88♉	11.51N	05.69♉	12.36N
03/02	18.16♈	08.10N	21.56♈	09.01N	25.08♈	09.91N	28.63♈	10.79N	02.28♉	11.65N	06.07♉	12.49N
03/12	18.68♈	08.28N	22.07♈	09.18N	25.58♈	10.09N	29.11♈	10.95N	02.76♉	11.80N	06.52♉	12.63N
03/22	19.24♈	08.48N	22.62♈	09.37N	26.12♈	10.27N	29.65♈	11.13N	03.28♉	11.97N	07.04♉	12.79N
04/01	19.82♈	08.69N	23.20♈	09.58N	26.70♈	10.47N	00.23♉	11.32N	03.85♉	12.16N	07.60♉	12.97N
04/11	20.42♈	08.90N	23.80♈	09.79N	27.30♈	10.67N	00.83♉	11.52N	04.45♉	12.35N	08.20♉	13.15N
04/21	21.01♈	09.11N	24.39♈	09.99N	27.90♈	10.88N	01.44♉	11.73N	05.07♉	12.55N	08.83♉	13.35N
05/01	21.59♈	09.32N	24.98♈	10.20N	28.51♈	11.08N	02.05♉	11.93N	05.70♉	12.74N	09.47♉	13.54N
05/11	22.14♈	09.52N	25.55♈	10.40N	29.09♈	11.28N	02.65♉	12.12N	06.32♉	12.93N	10.10♉	13.72N
05/21	22.65♈	09.71N	26.09♈	10.59N	29.65♈	11.47N	03.23♉	12.30N	06.92♉	13.12N	10.73♉	13.90N
05/31	23.13♈	09.88N	26.59♈	10.76N	00.16♉	11.64N	03.77♉	12.48N	07.49♉	13.29N	11.35♉	14.07N
06/10	23.54♈	10.03N	27.03♈	10.91N	00.63♉	11.79N	04.27♉	12.63N	08.01♉	13.44N	11.84♉	14.23N
06/20	23.89♈	10.15N	27.41♈	11.04N	01.03♉	11.92N	04.71♉	12.77N	08.49♉	13.58N	12.33♉	14.36N
06/30	24.17♈	10.25N	27.72♈	11.15N	01.37♉	12.03N	05.09♉	12.88N	08.90♉	13.69N	12.77♉	14.48N
07/10	24.36♈	10.32N	27.95♈	11.22N	01.63♉	12.11N	05.39♉	12.96N	09.24♉	13.78N	13.16♉	14.57N
07/20	24.47♈	10.36N	28.10♈	11.27N	01.82♉	12.16N	05.60♉	13.02N	09.50♉	13.85N	13.48♉	14.64N
07/30	24.49♈	10.36N	28.17♈	11.29N	01.91♉	12.17N	05.73♉	13.05N	09.68♉	13.88N	13.73♉	14.68N
08/09	24.43♈	10.34N	28.14♈	11.27N	01.90♉	12.18N	05.77♉	13.05N	09.77♉	13.89N	13.89♉	14.69N
08/19	24.29♈	10.28N	28.02♈	11.22N	01.81♉	12.16N	05.73♉	13.02N	09.76♉	13.87N	13.82♉	14.68N
08/29	24.06♈	10.19N	27.82♈	11.14N	01.64♉	12.11N	05.59♉	12.95N	09.65♉	13.81N	13.62♉	14.63N
09/08	23.75♈	10.07N	27.54♈	11.03N	01.38♉	12.05N	05.36♉	12.86N	09.46♉	13.73N	13.34♉	14.57N
09/18	23.39♈	09.93N	27.19♈	10.90N	01.06♉	11.96N	05.06♉	12.74N	09.19♉	13.63N	12.99♉	14.47N
09/28	22.98♈	09.77N	26.80♈	10.74N	00.67♉	11.83N	04.69♉	12.61N	08.84♉	13.50N	12.57♉	14.35N
10/08	22.52♈	09.59N	26.36♈	10.57N	00.24♉	11.68N	04.26♉	12.45N	08.43♉	13.35N	12.11♉	14.21N
10/18	22.07♈	09.41N	25.91♈	10.40N	29.78♈	11.52N	03.81♉	12.28N	07.99♉	13.19N	11.62♉	14.06N
10/28	21.62♈	09.23N	25.45♈	10.22N	29.30♈	11.34N	03.34♉	12.11N	07.51♉	13.02N	11.13♉	13.89N
11/07	21.19♈	09.06N	24.99♈	10.04N	28.85♈	11.16N	02.87♉	11.94N	07.03♉	12.85N	10.66♉	13.73N
11/17	20.81♈	08.90N	24.58♈	09.88N	28.42♈	10.99N	02.43♉	11.77N	06.55♉	12.68N	10.23♉	13.57N
11/27	20.47♈	08.75N	24.23♈	09.73N	28.05♈	10.83N	02.01♉	11.62N	06.12♉	12.54N	09.86♉	13.42N
12/07	20.22♈	08.64N	23.94♈	09.61N	27.74♈	10.68N	01.67♉	11.49N	05.75♉	12.40N	09.58♉	13.29N
12/17	20.04♈	08.56N	23.73♈	09.52N	27.50♈	10.56N	01.39♉	11.39N	05.44♉	12.30N	09.41♉	13.17N
12/27	19.96♈	08.51N	23.62♈	09.47N	27.35♈	10.46N	01.21♉	11.32N	05.22♉	12.22N	09.34♉	13.09N

DATE	1980 ⚷	1980 ⚷ Decl	1981 ⚷	1981 ⚷ Decl	1982 ⚷	1982 ⚷ Decl	1983 ⚷	1983 ⚷ Decl	1984 ⚷	1984 ⚷ Decl	1985 ⚷	1985 ⚷ Decl
01/01	09.29♉	13.06N	13.63♉	13.89N	18.24♉	14.68N	23.15♉	15.41N	28.43♉	16.06N	04.13♊	16.60N
01/11	09.16♉	13.02N	13.60♉	13.84N	18.03♉	14.63N	22.88♉	15.35N	28.11♉	16.01N	03.75♊	16.55N
01/21	09.13♉	13.01N	13.52♉	13.83N	17.91♉	14.61N	22.72♉	15.33N	27.89♉	15.98N	03.47♊	16.52N
01/31	09.20♉	13.04N	13.56♉	13.85N	17.91♉	14.62N	22.66♉	15.33N	27.78♉	15.98N	03.31♊	16.52N
02/10	09.39♉	13.10N	13.70♉	13.90N	18.01♉	14.66N	22.73♉	15.37N	27.78♉	16.01N	03.25♊	16.55N
02/20	09.65♉	13.18N	13.93♉	13.98N	18.21♉	14.73N	22.89♉	15.43N	27.89♉	16.06N	03.32♊	16.60N
03/01	10.01♉	13.30N	14.25♉	14.07N	18.49♉	14.82N	23.12♉	15.50N	28.11♉	16.13N	03.50♊	16.66N
03/11	10.44♉	13.43N	14.66♉	14.20N	18.88♉	14.93N	23.48♉	15.61N	28.44♉	16.23N	03.78♊	16.75N
03/21	10.94♉	13.58N	15.14♉	14.35N	19.34♉	15.06N	23.92♉	15.73N	28.88♉	16.34N	04.17♊	16.85N
03/31	11.50♉	13.75N	15.69♉	14.50N	19.88♉	15.21N	24.45♉	15.87N	29.39♉	16.47N	04.66♊	16.96N
04/10	12.10♉	13.93N	16.29♉	14.67N	20.47♉	15.37N	25.03♉	16.01N	29.97♉	16.60N	05.22♊	17.08N
04/20	12.73♉	14.11N	16.92♉	14.85N	21.11♉	15.53N	25.68♉	16.17N	00.61♊	16.74N	05.86♊	17.20N
04/30	13.38♉	14.30N	17.59♉	15.02N	21.79♉	15.70N	26.36♉	16.32N	01.30♊	16.88N	06.56♊	17.33N
05/10	14.04♉	14.48N	18.26♉	15.20N	22.48♉	15.87N	27.06♉	16.48N	02.03♊	17.02N	07.30♊	17.47N
05/20	14.68♉	14.65N	18.93♉	15.36N	23.17♉	16.03N	27.78♉	16.63N	02.77♊	17.16N	08.07♊	17.57N
05/30	15.31♉	14.82N	19.59♉	15.52N	23.86♉	16.18N	28.49♉	16.77N	03.52♊	17.29N	08.85♊	17.67N
06/09	15.90♉	14.97N	20.21♉	15.67N	24.52♉	16.32N	29.20♉	16.90N	04.27♊	17.40N	09.63♊	17.76N
06/19	16.45♉	15.11N	20.80♉	15.80N	25.15♉	16.44N	29.88♉	17.01N	04.99♊	17.50N	10.40♊	17.85N
06/29	16.95♉	15.22N	21.35♉	15.92N	25.74♉	16.55N	00.52♊	17.11N	05.67♊	17.59N	11.15♊	17.92N
07/09	17.38♉	15.32N	21.83♉	16.01N	26.27♉	16.64N	01.10♊	17.20N	06.31♊	17.66N	11.86♊	17.98N
07/19	17.73♉	15.39N	22.23♉	16.08N	26.73♉	16.71N	01.62♊	17.26N	06.89♊	17.72N	12.51♊	18.03N
07/29	18.00♉	15.43N	22.56♉	16.13N	27.12♉	16.76N	02.07♊	17.31N	07.40♊	17.75N	13.10♊	18.06N
08/08	18.18♉	15.45N	22.80♉	16.15N	27.41♉	16.79N	02.43♊	17.33N	07.83♊	17.77N	13.61♊	18.06N
08/18	18.27♉	15.44N	22.94♉	16.15N	27.61♉	16.79N	02.70♊	17.33N	08.17♊	17.76N	14.02♊	18.05N
08/28	18.26♉	15.41N	22.99♉	16.13N	27.71♉	16.76N	02.88♊	17.31N	08.40♊	17.74N	14.34♊	18.02N
09/07	18.15♉	15.35N	22.93♉	16.07N	27.71♉	16.72N	02.94♊	17.27N	08.53♊	17.70N	14.55♊	17.98N
09/17	17.95♉	15.26N	22.78♉	15.99N	27.61♉	16.65N	02.89♊	17.21N	08.54♊	17.64N	14.66♊	17.92N
09/27	17.66♉	15.15N	22.53♉	15.90N	27.40♉	16.56N	02.73♊	17.13N	08.44♊	17.57N	14.64♊	17.85N
10/07	17.29♉	15.02N	22.20♉	15.78N	27.10♉	16.46N	02.48♊	17.03N	08.24♊	17.48N	14.50♊	17.76N
10/17	16.86♉	14.88N	21.79♉	15.64N	26.72♉	16.33N	02.13♊	16.92N	07.93♊	17.38N	14.25♊	17.67N
10/27	16.39♉	14.73N	21.33♉	15.50N	26.27♉	16.20N	01.71♊	16.80N	07.53♊	17.27N	13.90♊	17.57N
11/06	15.90♉	14.57N	20.83♉	15.35N	25.76♉	16.06N	01.23♊	16.67N	07.06♊	17.15N	13.45♊	17.47N
11/16	15.40♉	14.41N	20.33♉	15.20N	25.25♉	15.92N	00.70♊	16.54N	06.54♊	17.03N	12.94♊	17.36N
11/26	14.92♉	14.27N	19.83♉	15.05N	24.73♉	15.78N	00.17♊	16.42N	05.97♊	16.91N	12.39♊	17.26N
12/06	14.46♉	14.13N	19.34♉	14.92N	24.22♉	15.66N	29.61♉	16.29N	05.41♊	16.81N	11.82♊	17.17N
12/16	14.08♉	14.01N	18.92♉	14.81N	23.76♉	15.54N	29.11♉	16.19N	04.88♊	16.71N	11.25♊	17.09N
12/26	13.77♉	13.93N	18.56♉	14.72N	23.35♉	15.45N	28.66♉	16.10N	04.39♊	16.64N	10.69♊	17.02N

DATE	1986	1986 Decl	1987	1987 Decl	1988	1988 Decl	1989	1989 Decl	1990	1990 Decl	1991	1991 Decl
01/01	10.39♊	16.99N	17.34♊	17.17N	25.12♊	17.06N	03.80♋	16.54N	13.79♋	15.46N	25.24♋	13.63N
01/11	09.95♊	16.95N	16.84♊	17.15N	24.53♊	17.05N	03.17♋	16.56N	13.13♋	15.52N	24.55♋	13.73N
01/21	09.61♊	16.93N	16.42♊	17.14N	24.03♊	17.07N	02.60♋	16.60N	12.48♋	15.59N	23.80♋	13.85N
01/31	09.37♊	16.93N	16.10♊	17.15N	23.62♊	17.09N	02.11♋	16.66N	11.86♋	15.66N	23.11♋	13.98N
02/10	09.26♊	16.96N	15.89♊	17.18N	23.32♊	17.13N	01.72♋	16.72N	11.35♋	15.78N	22.49♋	14.13N
02/20	09.26♊	17.00N	15.81♊	17.22N	23.15♊	17.18N	01.45♋	16.79N	10.95♋	15.89N	21.97♋	14.28N
03/02	09.39♊	17.06N	15.86♊	17.28N	23.13♊	17.25N	01.32♋	16.87N	10.68♋	15.99N	21.56♋	14.42N
03/12	09.63♊	17.14N	16.04♊	17.35N	23.24♊	17.33N	01.47♋	16.95N	10.57♋	16.09N	21.29♋	14.56N
03/22	09.98♊	17.23N	16.36♊	17.44N	23.48♊	17.41N	01.76♋	17.03N	10.62♋	16.18N	21.17♋	14.68N
04/01	10.45♊	17.33N	16.78♊	17.53N	23.85♊	17.48N	02.20♋	17.10N	10.81♋	16.26N	21.20♋	14.78N
04/11	11.01♊	17.44N	17.30♊	17.62N	24.34♊	17.56N	02.75♋	17.17N	11.14♋	16.33N	21.40♋	14.86N
04/21	11.64♊	17.55N	17.92♊	17.71N	24.94♊	17.64N	03.40♋	17.23N	11.60♋	16.37N	21.75♋	14.92N
05/01	12.35♊	17.66N	18.61♊	17.80N	25.63♊	17.70N	04.15♋	17.27N	12.20♋	16.40N	22.28♋	14.94N
05/11	13.10♊	17.76N	19.37♊	17.88N	26.39♊	17.76N	04.98♋	17.30N	12.91♋	16.41N	22.92♋	14.93N
05/21	13.89♊	17.86N	20.18♊	17.95N	27.22♊	17.80N	05.87♋	17.32N	13.72♋	16.39N	23.67♋	14.89N
05/31	14.71♊	17.95N	21.03♊	18.01N	28.10♊	17.83N	06.81♋	17.31N	14.62♋	16.35N	24.54♋	14.82N
06/10	15.53♊	18.02N	21.90♊	18.06N	29.00♊	17.85N	07.79♋	17.29N	15.58♋	16.29N	25.49♋	14.72N
06/20	16.36♊	18.09N	22.78♊	18.10N	29.93♊	17.85N	08.79♋	17.25N	16.58♋	16.20N	26.52♋	14.58N
06/30	17.16♊	18.13N	23.64♊	18.12N	00.87♋	17.83N	09.79♋	17.19N	17.61♋	16.09N	27.61♋	14.42N
07/10	17.93♊	18.17N	24.48♊	18.11N	01.79♋	17.79N	10.77♋	17.10N	18.71♋	15.95N	28.74♋	14.23N
07/20	18.65♊	18.18N	25.29♊	18.08N	02.68♋	17.74N	11.73♋	17.01N	19.79♋	15.80N	29.89♋	14.01N
07/30	19.32♊	18.18N	26.05♊	18.04N	03.53♋	17.67N	12.64♋	16.89N	20.85♋	15.62N	01.05♌	13.77N
08/09	19.91♊	18.17N	26.74♊	17.98N	04.33♋	17.59N	13.50♋	16.76N	21.89♋	15.43N	02.20♌	13.51N
08/19	20.42♊	18.14N	27.36♊	17.92N	05.05♋	17.50N	14.28♋	16.62N	22.88♋	15.23N	03.33♌	13.23N
08/29	20.84♊	18.10N	27.88♊	17.84N	05.69♋	17.40N	14.97♋	16.47N	23.81♋	15.02N	04.42♌	12.94N
09/08	21.14♊	18.04N	28.29♊	17.76N	06.23♋	17.30N	15.55♋	16.32N	24.66♋	14.80N	05.45♌	12.65N
09/18	21.32♊	17.97N	28.59♊	17.68N	06.67♋	17.18N	16.02♋	16.17N	25.43♋	14.59N	06.40♌	12.36N
09/28	21.37♊	17.90N	28.77♊	17.59N	06.97♋	17.07N	16.35♋	16.02N	26.08♋	14.38N	07.27♌	12.07N
10/08	21.31♊	17.81N	28.83♊	17.50N	07.13♋	16.97N	16.54♋	15.88N	26.63♋	14.18N	08.01♌	11.80N
10/18	21.13♊	17.73N	28.75♊	17.41N	07.16♋	16.87N	16.61♋	15.75N	27.01♋	14.00N	08.63♌	11.55N
10/28	20.84♊	17.64N	28.54♊	17.33N	07.05♋	16.78N	16.50♋	15.63N	27.25♋	13.85N	09.10♌	11.32N
11/07	20.44♊	17.55N	28.21♊	17.25N	06.81♋	16.70N	16.25♋	15.54N	27.33♋	13.72N	09.42♌	11.13N
11/17	19.96♊	17.46N	27.77♊	17.19N	06.45♋	16.63N	15.87♋	15.47N	27.25♋	13.63N	09.60♌	10.98N
11/27	19.41♊	17.38N	27.23♊	17.14N	05.98♋	16.58N	15.38♋	15.42N	27.02♋	13.56N	09.58♌	10.87N
12/07	18.79♊	17.30N	26.65♊	17.09N	05.42♋	16.55N	14.77♋	15.40N	26.65♋	13.55N	09.39♌	10.82N
12/17	18.19♊	17.24N	26.04♊	17.09N	04.81♋	16.53N	14.13♋	15.41N	26.16♋	13.54N	09.05♌	10.81N
12/27	17.61♊	17.19N	25.43♊	17.07N	04.13♋	16.53N	13.49♋	15.44N	25.56♋	13.60N	08.56♌	10.86N

DATE	1992 ⚷	1992 Decl	1993 ⚷	1993 Decl	1994 ⚷	1994 Decl	1995 ⚷	1995 Decl	1996 ⚷	1996 Decl	1997 ⚷	1997 Decl
01/01	08.25♌	10.90N	22.97♌	07.14N	09.20♍	02.46N	26.35♍	02.74S	13.64♎	07.83S	00.27♏	12.15S
01/11	07.61♌	11.01N	22.46♌	07.24N	08.93♍	02.50N	26.45♍	02.82S	14.07♎	07.99S	00.99♏	12.37S
01/21	06.91♌	11.16N	21.83♌	07.40N	08.48♍	02.61N	26.32♍	02.80S	14.29♎	08.08S	01.53♏	12.51S
01/31	06.19♌	11.33N	21.11♌	07.60N	07.90♍	02.79N	26.01♍	02.70S	14.32♎	08.08S	01.92♏	12.61S
02/10	05.48♌	11.53N	20.31♌	07.85N	07.23♍	03.02N	25.53♍	02.52S	14.17♎	08.02S	02.08♏	12.61S
02/20	04.78♌	11.74N	19.56♌	08.11N	06.49♍	03.30N	24.91♍	02.28S	13.83♎	07.87S	02.04♏	12.55S
03/01	04.21♌	11.95N	18.93♌	08.35N	05.80♍	03.58N	24.22♍	02.00S	13.33♎	07.65S	01.84♏	12.44S
03/11	03.75♌	12.14N	18.31♌	08.62N	05.00♍	03.92N	23.46♍	01.67S	12.70♎	07.37S	01.46♏	12.25S
03/21	03.44♌	12.32N	17.80♌	08.86N	04.30♍	04.25N	22.69♍	01.32S	11.97♎	07.05S	00.91♏	12.01S
03/31	03.30♌	12.47N	17.44♌	09.09N	03.71♍	04.55N	21.96♍	00.96S	11.15♎	06.67S	00.27♏	11.73S
04/10	03.35♌	12.58N	17.23♌	09.27N	03.25♍	04.82N	21.29♍	00.62S	10.37♎	06.31S	29.55♎	11.42S
04/20	03.54♌	12.66N	17.20♌	09.41N	02.96♍	05.04N	20.71♍	00.29S	09.65♎	05.95S	28.80♎	11.09S
04/30	03.90♌	12.70N	17.34♌	09.49N	02.87♍	05.20N	20.29♍	00.03S	09.01♎	05.63S	28.04♎	10.76S
05/10	04.41♌	12.69N	17.67♌	09.52N	02.94♍	05.30N	20.04♍	00.18N	08.50♎	05.35S	27.29♎	10.44S
05/20	05.07♌	12.65N	18.19♌	09.49N	03.19♍	05.34N	19.98♍	00.31N	08.14♎	05.12S	26.68♎	10.16S
05/30	05.87♌	12.56N	18.85♌	09.41N	03.61♍	05.31N	20.11♍	00.38N	07.95♎	04.96S	26.19♎	09.93S
06/09	06.78♌	12.42N	19.65♌	09.28N	04.21♍	05.22N	20.46♍	00.35N	07.94♎	04.87S	25.85♎	09.76S
06/19	07.79♌	12.25N	20.57♌	09.09N	04.98♍	05.05N	20.96♍	00.26N	08.11♎	04.85S	25.72♎	09.65S
06/29	08.88♌	12.04N	21.61♌	08.85N	05.89♍	04.83N	21.62♍	00.11N	08.47♎	04.91S	25.92♎	09.61S
07/09	10.03♌	11.80N	22.73♌	08.57N	06.91♍	04.55N	22.44♍	00.12S	09.04♎	05.06S	26.29♎	09.64S
07/19	11.23♌	11.52N	23.94♌	08.25N	08.05♍	04.22N	23.41♍	00.41S	09.75♎	05.26S	26.84♎	09.73S
07/29	12.47♌	11.21N	25.21♌	07.89N	09.28♍	03.84N	24.50♍	00.75S	10.62♎	05.53S	27.55♎	09.88S
08/08	13.72♌	10.88N	26.52♌	07.50N	10.57♍	03.42N	25.69♍	01.15S	11.62♎	05.85S	28.42♎	10.10S
08/18	14.97♌	10.52N	27.86♌	07.08N	11.92♍	02.97N	26.97♍	01.59S	12.73♎	06.23S	29.41♎	10.37S
08/28	16.21♌	10.15N	29.19♌	06.64N	13.31♍	02.49N	28.33♍	02.06S	13.95♎	06.64S	00.52♏	10.68S
09/07	17.40♌	09.78N	00.53♍	06.19N	14.73♍	01.98N	29.73♍	02.57S	15.25♎	07.09S	01.72♏	11.03S
09/17	18.54♌	09.40N	01.83♍	05.72N	16.15♍	01.46N	01.16♎	03.09S	16.62♎	07.56S	03.00♏	11.41S
09/27	19.61♌	09.02N	03.10♍	05.26N	17.54♍	00.94N	02.62♎	03.62S	18.04♎	08.05S	04.33♏	11.81S
10/07	20.59♌	08.66N	04.29♍	04.80N	18.90♍	00.42N	04.08♎	04.16S	19.48♎	08.55S	05.71♏	12.22S
10/17	21.46♌	08.32N	05.41♍	04.37N	20.22♍	00.09S	05.51♎	04.70S	20.93♎	09.06S	07.12♏	12.64S
10/27	22.22♌	08.00N	06.41♍	03.95N	21.46♍	00.59S	06.91♎	05.23S	22.37♎	09.55S	08.53♏	13.06S
11/06	22.81♌	07.72N	07.29♍	03.57N	22.60♍	01.06S	08.23♎	05.74S	23.79♎	10.04S	09.93♏	13.47S
11/16	23.24♌	07.48N	08.03♍	03.23N	23.65♍	01.49S	09.49♎	06.22S	25.17♎	10.50S	11.28♏	13.86S
11/26	23.49♌	07.30N	08.61♍	02.95N	24.54♍	01.88S	10.64♎	06.66S	26.47♎	10.94S	12.59♏	14.23S
12/06	23.57♌	07.18N	08.95♍	02.71N	25.27♍	02.20S	11.66♎	07.06S	27.69♎	11.34S	13.82♏	14.58S
12/16	23.48♌	07.11N	09.05♍	02.55N	25.83♍	02.47S	12.55♎	07.40S	28.79♎	11.69S	14.96♏	14.89S
12/26	23.21♌	07.11N	09.28♍	02.47N	26.21♍	02.66S	13.30♎	07.69S	29.76♎	12.00S	16.00♏	15.17S

DATE	1998 ♀	1998 ♀ Decl	1999 ♀	1999 ♀ Decl	2000 ♀	2000 ♀ Decl	2001 ♀	2001 ♀ Decl	2002 ♀	2002 ♀ Decl	2003 ♀	2003 ♀ Decl
01/01	15.59♏	15.31S	29.38♏	17.25S	11.64♐	18.14S	22.61♐	18.24S	02.24♑	17.78S	10.82♑	16.94S
01/11	16.54♏	15.51S	00.44♐	17.40S	12.75♐	18.22S	23.71♐	18.25S	03.30♑	17.72S	11.83♑	16.84S
01/21	17.33♏	15.67S	01.39♐	17.51S	13.77♐	18.27S	24.74♐	18.23S	04.32♑	17.65S	12.82♑	16.73S
01/31	17.96♏	15.77S	02.20♐	17.59S	14.69♐	18.29S	25.69♐	18.19S	05.28♑	17.56S	13.76♑	16.60S
02/10	18.41♏	15.82S	02.87♐	17.62S	15.49♐	18.28S	26.55♐	18.13S	06.17♑	17.45S	14.65♑	16.46S
02/20	18.68♏	15.81S	03.39♐	17.62S	16.15♐	18.25S	27.29♐	18.05S	06.97♑	17.34S	15.47♑	16.31S
03/02	18.78♏	15.76S	03.72♐	17.58S	16.70♐	18.19S	27.91♐	17.97S	07.66♑	17.21S	16.20♑	16.15S
03/12	18.68♏	15.65S	03.87♐	17.51S	17.03♐	18.11S	28.40♐	17.87S	08.23♑	17.08S	16.84♑	15.99S
03/22	18.39♏	15.50S	03.84♐	17.40S	17.22♐	18.02S	28.72♐	17.76S	08.66♑	16.96S	17.35♑	15.84S
04/01	17.95♏	15.30S	03.64♐	17.27S	17.22♐	17.91S	28.89♐	17.65S	08.96♑	16.83S	17.75♑	15.70S
04/11	17.38♏	15.06S	03.28♐	17.11S	17.06♐	17.78S	28.90♐	17.54S	09.13♑	16.71S	18.01♑	15.56S
04/21	16.67♏	14.80S	02.79♐	16.93S	16.74♐	17.65S	28.76♐	17.43S	09.14♑	16.60S	18.13♑	15.45S
05/01	15.94♏	14.53S	02.20♐	16.74S	16.29♐	17.52S	28.48♐	17.32S	09.00♑	16.51S	18.11♑	15.35S
05/11	15.20♏	14.26S	01.52♐	16.54S	15.71♐	17.38S	28.07♐	17.23S	08.72♑	16.43S	17.96♑	15.27S
05/21	14.48♏	14.01S	00.80♐	16.35S	15.07♐	17.25S	27.56♐	17.14S	08.33♑	16.37S	17.69♑	15.22S
05/31	13.83♏	13.78S	00.04♐	16.15S	14.39♐	17.13S	26.96♐	17.07S	07.82♑	16.33S	17.31♑	15.19S
06/10	13.25♏	13.58S	29.35♏	15.99S	13.70♐	17.02S	26.30♐	17.01S	07.25♑	16.30S	16.83♑	15.18S
06/20	12.81♏	13.43S	28.75♏	15.85S	13.03♐	16.93S	25.60♐	16.97S	06.63♑	16.30S	16.27♑	15.20S
06/30	12.53♏	13.33S	28.25♏	15.75S	12.39♐	16.86S	24.95♐	16.94S	05.99♑	16.33S	15.67♑	15.24S
07/10	12.41♏	13.29S	27.88♏	15.68S	11.86♐	16.81S	24.34♐	16.94S	05.36♑	16.37S	15.03♑	15.30S
07/20	12.46♏	13.30S	27.66♏	15.66S	11.45♐	16.79S	23.81♐	16.97S	04.74♑	16.44S	14.42♑	15.37S
07/30	12.73♏	13.37S	27.60♏	15.72S	11.17♐	16.80S	23.38♐	17.01S	04.22♑	16.51S	13.86♑	15.45S
08/09	13.13♏	13.49S	27.70♏	15.85S	11.04♐	16.84S	23.07♐	17.07S	03.78♑	16.58S	13.35♑	15.55S
08/19	13.70♏	13.66S	27.96♏	16.09S	11.09♐	16.90S	22.89♐	17.14S	03.46♑	16.66S	12.94♑	15.65S
08/29	14.42♏	13.86S	28.40♏	16.35S	11.28♐	16.98S	22.86♐	17.22S	03.27♑	16.74S	12.62♑	15.75S
09/08	15.28♏	14.10S	29.00♏	16.54S	11.62♐	17.08S	22.98♐	17.31S	03.23♑	16.83S	12.43♑	15.84S
09/18	16.26♏	14.38S	29.72♏	16.74S	12.10♐	17.20S	23.24♐	17.40S	03.31♑	16.90S	12.36♑	15.93S
09/28	17.35♏	14.67S	00.57♐	16.93S	12.73♐	17.33S	23.67♐	17.49S	03.54♑	16.97S	12.43♑	16.01S
10/08	17.52♏	14.97S	01.53♐	17.11S	13.49♐	17.46S	24.22♐	17.57S	03.90♑	17.03S	12.64♑	16.08S
10/18	19.76♏	15.29S	02.59♐	17.27S	14.35♐	17.60S	24.89♐	17.65S	04.39♑	17.08S	12.99♑	16.14S
10/28	21.06♏	15.60S	03.71♐	17.40S	15.31♐	17.73S	25.66♐	17.72S	05.00♑	17.11S	13.44♑	16.17S
11/07	22.37♏	15.91S	04.90♐	17.51S	16.34♐	17.85S	26.53♐	17.77S	05.72♑	17.13S	14.01♑	16.19S
11/17	23.71♏	16.20S	06.13♐	17.60S	17.44♐	17.96S	27.48♐	17.81S	06.52♑	17.15S	14.68♑	16.18S
11/27	25.05♏	16.48S	07.38♐	17.68S	18.57♐	18.06S	28.49♐	17.82S	07.40♑	17.13S	15.44♑	16.16S
12/07	26.35♏	16.74S	08.63♐	17.84S	19.73♐	18.14S	29.54♐	17.82S	08.34♑	17.12S	16.27♑	16.10S
12/17	27.62♏	16.96S	09.86♐	17.98S	20.90♐	18.20S	00.62♑	17.82S	09.32♑	17.05S	17.15♑	16.03S
12/27	28.81♏	17.16S	11.06♐	18.10S	22.05♐	18.23S	01.70♑	17.79S	10.32♑	16.98S	18.07♑	15.93S

DATE	2004 ⚷	2004 ⚷ Decl	2005 ⚷	2005 ⚷ Decl	2006 ⚷	2006 ⚷ Decl	2007 ⚷	2007 ⚷ Decl	2008 ⚷	2008 ⚷ Decl	2009 ⚷	2009 ⚷ Decl
01/01	18.54♑	15.88S	25.61♑	14.66S	01.97♒	13.39S	07.83♒	12.08S	13.26♒	10.77S	18.39♒	09.44S
01/11	19.48♑	15.75S	26.49♑	14.52S	02.79♒	13.23S	08.59♒	11.92S	13.96♒	10.61S	19.05♒	09.29S
01/21	20.42♑	15.61S	27.38♑	14.35S	03.63♒	13.06S	09.38♒	11.74S	14.70♒	10.42S	19.74♒	09.10S
01/31	21.34♑	15.45S	28.26♑	14.17S	04.47♒	12.86S	10.18♒	11.54S	15.46♒	10.22S	20.46♒	08.90S
02/10	22.22♑	15.28S	29.11♑	13.98S	05.29♒	12.66S	10.97♒	11.33S	16.22♒	10.01S	21.19♒	08.68S
02/20	23.04♑	15.10S	29.92♑	13.78S	06.09♒	12.45S	11.75♒	11.11S	16.98♒	09.78S	21.92♒	08.46S
03/01	23.79♑	14.92S	00.60♑	13.60S	06.77♒	12.25S	12.42♒	10.91S	17.70♒	09.55S	22.56♒	08.25S
03/11	24.46♑	14.74S	01.29♑	13.40S	07.46♒	12.04S	13.11♒	10.68S	18.39♒	09.32S	23.24♒	08.01S
03/21	25.03♑	14.56S	01.89♑	13.21S	08.09♒	11.83S	13.75♒	10.46S	19.03♒	09.09S	23.89♒	07.78S
03/31	25.49♑	14.40S	02.39♑	13.03S	08.63♒	11.64S	14.31♒	10.26S	19.60♒	08.88S	24.47♒	07.56S
04/10	25.83♑	14.25S	02.79♑	12.86S	09.08♒	11.46S	14.79♒	10.06S	20.10♒	08.68S	24.99♒	07.35S
04/20	26.04♑	14.12S	03.09♑	12.72S	09.41♒	11.30S	15.17♒	09.89S	20.51♒	08.50S	25.42♒	07.16S
04/30	26.13♑	14.01S	03.25♒	12.59S	09.64♒	11.16S	15.45♒	09.74S	20.82♒	08.34S	25.77♒	06.99S
05/10	26.09♑	13.93S	03.28♒	12.50S	09.75♒	11.06S	15.63♒	09.62S	21.03♒	08.21S	26.02♒	06.85S
05/20	25.91♑	13.87S	03.20♒	12.44S	09.75♒	10.98S	15.69♒	09.54S	21.13♒	08.12S	26.18♒	06.74S
05/30	25.63♑	13.84S	03.00♒	12.40S	09.63♒	10.94S	15.63♒	09.48S	21.13♒	08.05S	26.23♒	06.67S
06/09	25.23♑	13.84S	02.70♒	12.40S	09.40♒	10.93S	15.47♒	09.46S	21.03♒	08.03S	26.18♒	06.63S
06/19	24.74♑	13.87S	02.30♒	12.43S	09.07♒	10.95S	15.21♒	09.48S	20.82♒	08.03S	26.02♒	06.63S
06/29	24.20♑	13.92S	01.82♒	12.49S	08.66♒	11.01S	14.86♒	09.53S	20.51♒	08.08S	25.77♒	06.66S
07/09	23.63♑	14.00S	01.29♒	12.57S	08.16♒	11.10S	14.43♒	09.61S	20.13♒	08.16S	25.43♒	06.73S
07/19	23.03♑	14.09S	00.72♒	12.68S	07.64♒	11.20S	13.95♒	09.72S	19.68♒	08.27S	25.03♒	06.83S
07/29	22.45♑	14.20S	00.13♒	12.80S	07.09♒	11.33S	13.43♒	09.85S	19.18♒	08.40S	24.57♒	06.96S
08/08	21.89♑	14.32S	29.58♑	12.93S	06.54♒	11.48S	12.89♒	10.00S	18.66♒	08.55S	24.08♒	07.11S
08/18	21.41♑	14.44S	29.06♑	13.07S	06.01♒	11.63S	12.34♒	10.17S	18.14♒	08.72S	23.57♒	07.28S
08/28	21.02♑	14.56S	28.62♑	13.21S	05.52♒	11.79S	11.85♒	10.33S	17.64♒	08.89S	23.06♒	07.46S
09/07	20.73♑	14.67S	28.26♑	13.35S	05.10♒	11.94S	11.40♒	10.50S	17.18♒	09.07S	22.58♒	07.64S
09/17	20.55♑	14.78S	27.99♑	13.47S	04.78♒	12.08S	11.03♒	10.65S	16.77♒	09.24S	22.15♒	07.82S
09/27	20.51♑	14.87S	27.84♑	13.58S	04.55♒	12.21S	10.74♒	10.79S	16.44♒	09.39S	21.79♒	07.98S
10/07	20.58♑	14.95S	27.80♑	13.67S	04.43♒	12.31S	10.55♒	10.92S	16.20♒	09.52S	21.51♒	08.13S
10/17	20.78♑	15.01S	27.89♑	13.74S	04.43♒	12.40S	10.46♒	11.01S	16.06♒	09.63S	21.32♒	08.25S
10/27	21.11♑	15.04S	28.10♑	13.79S	04.55♒	12.45S	10.49♒	11.09S	16.03♒	09.72S	21.23♒	08.35S
11/06	21.55♑	15.06S	28.44♑	13.80S	04.77♒	12.48S	10.64♒	11.13S	16.12♒	09.77S	21.24♒	08.42S
11/16	22.10♑	15.04S	28.88♑	13.79S	05.11♒	12.48S	10.89♒	11.14S	16.31♒	09.79S	21.36♒	08.45S
11/26	22.74♑	15.01S	29.42♑	13.75S	05.56♒	12.44S	11.26♒	11.15S	16.60♒	09.77S	21.58♒	08.45S
12/06	23.46♑	14.94S	00.04♒	13.69S	06.10♒	12.38S	11.71♒	11.05S	16.99♒	09.72S	21.91♒	08.41S
12/16	24.25♑	14.85S	00.74♒	13.59S	06.71♒	12.29S	12.25♒	10.97S	17.47♒	09.64S	22.33♒	08.34S
12/26	25.09♑	14.74S	01.50♒	13.47S	07.40♒	12.17S	12.86♒	10.85S	18.03♒	09.53S	22.82♒	08.23S

DATE	2010 ♆	2010 ♆ Decl	2011 ♆	2011 ♆ Decl	2012 ♆	2012 ♆ Decl	2013 ♆	2013 ♆ Decl	2014 ♆	2014 ♆ Decl	2015 ♆	2015 ♆ Decl
01/01	23.15♒	08.16S	27.65♒	06.89S	01.94♓	05.65S	06.07♓	04.43S	10.00♓	03.25S	13.80♓	02.10S
01/11	23.75♒	08.00S	28.21♒	06.75S	02.44♓	05.52S	06.54♓	04.35S	10.42♓	03.14S	14.19♓	01.99S
01/21	24.40♒	07.83S	28.81♒	06.58S	03.00♓	05.35S	07.07♓	04.15S	10.92♓	02.99S	14.64♓	01.86S
01/31	25.08♒	07.63S	29.46♒	06.38S	03.61♓	05.17S	07.65♓	03.97S	11.47♓	02.81S	15.16♓	01.69S
02/10	25.78♒	07.41S	00.13♓	06.17S	04.25♓	04.96S	08.26♓	03.76S	12.06♓	02.62S	15.72♓	01.50S
02/20	26.49♒	07.18S	00.81♓	05.94S	04.96♓	04.74S	08.90♓	03.54S	12.67♓	02.40S	16.31♓	01.29S
03/02	27.19♒	06.95S	01.49♓	05.71S	05.64♓	04.48S	09.55♓	03.31S	13.30♓	02.18S	16.93♓	01.07S
03/12	27.86♒	06.71S	02.15♓	05.47S	06.29♓	04.24S	10.19♓	03.08S	13.93♓	01.94S	17.55♓	00.84S
03/22	28.50♒	06.48S	02.79♓	05.23S	06.92♓	04.01S	10.81♓	02.84S	14.55♓	01.71S	18.16♓	00.61S
04/01	29.08♒	06.25S	03.38♓	05.00S	07.51♓	03.77S	11.41♓	02.60S	15.15♓	01.47S	18.76♓	00.37S
04/11	29.61♒	06.04S	03.92♓	04.78S	08.06♓	03.55S	11.96♓	02.38S	15.71♓	01.24S	19.32♓	00.14S
04/21	00.06♓	05.84S	04.39♓	04.58S	08.54♓	03.35S	12.46♓	02.17S	16.22♓	01.03S	19.84♓	00.07N
05/01	00.43♓	05.67S	04.79♓	04.40S	08.95♓	03.16S	12.89♓	01.98S	16.67♓	00.83S	20.31♓	00.27N
05/11	00.71♓	05.52S	05.10♓	04.24S	09.28♓	03.00S	13.25♓	01.81S	17.05♓	00.66S	20.71♓	00.45N
05/21	00.90♓	05.40S	05.32♓	04.12S	09.53♓	02.87S	13.53♓	01.67S	17.35♓	00.51S	21.05♓	00.61N
05/31	00.98♓	05.32S	05.45♓	04.03S	09.69♓	02.76S	13.72♓	01.56S	17.58♓	00.39S	21.30♓	00.74N
06/10	00.97♓	05.27S	05.48♓	03.96S	09.75♓	02.70S	13.82♓	01.48S	17.71♓	00.31S	21.47♓	00.83N
06/20	00.85♓	05.27S	05.42♓	03.94S	09.72♓	02.67S	13.82♓	01.44S	17.76♓	00.25S	21.55♓	00.89N
06/30	00.65♓	05.29S	05.25♓	03.96S	09.59♓	02.70S	13.74♓	01.47S	17.71♓	00.24S	21.54♓	00.92N
07/10	00.35♓	05.35S	05.00♓	04.01S	09.37♓	02.72S	13.56♓	01.54S	17.57♓	00.26S	21.43♓	00.89N
07/20	29.99♒	05.45S	04.68♓	04.10S	09.04♓	02.80S	13.31♓	01.64S	17.35♓	00.32S	21.25♓	00.83N
07/30	29.56♒	05.57S	04.28♓	04.22S	08.71♓	02.91S	12.98♓	01.77S	17.05♓	00.41S	20.99♓	00.78N
08/09	29.09♒	05.72S	03.83♓	04.36S	08.30♓	03.05S	12.58♓	01.93S	16.69♓	00.53S	20.66♓	00.67N
08/19	28.58♒	05.90S	03.36♓	04.52S	07.84♓	03.21S	12.14♓	02.11S	16.28♓	00.68S	20.27♓	00.53N
08/29	28.09♒	06.07S	02.88♓	04.70S	07.36♓	03.39S	11.68♓	02.29S	15.83♓	00.85S	19.84♓	00.36N
09/08	27.61♒	06.26S	02.40♓	04.89S	06.87♓	03.59S	11.21♓	02.48S	15.37♓	01.04S	19.37♓	00.18N
09/18	27.17♒	06.44S	01.93♓	05.08S	06.41♓	03.77S	10.75♓	02.67S	14.91♓	01.23S	18.91♓	00.01S
09/28	26.78♒	06.61S	01.52♓	05.26S	06.00♓	03.96S	10.31♓	02.85S	14.45♓	01.42S	18.46♓	00.15S
10/08	26.46♒	06.77S	01.18♓	05.43S	05.63♓	04.13S	09.92♓	03.02S	14.05♓	01.61S	18.05♓	00.20S
10/18	26.24♒	06.91S	00.91♓	05.57S	05.34♓	04.28S	09.60♓	03.16S	13.70♓	01.78S	17.68♓	00.39S
10/28	26.10♒	07.01S	00.73♓	05.69S	05.13♓	04.41S	09.35♓	03.27S	13.42♓	01.93S	17.37♓	00.57S
11/07	26.07♒	07.09S	00.65♓	05.78S	05.01♓	04.51S	09.19♓	03.35S	13.22♓	02.05S	17.14♓	00.73S
11/17	26.14♒	07.13S	00.67♓	05.84S	04.98♓	04.58S	09.12♓	03.40S	13.12♓	02.14S	16.99♓	00.86S
11/27	26.32♒	07.14S	00.78♓	05.86S	05.06♓	04.61S	09.16♓	03.39S	13.10♓	02.19S	16.94♓	00.96S
12/07	26.59♒	07.11S	01.00♓	05.85S	05.23♓	04.61S	09.28♓	03.36S	13.18♓	02.21S	16.98♓	01.03S
12/17	26.95♒	07.06S	01.31♓	05.80S	05.51♓	04.58S	09.50♓	03.39S	13.36♓	02.20S	17.12♓	01.06S
12/27	27.40♒	06.95S	01.71♓	05.71S	05.86♓	04.48S	09.81♓	03.30S	13.63♓	02.14S	17.35♓	01.01S

Magi Astrochart for _____

Prepared by:

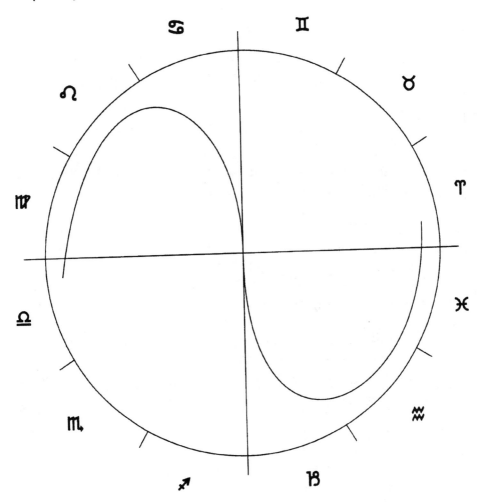

MAGI ASTROLOGY COMPUTER SOFTWARE

To help you take full advantage of the knowledge provided in this book, the Magi Society has developed unique computer software. The software is called MagiSoft and will allow you to obtain all of the types of astrological information presented in this book, as well as perform all the types of analyses that have been discussed. All of the charts in this book were created using the program. The software is completely compatible with Windows 95, Windows 98, and Windows NT.

MagiSoft provides the positions of all the planets, the Sun, Chiron, Moon, and true node, for the years 1900 through 2009. In addition, the program calculates the ascendant and midheaven, and will display and print birth charts like the ones in this book for any time and place within all those years, and will list all of the natal aspects. The program even gives you the ability to search for special types of Planetary Geometry.

MagiSoft also allows you to create and calculate a CAC (Combined Alignment Chart), as well as list and print all of the interaspects. The program helps you easily see if you have Romantic Super Linkages and Sexual Linkages with anyone. MagiSoft even calculates, displays, and prints Combined Planetary Geometry.

We want Magi Astrology to be as widely used as possible, so we have priced our software such that anyone will be able to afford it; however, it is only available for those who have bought this book and is therefore designed to be used in association with the Planetary Interpreter within. A special coupon for the software is on the following page. To obtain the software, fill out the coupon (or a copy of it), and send it to us with a check or money order for $38 plus appropriate shipping costs, as detailed on the coupon.

MAGI SOCIETY ®

Computer Software

MagiSoft™ is the Magi Society's special computer software for compatibility and Magi Astrology. MagiSoft was especially designed so that even a novice will find it easy to use. The cost is $38 plus shipping (please see below).

To order the Magi Society's MagiSoft, please fill out the form at the bottom of this page (or you may make a copy of this form), and send it along with a check or money order for the appropriate amount to:

> MAGI SOCIETY
> P.O Box 522
> Murray Hill Station
> New York, NY 10156

Magi Society: Please send one copy of MagiSoft to me at the address below. I understand that MagiSoft is your special computer software for the astrology of love and money and has all of the capabilities described on the previous page.

NAME: _____

ADDRESS: _____

_____

_____

I enclose my check or money order payable to The Magi Associates, Inc., for $38 plus $5 shipping and handling.

(Orders from areas outside of North America, please add $8 for shipping. New York State residents please add 8.25% sales tax.)

(MagiSoft is completely compatible with Windows 95 and 98, as well as Windows NT, and will be updated to be compatible with future versions of Microsoft operating systems. Apple computers that have the ability to run PC software will be able to run MagiSoft. Your program will be shipped to you on standard 3.5-inch disks.)

ABOUT THE MAGI SOCIETY

The Magi Society is an international organization of scientific astrologers. Our members include senior officers of some of the world's most influential financial institutions and many professionals with advanced degrees in the sciences. The Society was founded as a secret society in China in 1625, and its members have included some of the most legendary Chinese astrologers since that time.

The first American branch of the Magi Society was established in early 1995, and it is responsible for the compilation of the Society's first two published books, as well as this one. The Magi Society trains and certifies Magi Astrologers and provides all of its members with advanced computer software for astrology, which has unique capabilities in the analysis and interpretation of planetary geometry and interaspects.

If you're interested in information about our society or our services, if you wish to join us, or if you just want to be on our mailing list, please feel free to contact us at:

The Magi Society
P.O. Box 522
Murray Hill Station
New York, NY 10156
(212) 867-2905

(If the telephone number ever changes, it will be listed under Magi Associates, Inc., in New York City.)

We hope you enjoyed
this Hay House Astro Room book.
If you would like to receive a free catalog featuring additional
Hay House books and products, or if you would like information about
the Hay Foundation, please contact:

Hay House, Inc.
P.O. Box 5100
Carlsbad, CA 92018-5100

(760) 431-7695 or **(800) 654-5126**
(760) 431-6948 (fax) or **(800) 650-5115 (fax)**

Please visit the Hay House Website at: **www.hayhouse.com**